**SOUND & MUSIC PROJECTS FOR
EURORACK AND BEYOND**

SOUND & MUSIC PROJECTS FOR EURORACK AND BEYOND

Explorations in Teensy® Microcontroller Technology

Brent Edstrom

OXFORD
UNIVERSITY PRESS

Oxford University Press is a department of the University of Oxford.
It furthers the University's objective of excellence in research, scholarship,
and education by publishing worldwide. Oxford is a registered trade mark of
Oxford University Press in the UK and in certain other countries.

Published in the United States of America by Oxford University Press
198 Madison Avenue, New York, NY 10016, United States of America.

© Oxford University Press 2024

All rights reserved. No part of this publication may be reproduced, stored in a retrieval system,
or transmitted, in any form or by any means, without the prior permission in writing of Oxford
University Press, or as expressly permitted by law, by license or under terms agreed with the
appropriate reprographics rights organization. Inquiries concerning reproduction outside the scope
of the above should be sent to the Rights Department, Oxford University Press, at the address above.

You must not circulate this work in any other form
and you must impose this same condition on any acquirer

Library of Congress Cataloging-in-Publication Data
Names: Edstrom, Brent, author.
Title: Sound & music projects for Eurorack and beyond : explorations in
Teensy® microcontroller technology / Brent Edstrom.
Other titles: Sound and music projects for Eurorack and beyond
Description: [1.] | New York, NY : Oxford University Press, 2024. |
Includes bibliographical references and index.
Identifiers: LCCN 2024032001 (print) | LCCN 2024032002 (ebook) |
ISBN 9780197514474 (paperback) | ISBN 9780197514467 (hardback) |
ISBN 9780197514498 (epub)
Subjects: LCSH: Electronic musical instruments—Construction. |
Synthesizer (Musical instrument)—Construction. |
Teensy (Programmable controller)—Programming. | Computer sound processing.
Classification: LCC ML1092 .E38 2024 (print) | LCC ML1092 (ebook) |
DDC 786.7/1923—dc23/eng/20240830
LC record available at https://lccn.loc.gov/2024032001
LC ebook record available at https://lccn.loc.gov/2024032002

DOI: 10.1093/9780197514504.001.0001

Paperback printed by Sheridan Books, Inc., United States of America
Hardback printed by Bridgeport National Bindery, Inc., United States of America

To my daughter, Emily. You bring joy to my heart.

CONTENTS

ACKNOWLEDGMENTS   IX

PREFACE   XI

PART I   **EXPLORATIONS IN MUSIC SYNTHESIS AND DSP   1**

CHAPTER 1   LIGHT SYNTH   3

CHAPTER 2   WAVETABLE SYNTHESIS   21

CHAPTER 3   CREATING A SYNTHESIZER USER INTERFACE   32

CHAPTER 4   FM SYNTHESIS   50

CHAPTER 5   ADDITIVE SYNTHESIS   62

CHAPTER 6   GRANULAR SYNTHESIS   76

CHAPTER 7   DIGITAL SIGNAL PROCESSING   87

PART II   **EXPLORATIONS IN THE MUSICAL INSTRUMENT DIGITAL INTERFACE   109**

CHAPTER 8   MIDI I/O   111

CHAPTER 9   POLYPHONY   129

CHAPTER 10   INTERACTIVE MIDI ARPEGGIATOR   142

CHAPTER 11   GENETIC STEP SEQUENCER   161

PART III   **EURORACK CONCEPTS   187**

CHAPTER 12   MAKING CONNECTIONS: MICROCONTROLLER I/O   189

CHAPTER 13   POWERING EURORACK MODULES   205

CHAPTER 14   BUILDING EURORACK MODULES: PART I: STRIPBOARD   216

VIII CONTENTS

CHAPTER 15 BUILDING EURORACK MODULES
WITH PCBS **233**

CHAPTER 16 VOLTAGE CONTROL, GATES,
AND TRIGGERS **253**

PART IV EURORACK PROJECTS 275

CHAPTER 17 BUILDING A EURORACK EFFECTS UNIT **277**

CHAPTER 18 MIDI TO CONTROL-VOLTAGE
CONVERTER **293**

CHAPTER 19 BUILDING EUROSYNTH **312**

APPENDIX A: DATA TYPES 335

APPENDIX B: PRIMARY AUDIO OBJECTS 337

APPENDIX C: USING POLYPHONE TO CREATE CUSTOM WAVETABLES 339

NOTES 345

BIBLIOGRAPHY 351

INDEX 357

ACKNOWLEDGMENTS

Thank you to Norman Hirschy, Executive Acquisitions Editor, Oxford University Press, for your support and encouragement of this project. I am also grateful to the (anonymous) peer reviewers who provided valuable feedback and suggestions. A big thank you to Dr. Philip Measor and Dr. Matthew Skala (founder of North Coast Synthesis Ltd.), who provided feedback on several sections of the manuscript. And thank you, too, to my family who encouraged me through several years of research and writing. It takes a village (or at least a team of able professionals) to bring a book to fruition, and I am grateful to copyeditor Tim Rutherford-Johnson and the editorial and design team at Oxford University Press for your good work.

PREFACE

To invent, you need a good imagination and a pile of junk.[1]

Thomas Alva Edison

Why I Wrote This Book

In 2016 I published *Arduino for Musicians* (Oxford University Press). Although scholarly tomes are, by definition, labors of love, it was gratifying to hear from readers who were excited to learn how to create their own custom instruments and Musical Instrument Digital Interface (MIDI) controllers. The book seemed to resonate with many like-minded individuals who understand that the maker movement has created new expressive opportunities by expanding the creative musical palette into the realm of circuits and source code. A democratization of technical tools has blurred the line between design and creative application.[2]

This book builds on the theoretical foundations developed in *Arduino for Musicians*, with a focus on higher-end projects ranging from music synthesizers to digital signal processors and a step sequencer based on evolutionary algorithms. The book also explores many of those concepts in the context of Eurorack, a popular framework for mounting and interconnecting modular music synthesizers and related components. My hope is that this book will fill a much-needed gap between the disciplines of music, computer science, and electronics that will enable readers to envision and create professional instruments and sound-design tools.

Although previous experience with programming and electronics is helpful, topics are presented in building-block fashion throughout the book, so the primary requirement is a willingness to learn and to explore. Additional resources are provided at the Oxford University Press (OUP) website, including video tutorials and demonstrations.

What Is a Microcontroller?

In some respects, a microcontroller is akin to a simple computer. Where a computer contains components including memory, central processing unit, hard drive, and video card installed on a motherboard, the functionality of a microcontroller is found on a single chip.[3] Like a computer, microcontrollers can be programmed to do any number of interesting things. Microcontrollers provide multiple input and output pins that can interact with electronic components including pushbuttons, light and distance sensors, LEDs, and a host of other items that form the building blocks of powerful custom creations. The marriage of programming and electronics is a powerful combination that enables creators to envision and build unique synthesizers, MIDI devices, digital signal processors, and other instruments that can rival commercial offerings. Building custom electronic instruments is not only economical, but microcontrollers are also fascinating and open the door to a nearly limitless array of creative options. To quote author Charles Platt:

> *By learning how technology works, you become better able to control your world instead of being controlled by it.*[4]

What Is Eurorack?

Eurorack is a modular synthesizer format that is characterized by interconnectivity and a standardized form factor (see Figure P.1). Eurorack is also a compelling creative space where sound generators, modifiers, controllers, and processors from a wide variety of manufacturers can be connected in unique ways to produce compelling new music and sound designs. Finally, Eurorack represents a revival of an analog synthesis ethos where creative experimentation and spontaneous creation abound. It is as fun as it sounds.

FIGURE P.1 Custom Eurorack modules

What You Will Learn

This book is geared toward musicians, students, hobbyists, and other individuals who want to learn how to create custom synthesizers, MIDI controllers, Eurorack devices, and related instruments. Concepts including programming, circuitry, synthesis, and design are presented in building-block fashion to facilitate interactive learning. While some concepts will necessarily require an exploration of advanced topics, the book utilizes pre-existing code libraries when possible so readers can focus on the creative application of underlying technologies. To use a musical metaphor, it is not necessary to learn the intricacies of piano action regulation to become an accomplished pianist. Similarly, it is not always necessary to learn the nuts and bolts of fixed-point math or fast Fourier transform to use a digital oscillator. While the book does not shy away from advanced details, it does focus on the creative application of core concepts and will provide a solid basis for further study.

Why Teensy?

Although many microcontrollers are available to professionals and hobbyists, this book focuses on the Teensy products manufactured by PJRC. Teensy boards, which PJRC describes as "a complete USB-based microcontroller development system,"[5] are small USB devices that are easy to program. The boards offer many advantages to music makers:

- Teensy boards are relatively easy to use.
- The devices provide out-of-the-box support for audio and MIDI (including multiple ports of "driverless" USB MIDI).
- PJRC provides a convenient web-based audio design tool for visual creation of powerful audio projects.
- Teensy 3.x and 4.x devices are fast enough to support professional audio sample rates.
- An optional Audio Adapter Board provides the necessary circuitry for mic and line input, stereo buffered output, and streaming of audio files from an SD card.

Categories of Teensy Devices

Teensy microcontrollers are categorized as series 2.x, 3.x, 4.x, and LC devices, but the 2.x, 3.x, and LC boards are currently being phased out. Teensy 4.x Development Boards such as the 4.0 (see Figure P.2) are 32-bit devices with enough power for digital signal processing, physical modeling, and other audio tasks. Teensy 4.x boards also excel at MIDI and can be configured to send and receive MIDI via a USB connection or traditional 5-pin DIN connector.

Caution: Take care to avoid connecting voltages higher than 3.3V to the pins of a Teensy microcontroller.

FIGURE P.2 Teensy 4.0

Unlike teensy 3.x devices, Teensy 4.x microcontrollers do not contain a DAC, but audio output is easily achieved by attaching a Teensy Audio Adapter Board (see Figure P.3).

FIGURE P.3 Teensy Audio Adapter Board

PJRC also offers the Teensy 4.1 which, among other enhancements, provides additional digital and analog I/O and support for Ethernet (see Figure P.4).

FIGURE P.4 Teensy 4.1

My advice is to start with a Teensy 4.0 and Audio Adapter Board since I use that configuration throughout the book.

Organization of the Book

- **Part I: Explorations in Music Synthesis** and DSP introduces Teensy microcontrollers through hands-on projects that explore forms of music synthesis including subtractive, wavetable, frequency modulation, additive, and granular synthesis. The projects can be built, with a few inexpensive electronic components, on a solderless breadboard like the one shown in Figure P.5.

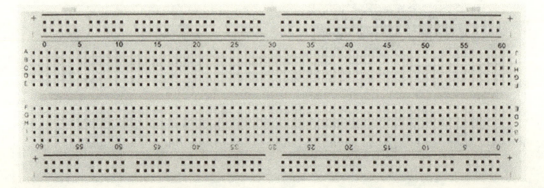

FIGURE P.5 Solderless breadboard

- **Part II: Explorations in the Musical Instrument Digital Interface** details the use of USB and 5-pin UART MIDI. As with Part I, the explorations in Part II can be built on a solderless breadboard and demonstration projects include an interactive arpeggiator and step sequencer based on generative genetic algorithms.
- **Part III: Eurorack Concepts** provides a foundation for designing custom Eurorack modules. Chapters detail circuits for connecting microcontrollers to standard +/−12V Eurorack power sources, control voltage and audio input and output, building modules, and designing PCBs and front panels.
- **Part IV: Eurorack Projects** applies core concepts to three DIY projects: a Eurorack effects unit, MIDI to control voltage converter, and an extensible EuroSynth FM synthesizer.

Readers are encouraged to experiment with and adapt core concepts to their own unique creations.

Electronic Components and Software

As detailed in the pages that follow, most Teensy projects utilize source code and circuitry as shown in Figure P.6. Circuits are connected to the pins of the microcontroller to handle signal input and output and to provide a means for users to interact with the microcontroller via switches, potentiometers, and other components. Code is written and uploaded to the microcontroller, and the code and circuitry are tested and revised until the device operates in the desired way. Projects can be finalized into a permanent circuit (e.g., printed circuit board, solder board, etc.) if desired, and the circuitry and microcontroller will run without a connection to a computer. This is one of the most compelling aspects of microcontroller technology—microcontrollers can function as *stand-alone* devices on stage or in the studio.

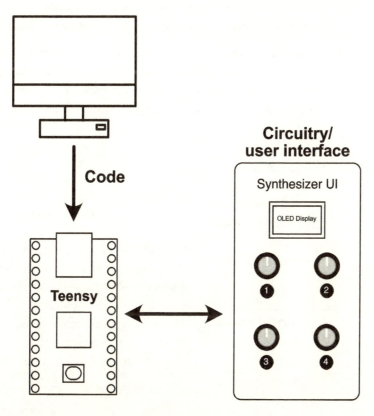

FIGURE P.6 Overview of a typical microcontroller project

Primary Equipment and Electronic Components

Microcontrollers such as Arduino and Teensy represent a blank slate that can be used to craft unique projects ranging from audio and MIDI devices to robots and autonomous performers. Although a bare-bones Teensy microcontroller can be programmed to output audio or MIDI, most users will want to connect switches, LEDs, and other components to enable real-time interaction with the device. Tables P.1 and P.2 represent a modest collection of equipment and electronic components that are suitable for the exploratory projects in the first section of the book. Parts can be purchased from hobbyist-friendly vendors such as Adafruit or Sparkfun. Bulk purchases may be more cost effective from larger vendors such as Digikey, but inventories are so vast that part selection can be daunting for beginners.

TABLE P.1 Primary equipment

Item	Description
Computer	A laptop or desktop computer is used to write source code and upload the compiled code to the microcontroller. Old or inexpensive used computers can often be repurposed for use in an electronic lab, and **I recommend that approach over connecting experimental circuits to an expensive computer.**
Solderless breadboard	A solderless breadboard provides a way to temporarily connect electronic components to form circuits. A breadboard is the creative workspace where microcontroller exploration and testing occur.
Hookup wire	Hookup wire connects electronic components to one another or to the pins of a microcontroller. A selection of male/male and male/female wires are useful for forming circuits using a variety of electronic components.
Digital Multimeter	An inexpensive multimeter provides a way to test voltage, current, and resistance, check for short circuits, and related tasks. Although projects can be completed without a multimeter, the device will enable a deeper understanding of core concepts and aid the troubleshooting process.

TABLE P.2 Primary electronic components

Item	Common Schematic Symbol	Description
Pushbutton or tactile switches		Pushbuttons connect to digital pins and provide a way to interact with the microcontroller. Common applications include start or stop buttons and menu selection. Tactile switches are often a good choice for breadboarding since many brands can be plugged directly into a solderless breadboard.

TABLE P.2 Continued

Item	Common Schematic Symbol	Description
Resistors		Resistors are inexpensive passive components that are used for a variety of tasks ranging from current reduction to voltage division. Consider purchasing a basic starter kit consisting of multiple through-hole resistors of common values.
Photoresistor		Photoresistors (or light-dependent resistors) are a type of variable resistor where resistance decreases in response to light. A photoresistor is used in the first chapter of the book for a simple Theremin-like synthesizer, and they provide unique opportunities for utilizing light to control synthesis parameters such as filter cutoff and resonance.
Capacitor		Capacitors represent another common passive component. They can be combined with resistors to form simple passive filters, used to smooth the output of a power supply, or for many other tasks. As with resistors, inexpensive through-hole capacitor kits consisting of common values are readily available from a variety of vendors.
Potentiometers		Potentiometers function as variable resistors or voltage dividers and are often used to control volume levels, adjust filter cutoff, and many other tasks. Small "trimmer" pots are a good choice for circuit design since many brands can be plugged directly into a breadboard. 10k ohm is a common resistance value for connecting to the analog pins of a microcontroller.
LEDs		Light emitting diodes provide visual feedback and are useful in indicating MIDI clock pulses, the tempo of a sequencer, or active status of a component or device.

(continued)

XVIII   PREFACE

TABLE P.2 Continued

Item	Common Schematic Symbol	Description
Rotary Encoders	CLK DT SW + GND	Rotary encoders look like potentiometers, but they function like a pair of tactile switches. Rotary encoders are a good choice for applications that require users to input precise values. The shaft of some encoders can also function as a pushbutton switch—which is useful for projects with limited front-panel space. Unfortunately, most encoders do not work well with solderless breadboards. Leads can be soldered to the encoder pins or female/male hookup wire can provide a connection between the encoder and a breadboard. It is also possible to purchase encoders that are pre-soldered to a PCB breakout board—an excellent option for prototyping.
OLED display (I2C)		Small OLED displays utilizing an I2C interface are available for a few dollars from many vendors. Although not an essential component for microcontroller projects, I find them useful and OLED displays are used in several projects in the book.

Other Components

Although many projects can be created with the primary equipment and components listed in Tables P.1 and P.2, additional components are required to complete projects in the final sections of the book. These are shown in Table P.3.

TABLE P.3 Other components and equipment

Item	Description
Integrated Circuits	A variety of ICs ranging from operational amplifiers (op amps) to DACs and ADCs are used in later chapters of the book. Most ICs are inexpensive and readily available from a variety of vendors, and parts lists are available for download from the OUP website.
Jacks	While Teensy audio adapters provide audio input and output jacks, audio or MIDI jacks are necessary for some applications. Some jacks can even be plugged into a breadboard enabling convenient connections to external devices.

PREFACE   XIX

TABLE P.3 Continued

Item	Description
Soldering equipment	A soldering iron, solder, and solid hookup wire are required if you intend to finalize a project by moving it from a solderless breadboard to stripboard, solder board, or printed circuit board.
Oscilloscope	Oscilloscopes are not essential, but they are useful tools that can verify the shape of a waveform, visualize relative signal levels, and other tasks. Used analog oscilloscopes are inexpensive and newer digital oscilloscopes may fit the budget of serious hobbyists.

Precautions

Although it is relatively safe to build and experiment with small-signal electronic projects, it is always prudent to be mindful of hazards and minimize the potential for mishaps that might result in an injury or cause damage to a microcontroller or other components.

- Always wear protective eyewear when soldering or using power tools.
- Always use a vise, clamps, etc., when working with cutting and drilling tools.
- Never attempt to build or modify a circuit while power is applied to a breadboard or solderless breadboard. While voltages are relatively low for the projects described in the book, connecting hookup wire while a circuit is powered will increase the odds of damaging a component.
- Always turn off (and unplug) power supplies after experimenting with breadboard or Eurorack projects. This is a good idea for any wall wart power supply, but especially for experimental circuits such as the ones detailed in this book.
- Be mindful of the fact that voltages over 3.3V can damage the pins of a microcontroller. Use the 3.3V regulated power provided by the microcontroller (not the 5V power provided by USB or Eurorack power supply) when connecting components such as pushbuttons or potentiometers to a microcontroller.
- Take time to double check wiring when experimenting on a breadboard or soldering a project before applying power. Look for solder bridges that can occur between adjacent solder points and take special care to avoid short circuits.
- Be mindful of the fact that microcontrollers and some ICs can be damaged by the DC and AC voltages produced by many commercial Eurorack products. Several chapters of the book are devoted to circuits that scale or reduce such voltages.
- Avoid connecting USB to a microcontroller that is powered by an external power supply such as a 5V Eurorack supply. The Teensy manufacturer, PJRC, provides instructions for disconnecting USB and external power so a microcontroller can be programmed via a USB cable while powered by an external supply.[6]
- A mis-wired project can damage components or equipment such as commercial Eurorack modules. Always use a multimeter to check that a project is functioning properly and that voltages are at an appropriate level before attempting to connect the project to other devices.
- A mis-wired project can damage a computer, so it is advisable to use an inexpensive second-hand computer in an experimental electronics lab. With that said,

I have never experienced such a mishap in many years of experimenting with microcontrollers.

- **Note that none of the projects in this book utilize mains power.** All the projects in the first part of the book can be powered by a low voltage 5V USB power supply, and the Eurorack projects in the second and third part of the book can be powered by relatively low voltage commercial Eurorack power supplies.

Looking Ahead

Like any worthwhile endeavor, it takes time to develop the skills to effectively utilize code and electronic circuits. My sincere hope is that the book will provide a useful starting point for individuals who wish to explore these exciting technologies and that it will provide new avenues of exploration for music makers who have already worked in the realm of code and electronics. Take your time, explore, and enjoy a journey that will lead to new avenues of creative expression. As an electronics and programming autodidact, there is no false modesty in saying if I can do it, you can, too.

PART I
EXPLORATIONS IN MUSIC SYNTHESIS AND DSP

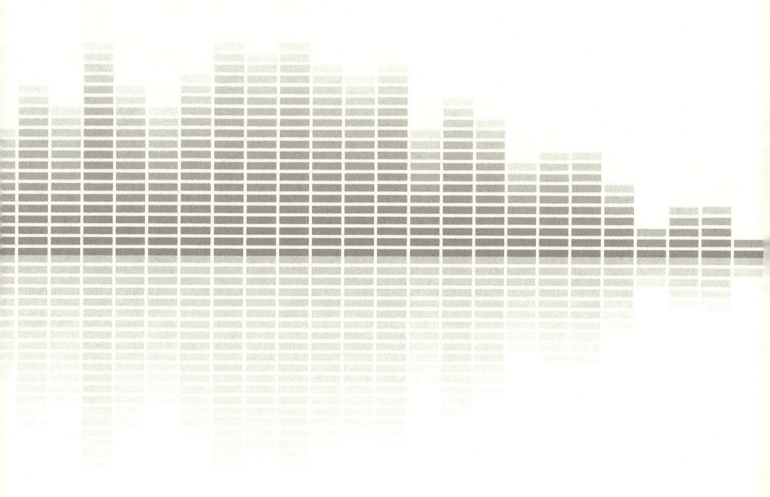

CHAPTER 1

LIGHT SYNTH

I do not think there is any thrill that can go through the human heart like that felt by the inventor as he sees some creation of the brain unfolding to success.[1]

NIKOLA TESLA

Light Synth: A First Project

This chapter provides a gentle introduction to the exciting world of Teensy microcontrollers. By the end of the chapter, you will create Light Synth—a synthesizer that responds to fluctuations in ambient light—and you will learn how to use a breadboard, an Integrated Development Environment (IDE), and an audio design tool that can facilitate a wide array of sound and synthesis projects.

GETTING STARTED

As you learned in the Preface, PJRC, the company that manufactures Teensy microcontrollers, provides several useful Teensy variants. This project (and many others in the book) uses a Teensy 4.0 microcontroller and Audio Adapter Board. Although Teensy boards are available with pre-soldered pins, you will want to give forethought to using the microcontroller and Audio Adapter Board on a solderless breadboard. One approach, shown in Figure 1.1, utilizes double-insulator header pins.

FIGURE 1.1 Teensy and Audio Adapter Board with double-insulator header pins

Sound & Music Projects for Eurorack and Beyond. Brent Edstrom, Oxford University Press. © Oxford University Press 2024.
DOI: 10.1093/9780197514504.003.0001

Another option, shown in Figure 1.2, combines a female header with pins that extend below the microcontroller. An Audio Adapter Board can be connected to the header with standard male pins. The headers are available from Adafruit, Sparkfun, and other vendors.

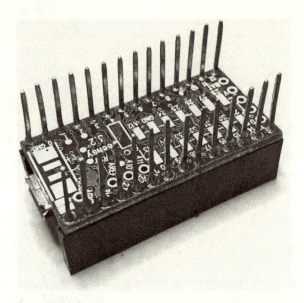

FIGURE 1.2 Teensy with female socket and extended pins

Tip: Although soldering isn't unduly difficult, it is best to practice with inexpensive components before attempting to solder header pins to a Teensy or Audio Adapter Board. Of course, many online video tutorials are available for various skill levels including my own Crash Course in Soldering, which is available from the Oxford University Press website.[2]

INSTALLING THE ARDUINO IDE

Teensy microcontrollers are programmed with the same Integrated Development Environment (IDE) as Arduino microcontrollers. To install the Arduino IDE, visit https://www.arduino.cc and download the environment for Windows, Linux, or macOS from the Software menu. Once the IDE is installed, select the Settings menu item, and add the following link to the "Additional boards manager URLs" section (see Figure 1.3):

https://www.pjrc.com/teensy/package_teensy_index.json

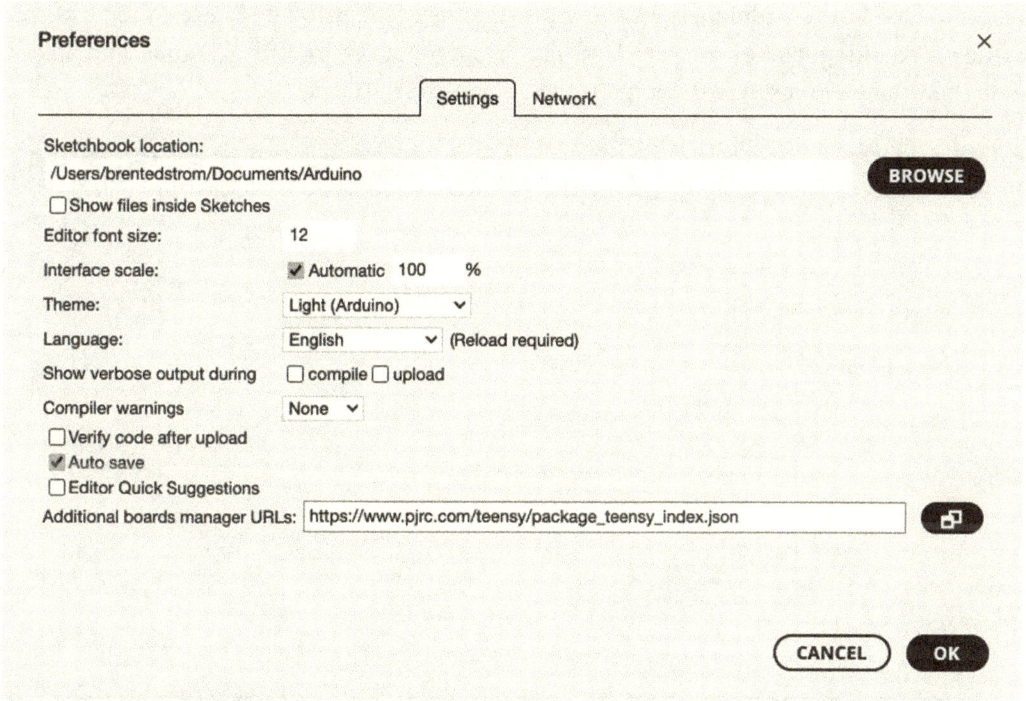

CHAPTER 1 LIGHT SYNTH

FIGURE 1.3 Adding a link to Teensy boards in the Arduino IDE

The configuration files for Teensy boards can then be installed via the Boards Manager in the Arduino IDE as shown in Figure 1.4. After installing the files, various Teensy boards will be available for use from the Tools->Board menu item.

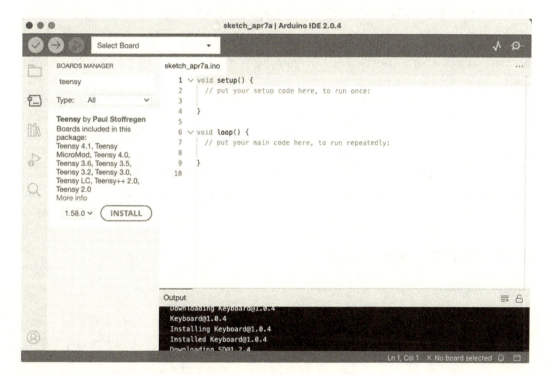

FIGURE 1.4 Installing Teensy boards via the Boards Manager

The interface of the Arduino IDE, shown in Figure 1.5, consists of a text editor used for writing and editing source code. The IDE also provides buttons to verify, compile, and upload code (known as a *sketch* in Arduino parlance) to a microcontroller.

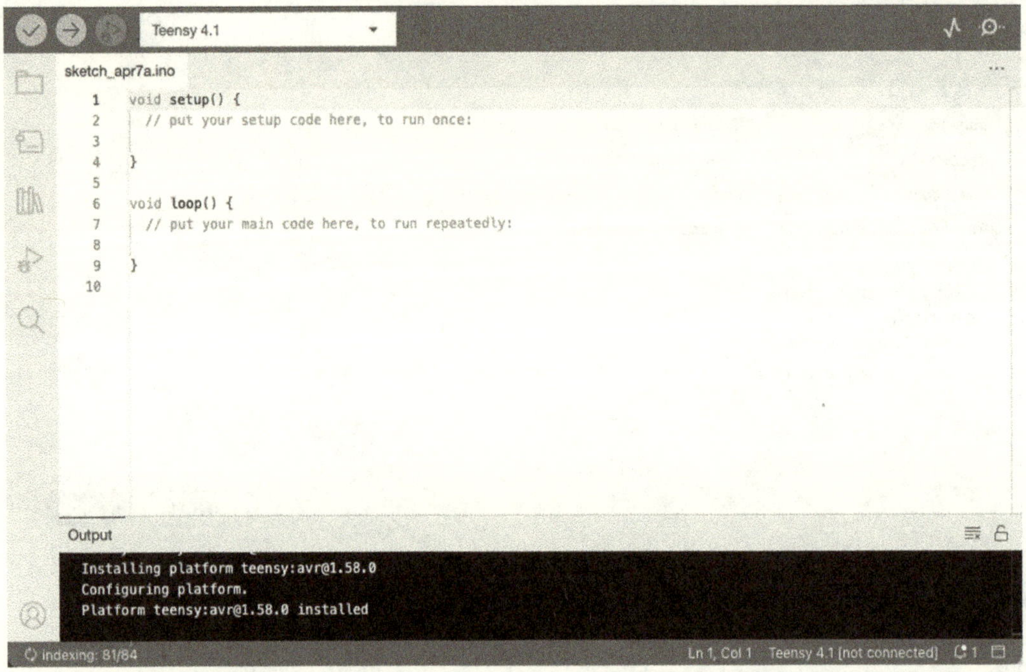

FIGURE 1.5 The Arduino IDE

LEARNING TO CODE THROUGH EXPLORATION

Before delving into a first synthesis project, it will be important to cover a few introductory programming concepts. Programming is a vast topic that rivals music in its expressive potential. However, it is not necessary to become a master coder to use the technology for your own creative pursuits. To use a musical analogy, lots of great music has been composed with just a few chords, and this section provides a "three-chord" introduction to microcontroller programming. While detailed coding instruction is beyond the scope of the book, your skills and understanding will develop through experimentation with the many source code listings provided throughout the text. And numerous programming tutorials are available online including several tutorials at the OUP website.

DEVELOPMENT PROCESS

Programming an Arduino or Teensy microcontroller typically involves four steps:

1. Typing source code in the IDE.
2. Clicking the Verify button to ensure the code is free of errors and can be compiled into a working application.

3. Clicking the Upload button to upload the compiled sketch to an attached microcontroller.
4. Repeating the process to add features or fix or improve the sketch.

A First Sketch

Programmers typically create a "Hello, world!" application to ensure that a newly installed language or IDE is working. For microcontroller programmers, the "Hello, world!" application is often in the form of the simple blinking LED sketch described in the following paragraphs.

Main Functions

Functions are blocks of code that can be called using the function name provided before an opening bracket. Teensy and Arduino programs always start with the two building-block functions shown in Listing 1.1.[3] The first line of a function contains its name—*setup()* and *loop()* in this instance—and opening and closing brackets indicate the start and end of each function. Instructions are added between the opening and closing brackets and execute one line at a time moving from the top of the function to the bottom bracket. Although the functions in Listing 1.1 don't contain any instructions, they do demonstrate the use of comments— non-executable text—that can be added to clarify code logic or for other purposes. To create a comment, simply type two forward slashes and the compiler will ignore the remainder of the text on the line. I often add comments to clarify logic or to indicate "To Do" items such as new features or bug fixes.

Listing 1.1 setup() and loop()

```
void setup()
{
    // put your setup code here, to run once:

}

void loop()
{
    // put your main code here, to run repeatedly:

}
```

The *setup()* and *loop()* functions have a special purpose for Arduino and Teensy microcontrollers. *setup()* is called *once* whenever the microcontroller powers up, and *loop()* is called *repeatedly* after any code is executed in the *setup()* function. Use *setup()* to initialize variables, configure hardware, allocate memory, or for other one-time tasks. The *loop()* function is used for everything else from checking MIDI input to tracking the state of pushbuttons and other components (see Figure 1.6).

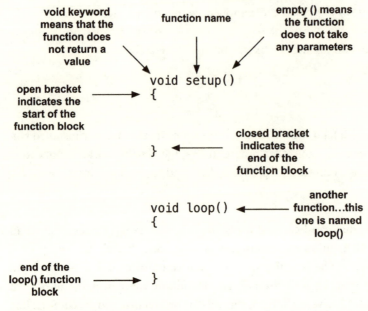

FIGURE 1.6 Visualizing functions

"Hello, World!" Blinking Sketch

Assuming you have installed the Arduino IDE and Teensy boards via the Boards Manager, follow these steps to program your microcontroller for the first time:

1. Connect the Teensy device to the computer via a USB cable.
2. Select the appropriate device from the Tools . . . Board Menu.
3. Select the device from the Tools . . . Port menu.
4. Enter the code shown in Listing 1.2, which is based on an example available via the Files . . . Examples . . . Teensy . . . Tutorial1 menu.
5. Click the compile button to turn the text into code that can be executed on the microcontroller.
6. Fix any typos and select the upload button to upload the compiled sketch to the Teensy device.

You should be greeted by a blinking LED. Collect ten points.

Listing 1.2 Blinking LED

```
//Use pin 11 for Teensy 2.0 or pin 6 for Teensy++ 2.0
int ledPin = 13;

void setup()
{
    // initialize the digital pin as an output.
    pinMode(ledPin, OUTPUT);
}

void loop()
{
    digitalWrite(ledPin, HIGH);  // set the LED on
    delay(1000);                 // wait for a second
    digitalWrite(ledPin, LOW);   // set the LED off
    delay(1000);                 // wait for a second
}
```

UNDERSTANDING THE BLINKING LED SKETCH

The blinking LED sketch illustrates several essential programming concepts. At the start of the program a variable named *ledPin* is assigned the value 13, a number that corresponds to a special digital pin that is connected to a built-in LED. We could have used any other valid name for the pin such as *TeensyLedPin* or *blinky_pin*, or some other descriptive name. The *int* keyword tells the compiler that the variable is an integer—a non-fractional number that can store positive or negative values. Other common data types include *float* (for fractional values) and *long* (for "large" integers), for example:

```
long big_number = 100000;
float pi = 3.14;
```

Additional data types are listed in Appendix A but rest assured that you can tackle most programming tasks with the types listed in this section.

A slight change to Listing 1.2 will improve the program and help to prevent hard-to-track bugs. Given that the pin assignment of the LED won't change, it makes better sense to declare *ledPin* as a *constant*, not a *variable*. Use the *const* keyword to tell the compiler that the assigned value will not change over the life of the program. Constants are useful in many contexts ranging from assigning pin numbers to categorizing MIDI messages:

```
const int ledPin = 13;
```

Moving back to the blinking LED sketch, notice how each instruction is followed by a semicolon but the function name and brackets are *not*. This distinction will become second nature after working through a few examples.

setup()

The setup function contains a comment and a single instruction. The instruction is a call to *pinMode()*, another built-in function available to Teensy and Arduino sketches. *pinMode()* takes two parameters representing the pin number and pin function, for example INPUT or OUTPUT—two constants that are pre-defined in the Arduino environment. Note that we could also pass the pin number directly, such as:

```
pinMode(13, OUTPUT); //Configure pin 13 for output
```

Although it is not a problem to pass pin numbers directly to a function, this can lead to logic errors in more complex applications—particularly if a sketch references a pin in more than one place.

WHAT'S WITH VOID?

A quick word about the *void* keyword. *void* indicates that a function does not return a value. A *void* function might be used to update a display or receive a MIDI note. In contrast, some functions return values. For example, you could create a custom function like the one shown in Listing 1.3 to calculate the square of a number. In this example, the function takes a single parameter, a temporary integer named *x*, and the *return* keyword returns the square of *x*. The *long* keyword at the start of the function specifies the return type—a *long* integer that can store larger values than a standard *int*.

Listing 1.3 Custom function

```
long square(int x)
{
    //Multiply x by itself and return the value
    return x * x;
}
```

Using functions, including the custom function shown above, is as simple as calling the function in code.

```
long myBigNumber = square(400); //myBigNumber = 160000
```

loop()

Most of the action happens in the loop function. Like *pinMode()*, *digitalWrite()* is another built-in function that takes two parameters: a number representing the microcontroller pin, and the pre-defined constant HIGH or LOW to indicate the status of the pin. The HIGH keyword indicates that the pin will output a voltage or, in the case of this sketch, light the built-in LED connected to the pin (see Listing 1.4).

Listing 1.4 Main loop() function

```
void loop()
{
    digitalWrite(ledPin, HIGH); // set the LED on
    delay(1000);                // wait for a second
    digitalWrite(ledPin, LOW); // set the LED off
    delay(1000);                // wait for a second
}
```

In this example, the *loop()* function also calls another built-in function named *delay()* that, unsurprisingly, delays the execution of the program for the given amount of milliseconds. This would be a good time to experiment by entering different delay values or, better yet, use a variable as shown in Listing 1.5.

> *Tip: It is generally a bad idea to use the delay function in code since it will prevent your sketch from responding to button presses, MIDI input, and other events. We will look at strategies for tracking time in other chapters.*

USING A VARIABLE

Make the following modifications to the blinking LED sketch to see the LED gradually blink faster and faster. Note how an "if" statement resets the variable to its initial state if *delay_amount* falls below 10 milliseconds (see Listing 1.5).

Listing 1.5 Using a variable

```
int delay_amount = 1000;

void loop()
```

```
    {
    digitalWrite(ledPin, HIGH);  // set the LED on
    delay(1000);                 // wait for a second
    digitalWrite(ledPin, LOW);   // set the LED off
    delay(1000);                 // wait for a second
    //Decrease the amount of delay by 1ms each loop
    delay_amount = delay_amount - 1;

    //Reset if delay_amount is less than 10 ms
    if(delay_amount < 10)
    {
    delay_amount = 1000;
    }
}
```

Of course, there is a lot more to programming than the code shown in this short example, but the sketch does illustrate many of the core concepts including program logic and the use of variables, constants, and functions. The sketch will provide a foundation for using the powerful Teensy Audio library to create custom synthesizers and other instruments and, as you will see in the pages that follow, it only takes about twenty-five lines of code to create your first interactive synthesizer!

Tip: Although this introduction to a first sketch is necessarily brief, video tutorials are available at the OUP website including "Crash Course in Teensy Programming."

MAKING SOUND

Now that we have explored the basics of a sketch, it is time to combine source code and a few electronic components to create a synthesizer that responds to light. Along the way you will learn to use PJRC's powerful Audio System Design Tool, and you will learn to read fluctuating voltages from photoresistors (also known as light-dependent resistors or LDRs) that are attached to the Teensy's analog pins. You will also learn that Teensy microcontrollers are robust and powerful devices that are surprisingly easy to use for a variety of interesting musical and sound-design tasks.

Audio System Design Tool

PJRC provides a helpful visual design tool that makes it easy to instantiate and connect audio components in the Teensy Audio Library. The tool, which provides many building block objects ranging from oscillators, amplifiers, mixers, and filters, is available at https://www.pjrc.com/teensy/gui/.

Tip: All the explorations in the first section of the book utilize a Teensy 4.0 with an appropriate Audio Adapter Board.

Making Sound: A First Synthesis Sketch

To get started with this project, run the Audio System Design Tool[4] via the internet and drag the following components into the workspace:

• Two waveform objects.
• One mixer.

- One i2s object.
- One sgtl5000 object.

Drag the rectangles on the right side of each object to make the connections shown in Figure 1.7.

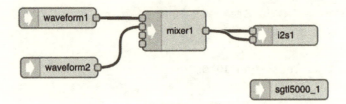

FIGURE 1.7 Two oscillators and a mixer

These objects, which are detailed in Appendix B, form the basis of many Teensy synthesis projects that utilize the Audio Adapter Board.

Select the Export button in the Audio System Design Tool and copy and paste the resulting code into the top of a newly created sketch in the Teensyduino IDE. Note that you can use the Import button to copy and paste an audio configuration from an existing sketch should you want to revisit a sketch that has been previously created in the Design Tool.

Boilerplate Initialization Code

Several lines of code must be added to initialize the audio system to produce sound from the Audio Adapter Board. Listing 1.6 demonstrates one way to initialize audio objects. Note that this code follows the *#include* statements and audio components that were copied and pasted from the Design Tool. In the C language, *#include* statements are typically added to incorporate a code library into a project. For example, libraries of pre-existing code are available through the #include mechanism to process MIDI messages, communicate with a serial connection, or for many other tasks.

Click the Upload button and connect headphones to the headphone jack of the Teensy Audio Adapter Board taking care not to wear the headphones until you are sure the output is at a comfortable level. You should hear a wonderfully "old school" synth bass sound. Don't worry if you don't understand the code in Listing 1.6. At this point, the nuances of the Audio System are less important than getting a feel for common tasks that are used to initialize the objects that were created with the Audio Design Tool.

Listing 1.6 Boilerplate initialization

```
void setup()
{
    AudioMemory(8);           //Reserve 8 blocks of audio memory
    sgtl5000_1.enable();      //Enable audio to the headphone jack
    sgtl5000_1.volume(0.40);  //Set headphone volume to 40%
    mixer1.gain(0, 0.35);     //Set mixer gain to 35% on channel 0
    mixer1.gain(1, 0.35);     //Set mixer gain to 35% on channel 1

    //Sawtooth wave at 35% and 80 Hz
    waveform1.begin(0.35, 80, WAVEFORM_SAWTOOTH);

    //Another sawtooth wave at 35% and 83 Hz
    waveform2.begin(0.35, 83, WAVEFORM_SAWTOOTH);
}
```

Member Selection Operator

Where functions such as *setup()* and *loop()* are used to organize code into useful blocks, Teensy audio objects provide similar functionality using blocks of code called *class methods* or *class functions*—a special type of function associated with a C++ class. For example, to set the gain of the *mixer1* object, use the variable name followed by a "." (dot) and the name of the method and include the channel (from 0 to 3) and volume (from 0.0 to 1.0) as parameters:[5]

```
mixer1.gain(0, 0.35); //Set channel 0 to 35% of maximum volume
```

Similarly, the *waveform1* and *waveform2* objects are initialized with the *begin()* method, which takes parameters representing the level (from 0.0 to 1.0), frequency, and waveform using one of the constants defined in *synth_waveform.h*, a file that is included with Teensyduino:

```
#define WAVEFORM_SINE              0
#define WAVEFORM_SAWTOOTH          1
#define WAVEFORM_SQUARE            2
#define WAVEFORM_TRIANGLE          3
#define WAVEFORM_ARBITRARY         4
#define WAVEFORM_PULSE             5
#define WAVEFORM_SAWTOOTH_REVERSE  6
#define WAVEFORM_SAMPLE_HOLD       7
```

Audio Memory

The only other parts of the boilerplate initialization that require an explanation are the calls to *AudioMemory()* and two calls to methods of the sgtl5000 class. As described in the Teensy Audio documentation, *AudioMemory()* allocates memory for all audio connections.[6] The function takes an integer indicating the number of audio blocks to be used. The documentation recommends starting with a reasonable default and adjusting the block size as necessary. Another function, *AudioMemoryUsageMax()*, can be called to optimize the memory-allocation values during the development process.

Stereo Codec

The SGTL5000 object refers to the onboard Stereo Codec that is used to stream audio input and output. In most cases, all that is required is to enable the device and set the volume in the *setup()* function:

```
sgtl5000_1.enable();
sgtl5000_1.volume(0.40); //Volume at 40% of max
```

Tip: Click on an object in the online Audio Design Tool to learn more about the available methods, variable ranges, and other information associated with a given object. Appendix B provides a summary of the waveform, mixer, i2s, and sgtl5000 objects that are central to many Teensy/Audio Adapter synthesis applications.

Example

Listing 1.7 demonstrates how the *frequency()* method of a waveform object can be configured to create a swooping effect. Other methods such as *pulseWidth()* and *amplitude()* function similarly:

Listing 1.7 Changing the frequency of a waveform object

```
float freq = 50.0;
const float rate = 1.05;

void loop()
{
        //Update waveform frequency
        waveform1.frequency(freq);
        //Multiply frequency by rate constant
        freq = freq * rate;

        //Reset freq to 50 Hz if frequency > 800 Hz
        if(freq > 800.0)
        {
            freq = 50.0;
        }
}
```

Tip: The Teensy 4.0 (and some other models) can also output audio over a USB connection. This is a powerful feature that enables the output of Teensy synthesis and audio projects to be recorded directly into a digital audio workstation. All that is required is to replace the i2S and sgtl5000 components with a single AudioOutputUSB component in the Audio System Design Tool, and to select the Tools . . . USB Type . . . Audio option in the Arduino IDE. Additional information is provided in Chapter 6.

Light Synth

This section builds on the previous audio demonstration to create an interactive *subtractive synthesizer* that responds to light or other forms of virtual voltage control. Subtractive synthesis is a popular synthesis typology where filters attenuate or "subtract" content from the harmonic spectrum to alter the timbre of a tone. To complete the project, it will be necessary to procure the following components:

- Teensy 3.2 or 4.0 microcontroller with Audio Adapter Board.
- Breadboard for prototyping.
- Hookup wire.

- Two or more photoresistors (also known as Light Dependent Resistors or LDRs).
- Two or more 10k resistors.

ADDING A DIGITAL FILTER TO LIGHT SYNTH

Although Teensy microcontrollers are digital devices—sounds are produced by converting digits to analog via a *Digital to Analog Converter* (DAC)—boards such as the Teensy 4.0 can emulate the components of an analog synthesizer including oscillator, filter, low-frequency oscillator (LFO), and envelope.

To add a filter to the Light Synth project, revisit the Audio System Design Tool and add the filter object as shown in Figure 1.8.

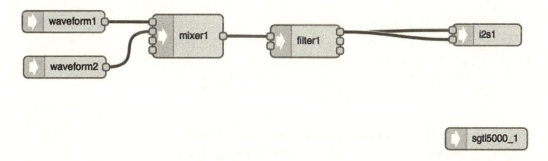

FIGURE 1.8 Adding a filter in the Audio System Design Tool

As with the previous synthesis example, use the export button and copy and paste from the Audio Design Tool into a newly created sketch (or download this or other examples from the OUP website).

The filter object, which is initialized using class methods, provides two inputs and three outputs. Connect a signal (e.g., the output of a mixer object) to the top input and (optionally) connect the output of an LFO to modulate the cutoff frequency of the filter. The outputs consist of low-pass, band-pass, and high-pass filters, respectively (see Table 1.1).

TABLE 1.1 Filter inputs and outputs.

Port	Purpose
In 0	Signal to Filter
In 1	Frequency Control
Out 0	Low-pass Output
Out 1	Band-pass Output
Out 2	High-pass Output

Enter the following code in the *setup()* function (this code should follow the code that was copied from the Design Tool), upload the sketch, and experiment with the filter parameters to get a feel for how filter cutoff and resonance alter the harmonic sound spectrum (see Listing 1.8).

Listing 1.8 Filter object configuration

```
void setup()
{
        AudioMemory(20);
        sgtl5000_1.enable();
        sgtl5000_1.volume(0.40);
        mixer1.gain(0, 0.50);

        //Configure filter cutoff frequency
        filter1.frequency(5000);
        //Resonance range is from 0.7 to 5.0
        filter1.resonance(4.8);
        //Alteration of corner freq. in octaves
        filter1.octaveControl(1);

        waveform1.begin(0.35, 80, WAVEFORM_SQUARE);
        waveform2.begin(0.35, 83, WAVEFORM_SQUARE);
}
```

USING A BREADBOARD

As fun as it is to hear powerful synthesized sounds emanating from the Teensy microcontroller, the real joy comes from using potentiometers and other components to control parameters in real time. An inexpensive breadboard like the one shown in Figure 1.9 provides a way to connect a variety of components to a Teensy or Arduino device and is akin to blank music manuscript in the hands of electrical engineers and music makers.

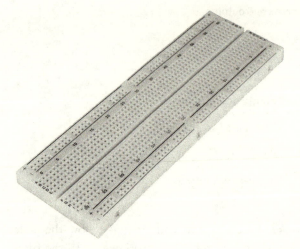

FIGURE 1.9 A solderless breadboard

Attach a Teensy 3.x or 4.x microcontroller (with Audio Board) to the breadboard (*making sure that the pins straddle each side of the center line of the board*) and use hookup wire to connect the ground pin to the blue ground rail and the 3.3V pin to one of the red rails (see Figure 1.10). Note that the power and ground rails are functionally akin to an auxiliary send on a mixer in that power and ground can be tapped at any point along the rail (left to right), a metaphor that will be familiar to many musicians.

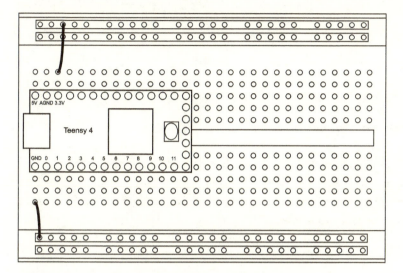

FIGURE 1.10 Connecting the Teensy to power and ground rails

The "strips" in the center of the breadboard are connected vertically but signals do not cross the center line. This is an important concept to remember when working with integrated circuits and microcontrollers **which *must* straddle the center line to avoid a short circuit.** Be mindful that the pins on components such as light detecting resistors are never connected to points on the same column (unless they straddle the center line) because electrons will follow the path of least resistance and simply bypass the component.

USING PHOTORESISTORS FOR PRIMITIVE VOLTAGE CONTROL

Connect a photoresistor and 10kΩ resistor as shown in Figures 1.11 (graphic representation) and 1.12 (circuit representation).[7] Note that one side of the photoresistor/light-detecting resistor is connected to the power 3.3V rail and the other side of the component connects to one side of a resistor before being attached to the A0 (Analog-0) pin of the Teensy. Connect the other side of the resistor to the ground rail.

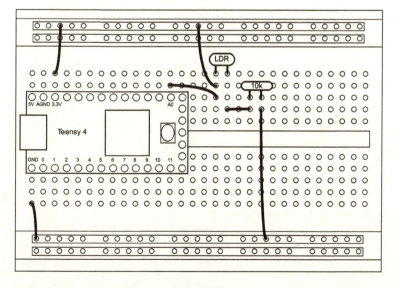

FIGURE 1.11 Photoresistor (graphic illustration)

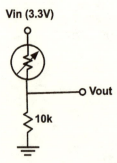

FIGURE 1.12 Photoresistor (schematic representation)

Connect another photoresistor to available slots on the breadboard and duplicate the previous circuit (but attach the output to the A1 pin on the Teensy).
Warning: Always connect LDRs, potentiometers, and related components to 3.3V (or lower) since higher voltages can damage your microcontroller.

Reading Values

It is now possible to read the output of the photoresistors and use those values to update audio parameters in the Audio System. This is easily achieved by calling the *analogRead()* function:

```
//Read the value of the first photoresistor
int value1 = analogRead(A0);
//Read the value of the second photoresistor
int value2 = analogRead(A1);
```

The values returned by *analogRead()* range from 0 to 1023 (10-bit resolution) and can be used "as is" for parameters such as frequency or filter cutoff or scaled to control a narrow range such as the range the 0.7 to 5.0 range used to control filter resonance in the Teensy Audio System.

One approach to real-time control is shown in Listing 1.9. In this example, the first photoresistor controls filter cutoff and the second photoresistor controls the frequency of the oscillators. To create a more authentic analog sound, the second oscillator is detuned by a constant defined at the start of the sketch.

Listing 1.9 Using the values returned from analogRead() to control synthesizer parameters

```
void loop()
{
        float filter_cutoff = analogRead(A0) + 1500;
        float freq = analogRead(A1) + 50;

        //Update filter and oscillator with new values
        filter1.frequency(filter_cutoff);
        waveform1.frequency(freq);
        waveform2.frequency(freq * detune);
}
```

Thinning Analog Input Data

In a complex program it can be helpful to avoid the overhead of calling *analogRead()* on every iteration of the main loop. One approach to thinning data is to use *elapsedMillis*, a timing object available to Teensy microcontrollers. As the name implies, *elapsedMillis* counts the number of milliseconds since the *elapsedMillis* object was instantiated. Listing 1.10, a complete listing of the main body of the Light Synth project, demonstrates how *elapsedMS* can query *analogRead()* at a slower rate such as every 50 milliseconds. Also note that two variables, *elapsedMS* and *detune*, are defined outside of any function body and, thus, have *global scope* see Listing 1.10). Global variables are useful when you want to track a value throughout the life of a program or when it is desirable for a variable to be visible to more than one function.

Listing 1.10 Main body of the Light Synth project

```
elapsedMillis elapsedMS;
const float detune = 1.01;

void setup()
{
        AudioMemory(20);
        sgtl5000_1.enable();
        sgtl5000_1.volume(0.40);
        mixer1.gain(0, 0.50);

        //Configure filter resonance
        filter1.resonance(4.8); //range is from 0.7 to 5.0
        filter1.octaveControl(1);
}

void loop()
{
        //Sample LDRs 20 times per second
        if(elapsedMS >= 50)
        {
            elapsedMS = 0; //Reset the counter
            float filter_cutoff = analogRead(A0) + 1500;
            float freq = analogRead(A1) + 50;

            //Update filter and oscillator with new values
            filter1.frequency(filter_cutoff);
            waveform1.frequency(freq);
            waveform2.frequency(freq * detune);
        }
}
```

Click the Upload button after entering and verifying Listing 1.10 and explore the variety of tones that can be produced by moving your hands in proximity to the photoresistors. It is also fun to experiment with a flashlight or phone to create dramatic effects.

Summary

The Light Synth project demonstrates the combined power of Teensy microcontrollers, the Audio System Design Tool, and the Teensy Audio Library. In this example, a unique synthesizer was created with a modest amount of source code (fewer than twenty-five lines excluding the code that was imported from the Audio Design Tool). It may be helpful to revisit the project after reading additional chapters to experiment with alternative approaches to synthesis such as frequency modulation, additive synthesis, or sample playback. The synthesizer could also be enclosed in a project box, cigar box, or finalized as a Eurorack instrument as described in Parts III and IV. Source code and demonstration videos for this and other projects are available from the OUP website.

Creative Challenge

Hands-on experimentation is the best way to develop fluency with a program language. To that end, consider how you might alter the code to incorporate additional features such as:

- Adding more oscillators to create light-dependent sound clusters.
- Adding another photoresistor for independent control of each oscillator.
- Adding a pushbutton for waveform selection.
- Adding a photoresistor or potentiometer to control amplitude levels.
- Adding additional oscillators that respond to light in unique ways such as individual frequency and amplitude scaling.

There are also many avenues of exploration beyond coding. For example, invite friends or an audience to interact with the device with the flashlight feature of their cell phones. Or place a slow-moving fan between the device and a light source to create unique oscillating effects.

CHAPTER 2

WAVETABLE SYNTHESIS

This chapter builds on concepts developed in Chapter 1 with a focus on *wavetable synthesis*, a category of music synthesis that is particularly useful for producing realistic sounds ranging from flutes and strings to percussion and sound effects. You will also learn how to use potentiometers to interact with the audio system and incorporate USB to process MIDI Note-On and Note-Off messages. Readers are encouraged to visit the OUP website to download source code and other resources.

The wavetable project detailed in this chapter is a simple synthesizer that uses two potentiometers (described later in the chapter) to control attack and release of an envelope.

The following components are required to complete the project:

- Teensy 3.2 or 4.0 microcontroller with Audio Adapter Board.
- Breadboard for prototyping.
- Hookup wire.
- Two or more 10k potentiometers.

Overview of Wavetable Synthesis

Unlike other forms of synthesis such as subtractive, additive, or frequency modulation that excel at creating unique synthetic sounds, sample-based synthesis is useful for producing acoustic sounds that would be difficult or impossible to produce with other synthesis methods. With wavetable synthesis, a table of samples is stored in a memory block and played back at a periodic rate to recreate a sound, in much the same way we perceive motion when the frames of a film are viewed at different speeds.[1] Although sample playback has several advantages, one distinct disadvantage—particularly regarding microcontrollers—is the fact that samples can require large amounts of memory. For this reason, I typically use samples only for short loops or percussive sounds.

ANATOMY OF A SAMPLE

As the name implies, wavetable oscillators contain a table or array of samples representing a waveform—a series of fluctuating voltage levels. The samples are created by taking periodic snapshots of a signal at a steady rate called the *sample rate* (see Figure 2.1). CD recordings, for example, utilize a sample rate of 44,100 samples per second although higher rates are routinely used in modern recording studios.

Sound & Music Projects for Eurorack and Beyond. Brent Edstrom, Oxford University Press. © Oxford University Press 2024.
DOI: 10.1093/9780197514504.003.0002

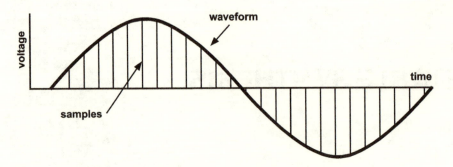

FIGURE 2.1 Sampling a sine wave

A related term, *bit depth*, refers to the number of bits used to represent incoming voltage levels. In an 8-bit sampling system, for example, fluctuating voltages are captured with one of only 256 possible voltage levels. In contrast, 16 bits are used to record samples in CD audio and provide 65,536 possible dynamic levels for a given range of voltages. Figure 2.2 illustrates how more bits provide better dynamic accuracy.

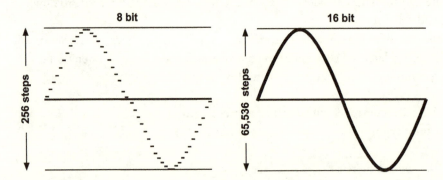

FIGURE 2.2 Conceptualization of low- and high-fidelity bit depth

PERIOD AND FREQUENCY

Musicians routinely deal with *frequency*, the measure of the number of occurrences of a wave in a given amount of time, but frequency is directly linked to *periodicity*—the length of time (in seconds) for a wave to complete a cycle. As is evident in Figure 2.3, frequency and periodicity have a reciprocal relationship: the period of a waveform decreases as frequency increases and vice versa, as described by the equation:

$$T = \frac{1}{f}$$

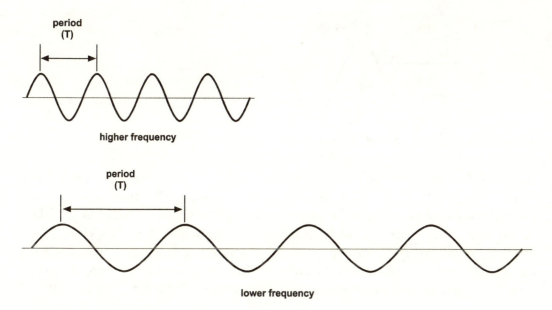

FIGURE 2.3 Frequency and periodicity

VISUALIZING A LOOKUP TABLE

The Teensy Audio Library provides a wavetable oscillator that stores an array of samples called a *lookup table*. With this approach, one period of the waveform is stored in the lookup table and the oscillator accesses the samples at a rate that will produce the desired frequency. Figure 2.4 provides a conceptualization of the process.

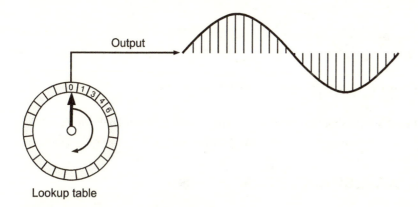

FIGURE 2.4 Conceptualization of a lookup table

SAMPLING INCREMENT

Once a signal has been digitized into a lookup table, the wavetable oscillator can output a variety of frequencies—just like other types of digital oscillators. This is achieved by adjusting the period of the wavetable. One way to visualize the process is to consider a one-second digitization of A-440 Hz performed on a piano. Assuming a sample rate of 44.1 kHz, 44,100 samples are required to capture the recording. Playing back the digitization is simply a matter of outputting the samples through a digital-to-analog converter at the same rate as the initial digitization—44.1 kHz in this case (see Figure 2.5). Here, the step-size or increment value has a one-to-one relationship with the wavetable, so the period (and frequency) remains the same as the original.

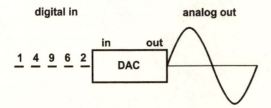

FIGURE 2.5 Conceptualization of playing samples through a DAC

Now, consider what would happen if the playback engine skipped every other sample when outputting the waveform at 44.1 kHz. Instead of incrementing one step for every sample, the increment value would increase to 2 and the waveform period would be halved, resulting in a doubling of frequency (880 Hz, in this example). Phrased another way, two iterations of the waveform are output in the same timespan as the original waveform by increasing the increment value. Similarly, the original frequency of 440 Hz would decrease to 220 Hz with an increment value of 0.5 since the period—the amount of time it takes to iterate the waveform—is doubled (see Figure 2.6).

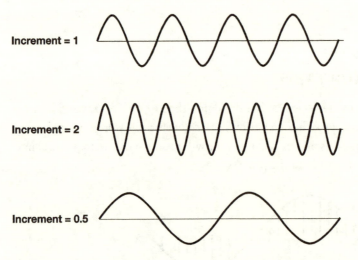

FIGURE 2.6 Conceptualization of wavetable increment value and frequency

Other frequencies can be achieved using fractional increment values but, fortunately, those details are conveniently handled by the wavetable audio objects provided by the Teensy Audio Library.

A WORD ABOUT WAVESHAPING SYNTHESIS

Waveshaping synthesis is an interesting evolution of wavetable or sample-playback synthesis. Where the accumulator of a sample-based synthesizer can be thought of as a ramp wave—the accumulator increments until it reaches a peak jumps to a lower value—waveshaping synthesis provides a mechanism for utilizing other waveform shapes to index a lookup table.[2] Although the wavetable object in the Teensy Audio Library doesn't provide a way to alter the indexing mechanism beyond selecting a given frequency, waveshaping synthesis can be achieved by coding custom audio objects. Chapter 7 provides an overview of writing custom DSP objects, and additional information on the use of fixed-point math for high-resolution indexing can be found in my own *Arduino for Musicians*.[3]

EXPLORING SAMPLE PLAYBACK

The WavetableSynth project provides a convenient way to experiment with wavetable synthesis. The project responds to USB MIDI input and provides two potentiometers to control the envelope or dynamic contour of the output. Start by downloading the WavetableSynth project from the OUP website and copy the folder to the appropriate Arduino sketch folder on your computer. The sketch includes wavetable samples that are extracted from SoundFont2 files and configured with the objects shown in Figure 2.7. Alternatively, read Appendix C to create a project with your own custom samples.

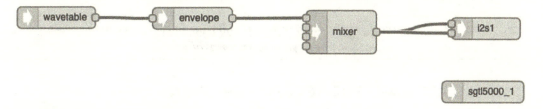

FIGURE 2.7 WavetableSynth objects

ADDING POTENTIOMETERS

The Wavetable synthesis project uses two potentiometers for real-time control of the attack and release parameters of an envelope. Potentiometers, also known as *variable resistors*, are functionally like the photoresistors described in Chapter 1 in that they provide a variable amount of resistance, but a knob controls the level of resistance instead of ambient light. Connect the potentiometers to a breadboard as shown in Figure 2.8. The amount of resistance is not critical for this application, but 10k is a common value.

Tip: Inexpensive trimmer potentiometers are a good option for breadboarding since the legs can usually be plugged directly into a solderless breadboard. Be sure to select trimmer pots with knobs since it is inconvenient to use a screwdriver to adjust a potentiometer.

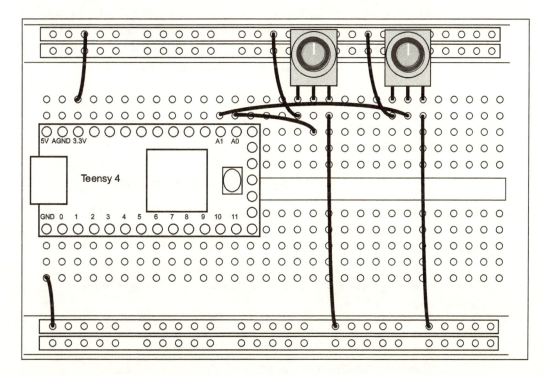

FIGURE 2.8 Wiring potentiometers

Note how one outer leg of the potentiometer connects to a positive voltage provided by the microcontroller and the other outer leg connects to ground. The middle leg provides a variable voltage based on the position of the knob, and this voltage is read via the Teensy analog pins—A0 and A1 in this example. You can flip the orientation of the potentiometer or swap the 3.3V and GND leads if the knob functions in the wrong direction. Or, to coin an audio recording phrase, "fix it in the mix" by altering source code. Also note how the top rail is connected to the 3.3V Teensy pin and the bottom rail connects to GND.

Warning: Always connect potentiometer pins to 3.3V (or lower) since higher voltages can damage your microcontroller.

CONFIGURATION IN THE SETUP() FUNCTION

The *setup()* function initializes the audio system using the boilerplate code shown in Listing 2.1, code that is similar to the boilerplate code from Chapter 1.

Listing 2.1 Initializing the audio system

```
void setup()
{

    AudioMemory(20);
    sgtl5000_1.enable();
    sgtl5000_1.volume(0.8);
    mixer.gain(0, 0.7);
    .
    .
    .
```

The *setup()* function also configures the wavetable oscillator to use digital samples supplied in the decoded header (.h) and source (.cpp) files, which are available as extra tabs in the Aurduino IDE. View the header file tab and look for the variable listed after *AudioSynthWavetable::instrument_data* (see the boldface **strings** variable shown in Listing 2.2).

Listing 2.2 Locating the name of wavetable data

```
//From strings_samples.h
#pragma once
#include <Audio.h>
extern const AudioSynthWavetable::instrument_data strings;
```

The variable provides a way to connect the wavetable object that was created by the Audio System Design Tool with the digital samples contained in the header (.h) and source (.cpp) files as shown in Listing 2.3:

Listing 2.3 Connecting a wavetable oscillator to Soundfont data stored in the sample header file

```
void setup()
{
        //Audio initialization goes here
        //Point to wavetable data
        wavetable.setInstrument(strings);

}
```

SETTING UP USB MIDI CALLBACK FUNCTIONS

One of the best features of Teensy microcontrollers is the ease with which USB MIDI can be incorporated into a project. Simply select "Tools . . . USB Type: MIDI" from the IDE menu and your project will be ready to function as a USB MIDI input or output device. However, it is necessary to tell the Teensy what to do with those messages. Other chapters provide more information regarding the use of USB and five-pin DIN MIDI but, for now, we will configure the Teensy to handle incoming Note-On and Note-Off messages.

One convenient approach to handling MIDI messages is to use a *callback* function.[4] The idea is to write a function with a specific prototype expected by the Teensy and ask the USB MIDI handler to automatically call that function when relevant MIDI data is received. As shown in Listing 2.4, use the *setHandleNoteOff()* and *setHandleNoteOn()* methods to pass a pointer to the your note-handling functions. Note that pointers will be detailed in later chapters but, for now, understand that the "setter" functions in Listing 2.4 receive the memory location of the callback functions when the function names are passed as a parameter.

Listing 2.4 Setting Note-On and Note-Off handlers

```
void setup()
{
    //Audio initialization and wavetable configuration goes here

    //MIDI Callback setup
    usbMIDI.setHandleNoteOff(onNoteOff);
    usbMIDI.setHandleNoteOn(onNoteOn);
}
```

*Tip: MIDI has been so seamlessly integrated into almost every music application that some users—at least many of my students—are not always aware of its purpose and function. Unlike audio recording or virtual synthesis applications that output digital audio **sound**, MIDI is a communications protocol that transmits **performance data**. MIDI can be used to send and receive numbers representing the pitch and loudness of a note or to determine when a damper pedal has been pressed (among many other things), but no sound is transferred in the process.*

WRITING MIDI NOTE HANDLERS

Using information provided by the Teensy MIDI documentation, write two functions with the expected parameters as shown in Listing 2.5. The functions can have any name, but the number and type of parameters must match the expected prototype.[5]

Listing 2.5 Note-On and Note-Off callback function prototypes

```
void onNoteOn(byte channel, byte note, byte velocity)
{
        //Handle Note-On messages here
}

void onNoteOff(byte channel, byte note, byte velocity)
{
        //Handle Note-Off messages here
}
```

Fleshing out the Note-On and Note-Off callback functions is easily achieved by passing the note and velocity values to the wavetable oscillator via its *playNote()* method (see Listing 2.6). The *playNote()* messages are followed by a call to the *noteOn()* method of the envelope—one of the other objects created in the Audio System Design Tool as shown in Figure 2.7. As you will see, the envelope object provides a convenient way to alter attack and release (and other parameters) in real-time via a potentiometer or other component. The value of the note is stored in a global variable named *last_note*—which makes it easier to coordinate Note-On and Note-Off messages. A key concept is that the *playNote()* and *envelope()* methods shown in Listing 2.6 correspond with objects created in the visual Audio Design Tool.

Listing 2.6 Complete onNoteOn() callback function

```
void onNoteOn(byte channel, byte note, byte velocity)
{
        wavetable.playNote(note, velocity);
        envelope.noteOn();
        last_note = note;
}
```

The Note-Off callback function is similarly simple (see Listing 2.7). In this case, the function checks to see if the incoming Note-Off message matches the current Note-On message—a technique that helps to prevent erroneous Note-Off events when playing with a legato touch.

Listing 2.7 The complete onNoteOff() callback function

```
void onNoteOff(byte channel, byte note, byte velocity)
{
        if(note == last_note)
        {

            envelope.noteOff();
        }
}
```

THE MAIN LOOP

Two tasks are all that are required of the main *loop()* to complete the monophonic wavetable synthesizer project:

1. Call *usbMIDI.read()* to force the MIDI system to read any incoming MIDI messages.
2. Call *analogRead()* to read the status of the potentiometers and use those values to update the attack and release of the envelope.

Calling usbMIDI.read()

Note how, in Listing 2.8, *usbMIDI.read()* is called during each iteration of the main loop. This is an easy step to forget, but it is necessary to tell the USB MIDI manager to read incoming messages and, in turn, trigger any necessary calls to the callback functions created in the previous step.

CHAPTER 2 WAVETABLE SYNTHESIS   29

Listing 2.8 Calling usbMIDI.read() in the main loop

```
void loop()
{
        while (usbMIDI.read()) {
        }
}
```

Calling analogRead()

Listing 2.9 shows how the value of each potentiometer is stored in the variables *knob1* and *knob2* via the *analogRead()* function. A common task when programming microcontrollers is to read the value of an analog input (such as the potentiometers attached to the A0 and A1 pins) and scale the value for use in a sketch. In its default configuration, *analogRead()* returns a 10-bit value in the range of 0–1,023—a range that will seem arbitrary for many applications. One way to scale values is to use floating point numbers to calculate a percentage based on the given voltage level. The percentage can then be multiplied by a desired range such as 0–4,000 (which represents a maximum duration of 4,000 milliseconds in the context of the wavetable sketch):

```
float knob1 = analogRead(A0);     //Read value from A0 pin (0-1,023)
float percent = knob1 / 1023.0;   //Calculate percentage: e.g. 0.75
float ms = percent * 4000;        //Apply percentage to desired range
```

Given that the task of scaling incoming voltages is so common, the Arduino library provides a function named *map()* that returns a scaled value based on a given input, expected range (0–1,023), and scaled range (0–4,000 for this example).[6]

```
//Scale potentiometer values (0-1023) to duration (0-4 seconds)
float attack = map(knob1, 0, 1023, 0, 4000);
```

A final step is to send the scaled values to the *attack()* and *release()* methods of the envelope object for real-time control of those parameters.

Listing 2.9 Reading potentiometers

```
void loop()
{
        while (usbMIDI.read()) {
        }

        //Read potentiometers
        int knob1 = analogRead(A0);
        int knob2 = analogRead(A1);

        //Scale potentiometer values (0-1023) to duration (0-4
            seconds)
        float attack = map(knob1, 0, 1023, 0, 4000);
        float release = map(knob2, 0, 1023, 0, 4000);
```

```
                    //Update the envelope
                    envelope.attack(attack);
                    envelope.release(release);

}
```

Amazingly, only 50 lines of code are required to produce a working monophonic wavetable synthesizer that responds to incoming USB MIDI messages and provides real-time control of attack and release parameters. This speaks to the power of the Teensy audio library as well as Object Oriented Programming (OOP) where powerful objects, such as the *AudioSynthWavetable* oscillator, handle the low-level details that can make real-time synthesis such a challenge.

> *Tip:* Appendix C details the process of using the Polyphone Soundfont Editor to derive your own custom samples from a Soundfont2 wavetable.

Using the Wavetable Synthesizer

Where traditional five-pin DIN MIDI will be more appropriate for most finished projects (and the circuits are covered in Chapter 8), USB MIDI provides a convenient way to interact with projects during the development phase. My preferred method is to use a digital audio workstation (DAW) as a USB MIDI source when breadboarding. Assuming the Teensy device has been programmed as a USB MIDI device using the Tools setting in the Arduino IDE as described earlier in the chapter, it should show up as a MIDI device in DAWs including Ableton Live, Logic Pro, Cubase, and others. There are even web-based options including Signal, an open-source online MIDI editor available at https://signal.vercel.app/ (see Figure 2.9).

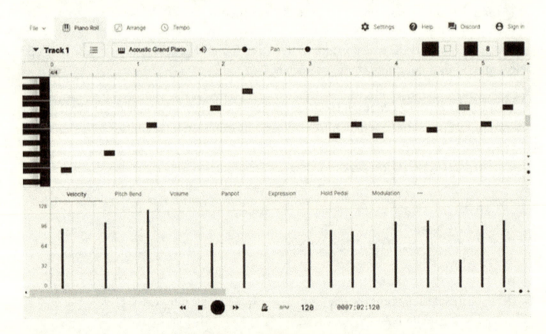

FIGURE 2.9 Using an online MIDI editor to send USB MIDI to a Teensy project

Alternatively, you can generate MIDI messages directly in the main loop by calling the appropriate MIDI handler. For example, the following code snippet will produce random MIDI notes with a velocity of 100 when placed in the main loop of the wavetable sketch:

```
onNoteOn(1, random(127), 100);
delay(500);
```

Summary

As with the Light Synth project from Chapter 1, components from the Teensy Audio System Design Tool simplify the process of using microcontrollers for music synthesis. The wavetable object can be used as the basis for a monophonic or polyphonic sample-based synthesizer, and the output can be processed by other objects in the library such as filers and digital signal processors.

CREATIVE CHALLENGE

Readers are encouraged to experiment with the source code provided on the OUP website. Consider the following programming challenges as a vehicle to develop programming fluency, or enjoy incorporating your own features:

- Use the tips from Appendix C to create your own custom samples for use in a Teensy audio project.
- Connect additional potentiometers to control envelope decay and sustain levels.
- Generate random notes in the main loop.
- Generate a series of ascending or descending notes in the main loop (e.g., ascending thirds or fourths).
- Incorporate additional oscillators to create a harmonization feature.
- Incorporate a second oscillator to respond to MIDI notes on another channel.

Also consider ways that the project could be used in conjunction with a DAW or free online sequencer. For example, you could create custom samples from objects around your home, bird calls, or nature. Or use digital editing software to mangle samples into a unique sound source for the instrument. It is fun and informative to adapt the technology for your own creative pursuits!

CHAPTER 3

CREATING A SYNTHESIZER USER INTERFACE

This chapter details the development of a synthesizer interface that can be used to experiment with a variety of synthesis topologies. We look at pushbuttons, rotary encoders, and an OLED display as well as programming concepts including arrays, references, and object pointers that form the basis of an extensible synthesizer interface. The user interface project utilizes the following components:

- Teensy 3.2 or 4.0 microcontroller.
- Breadboard for prototyping.
- Hookup wire.
- Four rotary encoders with built-in tactile switch. Encoder breakout modules are a good option for use on a solderless breadboard.
- Four through-hole tactile switches (only required if encoders do not contain a switch).
- Inexpensive 0.96-inch I2C OLED display compatible with the Adafruit SSD1306 library.

Developing a User Interface

The user interface (see Figure 3.1) consists of four rotary encoders (with integrated pushbuttons) and an OLED display. The pushbuttons are used for menu selection and the encoders are configured to control multiple parameters. The minimalist user interface is simple to breadboard but will provide enough flexibility to control the additive, frequency modulation, and granular synthesizers in the chapters that follow. The interface also forms the basis for one of the capstone projects in the last section of the book—a fully functional Eurorack FM synthesizer. Of course, many other designs could be developed with these or other components, but a primary benefit of the simple design is that it lends itself to Eurorack projects where rack space is often at a premium. We will begin with a discussion of pushbuttons, encoders, and OLED displays and then consider the underlying programming logic to create a useful interface.

Sound & Music Projects for Eurorack and Beyond. Brent Edstrom, Oxford University Press. © Oxford University Press 2024.
DOI: 10.1093/9780197514504.003.0003

CHAPTER 3 CREATING A SYNTHESIZER USER INTERFACE   33

FIGURE 3.1 Simple Eurorack user interface

PUSHBUTTONS

Bear in mind that standalone momentary pushbuttons can be used, or you can incorporate rotary encoders with built-in pushbuttons as shown in Figure 3.1. Small tactile switches can be a great choice for breadboarding if you don't have access to encoders with built-in switches.

Connecting Pushbuttons and Tactile Switches

To use a pushbutton in your sketch, connect one pin to ground and connect a corresponding pin to a digital pin on the microcontroller as shown in Figure 3.2. Pull-up resistors are often used with switches to avoid a *floating pin*, but an internal pull-up resistor can be configured for the purpose.[1]

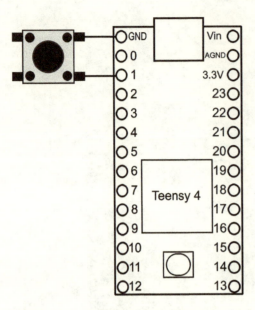

FIGURE 3.2 Connecting a tactile switch to a Teensy microcontroller

Using the Bounce Class

The term *class*, in the context of C++ programming, represents a user-defined data type. Many of the libraries available to Arduino and Teensy rely on one or more classes and can be used without an understanding of the inner workings of the code. This is the beauty of object-oriented programming where objects are designed to solve or simplify programming challenges by encapsulating functionality.

The *Bounce* class, provided by PJRC as part of the Teensyduino add-on, makes it easy to incorporate pushbuttons into projects.[2] All that is required is to include the *Bounce.h* header file and create an instance of a Bounce object. Incidentally, header files provide a mechanism for incorporating pre-existing code and classes into a project.

Listing 3.1 illustrates the creation of a *Bounce* object named *btn1* that connects to digital pin 1 and has a 15-millisecond debounce—the amount of time the object will ignore spurious voltage changes after the pushbutton is pressed. You can experiment with different debounce values as appropriate for a given application.

Listing 3.1 Creating a Bounce object

```
#include <Bounce.h>  //Include the Bounce.h header file

//Create a Bounce object named btn1 on pin 1
Bounce btn1 = Bounce(1, 15);
```

Switches will need a *pull-up resistor* to prevent random voltage levels that result from a floating pin, but that is easily achieved using the INPUT_PULLUP macro as shown in Listing 3.2. In this case, the pin is configured as an input with an internal pull-up resistor and a single call to *pinMode()* in the *setup()* function.

Listing 3.2 Configuring internal pull-up for a pin

```
void setup()
{
    //Configure pin 1 with an internal pull-up
    pinMode(1, INPUT_PULLUP);
}
```

Reading the status of a pushbutton switch involves calling the *update()* method of the *Bounce* object and then calling *fallingEdge()* to determine if the switch is engaged (see Listing 3.3). A method named *risingEdge()* is also available should you want to detect the release of a pushbutton.

Tip: *The update() method of the Bounce class should be called repeatedly from the main loop.*

Listing 3.3 Checking for a button press

```
void loop()
{
    btn1.update();
    if(btn1.fallingEdge())
    {
        //Button pressed! Do something interesting here.
    }
}
```

ROTARY ENCODERS

Rotary encoders are useful components that are conceptually like a coordinated pair of switches. Unlike potentiometers, encoders provide precision and an unlimited range. Where potentiometers bottom out at both ends of their range, encoders can travel an unlimited number of turns in either direction.

Connecting a Rotary Encoder

As shown in Figure 3.3, connect the two encoder outputs to digital pins on the Teensy and connect the GND pin of the encoders to GND on the microcontroller.

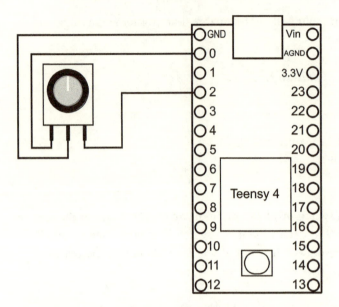

FIGURE 3.3 Connecting a rotary encoder to a microcontroller

Tip: Most rotary encoders are designed to be soldered to a PCB and can be challenging to work with on a breadboard. Several manufactures offer breakout modules with an encoder soldered to a small PCB and pins that are breadboard compatible (see Figure 3.4).

FIGURE 3.4 Encoder breakout modules on a breadboard

Using the Encoder Class

As with the *Bounce* class listed in the previous section, the *Encoder* class makes quick work of incorporating a rotary encoder in a sketch. Be sure to include the *Encoder.h* header file and instantiate an Encoder object, as shown in Listing 3.4.

CHAPTER 3 CREATING A SYNTHESIZER USER INTERFACE   37

Listing 3.4 Creating an Encoder object

```
#include <Encoder.h>

//Create an encoder that connects to digital pins 2 and 3
Encoder encoder1(2, 3);
```

Creating an Encoder Tracking Function (simple)

Listing 3.5 demonstrates a basic encoder tracking function. In this example a *static variable*—a non-volatile variable that has local scope—stores the most recent position of the encoder. The *read()* member function returns the accumulated position of the encoder and the difference is calculated by subtracting the previous position from the current position. One benefit of using an accumulated position is that the *same* encoder handler can be used to update multiple variables—something that will become clear as we use object references to expand the user interface in the pages that follow.

> **Tip:** *Listing 3.5 uses a long integer instead of a standard int to read values returned by the encoder. The long keyword signifies a variable that can store a larger range of values, and it is the best choice in this application since the Encoder class returns long integers.*

Listing 3.5 Encoder tracking function (basic)

```
long handleEncoder()
{
    //A static variable to store the last encoder position
    static long last_position = 0;

    //Read the position
    long pos = encoder1.read();

    if(pos == last_position)
    {
            //No need to continue, difference = 0
            return 0;
    }

    //Calculate the difference
    long difference = pos - last_position;
    //Remember the new position
    last_position = pos;
    return difference;
}
```

OLED DISPLAY

I2C OLED displays like the one shown in Figure 3.5 are a great choice for DIY Eurorack projects given their low cost, small form factor, and ease of use. The displays provide an inexpensive and flexible way to provide user feedback representing modes of operation, synthesizer parameters, and related information.

FIGURE 3.5 OLED display

Connecting an OLED Display

Displays such as Adafruit's SSD1306 can function as an I2C device and are connected to a Teensy using the pins listed in Table 3.1.[3] I2C is a serial protocol that utilizes two wires to connect low speed devices to a microcontroller, but note the following caution from PJRC regarding pull-up resistors:

TABLE 3.1 OLED I2C pin assignments.

Signal	Teensy 2.0	Teensy++ 2.0	Teensy LC	Teensy 3.0–3.6	Teensy 4.0, 4.1
SCL	Pin 5	Pin 0	Pin 19	Pin 19	Pin 19
SDA	Pin 6	Pin 1	Pin 18	Pin 18	Pin 18

Caution: "Normally a 4.7k pullup resistor is connected between each signal and power (+3.3V on Teensy 3.0, +5V on Teensy 2.0). On Teensy 2.0, 4.0, and 4.1, the weak internal pullup resistors may be sufficient for short wires to a single device. Because the internal resistors are so weak, communication may be slower or unreliable if the wires are long. Teensy LC & 3.0-3.6 requires pullup resistors to +3.3V. The on-chip pullups are not used. 4.7k resistors are recommended for most applications."[4]

To paraphrase, connect the device to the pins listed in Table 3.1, but also connect 4.7k resistors between the pins and +3.3V for better speed and reliability—particularly when moving from a solderless breadboard to finalized project (see Figure 3.6).

> ***Tip:*** *Be sure to check the pinout of any OLED you intend to purchase if it is to be used with the printed circuit boards presented in the last section of the book: the location of the ground and power pins are reversed on some units.*

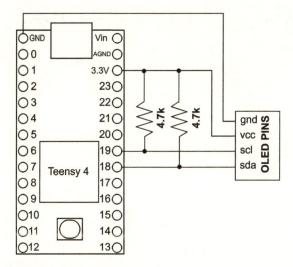

FIGURE 3.6 I²C OLED hookup

Configuring an OLED

Adafruit provides a library that makes it easy to incorporate a 1306 compatible I2C OLED display in your project. The library is available via the Library Manger in the Arduino IDE and requires the following header files to be included at the top of the sketch:

```
#include <Adafruit_GFX.h>
#include <Adafruit_SSD1306.h>
```

You will also need to create an instance of an *Adafruit_SSD1306* object and specify the reset pin, but note that a default of –1 (no reset) will work for the many displays that do not provide a reset pin:

```
const int OLED_RESET = -1;
Adafruit_SSD1306 display(OLED_RESET);
```

Finally, use the following boilerplate code to initialize the OLED display in the *setup()* function of your main sketch (see Listing 3.6).[5]

Listing 3.6 Setting up an OLED display

```
void setup()
{
    //Let circuitry stabilize then initialize OLED display
    delay(100);
    display.begin(SSD1306_SWITCHCAPVCC, 0x3C);
    display.setTextSize(1);
    //This mode overwrites text
    display.setTextColor(WHITE, BLACK);

}
```

Outputting Text

At this point the display is ready for action using the methods found in the Adafruit_SSD1306.h header file. For example, call the function shown in Listing 3.7 to print a ubiquitous "Hello, world!" message on the OLED screen using functions such as *clearDisplay()* and *setCursor()* from the header file.

Listing 3.7 "Hello, world!" example

```
void helloWorld()
{
    display.clearDisplay(); //Clear the display
    display.setCursor(0,0); //Set cursor to top left corner

    //Write a message
    display.print("Hello, world!");

    display.display(); //Tell the display to update contents
}
```

A Helper Function

You will likely find the display to be somewhat "kludgy" to use, so helper functions such as the one shown in Listing 3.8 can be convenient. This example takes a String object and floating-point value and prints the string and number to the location represented by x1, y1 and x2, y2 respectively—functionality that is useful when printing value and label pairs. As is evident in the listing, the *value* parameter is converted to a String with two decimal places. Remember that it is necessary to call *display.display()* after *printValue()* to see any text on the screen.

Listing 3.8 printValue() helper function

```
void printValue(String label, float value, int x1, int y1,
    int x2, int y2)
{
    display.setCursor(x1,y1);
    display.print(label);

    //Format the value as a string
    String val = String(value, 2);
    display.setCursor(x2, y2);
    display.print(val);
}
```

Connecting Code to Components

Now that we have explored pushbuttons, encoders, and an OLED display, it is time to combine those components into a complete user interface. Pin assignments for all switches and encoders are listed at the top of the source file, and the file will provide a useful vehicle for experimenting with menu systems and parameter manipulation.

This section provides an overview of enumerations, pointers, references, arrays, and other advanced programming concepts, so readers who are new to programming might want to skim the text and continue to the practical applications in the next chapter. It is not necessary to have a deep understanding of advanced programming techniques to experiment with the interface, and hands-on experimentation with the previous source code will provide a good foundation for further study.

Figure 3.7 illustrates one approach to wiring user interface elements. In this example, the OLED and rotary encoders are placed on a small solderless breadboard and hookup wire is used to connect the components to a Teensy microcontroller.

FIGURE 3.7 Connecting components on a solderless breadboard

A SIMPLE MENU SYSTEM

Connect four pushbuttons (or encoder pushbuttons) using the pin assignments shown in Listing 3.9. This example also features an *enumeration*, which provides a convenient way of naming modes of operation instead of hard-coding specific numbers. For example, mode1 equals 0, mode2 equals 1, and so on. The modes of operation that are selected by the pushbuttons are stored in the global variable *current_mode*. Each mode represents a virtual page or entry screen that will be useful in setting up a multi-page interface for a synthesizer. For example, you might use an enumeration to name volume, tuning, and envelope pages for a synthesizer project.

Listing 3.9 Configuring four pushbuttons

```
#include <Bounce.h>

//Set up push buttons
Bounce btn1 = Bounce(1, 15);
Bounce btn2 = Bounce(4, 15);
Bounce btn3 = Bounce(9, 15);
Bounce btn4 = Bounce(16, 15);

//Menu options:
enum{mode1, mode2, mode3, mode4};

int current_mode = mode1;

void setup()
{
    //Configure internal pull-up for pushbuttons
    pinMode(1, INPUT_PULLUP);
    pinMode(4, INPUT_PULLUP);
    pinMode(9, INPUT_PULLUP);
    pinMode(16, INPUT_PULLUP);
}
```

A Word About Pointers and References

Pointers and references can be tricky to work with, but they are helpful in many contexts and the basics are not hard to comprehend. The general idea is that it is sometimes helpful to use the *memory address* of a variable or object instead of directly calling the variable or object by name (or creating a copy of the object).

One way to think about pointers is to consider how physical mailing addresses are used. For example, a musician could design a snazzy promotional flyer and mail the flyer to 100 addresses to promote a concert of punk polka music. Addresses enable the musician to communicate a message to 100 households *without needing to know the names of the potential concertgoers*. In a similar way, C-language pointers and C++ references provide a means for communicating with a variable or object through a *memory address* without needing to know the name of a specific instance of a variable or object.

In the case of the user interface project, the four pushbuttons could be tracked with four nearly identical functions. That approach makes a lot of sense for certain applications, but we could also write a *single* function and pass a pointer or a reference to the Bounce object that is of interest. Although the difference is subtle, the function no longer needs to know the specific *name* of each instance of the Bounce object since the function uses the memory address of the object. In this case, using an address reduces redundant code and enables the same code to be used for multiple objects. Pointers and references may not make sense for simple projects, but they provide a helpful level of abstraction for this application where the same set of pushbuttons and encoders are used to select and update multiple operating modes, submenus, and variables.

References and pointers are functionally similar. Use an ampersand to find the memory address of a variable or object, and use an asterisk to declare a pointer of a given type.[6] In contrast, use an ampersand after an object type to declare a reference and assign the reference to a variable or object. Although the syntax is different, the pointer and reference examples are functionally equivalent.

```
//Create a Bounce object
Bounce myPushbutton(1, 15);

//Call a method of myPushbutton directly
myPushbutton.update();

//Create a pointer of type Bounce that
//points to myPushbutton
Bounce *myPushbuttonPointer = &myPushbutton;

//Call a method of myPushbutton indirectly with a pointer
myPushbuttonPointer->update();

//Create a reference of type Bounce that
//points to myPushbutton
Bounce& myPushbuttonReference = myPushbutton;

//Call a method of myPushbutton indirectly with a reference
myPushbuttonReference.update();
```

Handling Menu Selection

Note how a reference makes it possible to use a *single* function to track all the pushbuttons (see Listing 3.10).

Listing 3.10 *Using a single function to track multiple pushbuttons*

```
void trackButton(Bounce &rBtn, int mode)
{
    rBtn.update();
    if(rBtn.fallingEdge())
    {
        current_mode = mode;
        //Re-draw display or other action here
    }
}
```

The *trackButton()* function takes a reference to a Bounce object and uses the reference to call the *update()* and *fallingEdge()* methods to detect when a pushbutton is pressed. The beauty of this approach is that the same function could be used for dozens or even hundreds of switches *without ever needing to know the name of a specific instance of a Bounce object.* In this case, the syntax *Bounce &rBtn* indicates the first parameter is a reference to a Bounce object and the *update()* method can be called, as usual, using the object name and dot notation:

```
rBtn.update();
```

PASSING A REFERENCE AS A PARAMETER

Given that the Bounce parameter was declared as a reference in the function definition, nothing special is required to pass an object or variable as a reference to the function. Here, the four Bounce objects created in Listing 3.9 are passed to the button-tracking function along with a parameter representing the operation mode associated with the pushbutton.

Listing 3.11 *Passing references to objects*

```
void loop()
{
    //Pass references to Bounce objects to the tracking function
    trackButton(btn1, mode1);
    trackButton(btn2, mode2);
    trackButton(btn3, mode3);
    trackButton(btn4, mode4);
}
```

Don't worry if pointers and references are unfamiliar. They are used infrequently in the book and the important thing to remember is that pointers and references allow you to use or access objects without needing to know the specific name of the object or obtaining a copy of the object. They can also be useful when it is necessary to pass large objects (such as a stream of digital audio data) as a parameter to a function since only the memory address is required—*not the actual object.*

SOUND & MUSIC PROJECTS FOR EURORACK AND BEYOND

Parameter Arrays

The synthesizer UI demonstration sketch provides four modes or pages that are selected from the corresponding mode switches. Each page provides four variables that simulate parameters such as tuning and volume that might be used in a real synthesizer application. But how can all sixteen parameters be stored and updated in the sketch? Enter the array. One approach, shown in Listing 3.12, is to create an array of four floating-point variables for each mode. (Experienced programmers will point out that the parameters could also be stored in a single multi-dimensional array, but a single dimension is used here for clarity.)

Listing 3.12 Four arrays (one for each mode or "page")

```
float mode1Array[4];
float mode2Array[4];
float mode3Array[4];
float mode4Array[4];
```

Aside from the awkward-looking declaration, items in arrays can be used just like other variables. All that is required is to provide a zero-based index to read from or assign a value to an item in an array. For example, use the following syntax to update the first and last parameter of the array associated with mode1:

```
mode1Array[0] = 1.0; //Set the value of the first item to 1.0
mode1Array[3] = 5.5; //Set the value of the fourth item to 5.5
```

A NEW ENCODER HANDLER FUNCTION

As with the last section, references can help to minimize redundant code when tracking multiple encoders. Listing 3.13 demonstrates one such approach. In this example, a reference to an encoder, a reference to the encoder's last position, and an integer representing the encoder index are passed to the function. While a detailed discussion of the nuances of pointers and references is beyond the scope of this book, pointers are useful when you want to *pass an array* to a function or change a pointer assignment, and references—denoted by the ampersand in the function parameter list—are useful in most other situations where the reference can be initialized when is defined.[7]

As with the simple example presented earlier in the chapter, this *trackEncoder()* function stores the previous position of the encoder and uses that information to calculate a difference when the encoder changes position. However, this example updates the *last_position* parameter instead of storing the value as a static local variable.

Listing 3.13 Encoder tracking function (advanced)

```
void handleEncoder(Encoder &rEncoder, long &last_position,
    int index)
{
    long pos = rEncoder.read();
    if(pos == last_position)
```

```
    {
            //No need to continue: difference = 0
            return;
    }


    //Calculate the difference:
    long difference = pos - last_position;
    last_position = pos;


    //Update values based on the active mode
    switch(current_mode)
    {
        case mode1: mode1Array[index] += difference * 0.01; break;
        case mode2: mode2Array[index] += difference * 0.1; break;
        case mode3: mode3Array[index] += difference * 1.0; break;
        case mode4: mode4Array[index] += difference * 10.0; break;
    }
    updateDisplay = true;
}
```

Updating User Data

The second half of the function demonstrates an approach to updating variables based on the value of *current_mode*, a menu variable described earlier in the chapter. A switch statement compares *current_mode* with the defined modes and updates a variable corresponding to the given index and mode of operation. Also note the way that the *difference* variable is multiplied by various increment values to demonstrate how a single encoder can manipulate multiple variables with differing rates of change.

While this example would unnecessarily complicate encoder handling for a simple application, the incorporation of references enables the function to seamlessly update the many variables that would be found in a complex menu system.

SWITCH STATEMENTS

Listing 3.13 incorporates a *switch* statement to handle menu logic. Switch statements are functionally like a series of "if" statements, and they can improve the clarity of code in some contexts. The switch keyword compares a variable with any number of *case* statements and executes a relevant block of code if a match is found. Each block of code is followed by a *break* statement that moves program execution out of the case comparison.

> *Tip: For some applications, it may make better sense to move variable calculation out of the encoder handler and send the difference in encoder position as a return value from the handler (see Listing 3.10). The returned difference can be used from any calling function to calculate new values.*

Listing 3.14 Encoder handler: returning the difference

```
long handleEncoder(Encoder &rEncoder, long &last_position)
{
    long pos = rEncoder.read();
    if(pos == last_position)
    {
        //No need to continue: difference = 0
        return 0;
    }

    //Calculate the difference:
    long difference = pos - last_position;
    last_position = pos;
    return difference;
}
```

UPDATING THE OLED

The user interface demo provides a *redrawDisplay()* function that clears the display, prints the active mode, and calls *drawEncoderValues()* to print the values of the currently active mode (see Listing 3.15).

Listing 3.15 redrawDisplay()

```
void redrawDisplay()
{
    //Clear the display
    display.clearDisplay();

    //Print the current mode
    String mode = "MODE: " + String (current_mode +1);
    display.setCursor(0, 0);
    display.print(mode);

    drawEncoderValues();

    display.display();
    updateDisplay = false;
}
```

Passing an Array as a Parameter

The *drawEncoderValues()* function calls another helper function named *drawModeScreen()* to print value pairs for each of the four sets of arrays. Although separate functions could be provided for each mode—and that will likely be the best approach for complex applications—the function demonstrates how an array can be passed to a function. In this instance, a *single function* can print the contents of four (or more) arrays (see Listing 3.16).

CHAPTER 3 CREATING A SYNTHESIZER USER INTERFACE 47

Listing 3.16 drawEncoderValues() and drawModeScreen() functions

```
void drawEncoderValues()
{
    switch(current_mode)
    {
        case mode1: drawModeScreen(mode1Array); break;
        case mode2: drawModeScreen(mode2Array); break;
        case mode3: drawModeScreen(mode3Array); break;
        case mode4: drawModeScreen(mode4Array); break;
    }
}


void drawModeScreen(float valueArray[])
{
    printValue("E1: ", valueArray[0], 0, 10, 25, 10);
    printValue("E2: ", valueArray[1], 58, 10, 83, 10);
    printValue("E3: ", valueArray[2], 0, 20, 25, 20);
    printValue("E4: ", valueArray[3], 58, 20, 83, 20);
}
```

THE MAIN LOOP

The main loop, shown in Listing 3.17, is responsible for calling the button and encoder handlers and updating the display in response to user input. The sketch utilizes a global variable named *updateDisplay* that signals when the display should be redrawn.

Listing 3.17 main() loop

```
void loop()
{
  trackButtons();
  trackEncoders();
  if(updateDisplay == true)
  {
      redrawDisplay();
  }
}
```

To experiment with the demonstration project, download the source code from the OUP website and connect the switches, encoders, and OLED using the pin assignments listed in the comments at the beginning of the source code. The logical relationship of the pushbuttons, rotary encoders, and OLED display is shown in Figure 3.8 and will form the basis for the synthesis projects in the next several chapters. Don't be discouraged if concepts like pointers and arrays still feel unfamiliar. Source code is available from the OUP website, and it is not necessary to understand the inner workings of the interface to experiment with the synthesis projects that follow. Explore the concepts that are comfortable and your understanding of the inner workings of the source code will increase through experimentation and repetition.

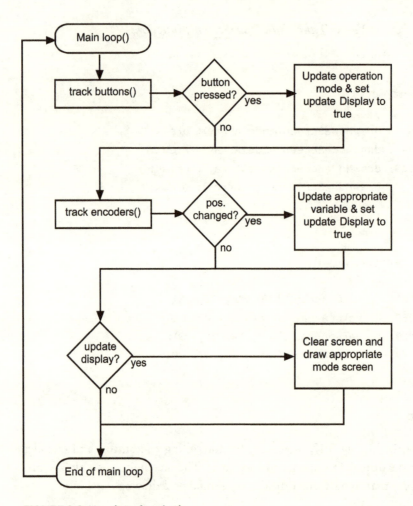

FIGURE 3.8 User interface logic

Summary

The source code, available for download from the OUP website, uses less than 200 lines of code to implement the interface described in this chapter. With that said, it is easy to lose sight of the underlying function as audio objects, MIDI input, and synthesis logic are added on top of the interface. Experimenting with the User Interface Demo project is a good start, but also consider enhancements or other approaches that might be useful for your own projects. Figure 3.9 illustrates a PCB version of the completed interface, which can be manufactured for about $1 per board using the concepts detailed in Chapter 15.

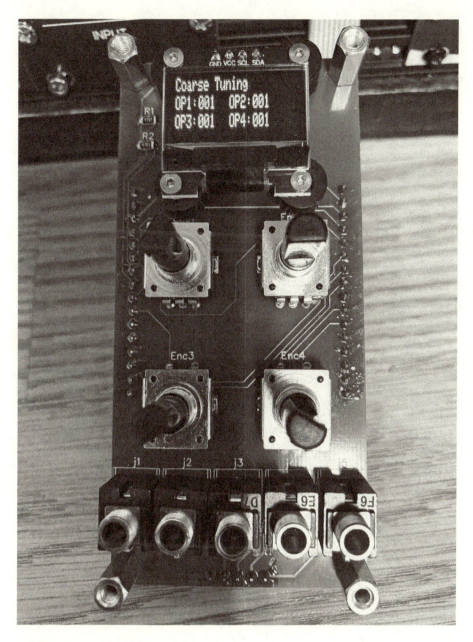

FIGURE 3.9 PCB interface in action

CREATIVE CHALLENGE

- Write code to create a welcome screen that is called from the *setup()* function.
- Experiment with the code by personalizing the OLED drawing functions.
- Alter source code to personalize the names of menu items.
- Alter the menu handler to accommodate submenus. Tip: use more enumerations.
- Revise the encoder handler to utilize other step sizes.
- Revise the interface to create a minimalist number guessing game.
- Advanced programmers might want to wrap the functionality in a class or utilize callback functions for buttons or encoders—an approach that could be useful for some applications.

CHAPTER 4

FM SYNTHESIS

Overview

Frequency Modulation (FM) is a category of synthesis popularized by Yamaha's DX7 in the 1980s. While the DX7 brought FM synthesis to the masses, its design was based on the work of John Chowning, who began his research in the 1960s.[1] This chapter provides a brief overview of FM synthesis and a description of how frequency modulation can be achieved with Teensy microcontrollers. The chapter concludes with a discussion of a fun FM synthesis project that will provide the basis for a fully featured Eurorack FM synthesizer in the final chapter of the book.

The simple FM synthesizer project requires the following components:

- Teensy 3.2 or 4.0 microcontroller with Audio Adapter Board.
- Breadboard for prototyping.
- Hookup wire.
- Two rotary encoders.
- I2C OLED display compatible with the Adafruit SSD1306 library.

Modulators and Carriers

A core concept of FM synthesis is that one periodic signal, usually a sine wave called the *modulator* or *modulating signal*, is used to modulate another signal called the *carrier wave* or *modulated signal*. In Figure 4.1, for example, the frequency of a modulator F_m modulates the phase or frequency of a carrier wave F_c.

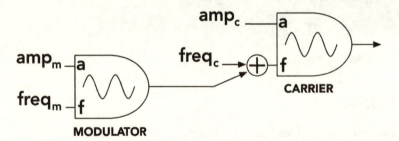

FIGURE 4.1 Modulator and Carrier (based on a diagram by Perry R. Cook in Real Sound Synthesis for Interactive Applications)

Sidebands

FM synthesis is easy to visualize if you have ever used a low-frequency oscillator (LFO) to modulate the pitch of an oscillator. Assuming the output of the LFO is a sine wave, when the frequency of the LFO is slow (below the audible range) the output of the carrier or modulated wave will sound like vibrato or a siren effect depending on the amplitude of the modulator (see Figure 4.2).

CHAPTER 4 FM SYNTHESIS   51

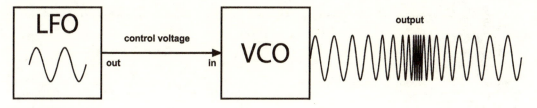

FIGURE 4.2 Using the output of an LFO to modulate frequency

As the frequency of the modulator increases into the audible range, new harmonics called *sidebands* are created "at frequencies equal to the carrier frequency plus and minus integer multiples of the modulator frequency" (see Figure 4.3).[2]

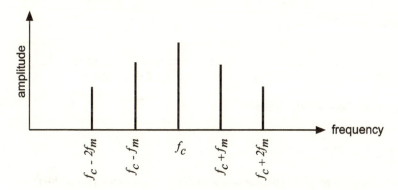

FIGURE 4.3 Sideband frequencies at multiples of the modulating frequency

Figure 4.4 shows the spectrum of an unmodulated 1,000 Hz signal and Figure 4.5 illustrates the same carrier signal modified by the application of a 100 Hz modulating signal. Note how sideband frequencies are created on each side of the fundamental frequency. These sideband frequencies affect the timbre of the tone by altering the harmonic spectrum. It is interesting to note that distinctive timbres—sometimes striking and unexpected ones—can be created with modulators and carriers consisting solely of sine waves that, by definition, lack harmonic content.

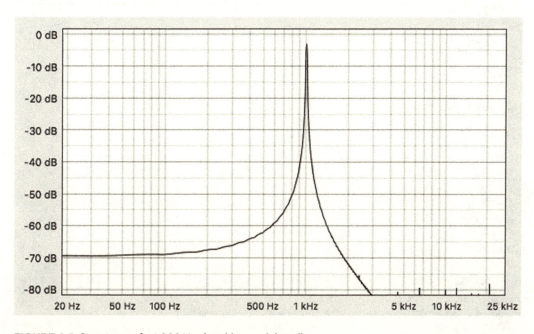

FIGURE 4.4 Spectrum of a 1,000 Hz signal (unmodulated)

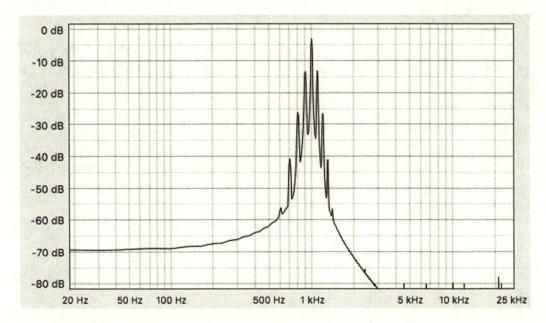

FIGURE 4.5 1,000 Hz signal modulated by a 100 Hz Signal

INHARMONIC SPECTRUM

Many interesting effects can be created when modulation and carrier signals are related by fractional ratios.[3] Such non-integer ratios produce *inharmonic* spectra as illustrated in Figure 4.6. This example shows the result of modulating a 1 kHz signal by a 770 Hz modulator. Bear in mind that the complex waveform shown in Figure 4.6 is the result of a *single* pair of sine waves configured as a modulator and carrier. Incidentally, a simple sketch titled FM-1KTEST is available for download from the OUP website. The sketch, which works with a Teensy 4 with Teensy Audio Shield, provides a convenient way to experiment with a single modulator and carrier wave.

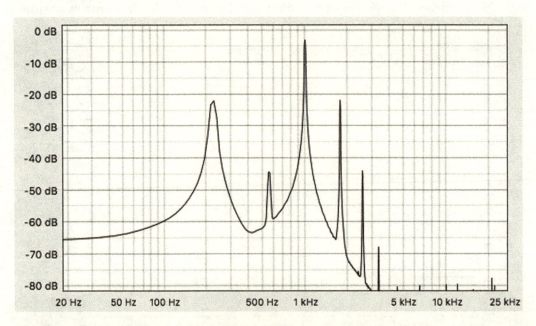

FIGURE 4.6 Inharmonic spectrum: 1 kHz carrier and 770 Hz modulator

EXPLORING FM SYNTHESIS: AN INTERACTIVE DEMONSTRATION SKETCH

Another demonstration sketch, available for download, provides a vehicle for exploring FM synthesis. The sketch utilizes a pair of rotary encoders and an OLED display as described in Chapter 3. The project, which can be built on a solderless breadboard, also features USB MIDI input provided by a DAW or other software. Alternatively, notes can be generated in the main loop.

The encoders control the frequency and amplitude of the modulator to provide unique timbres. While the output sounds like a typical LFO at slow speeds, increasing the frequency of the modulator produces sidebands as the modulator increases into the audible range. A surprisingly wide array of timbres can be achieved considering the simple demonstration is built on the interaction of two sine waves.

CONFIGURING THE AUDIO SYSTEM DESIGN TOOL FOR FM

Assuming you are using a Teensy 4 device (or similar) with the PJRC Audio Shield, visit the PJRC website and use the Audio System Design Tool to create the components shown in Figure 4.7.[4] The modulator and carrier waveforms are *AudioSynthWaveformModulated* objects, a type of oscillator that can be modulated by connecting the output of another source to its first input. Although the mixer object isn't used in this sketch, it provides a convenient way to control the output level of the shield with a potentiometer or rotary encoder if desired.

Tip: Any object from the Audio System Design Tool can be renamed by double-clicking on the object. For example, the modulatorOsc and carrierOsc objects in Figure 4.7 are the same type of object but have been renamed to show their function in the FM synthesis sketch.

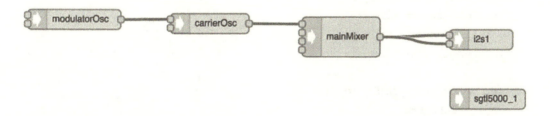

FIGURE 4.7 Configuring components in the Audio Design Tool

Use the export option from the Audio System Design Tool and copy the code to the top of your newly created sketch. The copied code includes header files for use by the Teensy audio system as well as instances of the objects created by the audio design tool.

Hardware and Configuration

The project makes use of an inexpensive OLED display as described in Chapter 3. Although the OLED is not required to experiment with the project on a solderless breadboard, it is helpful to view modulation and amplitude values to get a feel for how those values alter the timbre of a carrier wave. Use the pin assignments shown in Table 4.1.

TABLE 4.1 Pin assignments for OLED display.

Component Pin	Teensy 4 Pin
Encoder 1: A	2
Encoder 1: B	3
Encoder 2: A	5
Encoder 2: B	6
OLED: VCC	3.3V
OLED: GND	GND
OLED: SCL	19
OLED: SDA	18

Connect the rotary encoders to pins 2, 3 and 5, 6 as described in Chapter 3 and be sure to include the encoder header file at the top of the sketch to use the *Encoder* class:

```
#include <Encoder.h>
```

Create two instances of the encoder objects as well as four global *floating-point* variables representing the frequency and amplitude of the modulator and carrier.

```
Encoder encoder1(2, 3);
Encoder encoder2(5, 6);

float mod_factor = .5;
float mod_amp = 0.3;
float frequency = 100;
float amplitude = 0.3;
```

Also create an SSD1306 display object:
```
#define OLED_RESET 4
Adafruit_SSD1306 display(OLED_RESET);
```

Finally, use the boilerplate code from Chapter 1 to initialize the audio system and call the *begin()* method of each oscillator using the settings shown in Listing 4.1. The setup function also assigns MIDI callback functions which are described later in the chapter.

Listing 4.1 setup() function

```
void setup()
{
    //Configure audio
    AudioMemory(12);
    sgtl5000_1.enable();
    sgtl5000_1.volume(0.5);
```

```
        carrierOsc.begin(amplitude, frequency, WAVEFORM_SINE);
        modulatorOsc.begin(mod_amp, mod_factor * frequency,
           WAVEFORM_SINE);

        //OLED initialization not shown (see Chapter 3)

        //MIDI setup not shown

    }
```

Tracking Encoders

As shown in the main loop in Listing 4.2, all that remains is to write functions to track MIDI input and the status of the frequency and amplitude encoders.

Listing 4.2 The main loop

```
void loop()
{
    //Check for MIDI input
    while (usbMIDI.read()){
    }

    trackFreqEncoder();
    trackAmpEncoder();
}
```

As described previously in the book, a convenient way to handle encoder input is to read the status of the encoder during each iteration of the main loop. A *static* variable (e.g., a non-volatile variable that is only visible to the function) stores the position of the encoder and differences can be multiplied or added to variables such as the global variables used to store the frequency and amplitude of the modulator oscillator (see Listing 4.3). Both functions can be described by the following pseudo-code:

1. Read the encoder.
2. Return if the encoder position hasn't changed.
3. Calculate the difference between the current and previous positions.
4. Use the difference to update a variable.
5. Store the new position.
6. Add range constraints if necessary.

As shown in Listing 4.3, the frequency tracking function adds or subtracts 0.01 from the modulation factor depending on the direction the encoder is moving. The function also calls *updateScreen()*, a function that is described later in this chapter. One thing to note is how the new frequency for the modulator is calculated by multiplying the frequency of a tone by a modulation factor. This enables the effect of the frequency modulation to sound similar at all fundamental frequencies. Note that the code for *trackAmpEncoder()* is not shown since its functionality is nearly identical.

Listing 4.3 Function for modulation frequency

```
void trackFreqEncoder()
{
    static int last_position = 0;
    int pos = encoder1.read();

    if(pos == last_position)
    {
        //No need to continue
        return;
    }

    int difference = pos - last_position;
    last_position = pos;

    mod_factor += difference * 0.01;
    if(mod_factor < 0)
    {
        mod_factor = 0;
    }
    modulatorOsc.frequency(mod_factor * frequency);
    updateScreen();
}
```

Adding USB MIDI Input

As with the wavetable project in Chapter 2, this project responds to USB MIDI input. Although MIDI input and output are discussed in more detail later in the book, we will review the process of setting up two MIDI callback functions to handle MIDI Note-On and Note-Off messages.[5] The messages are handled by two creatively named *callback functions*: *onNoteOff()* and *onNoteOn()*. The idea behind a callback function is to create a function with an expected prototype and pass the function to a handler—in this case an object name *usbMIDI* that seamlessly handles the low-level details of MIDI input and output. The *usbMIDI* handler then "calls back" the corresponding function whenever MIDI Note-On or Note-Off messages are received. Connecting those functions to *usbMIDI* is easily achieved by passing the function name to *setHandleNoteOff()* and *setHandleNoteOn()*, two setter functions that are provided by *usbMIDI* (see Listing 4.4).

Listing 4.4 Passing callback functions to usbMIDI

```
//MIDI Callback setup
usbMIDI.setHandleNoteOff(onNoteOff);
usbMIDI.setHandleNoteOn(onNoteOn);
```

CHAPTER 4 FM SYNTHESIS   57

Tip: Be sure to select Tools->USB Type "MIDI" in the Arduino IDE or the usbMIDI object won't be available to the sketch.

Handling MIDI Note-On Messages

The code for MIDI input (see Listing 4.5) consists of the following steps:

1. Converting a MIDI note number to frequency.
2. Updating the frequency of the modulator and carrier oscillators.
3. Converting MIDI velocity to amplitude.
4. Updating the amplitude of the carrier oscillator.

Listing 4.5 MIDI input function

```
void onNoteOn(byte channel, byte note, byte velocity)
{
    //Convert MIDI note to frequency
    frequency = 440.0 * pow (2.0, (note-69) / 12.0);

    //Update the frequency of the modulator and carrier
    modulatorOsc.frequency(frequency * mod_factor);
    carrierOsc.frequency(frequency);

    //Convert MIDI velocity (0-127) to amplitude (0-1)
    amplitude = (float) velocity / 127.0;

    //Update the amplitude of the carrier
    carrierOsc.amplitude(amplitude);
}
```

CONVERTING MIDI NOTES TO FREQUENCY

Although comments clarify the function of most of the code in Listing 4.4, the MIDI conversion line is one of the most awkward lines of code in the book.[6] The underlying idea is that octaves are related by multiples of 2. For example, multiply a frequency such as 100 Hz by 2 to move to the next octave or multiply by 4 to move up by two octaves:

100Hz * 2 = 200Hz First octave
100Hz * 4 = 400Hz Second octave
100Hz * 8 = 800Hz Third octave

This idea can also be represented by powers of 2:

100Hz * 2^1 = 200Hz First octave
100Hz * 2^2 = 400Hz Second octave
100Hz * 2^3 = 800Hz Third octave

Given that semitones are equivalent to 1/12th of an octave, we can use fractional powers of 2 to calculate the fractions of an octave above a given base frequency such as A-440:

Three semitones above 440 Hz:
440Hz $*2^{(3/12)}$ = 523.25 Hz
Seven semitones above 440 Hz:
440Hz $*2^{(7/12)}$ = 659.26Hz

So far, so good, but how do we relate Hertz to MIDI notes? One approach is to use a known equivalency. For example, 440 Hz is a standard tuning note that corresponds to A4 on a piano or MIDI note number 69. We can use that information to create a fractional power based on the difference between an incoming MIDI note and the known value:

$2^{(n-69)/12}$

Applying that concept to the notes 67, 68, 69, 70, and 71 yields the following:

$2^{(67-69)/12}$ = 0.8909
$2^{(68-69)/12}$ = 0.9439
$2^{(69-69)/12}$ = 1.0
$2^{(70-69)/12}$ = 1.0595
$2^{(71-69)/12}$ = 1.1225

Multiplying the fractions from the preceding step by 440Hz yields the expected frequencies:

0.8909 * 440Hz = 392.0Hz [G4]
0.9439 * 440Hz = 415.3Hz [G#4]
1.0 * 440Hz = 440.0Hz [A4]
1.0595 * 440Hz = 466.2Hz [A#]
1.1225 * 440Hz = 494.0Hz [B4]

A function can now be devised to convert MIDI note values to their respective frequencies (see the citation in the chapter notes for a more thorough treatment of the topic):[7]

$$f(n) = 440*2^{(n-69)/12}$$

Handling MIDI Note-Off Messages

usbMIDI Note-Off messages are handled by the callback function shown in Listing 4.6. In contrast to the Note-On callback, *onNoteOff()* is blissfully simple and requires a single call that sets the amplitude of the carrier wave to 0. Note that we will incorporate a more expressive approach using an envelope in the next chapter.

Listing 4.6 usbMIDI Note-Off callback function

```
void onNoteOff(byte channel, byte note, byte velocity)
{
    carrierOsc.amplitude(0.0);
}
```

Updating the OLED display

A final task is to draw the amplitude and modulation values when the encoders change position (see Listing 4.7). The code follows four simple steps:

1. Clear the display.
2. Set the position of the cursor.
3. Draw text or numbers at the cursor position.
4. Call *display()* to update the contents of the display.

Listing 4.7 setup() and updateScreen()

```
void setup()
{
    //Audio and MIDI setup not shown

    //Set up display
    delay(100);
    display.begin(SSD1306_SWITCHCAPVCC, 0x3C);
    display.setTextSize(1);
    display.setTextColor(WHITE, BLACK);

    //Redraw the display
    updateScreen();
}

void updateScreen()
{
    display.clearDisplay();
    display.setCursor(0,0);
    display.print("Mod factor: ");
    display.print(mod_factor);
    display.setCursor(0, 10);
    display.print("Mod amp: ");
    display.print(mod_amp);
    display.display();
}
```

Tip: The approach to updating the display shown in Listing 4.7 is easy to follow but inefficient and can cause timing delays with complex streams of MIDI data. We will look at optimization strategies later in the book.

RUNNING THE SKETCH

Click the Upload button in the Arduino IDE to upload the demonstration sketch to the Teensy. Remember that it might be necessary to select your specific model from the Tools->Board submenu of the Arduino IDE and select its type as MIDI from the Tools->USB Type menu. Use an audio cable to connect the output of the Audio Shield to an amplifier or headphones but *be sure to turn the volume down* since the Teensy can generate a strong signal.

SENDING USB MIDI MESSAGES TO THE FM SYNTHESIZER

As described in Chapter 2, digital audio workstation software provides a convenient way to transmit USB MIDI messages to projects such as the basic FM synthesizer described in this chapter. Online MIDI editors (e.g., the Signal editor available at https://signal.vercel.app) are also a good choice for generating USB MIDI notes. Once the Teensy microcontroller has been programmed as a USB MIDI device, it should show up in the MIDI settings of your DAW or online editor. Select the device (or write your own code to generate notes in the main loop) and enjoy experimenting with a simple but fun FM synthesizer.

CONFIGURING TEENSY TO FUNCTION AS AN AUDIO INTERFACE

It is surprisingly easy to configure a Teensy microcontroller to function as a USB audio interface, enabling the device to, for example, receive USB MIDI messages from a DAW and return audio to the DAW over the same USB connection. All that is required is to revisit the Audio System Design Tool, change the *AudioInputI2S* object with *AudioOutputUSB*, and set the Teensy Type to MIDI+Audio in the Arduino IDE. Of course, it will also be necessary to re-import the header information from the design tool and recompile the sketch.

Figure 4.8 shows the output of the basic FM synthesizer in Ableton Live.

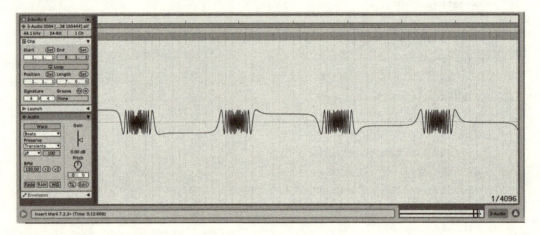

FIGURE 4.8 Output of the basic FM synthesizer in Ableton

Summary

Although the FM synthesizer project is relatively simple, hands-on experimentation will provide a good foundation for more advanced applications. Looking ahead to the final chapter of the book, the concepts detailed in this chapter form the basis of a powerful four-operator Eurorack FM synthesizer complete with multiple algorithms, four operators, control voltage input, and oscillator feedback (see Chapter 19). Additional details regarding FM algorithms and operators are provided in that chapter.

CREATIVE CHALLENGE

The Teensy Audio Library makes it relatively easy to create a primitive FM synthesizer. Consider ways that the source code could be improved or expanded such as:

- Use the *begin()* method of *AudioSynthWaveform* to configure the oscillator with alternative oscillator waveforms.
- Add a second modulator to modulate the first modulator.
- Generate notes programmatically in the main loop by directly calling the *onNoteOn()* and *onNoteOff()* functions.
- Generate and play random *frequencies* from the main loop.
- Revisit the Audio System Design Tool to incorporate additional components such as an audio effect.

Also consider creative applications of the project in the context of sound design and sequencing:

- Adjust the frequency and amplitude encoders to create a strident bass sound and sequence a bass line in a DAW or online sequencer.
- Design a soaring lead synth sound and run the output through a delay or other effects in a DAW.
- Create a slowly oscillating low-register pedal tone and use a virtual synthesizer to improvise a melody or harmonic "pads" over the pedal tone.
- Incorporate the concept of an *array* from Chapter 3 to output a repeating sequence of notes.
- Create a short monophonic melodic piece based solely around the simple FM synthesizer.

CHAPTER 5
ADDITIVE SYNTHESIS

Chapter 5 builds on the synthesis concepts presented in the previous chapters and the user interface from Chapter 3. Along the way, we will explore additive synthesis and how to marry components created in the Audio System Design Tool with code to create an interactive and expressive additive synthesizer. Be sure to visit the OUP website for complete source code and demonstration recordings and videos.

The additive synthesizer project requires the following components:

- Teensy 3.2 or 4.0 microcontroller with Audio Adapter Board.
- Breadboard for prototyping.
- Hookup wire.
- Four rotary encoders with built-in tactile switch.
- Four through-hole tactile switches (only required if encoders do not contain a switch).
- I2C OLED display compatible with the Adafruit SSD1306 library.

Brief Overview

Chapter 1 detailed the use of digital filters to modify the timbre of a tone using a process called subtractive synthesis. In contrast, *additive synthesis* uses sine waves of differing frequencies and amplitudes to create a unique harmonic spectrum.[1] The individual sine waves can, in some respects, be thought of as layers that work together to create new timbres (see Figure 5.1).[2]

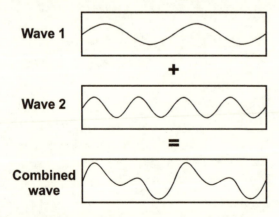

FIGURE 5.1 Waveform comprised of two "layers"

As Eduardo Reck Miranda notes in *Computer Sound Design*, "the idea of adding simple sounds to form complex timbres dates back to the time when people started to build pipe organs. Each pipe produced relatively simple sounds that combined to form rich spectra."[3] One way to visualize the power of additive synthesis is to combine a series of harmonics—or overtones as they are often referred to by musicians—at odd integer multiples of a fundamental pitch. In Figure 5.2, for example, I used an audio editor to combine sine waves at 100 Hz, 300 Hz, 500 Hz, and 700 Hz with each harmonic being −6db softer than the preceding harmonic. Note how a waveform resembling a square wave is starting to emerge with only *four* sine waves.[4]

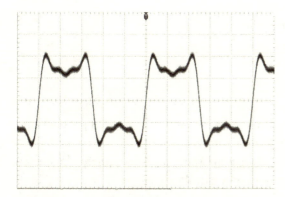

FIGURE 5.2 Combining odd harmonics

Another example can be seen in Figure 5.3, where harmonics at frequencies of 200 Hz, 300 Hz, and 400 Hz are combined—each at -3db less than the preceding harmonic—with a fundamental pitch at 100 Hz. Interestingly, a waveform resembling a sawtooth wave emerges.[5]

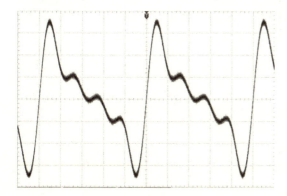

FIGURE 5.3 Creating a sawtooth wave from sine waves

But there is no reason the overtones need be harmonic. Figure 5.4 illustrates the complex waveform that is created when sine waves at 100 Hz, 225 Hz, 350 Hz, and 425 Hz are combined. Clearly, additive synthesis has a lot of potential to create interesting waveforms, and I have enjoyed creating custom sounds ranging from organ-like textures to strident inharmonic tones using the additive synthesizer detailed in this chapter.

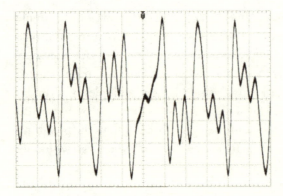

FIGURE 5.4 Complex waveform created from sine waves

Introducing AddiSynth

The additive synthesizer project consists of four rotary encoders with integrated pushbuttons and an OLED display and is built around a Teensy 4 with an Audio Adapter Board. The synthesizer features four sinusoidal oscillators whose amplitude can be modulated by one of four low-frequency oscillators to create unique undulating timbral changes. The pushbuttons select one of four entry modes: frequency multiplier, amplitude, LFO modulation rate, and LFO amplitude; and the four encoders provide a way to modify the selected parameter for each of the four paired oscillators and LFOs created with the Audio System Design Tool (see Figure 5.5).

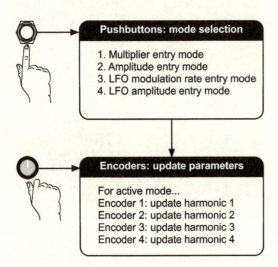

FIGURE 5.5 Additive synthesizer function

The synthesizer can be built on a solderless breadboard (see Figure 5.6) or finalized as a Eurorack or standalone synthesizer using the concepts from the final section of the book. But be sure to read Chapter 12 before attempting to connect the circuit to external gates or control voltages. The Teensy microcontroller can be damaged by overvoltage or undervoltage, so special processing circuitry must be used to reduce control voltage to an appropriate level.

FIGURE 5.6 Breadboarding AddiSynth

CONFIGURING THE AUDIO SYSTEM DESIGN TOOL

As with other projects in this section of the book, the additive synthesizer utilizes the Teensy Audio Shield for convenient output audio output via its audio jack. Use the Audio System Design Tool as described in Chapter 1 to create the objects shown in Figure 5.7:[6]

- Four pairs of *AudioSynthWaveformSine* and *AudioSynthWaveform* objects, each running through one of four *AudioEffectMultiply* objects.
- One AudioMixer4 object to receive the output of the *AudioEffectMultiply* objects.
- One *AudioEffectEnvelope* object connected to the input of an *AudioOutputI2S*.
- One *AudioControlSGTL5000* to coordinate audio streams on the Teensy Audio Shield.

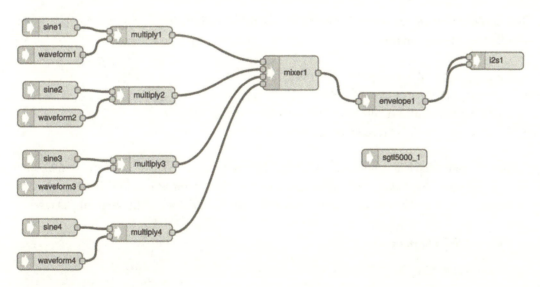

FIGURE 5.7 AddiSynth setup

The waveform objects (which are configured as sine waves) provide the fundamental pitch and harmonics, and the sine objects function as low-frequency oscillators to modulate the amplitude of each harmonic. This is accomplished with *AudioEffectMultiply*, an audio object that multiplies the signals together. Although it is more common to use individual envelopes for each harmonic, the LFOs provide an interesting sense of motion and ever-changing timbral color as harmonics increase and decrease in intensity.

A single envelope provides dynamic contour for a voice consisting of four waveforms. Although the envelope object is set to default values in the interest of clarity, it would be easy to apply concepts from Chapter 3 to incorporate an additional edit screen to adjust the attack, decay, sustain, and release of the envelope via the four encoders used in the project.

The relationship of fundamental pitch, oscillators, LFOs, and envelope is shown in Figure 5.8, which illustrates two of the four harmonic objects used in the project.

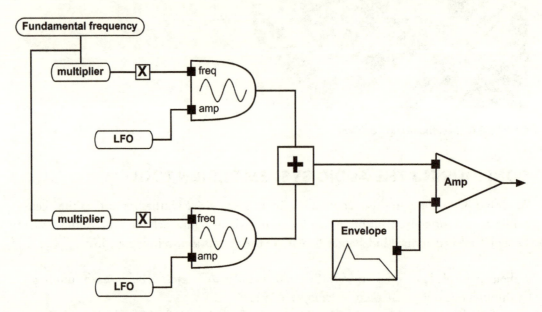

FIGURE 5.8 Conceptualization of oscillators and LFOs in the additive synthesizer

Coding AddiSynth

The additive synthesizer sketch is more complex than previous projects, but the logic can be distilled into four primary tasks:

- Responding to MIDI Note-On and Note-Off events.
- Changing the operating mode when a switch is pressed.
- Updating harmonic attributes when an encoder is moved.
- Redrawing the OLED display as needed.

In fact, the main loop is as simple as it sounds (see Listing 5.1). We will dive into the corresponding code in the pages that follow. Although there is more code to comprehend in this sketch than in other projects, remember that each segment of code completes a single (and often simple) task.

Listing 5.1 The main loop

```
void loop()
{
    //track MIDI input
    while (usbMIDI.read()) {
    }

    trackButtons();
    trackEncoders();
}
```

SETTING UP ENCODERS, SWITCHES, AND OLED DISPLAY

The additive synthesizer project utilizes the pin assignments shown in Table 5.1.[7]

TABLE 5.1 Teensy 4 pin assignments

Component Pin	Teensy 4 Pin
Encoder 1 switch	1
Encoder 1: A	2
Encoder 1: B	3
Encoder 2 switch	4
Encoder 2: A	5
Encoder 2: B	6
Encoder 3 switch	9
Encoder 3: A	14
Encoder 3: B	15
Encoder 1 switch	16
Encoder 1: A	17
Encoder 1: B	22
OLED: VCC	3.3V
OLED: GND	GND
OLED: SCL	19
OLED: SDA	18

We won't rehash content from previous chapters, but remember to include the Encoder.h and Bounce.h header files at the top of the sketch and create four Encoder objects and four Bounce objects using the pin assignments listed above. As with previous chapters, call the *pinMode()* function to set up internal pull-up resistors for each pushbutton:

```
//Set up internal pull-up resistors for switches
pinMode(1, INPUT_PULLUP);
pinMode(4, INPUT_PULLUP);
pinMode(9, INPUT_PULLUP);
pinMode(16, INPUT_PULLUP);
```

The code to configure the audio library and OLED display is nearly identical to previous chapters and can be viewed in the *setupAudioSystem()* and *setupDisplay()* sub functions available for download from the OUP website.

CREATING A HARMONIC DATA STRUCTURE

At the heart of the additive synthesizer are four sine waves that represent a fundamental tone and three harmonics. In this application the sine waves and LFOs have variable frequencies and amplitudes. Given that these variables relate to one another in a direct way, it makes sense to combine them into a logical grouping using a *structure*. In C++, a structure or *struct* is a data type that can contain multiple data members and, if desired, member functions to manipulate the variables or perform other tasks. For the additive synthesizer project, a structure will simplify the underlying logic of the sketch and prevent the headache of trying to track and manipulate over a dozen separate variables. Bear in mind that structures function just like C++ *classes* except that data members and member functions are *public*.[8] We don't need to dig into the nuances of C++ at this point, but classes are used in other sections of the book and function in a similar way.

As shown in Listing 5.2, create a structure with the *struct* keyword and declare each of its members within the braces. This is a good time to point out that structures can contain more than one data type such as integers and floating-point variables.

Listing 5.2 Defining a Harmonic structure

```
//A structure to represent a harmonic
struct Harmonic
{
    float multiplier;
    float amplitude;
    float modRate;
    float lfoAmp;
};
```

Next, create an array of harmonic structures representing the four oscillator and LFO pairs used in the sketch (see Listing 5.3):

Listing 5.3 Declaring an array of Harmonic structures

```
const int num_harmonics = 4;

//Create an array of harmonics
Harmonic harmonic[num_harmonics];
```

Although it took just a few lines of code to create a custom structure, it is hard to overstate how expressive this feature of C++ is. *Any* number of variables and functions can be combined as a logical grouping in a structure or class and used like built-in data types such as integers or floating-point variables. For example, use the following syntax to alter data members in the array created in the previous step:

```
//Increase the amplitude of the fundamental (first item in
    the array)
harmonic[0].amplitude += 0.2;

//Assign a multiplier value of 1.5 to the last harmonic in the array
harmonic[3].multiplier = 1.5;
```

OTHER GLOBAL VARIABLES

As shown in Listing 5.4, a few other global variables are declared to store the fundamental frequency, track the positions of the rotary encoders, and enumerate the menu system (see Chapter 3 for details).

Listing 5.4 Other global variables

```
//Floating point variable to store the fundamental pitch
float fundamental_frequency = 100;

//Initialize an array to store encoder positions
long lastPosition[] = {0, 0, 0, 0};

//Menu options
enum{multiplier_mode, amplitude_mode, lfo_mod_mode, lfo_amp_mode};

int currentMode = multiplier_mode;
```

Global Pointers

One of the challenges of working with the Audio System Design Tool is that audio objects are always handled as discrete objects. While that is undoubtedly the best approach for the tool, there are times where it is convenient to group like objects into an array. This enables the use of a loop to, say, update the frequency of each object without requiring the use of hard-coded object names.

One approach is to create an array of pointers and assign each pointer to the memory address to its respective object. Listing 5.5 demonstrates how pointers to *AudioSynthWaveformSine* and *AudioSynthWaveform* objects can be stored in an array. The object type is used to declare an array of pointers and each pointer in the array is assigned to the memory address of its corresponding object using the ampersand character as shown in the *setAudioPointers()* function below.[9]

Listing 5.5 Creating pointer arrays and assigning memory locations

```
//Create arrays to point to Audio Design Tool objects

AudioSynthWaveformSine *lfo[num_harmonics];

AudioSynthWaveform *wave[num_harmonics];

void setAudioPointers()
{
    //Point to sine objects
    lfo[0] = &sine1;
    lfo[1] = &sine2;
    lfo[2] = &sine3;
    lfo[3] = &sine4;
```

```
                    //Point to waveform objects
                    wave[0] = &waveform1;
                    wave[1] = &waveform2;
                    wave[2] = &waveform3;
                    wave[3] = &waveform4;
            }
```

This would be a good place to point out that these objects could be included as data members in the previously created *Harmonic* structure. Although that is a more elegant approach that I took in the first iteration of the sketch, I believe this approach will be clearer to most readers.

UPDATING HARMONICS

A single function, *updateHarmonics()*, provides the glue between the objects created in the Audio Design Tool and attributes stored in the array of *Harmonic* structures. The function is called whenever an attribute is changed via a rotary encoder and a loop passes the value of each harmonic attribute to the corresponding function of the audio object (see Listing 5.6). The only point of interest is that the frequency of each wave is calculated by multiplying the fundamental frequency (calculated in a MIDI handler function) by a multiplier. For example, the multiple of the fundamental will usually be 1 (unless a tuning offset is desired) and multipliers for each harmonic will be a desired offset above the fundamental (such as 2 for the second octave).

Listing 5.6 updateHarmonics() function

```
void updateHarmonics()
{
    for(int i = 0; i < num_harmonics; i++)
    {
        lfo[i]->amplitude(harmonic[i].lfoAmp);
        lfo[i]->frequency(harmonic[i].modRate);
        wave[i]->amplitude(harmonic[i].amplitude);
        wave[i]->frequency(harmonic[i].multiplier * fundamental_frequency);
    }
}
```

Although the function is concise, the lines of code within the loop may be unclear to some readers. In the interest of clarity, let's see what it would look like to directly code values using the first index of the *lfo* pointer array. We start by retrieving the corresponding amplitude from the first object in the harmonic array:

```
float lfo_amp = harmonic[0].lfoAmp;
```

The value can now be passed to the first object stored in the *lfo* array:

```
lfo[0]->amplitude(lfo_amp);
```

Those operations can be combined into a single step as shown in the first line in the loop. The only difference is that the relevant object is selected by the index of the loop and the harmonic value is passed directly to this *amplitude()* function instead of assigning it to a temporary variable.

```
lfo[i]->amplitude(harmonic[i].lfoAmp);
```

That's it! A single function coordinates values between Audio System objects and the array of *Harmonic* structures and provides most of the functionality of the synthesizer.

CODING THE USER INTERFACE

The final few tasks include functions for updating the display and handling pushbuttons, encoders, and MIDI input.

Pushbutton Handler

As with the user interface described in Chapter 3, a reference enables a single function to track the four pushbuttons used in this project (see Listing 5.7).

Listing 5.7 Pushbutton handler

```
void handleButton(Bounce &rBtn, int mode)
{
    rBtn.update();
    if(rBtn.fallingEdge())
    {
        currentMode = mode;
        updateDisplay();
    }
}
```

To call the function, send a *Bounce* object and an integer representing the corresponding operating mode to the pushbutton button handler. The ampersand in Listing 5.7 indicates the handler is receiving a reference to a Bounce object, and the integers are found in the enumeration described in Listing 5.4 (see Listing 5.8).

Listing 5.8 Calling the pushbutton handler

```
//Track each pushbutton
handleButton(multiplierBtn, multiplier_mode);
handleButton(amplitudeBtn, amplitude_mode);
handleButton(lfoModBtn, lfo_mod_mode);
handleButton(lfoAmpBtn, lfo_amp_mode);
```

Encoder Handler

The encoder handling functions are similar to code from Chapter 3. The handler takes a reference to the given encoder, a pointer to a corresponding harmonic object, and a reference to the last position of the encoder (see Listing 5.9). If the position of the given encoder has changed, the difference is applied to a corresponding attribute as determined by the active operating mode. The function also calls the *updateDisplay()* and *updateHarmonics()* functions as necessary.

Listing 5.9 Encoder Handler

```cpp
void handleEncoder(Encoder &rEncoder, Harmonic *pHarmonic,
            long &last_position, int index)
{
    long pos = rEncoder.read();
    if(pos == last_position || pHarmonic == NULL)
    {
        //No need to continue
        return;
    }

    //Calculate the difference:
    long difference = pos - last_position;
    last_position = pos;

    //Update the multiplier
    if(currentMode == multiplier_mode)
    {
        pHarmonic->multiplier += difference * 0.01;
            if(pHarmonic->multiplier <0)
            pHarmonic->multiplier = 0;
    }

    //Update amplitude
    if(currentMode == amplitude_mode)
    {
        pHarmonic->amplitude += difference * 0.01;
        if(pHarmonic->amplitude < 0)
            pHarmonic->amplitude = 0;
    }

    //Update modulation rate
    if(currentMode == lfo_mod_mode)
    {
        pHarmonic->modRate += difference * 0.01;
        if(pHarmonic->modRate < 0)
            pHarmonic->modRate = 0;
    }
    //Update lfo amplitude
    if(currentMode == lfo_amp_mode)
    {
        pHarmonic->lfoAmp += difference * 0.01;
        if(pHarmonic->lfoAmp < 0)
            pHarmonic->lfoAmp = 0;
    }

    updateDisplay();
    updateHarmonics();
}
```

As with the button handler, the encoder handler is called by passing the appropriate pointers and reference (see Listing 5.10).

Listing 5.10 Calling the encoder handler

```
//Track the encoders
handleEncoder(encoder1, &harmonic[0], lastPosition[0], 0);
handleEncoder(encoder2, &harmonic[1], lastPosition[1], 1);
handleEncoder(encoder3, &harmonic[2], lastPosition[2], 2);
handleEncoder(encoder4, &harmonic[3], lastPosition[3], 3);
```

UPDATING THE DISPLAY

The display is updated each time a harmonic variable is altered. This brute-force method is used for clarity, but the operation will create timing problems for tight streams of MIDI data. A more efficient approach is used in the final project, *Eurosynth*, in Chapter 19. For brevity, the *updateDisplay()* function and one of the sub-functions are shown in Listing 5.11:

Listing 5.11 Updating the display

```
void updateDisplay()
{
    display.clearDisplay();
    switch(currentMode)
    {
        case multiplier_mode: drawFreqScreen(); break;
        case amplitude_mode: drawAmplitudeScreen(); break;
        case lfo_mod_mode: drawLFOModScreen(); break;
        case lfo_amp_mode: drawLFOAmpScreen(); break;
    }
    display.display();
}

void drawFreqScreen()
{
    display.setCursor(0,0);
    display.print("Frequency Multiplier");
    printValue("OS1: ", harmonic[0].multiplier, 0, 10, 25, 10);
    printValue("OS2: ", harmonic[1].multiplier, 58, 10, 83, 10);
    printValue("OS3: ", harmonic[2].multiplier, 0, 20, 25, 20);
    printValue("OS4: ", harmonic[3].multiplier, 58, 20, 83, 20);
}
```

HANDLING USB MIDI EVENTS

MIDI input is handled by Note-On and Note-Off handlers as described in Chapters 2 and 4. The fundamental frequency is calculated in the *onNoteOn()* callback function shown in Listing 5.12, which also calls *updateHarmonics()* and the *noteOn()* method of the *envelope1* object created in the Audio System Design Tool. Where the FM project in Chapter 4 relies on the *amplitude()* function of an oscillator for MIDI Note-On and Note-Off events, the

AddiSynth calls the *noteOn()* and *noteOff()* method of the envelope that was created in the Audio System Design Tool.

Listing 5.12 onNoteOn() and onNoteOff() callback functions

```
void onNoteOn(byte channel, byte note, byte velocity)
{
    if(velocity == 0)
    {
        onNoteOff(channel, note, velocity);
        return;
    }
    //Convert MIDI note to frequency
    fundamental_frequency = 440.0 * pow (2.0, (note-69) / 12.0);
    updateHarmonics();
    envelope1.noteOn();
}

void onNoteOff(byte channel, byte note, byte velocity)
{
    envelope1.noteOff();
}
```

A final task is to activate MIDI input by attaching the MIDI callback functions to the *usbMIDI* object in the *setup()* function. See Chapters 4 and 8 for more details.

```
//MIDI callback setup
usbMIDI.setHandleNoteOff(onNoteOff);
usbMIDI.setHandleNoteOn(onNoteOn);
```

Figure 5.9 shows the output of AddiSynth in Ableton Live. In this example, AddiSynth received MIDI information from Ableton and functioned as a USB interface to send audio data back to the DAW. The process of configuring a Teensy sketch to function as a USB audio interface is detailed in the final paragraphs of Chapter 4. As is evident in the illustration, the AddiSynth project is capable of producing unique waveforms.

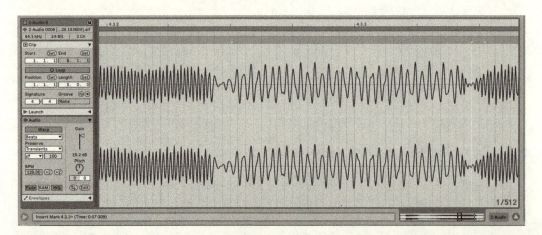

FIGURE 5.9 The output of AddiSynth in Ableton Live

Summary

We have covered a lot of ground in this chapter, ranging from additive synthesis and structures to elements of a user interface. Although there is more source code than in previous chapters, each segment of code represents a small, discrete task. It has been necessary to dig in the weeds in these initial chapters, but don't fret if some concepts still seem foreign. Hands-on experimentation will enhance learning, as will repetition. And many of the concepts, including structs, pointers, references, and callbacks, will become second nature as you gain more experience and see how the concepts are used in other projects throughout the book. Be sure to visit the OUP website for videos of this and other projects.

CREATIVE CHALLENGE

A good starting point in developing fluency is to download the source code from the OUP website and experiment by personalizing project. Customizations might include:

- Using different startup values for the *Harmonic* objects that are configured in the *initializeHarmonics()* function.
- Using a different approach to drawing information on the OLED.
- Using an alternative approach to harmonic modulation.
- Incorporating an element of randomness with object initialization or function.
- Advanced users might want to expand the project to incorporate an envelope for every harmonic (or provide an entry screen to adjust the voice envelope).
- Another option is to incorporate concepts from Chapters 8 and 9 to expand the project into a polyphonic synthesizer or use concepts from the final section of the book to create a fully featured Eurorack additive synthesizer.

Creative applications of the synthesizer might include:

- Creating a sound-design project that relies solely on the output of the additive synthesizer. For example, design, record, and layer slowly morphing sounds or create an interesting monophonic improvisation.
- Experimenting with harmonic and inharmonic offsets to create timbres that range from subtle to strident.
- Improvising a melody over a slowly morphing timbre.
- Recording the output of the synthesizer and incorporate the recording as a wave for a sample-based synthesizer.
- Experimenting with overtones to the minimum amplitude and modulation settings that are perceptible.

CHAPTER 6

GRANULAR SYNTHESIS

Granular synthesis is a category of synthesis with a theoretical foundation developed by composer Iannis Xenakis in the 1950s.[1] This chapter details two simple projects that utilize sample-based granular concepts: a wavetable synthesizer with granular processing and a project that utilizes a USB connection for the granular processing of a digital audio signal. I have found the second approach to be particularly useful since a 32-bit Teensy can function as an extension of a DAW into which interesting experiments can be recorded. As with other projects in the book, source code and video demonstrations are available from the OUP website.

The two granular synthesis projects require the following components:

- Teensy 3.2 or 4.0 microcontroller with Audio Adapter Board.
- Breadboard for prototyping.
- Hookup wire.
- Four rotary encoders with built-in tactile switch.
- Four through-hole tactile switches (only required if encoders do not contain a switch).
- I2C OLED display compatible with the Adafruit SSD1306 library.

Pitch Shifting

Pitch shifting, one of the core attributes of granular synthesis, is easy to visualize after completing the Wavetable Synthesis project in Chapter 2. In that project, a snippet of audio was digitized and turned into a wavetable and the frequency of the wavetable was determined by the step size of the index used to read samples from the table: larger increment values result in higher frequency playback since the wavetable is indexed at a faster rate and some samples are skipped. Similarly, smaller increment values result in lower-frequency playback as samples are effectively held as the indexer moves through the sample table at a slower rate (see Figure 6.1).

Original wavetable   **Index step size = 2**   **Index step size = 0.5**

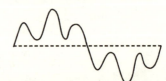

FIGURE 6.1 Conceptualization of pitch shifting

Sound Grains

Sound grains are created by looping small segments of digitized audio—often in the range of 5–100 milliseconds (see Figure 6.2).[2] Depending on the length of the grain, the loop may have a characteristic stuttering or robotic effect. A distinct pitch may be heard as the grain size decreases but, interestingly, the timbre often retains characteristics of the original samples.[2]

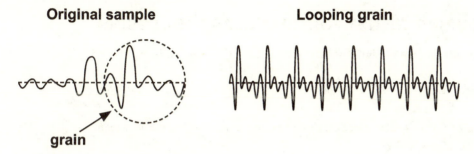

FIGURE 6.2 Looping sound grains

Getting Started

It is surprisingly easy to develop a basic granular synthesizer using the Teensy audio library. An audio effect, *AudioEffectGranular*, takes an incoming audio signal and provides class member functions that make it easy to adjust the pitch and grain size of the sampled material (see Table 6.1).[3] The input of the granular effect can be connected to the output of any audio object including USB audio, SPDIF, or even ADAT Toslink optical (depending on attached circuitry).

TABLE 6.1 AudioEffectGranular functions (from Audio System Design Tool documentation).

Function	Description
begin(array, length)	Initialize granular processing with an array of 16-bit integers used to store the sound grains. Until memory is allocated with this function, no audio appears at the output.
setSpeed(ratio)	Configure the relative speed grains will be played. 1.0 plays the grains without any change. Less than 1.0 slows the sound, and greater than 1.0 speeds up. The allowed range is 0.125 to 8.0, for ±3 octaves shift.
beginFreeze(grainLength)	Freezes the sound by sampling one grain, then repeatedly playing it. The grain length is specified in milliseconds, up to the size allowed by the array from begin().
beginPitchShift(grainLength)	Pitch shift by continuously sampling grains and playing them at an altered speed. The grain length is specified in milliseconds, up to one third of the memory from begin();
stop()	Stop granular processing. The input signal is passed to the output without any changes.

Wavetable Granular Project

This section describes how to configure a wavetable oscillator as the sound source for a granular synthesizer, an approach that is better suited to standalone synthesis where frequency and grain length settings could be saved as patches to non-volatile memory or an SD card.

CONFIGURING TEENSY FOR GRANULAR PROCESSING

Open the Audio System Design Tool and create the objects shown in Figure 6.3:

- One *AudioSynthWavetable* oscillator that will function as the sound source for the project.
- One *AudioEffectGranular* effect that will be used to process the audio stream.
- One *AudioMixer4* object.
- One *AudioOutputI2S* object and one *AudioControlSGTL5000* object to coordinate audio output with the Teensy Audio Shield.

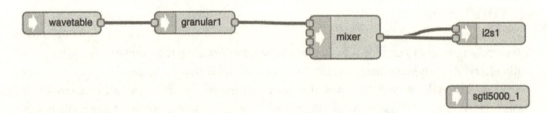

FIGURE 6.3 Objects for granular processing

PREPARING SAMPLES

Use the steps outlined in Chapter 2 to create .h and .cpp files containing samples of a short recording and add the files to the project using the Sketch . . . Add File option in Teensyduino. Alternatively, you can use the Wavetable Synthesis project from Chapter 2 as the basis for the granular project by importing components from the Audio System Design Tool and renaming the project. Use the *#include* directive to include the samples in the project and call *setInstrument()* to point to the *AudioSynthWavetable* object to the samples (see Listing 6.1):

Listing 6.1 Configuring the wavetable oscillator

```
#include "loop_samples.h"

void setup()
{
    //Audio, OLED, pin, and USB MIDI configuration goes here

    //Point to the sample set
    wavetable.setInstrument(my_loop);
}
```

CONFIGURING BUTTONS AND ENCODERS

The project utilizes two pushbuttons, two encoders (or two combined pushbuttons/encoders) and an OLED display as described in previous chapters. The choice of pins is not critical (aside from avoiding conflicts with the Audio Shield), but I used the pin assignments shown in Listing 6.2.

Listing 6.2 Configuring buttons and encoders

```
//Set up push buttons
Bounce beginFreezeBtn = Bounce(1, 15);
Bounce beginPitchShiftBtn = Bounce(4, 15);

//Set up encoders
Encoder lengthEncoder(2, 3);
Encoder speedEncoder(5, 6);
```

GLOBAL GRANULAR VARIABLES

Four global variables, shown in Listing 6.3, control the granular processor: *grainSpeed* and *grainLength* refer to the playback speed and length of the selected grain size, and the two Boolean variables indicate if the processor is in freeze or speed mode:[4]

Listing 6.3 Global variables

```
//Global granular variables
float grainSpeed = 1.0; //Default to normal speed
long grainLength = 250; //1/4 second loop
bool freezing = false;
bool speeding = false;
```

The granular object requires memory to process incoming data, so a block of memory is allocated in an array as shown in Listing 6.4.

Listing 6.4 Allocating an array for granular processing

```
//Memory for granular processing:
//290 ms at 44.1 kHz

#define GRANULAR_MEMORY_SIZE 12800
int16_t granularMemory[GRANULAR_MEMORY_SIZE];

void setup()
{
    //Other setup code goes here

    //Attach the buffer to the granular object
    granular1.begin(granularMemory, GRANULAR_MEMORY_SIZE);
}
```

MAIN LOOP()

As with other synthesis projects, the main loop handles a few basic tasks consisting of reading USB MIDI input, updating the display, and checking the status of buttons and encoders (see Listing 6.5):

Listing 6.5 Main loop()

```
void loop()
{
    while (usbMIDI.read()) {
    }

    handleLengthEncoder();
    handleSpeedEncoder();

    handleFreezeBtn();
    handlePitchShiftBtn();

    //Update the display if necessary
    if(updateDisplay)
    {
        drawDisplay();
    }
}
```

BUTTON HANDLERS

The button handlers, shown in Listing 6.6, are functions that toggle the status of the *freezing* and *speeding* variables. Note how freeze mode is started with a call to the *beginFreeze()* function and *beginPitchShift()* initiates pitch shifting. According to the documentation, the grain length must be less than a third of the size of the amount of memory reserved for granular processing, so *handlePitchShiftBtn()* provides a range check prior to calling *beginPitchShift()*.

Listing 6.6 Button handlers to toggle freezing and pitch shifting

```
void handleFreezeBtn()
{
    //Track the freeze button
    beginFreezeBtn.update();
    if (beginFreezeBtn.fallingEdge())
    {
        if(!freezing)
        {
            granular1.beginFreeze(grainLength);
            freezing = true;
```

```
        }else{
            granular1.stop();
            freezing = false;
        }
        updateDisplay = true;
    }
}

void handlePitchShiftBtn()
{
    //Track the speed button
    beginPitchShiftBtn.update();
    if (beginPitchShiftBtn.fallingEdge())
    {
        if(!speeding)
        {
            float temp_grain_length = grainLength;
            if(temp_grain_length > (GRANULAR_MEMORY_SIZE -1) /3)
            {
                temp_grain_length = (GRANULAR_MEMORY_SIZE -1) / 3;
            }
            granular1.beginPitchShift(temp_grain_length);
            speeding = true;
        }else{
            granular1.stop();
            speeding = false;
        }
        updateDisplay = true;
    }
}
```

ENCODER HANDLERS

The real fun of granular processing occurs when rotary encoders are used to alter playback speed or grain size. The code for handling encoders is similar to the code in previous chapters and consists of the following steps:

1. Calculate a difference if the encoder position has changed.
2. Use the difference to update the *grainSpeed* or *grainLength* global variables.
3. Ensure that the variables are within appropriate boundaries.
4. Update the granular processer with the new values.

Speed Encoder

Listing 6.7 follows the previous steps and calls the *setSpeed()* method of *AudioEffectGranular* to alter the playback speed of the audio stream:

SOUND & MUSIC PROJECTS FOR EURORACK AND BEYOND

Listing 6.7 handleSpeedEncoder()

```
void handleSpeedEncoder()
{
    static int last_position = 0;
    int pos = speedEncoder.read();

    if(pos == last_position)
    {
        return; //no need to continue
    }

    int difference = pos - last_position;
    last_position = pos;

    grainSpeed += difference * 0.02;
    if(grainSpeed > 8.0)
    {
        grainSpeed = 8.0;
    }
    if(grainSpeed < 0.125)
    {
        grainSpeed = 0.125;
    }

    granular1.setSpeed(grainSpeed);

    //Value changed...update the display
    updateDisplay = true;
}
```

Length Encoder

The *handleLengthEncoder()* function calls *beginFreeze()* and *beginPitchShift()*, two member functions of *AudioEffectGranular*, if either of those global variables has been set to "true" (see Listing 6.8):

Listing 6.8 handleLengthEncoder() function

```
void handleLengthEncoder()
{
    static int last_position = 0;
    int pos = lengthEncoder.read();
    if(pos == last_position)
    {
        return; //no need to continue
    }

    int difference = pos - last_position;
    last_position = pos;
```

```
    //increment by 1/100th of a second
    grainLength += difference * 5;

    if(grainLength > 290 /* cap at 290 ms as per array size*/)
    {
        grainLength = 290;
    }
    if(grainLength < 1)
    {
        grainLength = 1;
    }

    //Comment this section to prohibit a re-start
    //of freezing and shifting as length changes
    if(freezing)
    {
        granular1.beginFreeze(grainLength);
    }
    if(speeding)
    {
        granular1.beginPitchShift(grainLength);
    }

    //Value changed...update the display
    updateDisplay = true;
}
```

DRAWDISPLAY()

A final touch is to use the OLED to print the global variables that control the granular processor. Listing 6.9 shows one approach that utilizes an overloaded *printValue()* function. Here, the OLED displays the global variables as a pair of rows and columns.

Listing 6.9 drawDisplay()

```
void drawDisplay()
{
    display.clearDisplay();

    display.setCursor(0,0);
    display.print("Granular Synth");
    printValue("GRN: ", grainLength, 0, 10, 25, 10);
    printValue("SPD: ", grainSpeed, 58, 10, 83, 10);
    printValue("FR?: ", freezing, 0, 20, 25, 20);
    printValue("SP?: ", speeding, 58, 20, 83, 20);

    display.display();
    updateDisplay = false;
}
```

TESTING THE GRANULAR WAVETABLE PROJECT

Use a DAW or other software capable of outputting USB MIDI notes (or create notes algorithmically in the main loop) and experiment by toggling speed and loop modes and changing the length of the audio grain that controls granular looping. Although the project is primitive, it is still a fun and engaging way to explore real-time granular synthesis, and additional features and enhancements could be added using concepts presented throughout the book.

Granular USB Audio

Granular USB Audio, the second project in this chapter, is a simple revision of the Granular Wavetable project. Instead of using a wavetable oscillator as a sound source, this iteration of the project utilizes incoming audio via a USB connection.

CONFIGURING THE AUDIO SYSTEM DESIGN TOOL

The conversion to USB Audio is made possible by the *AudioInputUSB* object shown in Figure 6.4.[5] This configuration is slightly different than the wavetable version since incoming audio is in stereo. For simplicity, the stereo signal is mixed to a single channel before being processed by the *AudioEffectGranular* object. Although this version outputs audio via the Audio Shield, USB audio output can be achieved by routing the output of the granular object to a USB Output object.

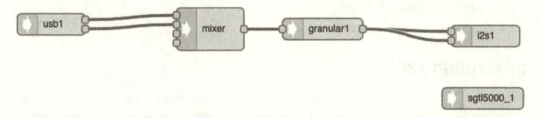

FIGURE 6.4 Configuring the Teensy for USB audio input

CONFIGURING TEENSY FOR AUDIO

Thanks to the power of the Teensy Audio library, all that is required for the Teensy to input audio via USB is to include a USB Input object and use the Tools . . . Type menu of Teensyduino to set the type to Audio. I can't overstate the power of that feature: 32-bit Teensy microcontrollers can function as driverless USB audio interfaces by simply including USB Input and Output objects in the Audio System Design Tool!

INTERACTING WITH A DAW

Other than the slightly different configuration above (and the lack of a wavetable oscillator and MIDI input), the Granular-USB project uses a similar codebase as the Granular Wavetable project. One slight variation can be seen in the main loop in Listing 6.10. Here, the *volume()* function of the *AudioInputUSB* object updates the output level based on settings that are returned by a DAW or other audio software, and the level is halved since the left and right channels are summed into a single channel.

Listing 6.10 Main loop()

```
void loop()
{
    float half_vol = usb1.volume() / 2.0;
    mixer.gain(0, half_vol);
    mixer.gain(1, half_vol);

    handleLengthEncoder();
    handleSpeedEncoder();

    handleFreezeBtn();
    handlePitchShiftBtn();

    //Update the display if necessary
    if(updateDisplay)
    {
        drawDisplay();
    }
}
```

To explore the capabilities of real-time granular processing on the Teensy, select the Teensy as an audio output destination in any audio software and play a recording or other sound source through the Teensy (see Figure 6.5). Depending on preference, use the Audio System Design Tool to create a USB output device and connect the output of the granular object to the input of *AudioOutputUSB* to record experiments back into the DAW.

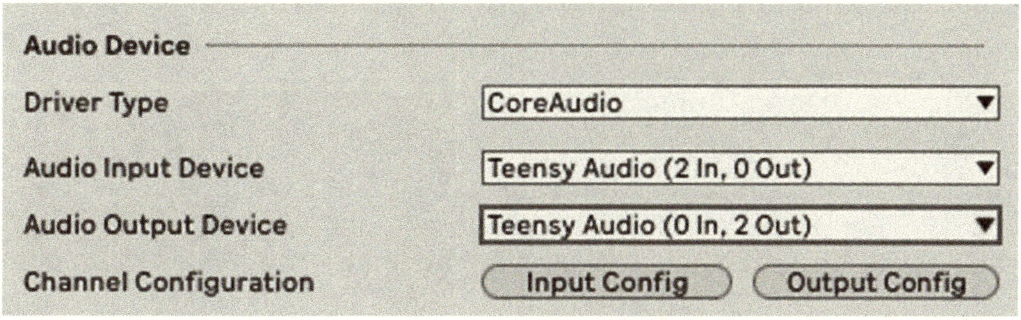

FIGURE 6.5 Teensy as an audio output device in Ableton Live

Summary

Granular processing provides unique opportunities for building custom instruments and sound-processing devices, and the potential for unique sounds is vast—even with the simple projects presented in this chapter. Potential enhancements might include using multiple wavetable oscillators to create granular sound clusters. Alternatively, multiple sound banks could be used as the basis for a unique granular MIDI instrument (particularly with the memory and processing capabilities of the newer Teensy 4.0 and 4.1 microcontrollers). Readers are also encouraged to experiment by combining synthesis typologies. For example, a hybrid FM/granular or additive/granular synthesizer could provide a unique music-making opportunity.

CREATIVE CHALLENGE

Granular synthesis provides many opportunities for sound design and composition. Configure the Teensy to receive USB audio and consider these composition starters as a jumping-off point for your own creative applications:

- Use a DAW to send a unique audio track such as industrial sounds, human voice, whale sounds, and so on, to the Teensy. Record the output in a DAW and manipulate the snippets to create *musique concrète*.
- Connect a microphone to an audio interface and use a DAW or other software to route the output to the Teensy. Ask a friend to speak, sing, or play into the microphone and experiment with the speed and length settings on the granular processor.
- Create a drum groove and use the granular processor to improvise "fills."
- Use a DAW to create an entire piece based on a single audio file. Use the file to create granular resources and layer those resources in an interesting way.
- Use the granular processor to create unique samples that can be loaded into a sample player (or used with the wavetable synthesizer described in Chapter 2).

CHAPTER 7

DIGITAL SIGNAL PROCESSING

I have fond memories of halcyon days playing in a rock band in the 1980s. Most weekends were spent lugging a large truck full of equipment and lights to venues around the state, and soundcheck started hours before the gig as we worked to dial in the perfect mix for our well-oiled sets of popular dance tunes. Although the bulk of the mix involved setting levels and adjusting EQ, the exciting part of the process occurred when the engineer added judicious amounts of "verb" from our trusty spring-reverb unit. Fast-forward forty years and it is clear that signal processing is still a central component of modern music production given the plethora of processing tools available to musicians.

Audio signals can be processed on the Teensy platform in the form of *digital signal processing* (DSP). However, unlike the expensive analog processors of yore, Teensy microcontrollers can do the job with better fidelity and for a modest cost (see Figure 7.1).

Sound & Music Projects for Eurorack and Beyond. Brent Edstrom, Oxford University Press. © Oxford University Press 2024.
DOI: 10.1093/9780197514504.003.0007

88   SOUND & MUSIC PROJECTS FOR EURORACK AND BEYOND

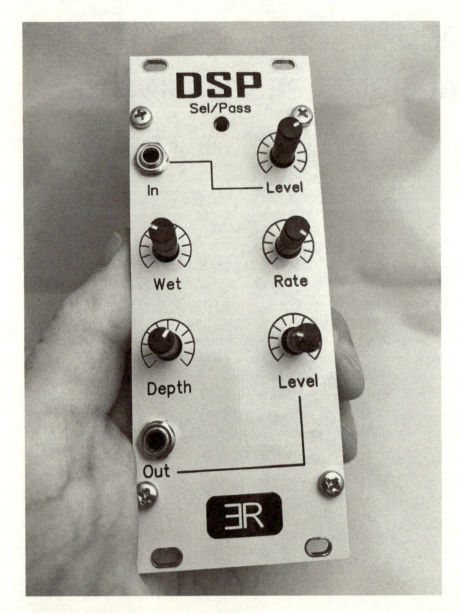

FIGURE 7.1 A finished Eurorack audio project

This chapter details the use of two DSPs from the Teensy Audio Library and the creation of two custom DSPs that are not currently available in the library. As with creating custom synthesizers, the Teensy platform affords an opportunity to develop unique processing units that can function as a component of a Eurorack setup, live rig, or guitar effects pedal. The process of creating custom effects processors can not only open the door to new forms of self-expression but also provide a deeper understanding of the digital and audio effects processors you may already own. And Teensy processors play well with other devices; the standalone DSP project can, for example, be configured to work with a DAW via a USB connection.[1]

Hardware Configuration

Components required for the DSP projects detailed in this chapter:

- Teensy 3.2 or 4.0 microcontroller with Audio Adapter Board.
- Breadboard for prototyping.

- Hookup wire.
- At least three 10k potentiometers.
- One through-hole tactile switch suitable for a breadboard.

The examples in this chapter use a single pushbutton to control *passthrough*—the state when an effect is inactive and "passes through" incoming samples. Each exploratory project also utilizes one, two, or three potentiometers which can be breadboarded using the diagram in Figure 7.2.

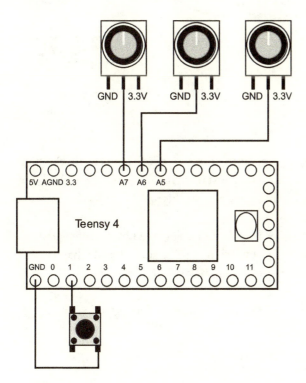

FIGURE 7.2 Breadboard diagram for pushbutton and potentiometers

Using Audio Effects from the Teensy Audio Library

The Audio System Design Tool provides a nice set of effects ranging from modulators such as chorus and flange to spatial effects including reverb and delay. As expected, signals flow from a sound source, through one or more effects, and ultimately reach a destination such as a line out or USB connection. Figure 7.3 illustrates one such approach where an *AudioInputUSB* component functions as a sound source and processed signals are sent to a Teensy Audio shield via the *AudioOutputI2S* and *AudioControlSGTL5000* objects.[2] I generally prefer to use USB audio input while coding custom processors since it is convenient to use a DAW or other audio software as a sound source, and Teensy can be configured as a driverless interface by selecting the Audio device setting in the IDE.

FIGURE 7.3 A basic effect configuration

Once you are happy with the function of an effect prototype, I recommend utilizing an *AudioInputI2S* component as a convenient line-input connection to virtual mixers and other audio components.[3] A stereo effect, shown in Figure 7.4, illustrates the use of the *AudioInputI2S* component as a sound source.

FIGURE 7.4 Using AudioInputI2S for line input

LINE INPUT

The I2S audio component can be configured for line (or microphone) input using the boilerplate code shown in Listing 7.1. In this case, the constants *AUDIO_INPUT_LINEIN* or *AUDIO_INPUT_MIC* are used to select the appropriate input. Figure 7.5 shows the pins that are dedicated to left and right line input.

Warning: Be aware that the Audio Adapter Board can be damaged by overvoltage (such as the signals that are typically available in a Eurorack setup), so be sure to read Chapter 12 if you intend to adapt the concepts in this chapter to a Eurorack project.[4]

Listing 7.1 Boilerplate for configuring the I2S Audio Shield for line input

```
sgtl5000.enable();
sgtl5000.inputSelect(AUDIO_INPUT_LINEIN);
sgtl5000.volume(0.5);
```

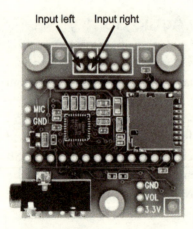

FIGURE 7.5 Line inputs on Teensy Audio Shield

EXAMPLE 1: CREATING A REVERB EFFECT

Figure 7.6 shows a configuration for a monophonic reverb. In this example, the left and right USB audio inputs are combined to mono in *mixer1* and wet and dry signals are combined by *mixer2* prior to reaching the Audio Shield. Incredibly, only twenty lines of code (sans the code generated by the Audio System Design Tool) are required to create a great-sounding reverb with controls for the balance of wet and dry signals, reverberance, and damping. We have certainly come a long way since the days of cumbersome spring reverbs!

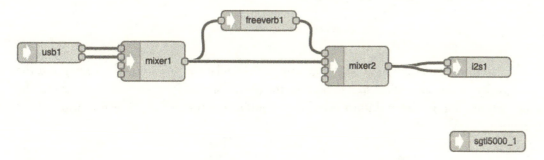

FIGURE 7.6 Setup for monophonic reverb

Listing 7.2 shows the setup code that is needed to configure the audio shield and mixer. The code allocates memory, enables the audio shield, and sets the gain for the shield and the left and right channels of the USB audio input.

Listing 7.2 Setup code for reverb prototype

```
void setup()
{
    AudioMemory(10);
    sgtl5000_1.enable();
    sgtl5000_1.volume(0.5);

    //Left and Right channels each at 50%
    mixer1.gain(0, 0.5);
    mixer1.gain(1, 0.5);
}
```

Real-time control of room size, damping, and wetness is provided by three potentiometers connected to pins A5–A7 (pins 19–21 on a Teensy 4.0). The values returned by the potentiometers are converted to floating-point numbers in the range of 0–1 and sent as parameters to the *roomsize()* and *damping()* methods of the *AudioEffectFreeverb* object.[5] The *mixer2* object blends the amount of wet and dry signal with mixer channel 0 corresponding to the *wetness* variable: As *wetness* increases, the level of channel 0 increases. However, the dry channel (channel 1) increases as wetness decreases (the amount of dry signal = *1.0 – wetness*). This is a useful trick whenever you want to fade between two signals using a single potentiometer.

Listing 7.3 Main loop of reverb project

```
void loop()
{
    float wetness = (float)analogRead(A7) / 1023.0;
    float size = (float)analogRead(A6) / 1023.0;
    float damping = (float)analogRead(A5) / 1023.0;
```

```
        freeverb1.roomsize(size);
        freeverb1.damping(damping);
        mixer2.gain(0, wetness);
        mixer2.gain(1, 1.0 - wetness);

}
```

The reverb effect sounds surprisingly good given the relatively low cost of a Teensy and the simplicity of the code. This speaks both to the power of the Teensy platform as well as the opportunity for unique multi-processors that combine multiple effects or utilize custom DSP effects.

EXAMPLE 2: FLANGING

A *flanger* is a device that splits a signal into two channels and modulates the phase of one of the channels. Apocryphal accounts of its origin sometimes cite Jimi Hendrix's experiments in manually slowing and speeding up the reels of two synchronized tape machines, but the effect is generally attributed to Les Paul in the 1950s. Origins aside, flanging can be a wonderful effect when applied to a guitar, synthesizer, or even a human voice!

A simple setup for a stereo flanger is illustrated in Figure 7.7. In this example, the left and right inputs (either USB or line) are routed through a flanger/mixer pair. As with the preceding code, a single potentiometer blends the amount of wet and dry signal—but the settings are applied to both input channels in this example.

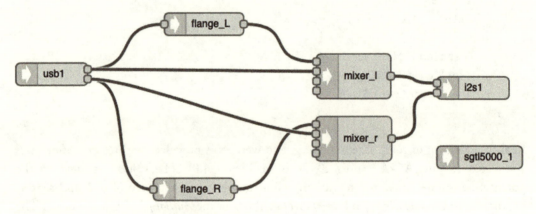

FIGURE 7.7 Stereo flange configuration

setup() function

The Teensy Audio Library configuration for a flanger is slightly more complicated since two arrays of *short* integers (signed 16-bit integers) must be created and attached to each *AudioEffectFlange* object (see Listing 7.4).[6] Three variables representing the sample offset (the amount of delay), flanger depth, wetness, and frequency are also defined in the "preamble" of the sketch (as are variables representing a passthrough toggle button):

CHAPTER 7 DIGITAL SIGNAL PROCESSING   93

Listing 7.4 Allocating memory for flanger delay lines

```
#define FLANGE_DELAY_LENGTH (6*AUDIO_BLOCK_SAMPLES)
// Allocate the delay lines for left and right channels
short l_delayline[FLANGE_DELAY_LENGTH];
short r_delayline[FLANGE_DELAY_LENGTH];

int s_offset = FLANGE_DELAY_LENGTH/4;
int s_depth = FLANGE_DELAY_LENGTH/4;

//A range of 0.05 to 5.0 works well
double s_freq;
float wetness;

bool passthrough = false;
Bounce passthroughBtn = Bounce(1, 15);
```

Setup consists of initializing the audio shield and calling the *begin()* method of the *AudioEffectFlange* objects (see Listing 7.5). Note how the *begin()* method takes a pointer to the delay array that was created in the previous step (as well as parameters representing the length of the delay, offset, flange depth, and rate of oscillation).

Listing 7.5 setup() function

```
void setup()
{
    //Set up passthrough pushbutton
    pinMode(0,INPUT_PULLUP);

    //Configure the Audio Shield
    AudioMemory(12);
    sgtl5000_1.enable();
    sgtl5000_1.volume(0.6);

    //Configure the flange effect:
    //buffer, length, offset, depth, delay rate
    flange_L.begin(l_delayline,FLANGE_DELAY_LENGTH,s_offset,
        s_depth,s_freq);
    flange_R.begin(r_delayline,FLANGE_DELAY_LENGTH,s_offset,
        s_depth,s_freq);

    //no effect until passthrough == false
    flange_L.voices(FLANGE_DELAY_PASSTHRU,0,0);
    flange_R.voices(FLANGE_DELAY_PASSTHRU,0,0);
}
```

For simplicity, two potentiometers provide real-time control of modulation frequency and the mix of wet and dry signals. Unlike the rotary encoders that were used for many of the previous projects, potentiometers sometimes return spurious values that can overload an object such as *AduioEffectFlange*, so a separate function—shown in Listing 7.6—provides a convenient way to apply a sensitivity range for which the function will *not* report a change. The function takes parameters corresponding to the potentiometer pin and sensitivity as well as references to integers that store the last value and new value. As is evident in the listing, the function returns *false* if the voltage returned from the pot does not meet the sensitivity threshold.

Listing 7.6 Function to read potentiometers

```
bool checkPot(int pot_pin, int &last_value, int &new_value,
        int sensitivity)
{
    int val = analogRead(pot_pin);
    if(val < last_value - sensitivity || val > last_value + sensitivity)
    {
        last_value = val;
        new_value = val;
        return true; //value changed
    }
    return false; //no value change
}
```

Main loop() function

The main loop of the flanger project is shown in Listing 7.7 and consists of code to update the modulation rate and the ratio of wet and dry signals based on the values returned by the *checkPot()* function. The code for handling the passthrough button is not shown since it is similar to the previous example. One strategy to be aware of is the use of the *AudioNoInterrupts()* and *AudioInterrupts()* functions, which "allows you to briefly suspend the audio library," a strategy that can reduce audio artifacts when multiple audio objects are changed at one time.[7]

Listing 7.7 Main loop of flanger project

```
void loop()
{
    int wet_pot;
    int freq_pot;
    static int last_wet_pot = 0;
    static int last_freq_pot = 0;

    if(checkPot(A7, last_wet_pot, wet_pot, 10))
    {
        wetness = (float) wet_pot / 1023.0;
        mixer_l.gain(0, wetness);
        mixer_l.gain(1, 1.0 - wetness);
        mixer_r.gain(0, wetness);
        mixer_r.gain(1, 1.0 - wetness);
    }else if(checkPot(A6, last_freq_pot, freq_pot, 10))
    {
        s_freq = ((float)freq_pot / 1023.0) * 5.0;
        if(s_freq < 0.05)
```

```
            {
                s_freq = 0.05;
            }
            if(!passthrough)
            {
                AudioNoInterrupts();
                flange_L.voices(s_offset,s_depth,s_freq);
                flange_R.voices(s_offset,s_depth,s_freq);
                AudioInterrupts();
            }
        }

        //Passthrough code not shown
    }
```

While the flanger effect might elicit a desire for tie-dye and go-go boots, the effect is still fun to use and has its place in the sound-processing arsenal of modern-day musicians.

Creating Custom Effects

While the Teensy Audio Library includes some wonderful effects, it is surprisingly easy to create new custom DSP objects for use with the library. In this section, we look at two simple effects—a clipper/fuzz distortion effect and a custom tremolo DSP object. Although these DSP objects won't win any awards for innovation, they provide a good foundation for your own explorations.

CUSTOM DSP EXAMPLE 1: CLIPPER

One way that distortion can occur is when analog or digital signals are driven to the point where the signals start to deform (see Figure 7.8). That functionality can be easily incorporated into a custom DSP object that plays nicely with other objects in the audio library.

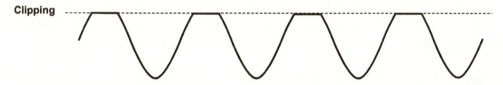

FIGURE 7.8 Distortion created by clipping

Template for New DSP Objects

Custom Teensy DSP objects start as inherited child classes of *AudioStream*—one of the core components in the Teensy library. The minimum requirements are that the new DSP object provides a default constructor (that calls the parent constructor) and implements a custom *virtual void* function named *update()*. Implementing a virtual *update()* function ensures that your custom DSP object will receive digital audio data when it is available.

A template for a new object, shown in Listing 7.8, consists of the new class definition (*AudioEffectClipper*), a constructor, a virtual *update()* function, and an array of audio block pointers:[8]

Listing 7.8 Basic template for a custom DSP object

```
#include <AudioStream.h>

class AudioEffectClipper: public AudioStream
{

    public:
    AudioEffectClipper(): AudioStream(1, inputQueueArray)
    {
        //Initialize member variables here
    }

    //Add public methods here
    virtual void update()
    {
            //DSP code goes here
    }

    private:
    audio_block_t *inputQueueArray[1];

    //Add other private member variables here

};
```

Data Members

Of course, most useful DSP projects will contain a variety of class variables and methods. In the case of the clipper effect, a signed 16-bit integer stores the value of the clip point—the amplitude at which incoming samples will be attenuated. The class also includes a Boolean variable to track passthrough or active status of the device (see Listing 7.9).

Listing 7.9 Data members of AudioEffectClipper

```
class AudioEffectClipper: public AudioStream
{
    bool pass;
    int16_t clip_point;
```

CHAPTER 7 DIGITAL SIGNAL PROCESSING 97

Setting the Clip Point

The derived *audioEffectClipper* class provides a member function named *setClipPoint()* tasked with setting the point at which incoming samples are attenuated. Most of the member functions in the Teensy Audio Library take floating point values in the range of 0–1 but, behind the scenes, the library uses signed 16-bit integers for many calculations, so *setClipPoint()* takes a floating-point number representing the *fractional* value of the maximum dynamic level. Listing 7.10 shows how *setClipPoint()* converts that value to an absolute amplitude based on the maximum value of a 16-bit signed integer.

Listing 7.10 setClipPoint() member function

```
void setClipPoint(float cp)
{
    //Clip point represents a fractional value of
    //maximum absolute 16-bit dynamic level
    clip_point = cp * 32767.0;
}
```

Setting the Active Status

As with other effects in this chapter, a simple passthrough "setter" function provides a mechanism to set the active status of the effect (see Listing 7.11):

Listing 7.11 passthrough() "setter" function

```
void passthrough(boolean p)
{
    pass = p;
}
```

update() function

The virtual *update()* function handles incoming blocks of samples and consists of two primary tasks: passing signals along in unmodified form when passthrough mode is true, and altering incoming samples, as necessary when the clipping effect is active.

PASSTHROUGH

As shown in Listing 7.12, passthrough mode consists of the following steps:

1. Calling *receiveReadOnly()* to request a block of samples.
2. Exiting the function if the block is empty.
3. Transmitting the sample block.
4. Releasing the sample block to avoid a memory leak.
5. Exiting the function.

SOUND & MUSIC PROJECTS FOR EURORACK AND BEYOND

Listing 7.12 Passthrough section of update() function

```
void AudioEffectClipper::update()
{
    audio_block_t *block;

    //Handle passthrough
    if(pass)
    {
        block = receiveReadOnly();
        if (!block) return;
        transmit(block);
        release(block);
        return;
    }
    .
    .
    .
```

The important thing to note in the preceding code is the use of *receiveReadOnly()*, which is the preferred method of receiving sample data when samples will not be modified (such as analyzing signal peaks or calculating RMS amplitude). As noted in the documentation, *receiveReadOnly()* is preferred "since it allows the library to avoid copying data when multiple objects receive the same data."[9]

CLIPPING FUNCTION

Implementing the clipping function consists of several steps that can be visualized with pseudo-code:

1. Calling *receiveWritable()* to request a block of samples.
2. Iterating through each sample in the block.
3. Setting each sample to the clip point (either positive or negative) if the sample value exceeds the clip point.
4. Transmitting the (modified) block.
5. Releasing the block to avoid a memory leak.

The implementation of the clipping algorithm, shown in Listing 7.13, follows the preceding steps with one small caveat: The clip point is an absolute value, so samples must be checked against a positive and negative value to ensure the waveform is clipped, as necessary, on positive and negative swings. Also, note how modified samples are written back to the sample block by assigning a value to the data array stored in the *audio_block_t* structure.

Listing 7.13 Clipping algorithm in update()

```
//Handle active mode
block = receiveWritable();
if (!block) return;

    for(int i = 0; i < AUDIO_BLOCK_SAMPLES; i++)
    {
```

```
        int32_t sample = block->data[i];

        //Clip samples if necessary
        if(sample > clip_point)
        {
            block->data[i] = clip_point;
        }else if (sample < -clip_point)
        {
            block->data[i] = -clip_point;
        }
    }

    transmit(block, 0);
    release(block);
```

Incorporating a Custom DSP Object in a Project

Incorporating custom DSP objects into the Audio Design Tool is beyond the scope of this book, but the process of incorporating the objects into a project is simple. I generally use the Audio Design Tool, as usual, to configure inputs, outputs, mixers, and related objects and include one or more placeholders for the new object using a similar audio object. It is then a simple matter to include the header and source files for the new DSP object and replace the placeholder with the name of the custom object. Listing 7.14 shows how an *AudioEffectFlange* object named *flanger* was replaced with the custom *AudioEffectClipper* object (see bold typeface).

Listing 7.14 Using a custom object

```
// GUItool: begin automatically generated code
AudioInputUSB          usb1;        //xy=99,115
//AudioEffectFlange     flanger;     //xy=274,109
AudioEffectClipper     clipper;
AudioOutputI2S         i2s1;        //xy=513,114
AudioConnection        patchCord1(usb1, 0, clipper, 0);
AudioConnection        patchCord2(clipper, 0, i2s1, 0);
AudioConnection        patchCord3(clipper, 0, i2s1, 1);
AudioControlSGTL5000   sgtl5000_1;  //xy=499,226
// GUItool: end automatically generated code
```

The custom *AudioEffectClipper* class is fun to use. The effect can range from applying a subtle amount of distortion to full-on "wall of sound" distortion suitable for a death metal set. Although the clipper algorithm is exceedingly simple, the code provides a good foundation for other explorations including the modulation effect detailed in the next section.

EXAMPLE 2: TREMOLO

I am showing my age when I say that I love the sound of a good tremolo. This might stem from the fact that I have enjoyed a lifelong interest in keyboards—including classic Fender Rhodes keyboards with their ubiquitous tremolo effect. For our purposes, tremolo is an audio effect that occurs when the amplitude of a signal is modulated at a relatively slow rate as shown in Figure 7.9.

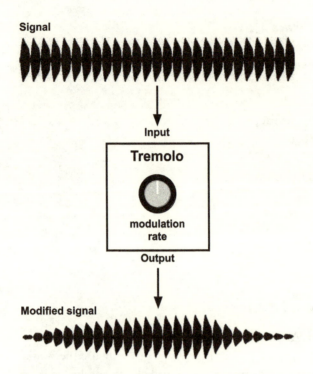

FIGURE 7.9 Tremolo diagram

Low-Frequency Oscillator

Translating the diagram from Figure 7.9 into code requires the use of a low-frequency oscillator to modulate the amplitude of a signal, so a brief diversion will help provide context for the code that is to follow. While a thorough treatment of custom LFOs and oscillators is beyond the scope of this book, a brief introduction to fixed-point numbers will be useful for readers who want to dig into the bowels of the Teensy Audio Library and create custom audio objects.

FIXED-POINT MATH

A truism is that floating-point math is often expensive in terms of processing time, and this is especially so on microcontrollers like Teensy and Arduino. One strategy, which harkens back to the early days of video games, is to use a fixed-point representation of a fractional value. An easy way to visualize the process is to consider how we read an analog clock: The second hand provides the accuracy that drives the clock for days or weeks at a time, but we usually round the minute hand when reading the time. Now imagine that the second hand represents the least significant byte of a 16-bit number so, instead of sixty seconds per minute, 256 "seconds" must pass before the minute hand changes. Figure 7.10 illustrates how this concept could be applied to a fixed-point number. Here, fractional values are accumulated in the lowest eight bits (after an imaginary "fixed" decimal point) as the highest eight bits are read. Such numbers can be described with "dot" notation. For example, the fixed-point number shown below is an "8.8" number consisting of a significant 8-bit byte followed by an imaginary decimal point with eight bits of precision. Although rounding occurs when the byte is read, the *overall* counting precision is more accurate (and faster) than using floating-point numbers.

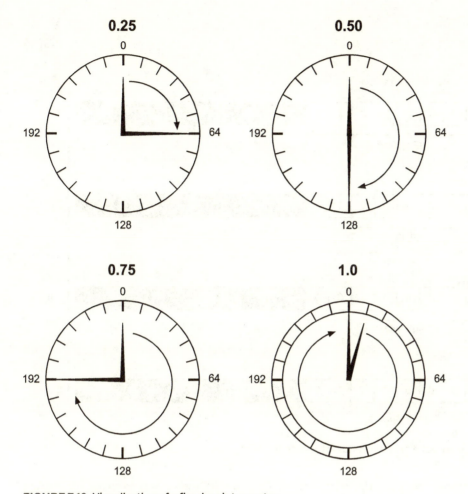

FIGURE 7.10 Visualization of a fixed-point counter

Figure 7.11 illustrates the same concept in a different way. The column on the left shows the actual 16-bit (8.8) fixed-point value and the column on the right shows its floating-point equivalent. The value that is used is the high byte shown in the middle. Although fixed-point numbers might seem antiquated, such numbers are used extensively in the Teensy audio library.[10]

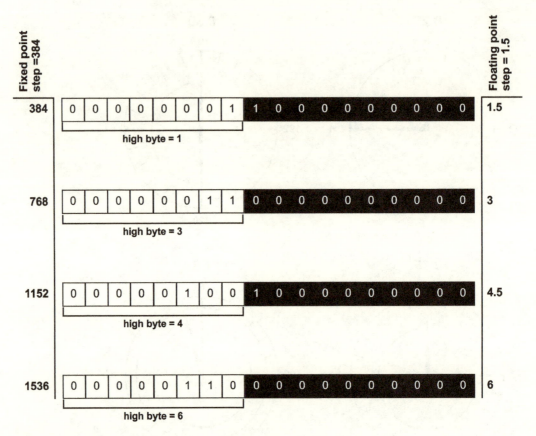

FIGURE 7.11 Fixed-point example: adding fractional values

By way of example, the code snippet in Listing 7.15 demonstrates one way to create an accurate 8.24 ramp oscillator. Note that the *tick()* function is assumed to be called by a steady timer—for example, from an audio object's *update()* function. In this example, the increment value determines the speed of oscillation where higher numbers correspond to higher frequency.

Listing 7.15 Code for a fixed-point ramp oscillator

```
uint32_t m_accumulator;
uint32_t m_increment;

inline virtual uint8_t tick()
{
    m_accumulator += m_increment;
    return m_accumulator >>24; //Right shift to retrieve high byte
}
```

GENERATING A TRIANGLE WAVE FROM A RAMP WAVE

While the ramp oscillator shown in Listing 7.15 could be used to modulate amplitude, the sudden change from maximum to minimum amplitude produces audio artifacts without extra code to handle interpolation. However, just as in the world of electronics, a ramp oscillator makes a perfect base to create other waveforms such as a triangle wave or, with the use of a lookup table, a sine wave. In my tests, I preferred the sound of a triangle wave as a modulation source (with the sine wave as a close second), so that is the approach I used for the *AudioEffectTremolo* object.

One of the geekier algorithms in the book is shown in Listing 7.16.[11] In this example a second accumulator tracks virtual voltage levels for a triangle waveform based on the underlying ramp waveform. The code, which is liberally commented, shows how right and left-shift operators can force the triangle wave to increase and decrease at twice the rate of the ramp accumulator. (Remember that the ramp wave reaches maximum amplitude at the *end* of each cycle, but the triangle must reach that point in the *middle* of each cycle.)

Listing 7.16 Generating a triangle wave from a ramp accumulator

```
inline virtual uint8_t tick()
{
    //Increase the ramp accumulator
    m_accumulator += m_increment;

    //Use left shift to compare the accumulator against half
    //the full amplitude (in 32 bits)
    if(m_accumulator < max_32 >>1)
    {
        //Use left shift to multiply the accumulator by two
        //if we are less than 1/2 the maximum amplitude
        m_triAccumulator = m_accumulator <<1;
    }else{
        //If we are over the halfway point, subtract the
        //accumulator from maximum amplitude and use
        //left shift to multiply by two.
        m_triAccumulator = (max_32 - m_accumulator) <<1;
     }
    return m_triAccumulator >>24;
}
```

There are many other details going on behind the scenes in the LFO class including calculating increment values, but the preceding code will provide a good overview for further exploration. The full code is available for download from the OUP website.

AudioEffectTremolo

The full listing of the *AudioEffectTremolo* header file (*effect_tremolo.h*) is shown in Listing 7.17. Aside from the inclusion of an *LFO* object, an amplitude member variable, and new setter methods; the code looks almost identical to the header file for the custom *AudioEffectClipper* class from the last section.

Listing 7.17 effect_tremolo.h

```
#ifndef_TREMOLO
#define_TREMOLO

#include <Arduino.h>
#include <AudioStream.h>
#include "lfo.h"
```

```
class AudioEffectTremolo: public AudioStream
{
    bool pass;
    LFO lfo;
    uint8_t amplitude;

    public:
    AudioEffectTremolo(): AudioStream(1, inputQueueArray)
    {
        pass = false;
        lfo.setSampleRate(AUDIO_SAMPLE_RATE);
        amplitude = 255;
    }

    void passthrough(boolean p);
    void setFrequency(float freq);
    void setAmplitude(float amp);

    virtual void update();
    private:
    audio_block_t *inputQueueArray[1];
};

#endif
```

Setting Amplitude Levels

One useful feature of the tremolo class is that the output level can be scaled between full amplitude and off using the value stored in the *amplitude* variable. As with other Teensy audio objects, a setter function is provided that takes a floating-point value in the range of 0–1. Unfortunately, using floating-point numbers should generally be avoided in the *update()* function, so a workaround is to apply the value as a percentage of an integer that is used to modulate amplitude levels (see Listing 7.18). As you will see in the next example, an 8-bit byte provides a convenient (and fast) way to alter the amplitude of a digital audio signal.

Listing 7.18 setAmplitude() member function

```
void AudioEffectTremolo::setAmplitude(float amp)
{
    //Scale amplitude to an 8-bit value
    amplitude = amp * 255.0;
}
```

Tremolo Algorithm

The tremolo algorithm is found in the *update()* member function of *AudioEffectTremolo* shown in Listing 7.19. Aside from some level shifting, the process is straightforward and consists of:

1. Retrieving a "voltage" value from the LFO that will be used to scale an amplitude.
2. Retrieving a sample from the sample block.
3. Multiplying the sample by the LFO scale and amplitude.

4. Using a right-shift to return the sample to a 16-bit range.
5. Updating the sample block with the altered sample.

The use of multiplication to attenuate a signal might seem counterintuitive at first glance, but the process is faster than using floating-point numbers to alter signal level. Consider how a 16-bit signed sample with a maximum positive value of 32727 could be reduced by 50% by multiplying it by an 8-bit byte in the range of 0–255. Using a scale value of 127 (approximately half the maximum modulation value) yields the following:

> sample = 32767 (maximum positive value)
> scale = 127 (half the possible scaled value)
> new value = 4161409 (sample * scale)
> processed sample = 16319 (new value / 255)

Translating this concept into code results in the algorithm shown in Listing 7.19. In this example the sample is multiplied by the scale factor and a right shift (>>8) provides a fast way to reduce the sample back to a 16-bit range. One important thing to note is that the results of the multiplication are assigned to a 32-bit value—which makes sense considering that the multiplication will result in values that exceed the range of a 16-bit integer.

Listing 7.19 Scaling amplitude

```
int16_t sample = 32767;
uint8_t scale = 127;
int32_t scaled_sample = sample * scale;
int16_t processed_sample = scaled_sample >> 8;


//processed_sample = 16255 (about half the maximum value)
```

Astute readers might wonder how negative samples are handled. The beauty of integer math is that the sign can be ignored for this application since it will be handled by *overflow*—which occurs when a value exceeds the range of an integer. Let's look at the output of a short C++ computer program to see how this works. This example illustrates the results of scaling the maximum positive value of a sample by the maximum scale factor. (Division is used in this example for better accuracy although the operation is slower than using right shift.) As is evident in the output, the maximum value of the integer is maintained through the process.

Listing 7.20 Scaling a positive 16-bit signed value

```
int16_t sample = 32767; //Maximum positive value
uint8_t scale = 255; //Maximum scale value
int32_t scaled_sample = sample * scale;
int16_t processed_sample = scaled_sample / 255;

//Show results
cout << processed_sample << endl;

Output:
32767
```

106 SOUND & MUSIC PROJECTS FOR EURORACK AND BEYOND

Let's now apply the process again using the maximum negative value of –32,768 (see Listing 7.21). Note how, even though the sign was ignored through the process of multiplication and division, overflow forces the sample back to a negative value in the final assignment to a signed 16-bit value.

Listing 7.21 Scaling a negative 16-bit value

```
int16_t sample = -32768; //Maximum positive value
uint8_t scale = 255; //Maximum scale value
int32_t scaled_sample = sample * scale;
int16_t processed_sample = scaled_sample / 255;

//Show results
cout << processed_sample << endl;

Output:
-32768
```

One final note: The *amplitude* member variable (which determines the overall signal level) and *scale* variable returned by the LFO are both 8-bit bytes in the range of 0–255, so applying the previous concepts to the tremolo algorithm means the sample is multiplied by both variables and requires a right-shift of >> 16 (division by 255x255) instead of a right-shift of >> 8. This process can be seen in the four commands within the "for" loop.

Listing 7.22 Tremolo algorithm

```
void AudioEffectTremolo::update()
{
    audio_block_t *block;

    //Passthrough code goes here

    //Retrieve sample block
    block = receiveWritable();
    if (!block)return;

    //Loop through sample block
    for(int i = 0; i < AUDIO_BLOCK_SAMPLES; i++)
    {
        //Retrieve values from the LFO & sample block
        uint8_t scale = lfo.tick();
        uint32_t sample = block->data[i];

        //Alter level by multiplying the sample
        //by scale and amplitude
        uint32_t processed_sample = sample * scale * amplitude;

        //Divide by 65536 to scale back down to 16-bit range
        block->data[i] = (processed_sample >> 16);
```

```
    }

    transmit(block, 0);
    release(block);
}
```

Summary

The Teensy audio library provides opportunities for electronic musicians and makers at all skill levels. Very little work is required to create powerful single- or multi-effects using the Audio System Design Tool, and advanced users can roll their own DSPs, opening the door to many possibilities for custom effects. The platform also offers opportunities for teachers to build DSP or synthesis classes around Teensy microcontrollers and for students to get a leg-up on a new marketable skill. On a practical level, building custom effects can also be economical. For example, basic commercial tremolo pedals start at about $100 and can easily run into hundreds of dollars—easily exceeding the cost of a Teensy, audio shield, project enclosure, and other components.

Many books and online resources are available for more information on the vast topic of DSP. Mark Owen's *Practical Signal Processing* provides excellent conceptual details about signal processing, and I have enjoyed spending time with Perry R. Cook's *Real Sound Synthesis for Interactive Applications*, which provides helpful information on various forms of synthesis, digital filters, and related concepts. Several old game programming books provided information on the fixed-point math described in this chapter, however, one of the most useful sources of information is the Teensy audio library itself. Browse through the many header and source files devoted to effects processing to learn how filters, delays, and many other effects are created. Explore. Create. Enjoy.

Code for the projects in this chapter (including the multi-effect processor shown at the start of the chapter) is available for download from the OUP website as are many demonstration videos and audio files.

CREATIVE CHALLENGE

It is often helpful to limit choices when composing music—an *economy of selection*—and that concept is at the heart of the creative challenges for this chapter. Experiment by using a single effect to process a sound or instrument and focus on the boundaries of the selection:[12]

- How subtly can an effect be applied before it is perceptible?
- Can a single effect make a sound unrecognizable? How? Why?
- Does a given effect change your perception of timbre, pitch, or loudness?
- Experiment by applying an effect in an unexpected way. For example, apply a clipper or tremolo to an acoustic recording or use expansive reverb on an EDM track.
- Experiment with an effect as a compositional element. For example, change the wetness of a reverb effect to enhance certain sections of an acoustic recording or add a subtle and changing amount of flange to a vocal track.

PART II
EXPLORATIONS IN THE MUSICAL INSTRUMENT DIGITAL INTERFACE

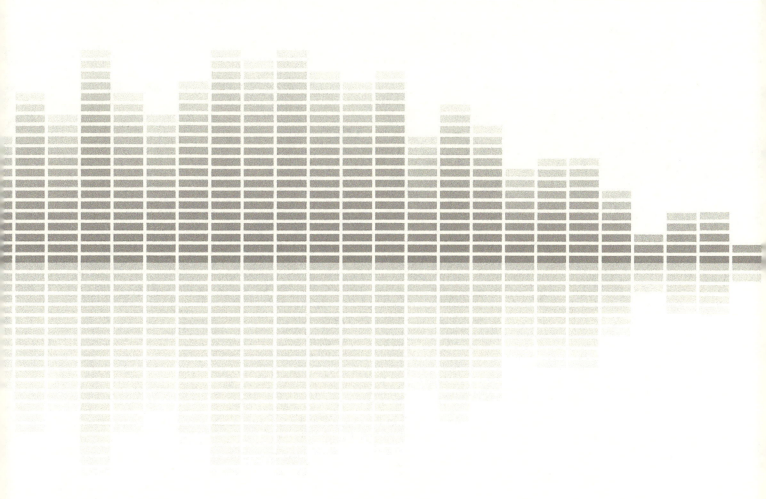

CHAPTER 8

MIDI I/O

> Yet these devices can also, in the hands of a sensitive musician, give
> rise to that wonder which is not an insignificant part of our experience
> of electronic music. The wonder of new discovery, of having one's
> preconceptions overturned is part of the excitement of the art.[1]
>
> PAUL GRIFFITHS, *A Guide to Electronic Music*

The Musical Instrument Digital Interface is a "digital communications language" that enables computers, keyboards, synthesizers, and other devices to transmit performance information as a series of bytes.[2] Since its inception in 1983, MIDI has become a core technology for many of the tasks that musicians undertake daily. MIDI is used for note-entry in DAWs and score-writers, as a communication network between sequencers and synthesizers, for real-time control of synthesizers and virtual mixers, and much more. With its slow baud rate and serial protocols, MIDI 1.0 has never had the cachet of snazzier technologies but make no mistake—few music technologies have provided such broad and long-lasting support for a wide range of musical activities.

This chapter provides an overview of the code and circuitry that are required to transmit and receive messages via USB and five-pin UART connections. The goal is not to delve into the minutia of messages—such information is available from sources including the MIDI Manufacturer's Association and books including my own *Arduino for Musicians*—but rather to provide a useful overview of MIDI input and output as a foundation for creative exploration.

USB MIDI

It is surprisingly easy to handle USB MIDI input and output on Teensy microcontrollers. Simply connect the Teensy device via USB and select the USB Type: MIDI option from the Tools menu in the Arduino IDE.

USB MIDI OUTPUT

When set to USB Type: MIDI, an object named *usbMIDI* will be available to sketches and can transmit and read MIDI messages as a driverless MIDI device. I can't overstate what a powerful feature this is for electronic musicians. With just a few lines of code, a Teensy can function as a powerful driverless MIDI interface to a computer or other USB device.

Sound & Music Projects for Eurorack and Beyond. Brent Edstrom, Oxford University Press. © Oxford University Press 2024.
DOI: 10.1093/9780197514504.003.0008

Listing 8.1 demonstrates one approach to MIDI output. In this example, a pushbutton is connected to a digital input of a Teensy microcontroller that outputs a chord when the pushbutton is pressed. Corresponding Note-Off messages are output when the switch is released. Although the example is simplistic, it does represent an incredible potential for real-time input and control.

Listing 8.1 One-finger chord sketch

```
#include <Bounce.h>

Bounce button0 = Bounce(0, 15);
const int channel = 1;
const int velocity = 100;

void setup()
{
    pinMode(0, INPUT_PULLUP);

}


void loop()
{
    button0.update();
    if (button0.fallingEdge()) {
        //Output a C-major triad
        usbMIDI.sendNoteOn(60, velocity, channel); // 60 = C4
        usbMIDI.sendNoteOn(64, velocity, channel);
        usbMIDI.sendNoteOn(67, velocity, channel);
    }

    if (button0.risingEdge()) {
        //Turn off the C-major triad
        usbMIDI.sendNoteOff(60, 0, channel);
        usbMIDI.sendNoteOff(64, 0, channel);
        usbMIDI.sendNoteOff(67, 0, channel);
    }

    //Controllers should discard incoming MIDI messages
    while (usbMIDI.read()) {

    }


}
```

All the standard MIDI messages, shown in Table 8.1, can be sent via USB using the process described above.

TABLE 8.1 Functions for sending MIDI messages

Message Type	usbMIDI Function
Note-On	sendNoteOn(note, velocity, channel);
Note-Off	sendNoteOff(note, velocity, channel);
Polyphonic Aftertouch	sendAfterTouchPoly(note, pressure, channel);
Control Change	sendControlChange(control, value, channel);
Program Change	sendProgramChange(program, channel);
Aftertouch	sendAfterTouch(pressure, channel);
Pitch Bend	sendPitchBend(value, channel);
System Exclusive	sendSysEx(length, array, hasBeginEnd);
Time Code	sendTimeCodeQuarterFrame(index, value);
Song Position Pointer	sendSongPosition(beats);
Song Select	sendSongSelect(song);
Tune Request	sendTuneRequest();
Real-time message: Clock	sendRealTime(Clock);
Real-time message: Start	sendRealTime(Start);
Real-time message: Continue	sendRealTime(Continue);
Real-time message: Stop	sendRealTime(Stop);
Real-time message: Active sensing	sendRealTime(ActiveSensing);
Real-time message: System reset	sendRealTime(SystemReset);

Listing 8.2 demonstrates the use of the *sendProgramChange()* method to select a program or "patch" from a connected device. In this example, four pushbuttons are connected to digital pins on a Teensy device and output a program change when selected. As with the previous example, the code is surprisingly simple for such a powerful potential. For example, the project could easily be expanded to include switches for bank selection and multiple favorites for use with an on-stage performance rig.

Listing 8.2 4-button patch changer

```
#include <Bounce.h>

Bounce button0 = Bounce(0, 15);
Bounce button1 = Bounce(1, 15);
Bounce button2 = Bounce(2, 15);
Bounce button3 = Bounce(3, 15);
```

```
const int channel = 1;
const int velocity = 100;
const int patch1 = 0;
const int patch2 = 1;
const int patch3 = 2;
const int patch4 = 3;

void setup()
{
    pinMode(0, INPUT_PULLUP);
    pinMode(1, INPUT_PULLUP);
    pinMode(2, INPUT_PULLUP);
    pinMode(3, INPUT_PULLUP);

}

void loop()
{
    button0.update();
    if (button0.fallingEdge()) {
        usbMIDI.sendProgramChange(patch1, channel);
    }

    button1.update();
    if (button1.fallingEdge()) {
        usbMIDI.sendProgramChange(patch2, channel);
    }

    button2.update();
    if (button2.fallingEdge()) {
        usbMIDI.sendProgramChange(patch3, channel);
    }

    button3.update();
    if (button3.fallingEdge()) {
        usbMIDI.sendProgramChange(patch4, channel);
    }

    //Controllers should discard incoming MIDI messages
    while (usbMIDI.read()) {

    }

}
```

CHAPTER 8 MIDI I/O   115

USB MIDI INPUT

Raw Input

Teensy microcontrollers can also function as driverless MIDI input devices. One approach, shown in Listing 8.3, uses the *read()* method of *usbMIDI* to check for available MIDI messages and unpacks the message using the *getType(), getChannel(), getData1(),* and *getData2()* methods. This example checks to see if the message type matches the *NoteOn* or *NoteOff* constants stored in the *usbMIDI* class and outputs a note a major third higher (four semitones) in response to any Note-On or Note-Off events.

Listing 8.3 Raw MIDI input (transposition example 1)

```
void setup()
{

}

void loop()
{

    if(usbMIDI.read())
    {
        byte type = usbMIDI.getType();
        byte channel = usbMIDI.getChannel();
        //Note: data1 and data2 correspond to MIDI note
        //number and velocity in this context:
        byte data1 = usbMIDI.getData1();
        byte data2 = usbMIDI.getData2();

        if(type == usbMIDI.NoteOn)
        {

            //Output the note
            usbMIDI.sendNoteOn(data1, data2, channel);
            //Output a Note-On a major third higher
            usbMIDI.sendNoteOn(data1 + 4, data2, channel);
        }

        if(type == usbMIDI.NoteOff)
        {

            //Turn off the note
            usbMIDI.sendNoteOff(data1, data2, channel);
            //Output a Note-Off a major third higher
            usbMIDI.sendNoteOff(data1 + 4, data2, channel);
        }
    }
}
```

Callback Functions

Although the preceding code for "raw" MIDI input works well for small sketches, callback methods provide an elegant solution for more complex projects. The idea is to write one or more functions to handle MIDI messages such as incoming Note-On or Note-Off events and pass a *function pointer* to the *usbMIDI* object, which will automatically call the function in response to the given message type.

The process of writing and registering callback functions is shown in Listing 8.4. Two MIDI functions are defined and passed as pointers in the *setup()* method, and the functions are automatically called by *usbMIDI* in response to incoming messages. This example, which is the functional equivalent of Listing 8.3, demonstrates how callbacks can simplify program design in some cases.

Listing 8.4 MIDI Callback functions (transposition example 2)

```
void setup()
{
    //Register callback functions with usbMIDI
    usbMIDI.setHandleNoteOn(myNoteOnHandler);
    usbMIDI.setHandleNoteOff(myNoteOffHandler);
}


void loop()
{
    //Check for MIDI messages.
    //Registered callback functions will be automatically called.
    usbMIDI.read();
}


//Note-On callback function
void myNoteOnHandler(byte channel, byte note, byte velocity)
{
    //Output the note
    usbMIDI.sendNoteOn(note, velocity, channel);
    //Output a Note-On a major third higher
    usbMIDI.sendNoteOn(note + 4, velocity, channel);
}


//Note-Off callback function
void myNoteOffHandler(byte channel, byte note, byte velocity)
{
    //Turn off the note
    usbMIDI.sendNoteOff(note, velocity, channel);
    //Output a Note-Off a major third higher
    usbMIDI.sendNoteOff(note + 4, velocity, channel);
}
```

USB HOST

Some Teensy microcontrollers such as the Teensy 3.6 and 4.1 are capable of functioning as a USB host and can receive data from a USB MIDI device without the need for a computer. This is a powerful feature that opens the door to a wide range of projects ranging from USB MIDI to CV conversion to projects that incorporate commercial devices. For example, I was able to read incoming MIDI messages from a Novation Launch Pad-Mini controller with just a few lines of code.

Five pins are provided on USB host-compatible Teensy microcontrollers that can be connected to a USB host cable (see Figure 8.1). Solder the pins so that they are accessible on the top of the Teensy board.

FIGURE 8.1 USB Host pins

Attach a USB host cable, shown in Figure 8.2, so that the power pin is closest to the USB port and the device will be ready to receive data from a variety of USB devices.

FIGURE 8.2 USB host cable

Code for Hosting a USB Device

The code for communicating with a host device is similar to the code used for other USB connections. As shown in Listing 8.5, the functionality relies on a header file named *USBHost_t36.h* and involves instantiating three objects: *USBHost*, *USBHub*, and *MIDIDevice*. As is evident in the listing, the *USBHub* and *MIDIDevice* objects take a pointer to a *USBHost* object when they are instantiated. In this example, the *setup()* function configures a *Serial* object for visual communication, starts the *USBHost* object, and attaches function callbacks to *MIDIDevice*. The main *loop()* is similarly brief and calls the *Task()* and *read()* methods of *USBHost* and *MIDIDevice* to handle communication with the devices. The brevity of the code speaks to the power of the Teensy platform for music making: Just twenty-five lines of code (sans callback functions) are required to configure a compatible Teensy to function as a host with a compatible USB MIDI device.

Listing 8.5 Source code for a USB host

```
#include <USBHost_t36.h>

USBHost myusb;
USBHub hub1(myusb);
USBHub hub2(myusb);
MIDIDevice midi1(myusb);
```

CHAPTER 8 MIDI I/O

```cpp
void setup()
{
    Serial.begin(115200);
    //Delay before turning on host
    delay(1500);
    Serial.println("MIDI USB Host input test");
    delay(10);
    myusb.begin();

    //Set up callbacks
    midi1.setHandleNoteOn(myNoteOn);
    midi1.setHandleNoteOff(myNoteOff);

}

void loop()
{
        myusb.Task();
        midi1.read();
}

void myNoteOn(byte channel, byte note, byte velocity)
{
    printMessage("Note On: ", channel, note, velocity);
}

void myNoteOff(byte channel, byte note, byte velocity)
{
    printMessage("Note Off: ", channel, note, velocity);
}

void printMessage(String msg, byte channel, byte note, byte
    velocity)
{
    Serial.print(msg);
    Serial.print("Channel: "); Serial.print(channel);
    Serial.print(" Note: "); Serial.println(note);
    Serial.print(" Velocity: "); Serial.println(velocity);
}
```

Five-pin DIN Connections

While it is convenient to transmit and receive MIDI messages via a single USB port, it is important to note that the traditional five-pin DIN connections found on many synthesizers have one or more MIDI *ports* to transmit or receive messages.

MIDI OUT and IN Ports

Unsurprisingly, MIDI OUT ports transmit messages *to* another device via a five-pin DIN cable (see Figure 8.3). The bytes representing MIDI messages are *serial* and travel, one at a time, through the MIDI cable to a receiving device. On the other end of the connection, a MIDI IN port receives messages from an OUT port. The incoming bytes are received, one at a time, to form corresponding MIDI messages which may (or may not) be intended for the given device depending on its channel assignment.

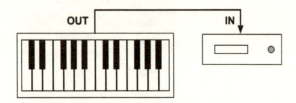

FIGURE 8.3 MIDI Out and In ports

MIDI THRU PORT

MIDI THRU Ports function like OUT ports in that they transmit MIDI messages. However, the role of a MIDI THRU port is to pass an *exact copy* of incoming messages to an attached device. As you will learn later in the chapter, THRU ports generally consist of a simple circuit extension of an INPUT port—but the function of a THRU port can also be mimicked in code. Figure 8.4 illustrates how the output of a single MIDI device could be connected to multiple devices via one or more THRU ports.

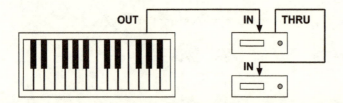

FIGURE 8.4 MIDI THRU port connected to two devices

Circuits for UART MIDI Output

The circuitry for five-pin MIDI is not unduly difficult to build on breadboard or soldering board, but it is important to be aware that the circuits for 5V microcontrollers (e.g., Teensy 2) and 3.3V (e.g., Teensy 3.x and 4.x) boards require slightly different approaches.

5V MIDI OUTPUT

A typical UART circuit for MIDI output on a 5V microcontroller is shown in Figure 8.5. A serial transmit pin connects to the input of a series of two inverting gates (such as a 7404 Hex inverter) and through a 220 Ohm resistor to pin 5 of a five-pin DIN jack. As shown in the illustration, pin 4 of the MIDI jack connects through a 220 Ohm resistor to 5V on the microcontroller, and pin 2 of the jack connects to GND. Note that, although the official MIDI specification recommends the Hex inverter, some implementations (including the 3.3V transmission circuit shown in the next section) use resistors but omit the inverting gates.

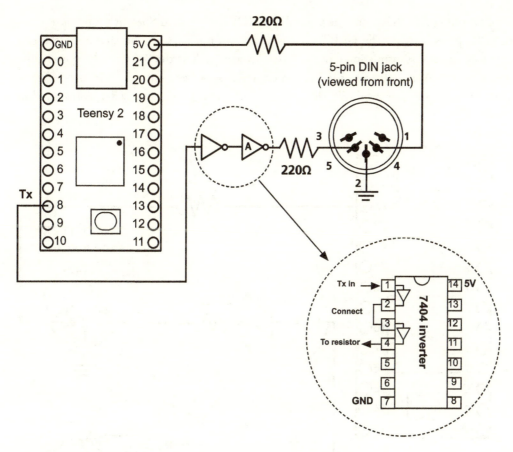

FIGURE 8.5 5V MIDI transmission circuit (for use with Teensy 2.x)

3.3V MIDI OUTPUT

Teensy manufacturer, PJRC, recommends the transmission circuit shown in Figure 8.6 for Teensy 3.x, 4.x, and LC microcontrollers.[3] Note the proportionally smaller resistors and omission of a Hex inverter.

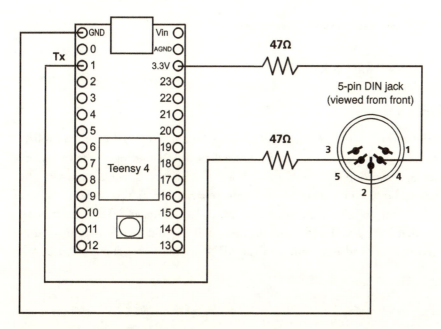

FIGURE 8.6 3.3V Basic MIDI transmission circuit (for use with Teensy 3.x or 4.x)

The 5V output circuit shown in The Complete MIDI 1.0 Detailed Specification places transistor or IC gates between the UART output and 220-ohm resistor, and that approach can be applied to a 3.3V transmission circuit. A hex inverter such as the 7404 can be powered by 5V but receive 3.3V signals from the TX pin on a Teensy 4 (see Figure 8.7). In my tests, the output of the hex inverter produced sharp edges with virtually no jitter when configured in this way.

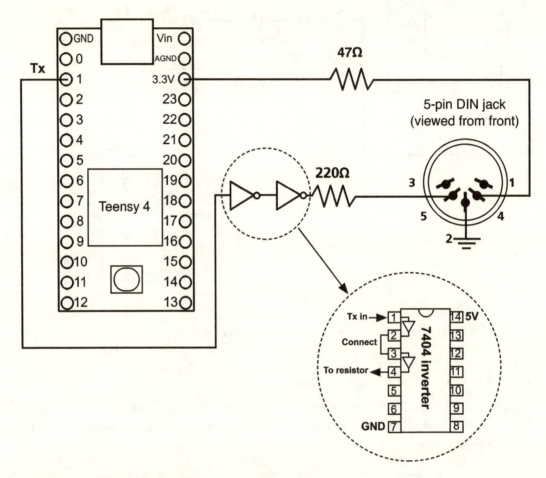

FIGURE 8.7 3.3V MIDI transmission circuit with hex inverter

Circuits for UART MIDI Input

5V MIDI RECEIVER

A standard 5V MIDI receiver circuit for use with Teensy 2.x and other 5V microcontrollers is shown in Figure 8.8 (schematic) and Figure 8.9 (breadboard).[4] According to the Complete MIDI 1.0 Detailed Specification, "to avoid ground loops, and subsequent data errors, the transmitter circuitry and receiver circuitry are internally separated by an opto-isolator (a light emitting diode and a photo sensor which share a single, sealed package)."[5] The specification also expressly states that DIN pins 1 and 3 are not used, and "should be left unconnected in the receiver and transmitter" and that "pin 2 of the MIDI In connector should also be left unconnected."

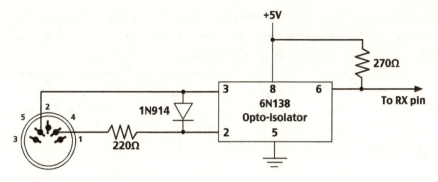

FIGURE 8.8 5V MIDI receiver schematic for use with Teensy 2.x or other 5-volt microcontrollers

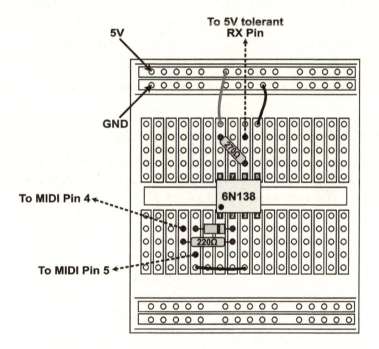

FIGURE 8.9 5V MIDI receiver on a breadboard. For use with Teensy 2.x or other 5-volt microcontrollers

Sidebar: Translating Circuit Diagrams to a Solderless Breadboard

Like any domain of knowledge, circuit diagrams can be a challenge to read and understand in the initial stages of learning. However, it is not unduly difficult to transfer a schematic to a solderless breadboard if you remember that the outer rows of most breadboards form a *horizontal* electrical connection and the columns in the middle part of the breadboard form a *vertical* electrical connection. The top and bottom columns are *not* connected electrically, which enables microcontrollers, integrated circuits, and other components to bridge the top and bottom columns without a short circuit.

It is also helpful to remember that the leads of components such as diodes, resistors, and capacitors will never be placed inline in the same column since signals or power will bypass the component. For example, in Figure 8.9, the cathode of the diode (indicated by a stripe) is placed on the same breadboard column as pin 2 of the opto-isolator and one lead of the 220-ohm resistor. This forms the electrical connection shown in the circuit schematic. The other lead of the resistor is inserted into a hole of another available column and a hookup wire can be used to connect any of the holes in that column and to pin 4 of a MIDI DIN connector. Similarly, the hookup wire connects pin 3 of the opto-isolator to the anode of the diode, and that column provides a tie-in point to pin 5 of the DIN connector.

Moving on to power and ground, the hookup wire connects 5V power on the power rail to pin 8 of the opto-isolator and, as indicated in the illustration, a 270-ohm resistor is placed between the 5V power column on pin 8 and pin 6 of the opto-isolator. Again, these connections mimic the electrical connections shown in the schematic. Finally, the hookup wire connects the ground rail to pin 5 on the opto-isolator.

Tip: Although the process of laying out a project on a solderless breadboard can feel like a puzzle, work methodically and follow the path of each signal and power connection as you mimic those connections on the breadboard. If a signal flows through a component such as a resistor or a capacitor, the leads will need to be plugged into separate columns on the breadboard (or straddle the non-conductive divider between the top and bottom columns). However, the leads of multiple components can be connected to a single column when those connections are shown in a schematic.

5V MIDI RECEIVER WITH MIDI THRU

Figure 8.10 illustrates how a 5V receiver circuit can be expanded to include a THRU port. In this example, incoming signals destined for the receive pin on a microcontroller are tapped and sent to a THRU port through a transmission circuit like the one shown in Figure 8.9.

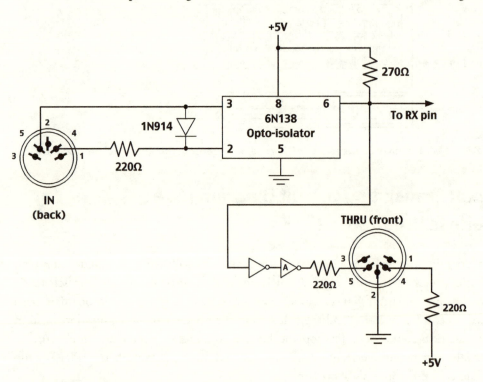

FIGURE 8.10 5V MIDI Receiver with THRU port

3.3V MIDI RECEIVER

The circuit shown in Figure 8.11 is based on a circuit provided by PJRC and illustrates an approach to using a 5-volt opto-isolator with a 3.3-volt microcontroller such as a Teensy 3.x or Teensy 4.x. While the circuit looks like it might create an overvoltage on the input pin of the microcontroller, the output of the opto-isolator is an *open collector* so the output floats when it goes high. When the output floats, the pull-up resistor "pulls" the output to the external 3.3V level.[6]

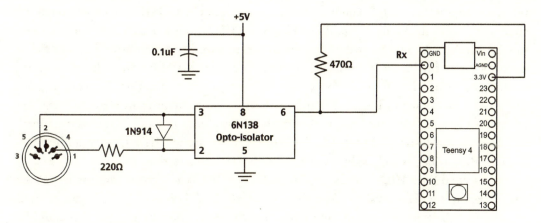

FIGURE 8.11 3.3V MIDI receiver circuit for Teensy 3.x of 4.x

UART Eurorack I/O

Although the circuits shown in the preceding examples are appropriate for Eurorack projects, there are several disadvantages of using five-pin DIN jacks in that context including the relatively large size of the connectors and limited options for vertical PCB-mounted components. One solution has emerged that utilizes standard 3.5 mm TRS stereo jacks and plugs (see Figure 8.12). Unfortunately, manufacturers utilized two contrasting approaches prior to standardization by the MIDI Manufacturer's Association, so consider a flexible approach to circuit design that enables signals to the tip and ring to be swapped if you intend to use the connection with non-standardized equipment.[7] One negative of using 3.5 mm jacks, and one of the reasons I prefer dedicated five-pin DIN jacks, is the potential for damage if a CV or higher voltage audio signal is connected to a MIDI circuit. The MIDI Manufacturers Association strongly advises protection circuitry when TRS connectors are used for MIDI input and output.

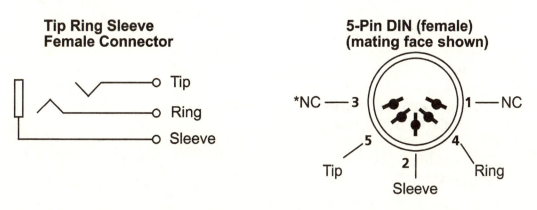

FIGURE 8.12 TRS MIDI Connection

MIDI Code

RECEIVING UART MIDI MESSAGES

The code for handling "old school" UART MIDI messages is like the code for USB MIDI input and output. Listing 8.6 demonstrates an approach to UART MIDI input. Although the code is only a few lines long, the project will convert MIDI Note-On and Note-Off messages to USB MIDI and could form the basis for an inexpensive MIDI converter. Given society's focus on greener living, it is rewarding to repurpose older MIDI hardware for use in a recording studio, as a MIDI to CV converter, or for some other application. For example, this snippet of code shown in Listing 8.6 and the UART input circuit from Figure 8.9 enabled me to use a Roland keyboard from 1998 with the most recent OSX and Windows machines!

As shown in Listing 8.6, serial MIDI projects make use of MIDI Library, a library by Francois Best, which is included via the *#include <MIDI.h>* directive.

The second line, *MIDI_CREATE_DEFAULT_INSTANCE()*, creates an instance of the MIDI class using default values. Alternatively, *MIDI_CREATE_INSTANCE*, can be used to configure the type, serial port, and name. For example, alternative input pins could be configured using *SoftwareSerial*:

```
#include <SoftwareSerial.h>
SoftwareSerial midiSerial(2,3);
MIDI_CREATE_INSTANCE(SoftwareSerial, midiSerial, MIDI);
```

As expected, MIDI input is started with a call to the *begin()* method in the *setup()* function. A specific channel can be selected for input, or all channels (omni) can be read as shown.

While callback functions can be configured as previously described, Listing 8.6 shows a more direct approach that could be useful for a comprehensive UART MIDI to USB MIDI converter. As shown at the start of the chapter, MIDI events are read with the *MIDI.read()* method and the *MIDI.getType()* method returns the message type. As is evident in code, the *MIDI* class also provides methods for determining the channel and data bytes.

Listing 8.6 UART MIDI input to USB MIDI output

```
#include <MIDI.h>

MIDI_CREATE_DEFAULT_INSTANCE();

void setup()
{
    //Start MIDI and listen to all channels
    MIDI.begin(MIDI_CHANNEL_OMNI);
}

void loop()
{
    if(MIDI.read())
    {
        switch(MIDI.getType())
        {
```

```
                case midi::NoteOn:
                    usbMIDI.sendNoteOn(MIDI.getData1(),
                                          MIDI.getData2(),
                                          MIDI.getChannel());
                break;
                case midi::NoteOff:
                    usbMIDI.sendNoteOff(MIDI.getData1(),
                                          MIDI.getData2(),
                                          MIDI.getChannel());
                break;
                default:
                    break;
            }
        }
}
```

SENDING UART MIDI MESSAGES

Aside from calling *MIDI_CREATE_DEFAULT_INSTANCE()* to create an instance of the MIDI class, outputting serial MIDI is almost the same as handling USB MIDI output. For example, Listing 8.7 demonstrates how Listing 8.1 could be revised to provide serial MIDI output.

Listing 8.7 UART MIDI Output

```
#include <Bounce.h>
#include <MIDI.h>

Bounce button0 = Bounce(0, 15);
const int channel = 1;
const int velocity = 100;

MIDI_CREATE_DEFAULT_INSTANCE();

void setup()
{
    pinMode(0, INPUT_PULLUP);
    MIDI.begin(MIDI_CHANNEL_OMNI);

}

void loop()
{
    button0.update();
    if (button0.fallingEdge()) {
        //Output a C-major triad
        MIDI.sendNoteOn(60, velocity, channel); // 60 = C4
```

```
            MIDI.sendNoteOn(64, velocity, channel);
            MIDI.sendNoteOn(67, velocity, channel);
        }

        if (button0.risingEdge()) {
            //Turn off the C-major triad
            MIDI.sendNoteOff(60, 0, channel);
            MIDI.sendNoteOff(64, 0, channel);
            MIDI.sendNoteOff(67, 0, channel);
        }

        //Controllers should discard incoming MIDI messages
        while (MIDI.read()) {
            // ignore incoming messages
        }
    }
```

Summary

It is worth repeating that Teensy microcontrollers are fantastic tools for working with MIDI. The devices can handle multi-port USB and UART input and output, and some Teensy devices can even function as USB MIDI hosts. Connecting components such as switches, potentiometers, light-detecting resistors, pressure sensors, and the like opens the door to unique and expressive interactive instruments. Other chapters in this section detail several MIDI projects including polyphony, arpeggiation, and genetic step sequencing.

CREATIVE CHALLENGES

There are many opportunities to use MIDI in the context of a live performance or in the studio. Here are a few project starters to consider:

- Create a multi-button patch changer to select sounds in live performance.
- Create a simple MIDI transposer to make it easier to play in different keys.
- Use MIDI pitch bend messages to create a MIDI transformer that changes standard MIDI Note-On messages into microtonal scale resources.
- Use the concepts from Chapter 1 to create a MIDI device that responds to changes in ambient light.
- Create a MIDI transformer that emits chords for each Note-On message.

CHAPTER 9

POLYPHONY

This chapter expands music synthesis into the realm of polyphony—where multiple voices combine to create harmony. We look at strategies for organizing audio objects into polyphonic data structures and consider three approaches to note prioritization, a necessary feature in any synthesis architecture with a finite number of voices. The discussion details the creation of a basic polyphonic synthesizer.

The following components are required to complete the polyphony project:

- Teensy 3.2 or 4.0 microcontroller with Audio Adapter Board.
- Breadboard for prototyping.
- Hookup wire.
- At least two 10k potentiometers.

Data Structures

The approach to polyphony detailed in this chapter is built around two data structures. The first structure, *SynthVoice*, is an object that encapsulates the characteristics of a musical voice and works in conjunction with audio objects created in the Audio System Design Tool. The second data structure, *SimpleSynth*, is a container class that stores multiple voices and coordinates MIDI messages and other user input with the voices contained within the class. Figure 9.1 illustrates the relationship between the data structures, main sketch, and audio objects.

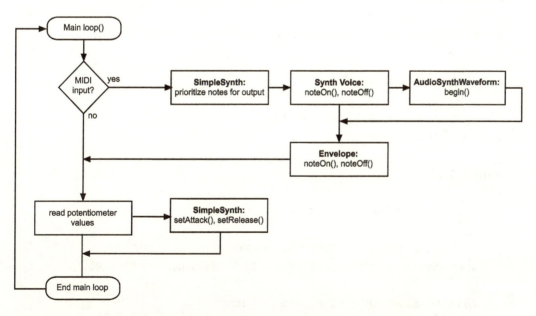

FIGURE 9.1 Relationship between data structures, main sketch, and audio objects

Sound & Music Projects for Eurorack and Beyond. Brent Edstrom, Oxford University Press. © Oxford University Press 2024.
DOI: 10.1093/9780197514504.003.0009

Configuring the Audio System Design Tool

Open a new sketch and use the Audio System Design Tool to create the objects shown in Figure 9.2:

- Four *AudioSynthWaveform* objects to function as the sound source for each voice.
- Four *AudioEffectEnvelope* objects that provide independent amplitude envelopes for each voice.
- One *AudioMixer4* object to blend the four voices.
- One *AudioOutputI2S* object and 1 *AudioControlSGTL5000* object to coordinate audio output with the Teensy Audio Shield.

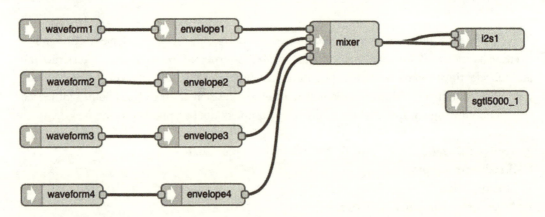

FIGURE 9.2 Configuring the Audio System Design Tool

SimpleSynth

Let's take a bird's-eye view of how the custom *SimpleSynth* class is used in a sketch before delving into the underlying data structures. As is evident in Listing 9.1, *SimpleSynth* coordinates the audio objects created in the Audio System Design Tool. All that is required is to instantiate an instance of the class, select a note prioritization method, and connect the class to the waveform and envelop objects created by the Audio System Design Tool.

Listing 9.1 Using SimpleSynth in a sketch (boilerplate code for audio objects not shown)

```
#include "SimpleSynth.h"

//Create an instance of SimpleSynth
SimpleSynth simpleSynth;

void setup()
{
    //Audio initialization not shown

    //Select a note prioritization method
    simpleSynth.notePrioritization = SimpleSynth::oldest_note;

    //Attach audio objects to simpleSynth
    simpleSynth.voices[0].attachAudioObjects(&waveform1, &envelope1);
```

```
    simpleSynth.voices[1].attachAudioObjects(&waveform2, &envelope2);
    simpleSynth.voices[2].attachAudioObjects(&waveform3, &envelope3);
    simpleSynth.voices[3].attachAudioObjects(&waveform4, &envelope4);

    //MIDI Callback setup
    usbMIDI.setHandleNoteOff(onNoteOff);
    usbMIDI.setHandleNoteOn(onNoteOn);
}

void loop()
{
    while (usbMIDI.read()) {
    }
}
```

Readers who are new to programming can use the *SimpleSynth* class as the basis for a robust polyphonic synthesizer, or you can read on to get a feel for the underlying data structures and how those objects can be adapted to other polyphonic projects.

STRUCTURES AND CLASSES

C++ provides two user-defined types that can combine data and functions into useful objects: *classes* and *structures*. One of the advantages (or disadvantages depending on context) of a structure is that all the data members are visible outside of the object, so all that is required is to create an instance of the structure and values can be assigned or read from any data member. In fact, the only difference between a class and a struct is that structs are public by default.[1]

SynthVoice

SynthVoice is a custom structure that contains pointers to two audio objects, *AudioSynthWaveform* and *AudioEffectEnvelope*, that are created in the Audio System Design Tool.[2] As shown in Listing 9.2, the class also contains a byte and a long integer representing the last MIDI Note-On and its timestamp—information that will be useful in handling Note-On and Note-Off messages. As is evident in the listing, the keyword *struct* is combined with a structure name and data members—either built-in types or other structures or classes—are added between the opening and closing brackets.

Listing 9.2 Data members of SynthVoice

```
struct SynthVoice
{
    //Pointers to audio objects
    AudioSynthWaveform *pWaveform;
    AudioEffectEnvelope *pEnvelope;
    //Variables to track the last note and its timestamp
    byte last_note;
    long timestamp;

    //Constructor and functions go here
};
```

Once you have defined a struct, it can be used just like built-in types (see Listing 9.3). In this example, the structure is instantiated with the name *synth_voice* and values are assigned to the data members just like any other variable.

Listing 9.3 Using a structure

```
SynthVoice synth_voice;

void setup()
{
    synth_voice.pWaveform = NULL;
    synth_voice.pEnvelope = NULL;
    synth_voice.last_note = 0;
    synth_voice.timestamp = 0;
}
```

CONSTRUCTORS

Classes and structures can also contain one or more *constructors*. Constructors are a special category of functions that are called when an object is instantiated.[3] While a detailed discussion of the power of constructors is beyond the scope of the book, a common application of the concept is to create a *default constructor* to initialize data members. Note how, in Listing 9.4, a default constructor initializes member variables and is automatically called when an instance of the structure is created. Listings 9.3 and 9.4 are functionally equivalent but Listing 9.4 is more elegant in my opinion.

Listing 9.4 Default constructor

```
Struct SynthVoice
{
    //Default constructor
    SynthVoice()
    {
        pWaveform = NULL;
        pEnvelope = NULL;
        last_note = timestamp = 0;
    }
    //Other code added here
    .
    .
    .
}


//Main sketch
//Default constructor automatically called:
SynthVoice synth_voice;
```

MEMBER FUNCTIONS

Structures and classes can also contain *member functions*—functions that reside inside the class. The real power of structures and classes becomes apparent when you realize that data members and member functions can work together to form functional building blocks. For example, let's add two convenience functions (see Listing 9.5). The *attachAudioObjects()* method provides a way to attach pointers to waveform and envelope objects created in the Audio System Design Tool, and *isActive()* returns the active state of the amplitude envelope—a feature that signifies when a voice is ready to emit another tone. These functions reside within the enclosing brackets of the structure.

Listing 9.5 Constructor and convenience methods

```
void attachAudioObjects(AudioSynthWaveform *pWave,
    AudioEffectEnvelope *pEnv)
{
    pWaveform = pWave;
    pEnvelope = pEnv;
}
bool isActive()
{
    return pEnvelope->isActive();
}
```

Another member function, *noteOn()*, is shown in Listing 9.6. This function forms the heart of the voice object and can be described with the following pseudo-code:

1. Convert incoming Note-On messages to the frequency and amplitude values required by the *AudioSynthWaveform* object.
2. Update the oscillator with the new amplitude and frequency values.
3. Call the envelope's *noteOn()* method.
4. Store the note.
5. Update the timestamp by calling the *millis()* function.
6. Call *noteOff()* if the velocity of the Note-On event is zero.

Listing 9.6 noteOn() method of SynthVoice

```
void noteOn(byte note, byte velocity)
{
    if(velocity > 0)
    {
        //Convert MIDI note to frequency
        float freq = 440.0* pow (2.0, (note-69) / 12.0);

        //Convert MIDI velocity (0-127) to amplitude (0-1)
        float amp = (float) velocity / 127.0;

        //Output a tone
        pWaveform->begin(amp, freq, WAVEFORM_SAWTOOTH);
        pEnvelope->noteOn();
        last_note = note;
        timestamp = millis();
```

```
    }else{
        noteOff(note);
    }


}
```

As shown in Listing 9.7, the *noteOff()* method resets the values of *last_note* and *timestamp* and calls the *noteOff()* method of the envelope. The function also checks to see if the envelope is currently active, which is useful in preventing erroneous Note-Off messages if two voices happen to share the same note.

Listing 9.7 noteOff() method of SynthVoice

```
void noteOff(byte note)
{
    //Note: This method will not turn the voice off if
    //a newer note is active or the envelop is inactive.
    if(note == last_note && pEnvelope->isActive())
    {
        pEnvelope->noteOff();
        timestamp = 0;
        last_note = 0;
    }
}
```

There isn't much to the *SynthVoice* struct, but that is generally a good thing in programming. The struct encapsulates the necessary components of a voice and can be easily adapted to a wide variety of polyphonic synthesis projects. Advanced programmers might consider using the C++ inheritance mechanism to develop a base class and derive new classes for other projects, but that approach—while powerful—is beyond the scope of the book.

We are just scratching the surface of structures and classes, but the underlying concept *is* as simple as it seems: Use a struct when you want to combine variables into a single object where the data members are publicly visible and add member functions—as needed—to enhance the utility of the data structure. Use a class when you want to control access to some of the data members or class functions.*SimpleSynth*

SimpleSynth provides an example of a *container class*. The class contains an array of *SynthVoice* objects and provides four methods:

1. *setAttack():* sets envelope attack values.
2. *setRelease():* sets envelope release values.
3. *noteOn():* prioritizes incoming Note-On messages.
4. *noteOff():* Handles incoming Note-Off messages.

SimpleSynth uses a combination of a class enumeration and an array to define and store four voices (see Listing 9.8). A second enumeration describes each of the three note prioritization methods used by the voice container: oldest note, highest note, and lowest note. As with structures, classes are defined with the *class* keyword, a class name, and opening and closing brackets. Advanced programmers will note that the *Standard Template* Library provides more elegant solutions for working with collections of objects, but a simple array is sufficient for this application. Also, note that STL is unavailable for many microcontrollers.

Listing 9.8 SimpleSynth data members

```cpp
class SimpleSynth
{
    enum{numVoices = 4};

    public:
    SynthVoice voices[numVoices];

    enum{oldest_note, highest_note, lowest_note};

    int notePrioritization = oldest_note;

    //Other methods go here
};
```

SETTING ATTACK AND RELEASE VALUES

The *setAttack()* and *setRelease()* methods shown in Listing 9.9 iterate through each of the voices stored in the voice array and call the *attack()* and *release()* methods of their respective envelopes.[4] Although the voice array is public and those methods could be called directly, the functions are convenient to use and serve to encapsulate core functionality in the class.

Listing 9.9 setAttack() and setRelease() methods

```cpp
void setAttack(int attack)
{
    for(int i = 0; i < numVoices; i++)
    {
        voices[i].pEnvelope->attack(attack);
    }
}

void setRelease(int release)
{
    for(int i = 0; i < numVoices; i++)
    {
        voices[i].pEnvelope->release(release);
    }
}
```

HANDLING NOTE-OFF MESSAGES

The *SimpleSynth noteOff()* method is one of the simplest in the book since the function need only call the *noteOff()* method for each voice in the array (see Listing 9.10).

Listing 9.10 noteOff method of SimpleSynth

```
void noteOff(byte channel, byte note, byte velocity)
{
    for(int i = 0; i < numVoices; i++)
    {
        voices[i].noteOff(note); //Pass message to SynthVoice
    }
}
```

Although channel and velocity parameters are not used in this example, those parameters will be useful should you want to expand the project to respond to specific MIDI channels or do something interesting based on release velocities that are produced by some MIDI controllers. Adding MIDI channel information at the voice level will provide a more robust solution when multiple overlapping unisons are used, but the approach shown in this chapter is a good starting point for polyphonic playing on a single keyboard or other MIDI device.

NOTE PRIORITIZATION ALGORITHM

The note-prioritization algorithm shown in Listing 9.11 is not unduly complicated, but a few steps are required to prioritize note replacement based on the lowest, highest, and oldest values of an array of voices. Figure 9.3 illustrates one approach to a prioritization algorithm. In this example, the algorithm iterates through the voice array to find any empty slots and tracks the index of the lowest, highest, and oldest notes so that the voice at that index can be replaced as needed.

CHAPTER 9 POLYPHONY 137

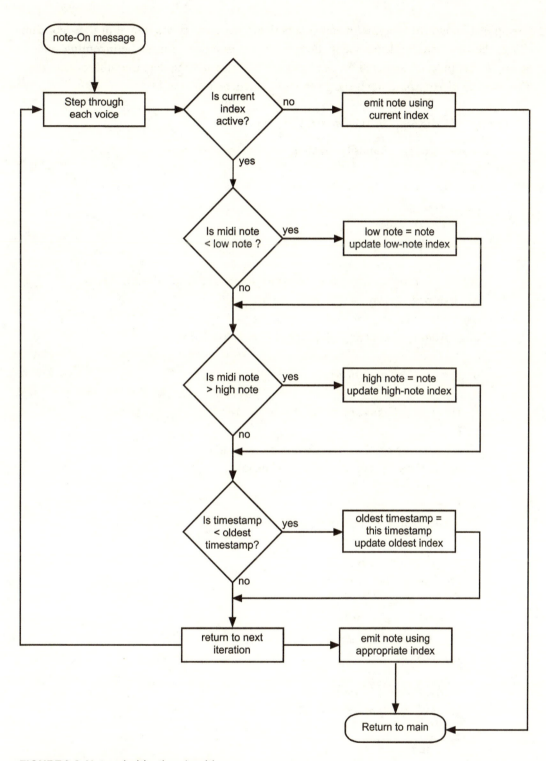

FIGURE 9.3 Note prioritization algorithm

Listing 9.11 shows the *noteOn()* member function in its entirety. As shown in the algorithm above, the function checks to see if the given voice is active. If not, the incoming note is slotted at that index. Also note how the series of "if" statements update the value of *low_note, high_note,* or *oldest_timestamp* if the given logical statement is true.

Listing 9.11 noteOn() method of SimpleSynth

```
void noteOn(byte channel, byte note, byte velocity)
{
    //Variables for index tracking
    int lowest_index = 0;
    int highest_index = 0;
    int oldest_index = 0;

    //Set starting values for lowest, highest, and oldest notes
    int low_note = voices[0].last_note;
    int high_note = voices[0].last_note;
    long oldest_timestamp = voices[0].timestamp;

    for(int i = 0; i < numVoices; i++)
    {
        if(voices[i].isActive()!= true)
        {
            //An "empty" note: output and return
            voices[i].noteOn(note, velocity);
            return;
        }
        byte note = voices[i].last_note;

        //Check for lowest note
        if(note < low_note)
        {
            low_note = note;
            lowest_index = i;
        }

        //Check for highest note
        if(note > high_note)
        {
            high_note = note;
            highest_index = i;
        }

        //Check for oldest note
        long timestamp = voices[i].timestamp;
        if(timestamp < oldest_timestamp)
        {
            oldest_timestamp = timestamp;
```

```
        oldest_index = i;
    }
}

switch(notePrioritization)
{
    case oldest_note: voices[oldest_index].noteOn(note,
        velocity); break;
    case highest_note: voices[highest_index].noteOn(note,
        velocity); break;
    case lowest_note: voices[lowest_index].noteOn(note,
        velocity); break;
}
}
```

Connecting *SimpleSynth* to the main sketch

Aside from the code that is generated by the Audio System Design Tool, very little code is required to complete the Simple Synth polyphonic synthesizer. The primary setup code consists of including *SimpleSynth.h* and creating an instance of a SimpleSynth object. Listing 9.12 also shows how the mixer object is used to set the gain for each voice and how pointers to audio objects are attached to the *SynthVoice* objects contained in *SimpleSynth*.

Listing 9.12 Setup code

```
#include "SimpleSynth.h"

//Create an instance of SimpleSynth
SimpleSynth simpleSynth;

void setup()
{
    AudioMemory(20);
    sgtl5000_1.enable();
    sgtl5000_1.volume(0.8);

    //Set voice levels
    mixer.gain(0, 0.25);
    mixer.gain(1, 0.25);
    mixer.gain(2, 0.25);
    mixer.gain(3, 0.25);

    //Set note prioritization
    simpleSynth.notePrioritization = SimpleSynth::oldest_note;

    //Attach audio objects
    simpleSynth.voices[0].attachAudioObjects(&waveform1, &envelope1);
    simpleSynth.voices[1].attachAudioObjects(&waveform2, &envelope2);
```

140 SOUND & MUSIC PROJECTS FOR EURORACK AND BEYOND

```
simpleSynth.voices[2].attachAudioObjects(&waveform3, &envelope3);
simpleSynth.voices[3].attachAudioObjects(&waveform4, &envelope4);

//MIDI Callback setup
usbMIDI.setHandleNoteOff(onNoteOff);
usbMIDI.setHandleNoteOn(onNoteOn);
}
```

MAIN LOOP() AND MIDI HANDLERS

The remaining code requires little discussion since similar snippets have been used in previous projects. The primary task of the loop is to call *usbMIDI.read()* and track the values returned by two potentiometers to set the attack and release parameters of the voice envelopes.[5] The note handlers are similarly simple, consisting of a single line that passes the bytes on to *SimpleSynth* for note prioritization (see Listing 9.13).

Listing 9.13 Main loop and MIDI handlers

```
void loop()
{
    while (usbMIDI.read()) {
    }

    int attackKnob = analogRead(A0);
    int releaseKnob = analogRead(A1);

    //Scale values from analogRead() to 0-1000
    int attack = map(attackKnob, 0, 1023, 0, 1000);
    float release = map(releaseKnob, 0, 1023, 0, 1000);
    simpleSynth.setAttack(attack);
    simpleSynth.setRelease(release);

}

void onNoteOn(byte channel, byte note, byte velocity)
{
    simpleSynth.noteOn(channel, note, velocity);
}

void onNoteOff(byte channel, byte note, byte velocity)
{
    simpleSynth.noteOff(channel, note, velocity);
}
```

Summary

The *Simple Synth* polyphonic synthesizer demonstration is purposefully minimal so core concepts can be more readily understood and applied to other projects. However, very little work would be required to add additional potentiometers for envelope decay and sustain, a pushbutton for waveform selection, or other features such as LFOs or digital filters. Depending on personal preference, it could be interesting to expand the synthesizer to use a non-tempered tuning system or incorporate additional components for real-time control. The fact that only 200 lines of code are required to create a basic polyphonic synthesizer not only speaks to the power of modern microcontroller technology and the Teensy audio library but also provides a glimpse of the creative potential of the technologies for modern-day musicians.

CREATIVE CHALLENGE

The concepts from this chapter can be applied in several ways. Consider the following project starters:

- Apply polyphony to one of the synthesizer projects in the first section of the book.
- Create a polyphonic MIDI to CV converter using the concepts from Chapter 18.
- Adapt source code for a creative application such as a MIDI device that outputs on different MIDI channels or produces MIDI continuous controller messages depending on the lowest, highest, or oldest note status (or some other qualifier).
- Enhance the source code to create an analytical function to identify chord qualities.
- Add an analytical feature to output MIDI messages based on strident intervals. For example, seconds, tritones, and sevenths might produce modulation or other continuous controller messages.

CHAPTER 10

INTERACTIVE MIDI ARPEGGIATOR

I am enough of the artist to draw freely upon my imagination. Imagination
is more important than knowledge. Knowledge is limited. Imagination
encircles the world.[1]

ALBERT EINSTEIN

The Interactive MIDI Arpeggiator project demonstrates several concepts including memory
buffers, MIDI I/O, and clock synchronization; and it is one of my favorites for its utility in
creating interactive musical patterns. Although this version utilizes MIDI, it would be easy to
add control voltage and gate output using the concepts outlined in later chapters. The project
also demonstrates the creative potential of microcontroller technology, where unique interactive playback algorithms are only limited by imagination.

The following components are required to complete the Interactive MIDI Arpeggiator
project:

- Any Teensy microcontroller.
- Breadboard for prototyping.
- Hookup wire.
- One 10k potentiometer.
- Twelve through-hole tactile switches.
- Built-in Teensy LED or optional through-hole LED and resistor.

Overview

The arpeggiator is comprised of four pairs of buttons that control pattern selection, rate (as a
division of tempo), note duration, and note repetitions. Four additional switches control the
project's active status, chord-hold mode, internal or external clock selection, and arbitrary
restart. My experiments were based on a Teensy LC microcontroller, but the project is easily
adaptable to a Teensy 3 or 4 series microcontroller as described in other chapters.

Circuit Overview

Figure 10.1 illustrates connections for the twelve switches, an LED, and a potentiometer.
Although the project is intended for breadboard experimentation, it could be completed as a
standalone project or Eurorack device using the concepts described in later chapters. Figure 10.2
illustrates one approach to connecting components on a solderless breadboard.

Sound & Music Projects for Eurorack and Beyond. Brent Edstrom, Oxford University Press. © Oxford University Press 2024.
DOI: 10.1093/9780197514504.003.0010

CHAPTER 10 INTERACTIVE MIDI ARPEGGIATOR 143

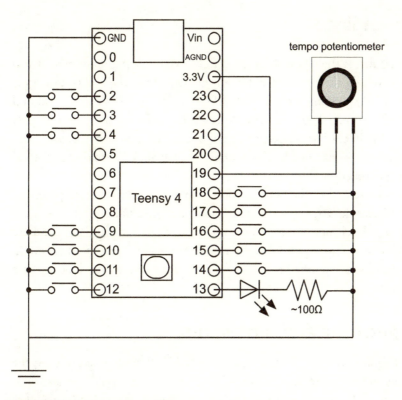

FIGURE 10.1 Teensy connections

FIGURE 10.2 Switches and potentiometer on a solderless breadboard

Developing ArpEngine

A custom *ArpEngine* class forms the heart of the Interactive MIDI Arpeggiator, which will be referred to as IMA throughout the chapter. Design goals include the ability to trigger arpeggiated patterns by playing chords on a MIDI device, a hold mode that can add and remove notes from a buffer in real time, multiple arpeggiation patterns, and the ability to synchronize to incoming MIDI clock messages. As you will see in the text that follows, arpeggiation and note management are handled by the *ArpEngine* class while internal and external MIDI clock messages are handled by the main sketch.

As with other classes presented in the book, readers who are relatively new to programming can download and use the *ArpEngine* class without an understanding of the inner workings of the class. A mid-level approach is to focus on the arpeggiation algorithms and use them as a template for customized arpeggiation patterns. More advanced programmers might find it useful to utilize the class as a point of reference for an entirely new approach or as a base class for an inherited class.

CREATING A STRUCTURE FOR MIDI NOTES

The header file for *ArpEngine* defines a C++ structure to store MIDI byte values. In C++, the primary difference between a *struct* and a *class* is that data members are public in a struct.[2] Given that the ArpEngine will contain and manipulate an array of MIDI bytes, it makes sense to open the bytes to the main sketch and other classes instead of relying on accessor methods.

The structure, shown in its entirety in Listing 10.1, is comprised of three bytes that represent a MIDI Note-On message. The class also provides a default constructor that initializes each byte to 0:

Listing 10.1 MidiNote struct

```
struct MidiNote{
    byte note;
    byte velocity;
    byte channel;
    MidiNote(): note(0), velocity(0), channel(0){};
};
```

Data Members

The *ArpEngine* header file declares several data members including an array and variables that track the status of MIDI Note-On messages in the message buffer. One of the benefits of object-oriented programming is that objects can minimize global variables and constants that tend to obfuscate complex procedural-based projects. In this example, a static constant representing the maximum size of the note buffer is defined inside the class. Each of the data members in Listing 10.2 is private and remains hidden from the calling program, simplifying the use of *ArpEngine* in other projects. Note that the internal constant is used to create an array of *MidiNote* objects that store incoming MIDI Note-On messages. As you will see, the *last_note* variable is used by *ArpEngine* to send Note-Off messages as the arpeggiator is running.

CHAPTER 10 INTERACTIVE MIDI ARPEGGIATOR   145

Listing 10.2 Arp Engine data members

```
static const int MAX_NOTES = 24;
MidiNote notes[MAX_NOTES];
int current_index;
int num_notes;
MidiNote last_note;
```

ArpEngine Header File

The entire *ArpEngine* header file is shown in Listing 10.3. As is evident in the source code, *ArpEngine* provides a default constructor and three categories of methods that manipulate the note buffer, process incoming and outgoing MIDI messages, and handle real-time arpeggiation.

Listing 10.3 Arp Engine Header File

```
#ifndef __ARPENGINE
    #define __ARPENGINE

#include <Arduino.h>

struct MidiNote{
    byte note;
    byte velocity;
    byte channel;
    MidiNote(): note(0), velocity(0), channel(0){};
};

class ArpEngine
{
    static const int MAX_NOTES = 24;
    MidiNote notes[MAX_NOTES];
    int current_index;
    int num_notes;
    MidiNote last_note;

    public:
    //Constructor
    ArpEngine():current_index(0), num_notes(0){};

    //Utility functions
    void addNote(byte note, byte velocity, byte channel);
    bool removeNote(byte note);
    void sortNotes();
    int getNumNotes(){return num_notes;};
    void clearAllNotes(){num_notes = 0;};

    //MIDI functions
    virtual void sendNoteOn(byte note, byte velocity, byte channel);
```

```
virtual void sendNoteOff(byte note, byte velocity, byte channel);
void sendLastNoteOff();
void allNotesOff();

//Playback functions
void restartArp(){current_index = 0;};
void doUpwardArp(int reps);
void doDownwardArp(int reps);
void doRandomArp(int reps);
void doWrap(int reps, int inc_value);
};


#endif
```

The remainder of this section focuses on the implementation of the methods that are declared in the header file. For this project, the methods for sending MIDI Note-On and Note-Off messages are declared as *virtual* functions. This simplifies the process of adapting *ArpEngine* for other forms of MIDI output, channel filtering, transposition, or other enhancements that could be easily implemented using the C++ inheritance mechanism.

Utility Member Functions

The *addNote()* method takes three bytes representing a Note-On message and increments num_notes, a member variable that tracks the number of notes currently stored in the note buffer. A range check ensures that notes are not added beyond the end of the buffer defined by MAX_NOTES (see Listing 10.4). Once a note has been added to the buffer, the buffer is resorted using the *sortNotes()* method described in the next section. Note that all the source code described in this section are found in *ArpEngine.cpp*, a file that is available for download at the OUP website.

Listing 10.4 addNote() method

```
void ArpEngine::addNote(byte note, byte velocity, byte channel)
{
    num_notes++;
    if(num_notes >= MAX_NOTES)
    {
        num_notes = MAX_NOTES-1;
    }
    notes[num_notes -1].note = note;
    notes[num_notes -1].velocity = velocity;
    notes[num_notes -1].channel = channel;

    //Do a simple bubble sort based on note number
    sortNotes();
}
```

Bubble Sort

The sortNotes() member function is based on a standard sorting algorithm known as a *bubble sort*.[3] In this algorithm, a primary loop counts from 0 to *num_notes*, and an inner loop counts from 0 to *num_notes* minus the current index of the main loop minus 1 on each iteration of the primary loop. Notes are swapped if the note value of a given MIDI message is higher than the next note in the array. Listing 10.5 demonstrates an implementation of the sorting algorithm, and Figure 10.3 provides a visual conceptualization of the process.

Listing 10.5 Bubble sort algorithm

```
void ArpEngine::sortNotes()
{
    for (int i = 0; i < num_notes; i++)
    {
        for (int j = 0; j < (num_notes - i - 1); j++)
        {
            if (notes[j].note > notes[j + 1].note)
            {
                MidiNote temp = notes[j];
                notes[j] = notes[j + 1];
                notes[j + 1] = temp;
            }
        }
    }
}
```

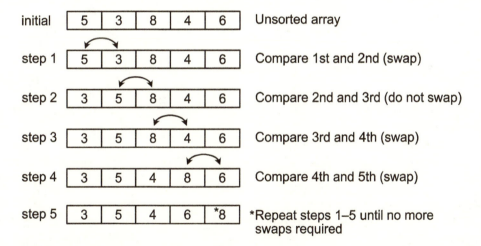

FIGURE 10.3 Bubble sort conceptualization

Notes are "virtually" removed from the note array using the *removeNote()* member function (see Listing 10.6). I use the term "virtual" because the notes are not actually deleted using real-time memory deallocation. The function overwrites the note by subtracting 1 from the index of any notes that are at a higher index and decreasing *num_notes*, the data member responsible for tracking the number of notes in the buffer. In my opinion, a fixed-length buffer is a good option for a microcontroller class like *ArpEngine*. It is also interesting to note that the function returns a Boolean indicating if the note was found in the note array, a functional detail that is useful in implementing a hold and release mechanism in the main sketch.

Tip: The increment and decrement operators provide a convenient shorthand for increasing or decreasing the value of a variable by one. For example, the following statements are equivalent:

variable++;   //variable = variable + 1;
variable--;   //variable = variable -1;

Listing 10.6 removeNote() method

```
bool ArpEngine::removeNote(byte note)
{
    bool note_found = false;

    //Loop through the note array
    for(int i = 0; i < num_notes; i++)
    {
        //See if the note is in the array
        if(notes[i].note == note)
        {
            note_found = true;
            //Remove the note by moving higher notes
            //down one slot in the array
            for(int c = i; c < num_notes; c++)
            {
                notes[c] = notes[c+1];
            }
            //Update the note counter
            num_notes--;
            if(num_notes < 0)
            {
                num_notes = 0;
            }
            //Break out of the loop
            break;
        }
    }
    //Return the status of note_found
    return note_found;
}
```

MIDI METHODS

As described previously in the chapter, the methods for sending Note-On and Note-Off messages are declared as *virtual* and simply wrap the standard Teensy *usbMIDI.sendNoteOn()* and *usbMIDI.sendNoteOff()* methods to provide an easily extensible class that can be used for other forms of MIDI output (see Listing 10.7). For example, all that is necessary to adapt the

CHAPTER 10 INTERACTIVE MIDI ARPEGGIATOR   149

class for five-pin DIN output is to create a new C++ subclass and override the functions for sending Note-On and Note-Off messages.[4]

Listing 10.7 sendNoteOn() and sendNoteOff() methods

```
void ArpEngine::sendNoteOn(byte note, byte velocity, byte channel)
{
    usbMIDI.sendNoteOn(note, velocity, channel);
}

void ArpEngine::sendNoteOff(byte note, byte velocity, byte channel)
{
    usbMIDI.sendNoteOff(note, velocity, channel);
}
```

As you will see in the next section, the arpeggiation algorithms store the previously played note using the member variable *last_note*, so the *sendLastNoteOff()* method is called to output a Note-Off message if necessary (i.e., when the value of *last_note.note* is not equal to 0). See Listing 10.8:

Listing 10.8 sendLastNoteOff() method

```
void ArpEngine::sendLastNoteOff()
{
    if(last_note.note != 0)
    {
        sendNoteOff(last_note.note,
        last_note.velocity, last_note.channel);
    }
}
```

Finally, the *allNotesOff()* member function outputs a Note-Off message for any notes that are currently stored in the note buffer. The *allNotesOff()* function is useful when a sequence is paused or when changing between hold or real-time input modes to prevent stuck notes that can occur when a receiving device does not receive a corresponding Note-Off message.

Listing 10.9 allNotesOff() method

```
void ArpEngine::allNotesOff()
{
    for(int i = 0; i < num_notes; i++)
    {
        sendNoteOff(notes[i].note, 0, notes[i].channel);
    }
}
```

EXAMPLES OF PLAYBACK METHODS

The real fun of developing *ArpEngine* is in writing the playback methods. After all, these functions are the only algorithms in the class that can be heard. This section focuses on two algorithms, *doUpwardArp()* and *doRandomArp()*, but other functions are available for download as part of the IMA project from the OUP website. Ideally, the boilerplate code shown in the following section will provide a foundation for personalizing the algorithms in new and interesting ways.

The playback member functions are called by the main sketch in response to clock messages. For example, to arpeggiate a buffer of notes, instantiate *ArpEngine* in the main sketch and call one of the arpeggiation methods in response to a MIDI clock message or an internal timer:

```
//Global instance of ArpEngine
ArpEngine myEngine;

//Call this method in response to MIDI clock messages
//Output 4 repetitions of each note in the buffer
myEngine.doUpwardArp(4);
```

doUpwardArp() algorithm

One point of interest in the arpeggiation algorithms is that they can handle an arbitrary number of repetitions of each note in the note buffer. The number of repetitions is given as a function parameter each time one of the arpeggiation algorithms is called from the main sketch.

Each of the arpeggiation algorithms functions similarly, so it will be helpful to consider the arpeggiation process in general terms with the pseudo-code outlined below:

1. Emit the note stored at the current index of the note array.
2. Store the value of the given note in the variable named *last_note*.
3. Increase the repeat count, a static variable that resides in each of the arpeggiation functions, as necessary.
4. Adjust the buffer index if the repeat count is greater than or equal to the number of repetitions given as a function parameter. For example, increase the index for upward arpeggiation or decrease the index for downward arpeggiation.
5. Reset the index as necessary to prevent an index that is out of bounds or use the modulus operator to wrap an index within the bounds of the array.

As is evident in Listing 10.10, the *doUpwardArp()* method follows the pseudo-code presented above and can be used as a boilerplate for any number of interesting arpeggiation patterns such as up and down arpeggiation, alternating indices, and the like.

Listing 10.10 doUpwardArp() method

```
void ArpEngine::doUpwardArp(int reps)
{
    static int repeats = 0;

    //Emit the note at the current
    index sendNoteOn(notes[current_index].note,
    notes[current_index].velocity, notes[current_index].channel);
```

```
    //Store the value as last_note
    last_note = notes[current_index];

    //Increase repeat counter
    repeats++;
    //Move to next index if repeat count is >= reps
    if(repeats >= reps)
    {
        repeats = 0;
        current_index++;
        //Restart at 0 if the index is out of bounds.
        if(current_index >= num_notes)
        {
            current_index = 0;
        }
    }
}
```

doRandomArp() algorithm

The *doRandomArp()* method is similar to *doUpwardArp()*, but the function selects a random index instead of looping from 0 to *num_notes* –1. The *random()* function, a stock Arduino function, is used for the task (see Listing 10.11):

Listing 10.11 doRandomArp() method

```
void ArpEngine::doRandomArp(int reps)
{
    static int repeats = 0;
    //Emit the note at the current index
    sendNoteOn(notes[current_index].note,
    notes[current_index].velocity, notes[current_index].channel);

    //Store the value of the note for the next iteration
    last_note = notes[current_index];

    //Increase repeat counter
    repeats++;

    //Select a new random index if necessary
    if(repeats >= reps)
    {
        repeats = 0;
        current_index = random(0, num_notes);
    }
}
```

Putting It All Together

The final section of the chapter details the essential functions of the main sketch including synchronizing with the MIDI clock, providing an internal clock, hold and release modes of operation, and connecting *ArpEngine* to pushbuttons, LED, and potentiometer.

HOLD AND RELEASE MODES

The IMA provides two input modes: release and hold. In release mode, MIDI Note-On messages are added to the note buffer and removed from the buffer when a corresponding MIDI Note-Off message is received. In contrast, the hold mode provides a way to sustain an arpeggiated pattern without holding the keys of a MIDI controller. In this mode, MIDI Note-On messages are added to the playback buffer, but the notes are not removed until a second MIDI Note-On message (of the same note value) is received. In this way, it is possible to initialize the arpeggiator and let it run until the notes are removed with a second Note-On message (or additional notes are added).

HANDLING MIDI MESSAGES

The main sketch provides MIDI functions to handle incoming Note-On and Note-Off messages and process MIDI Clock messages using the *usbMIDI* handler mechanism described in previous chapters. As is evident in Listing 10.12, six MIDI handlers are set to receive messages from *usbMIDI*:

Listing 10.12 Setting MIDI Handlers

```
usbMIDI.setHandleNoteOn(noteOnHandler);
usbMIDI.setHandleNoteOff(noteOffHandler);

//Handle MIDI clock
usbMIDI.setHandleRealTimeSystem(handleRealTimeSystem);
usbMIDI.setHandleStart(handleStart);
usbMIDI.setHandleStop(handleStop);
usbMIDI.setHandleSongPosition(handleSongPosition);
```

RESPONDING TO MIDI NOTES

The Note-On and Note-Off handlers are responsible for coordinating MIDI input with the *ArpEngine* and provide the underlying logic for the hold and real-time modes described in this section. The Note-On handler, shown in Listing 10.13, handles three tasks that are described in the pseudo-code below:

1. Echo the note to usbMIDI if the Boolean variable *midiThru* is true.
2. Attempt to remove the note from ArpEngine if the engine is currently in *hold* mode. (Notes are removed if they are pressed a second time in this mode.) Exit the handler if the note was removed.
3. Add the note to the *ArpEngine* buffer if it is a new note.

CHAPTER 10 INTERACTIVE MIDI ARPEGGIATOR   153

Listing 10.13 noteOnHandler() method

```
void noteOnHandler(byte channel, byte note, byte velocity)
{
    if(midiThru)
    {
        usbMIDI.sendNoteOn(note, velocity, channel);
    }

    if(holding)
    {
        //Pressing a note a second time will remove
        //it from the note from array
        if(arpEngine.removeNote(note))
        {
            //Exit if the note was removed from the array
            return;
        }
    }

    arpEngine.addNote(note, velocity, channel);
}
```

MIDI CLOCK AND INTERNAL CLOCK

A function named *doClock()* is provided in the main sketch to handle incoming MIDI clock or internal clock messages.[5] The function takes a byte representing the type of real-time message. When a clock message is received, the function increments *clock_ticks*, a global variable that tracks the current MIDI clock position. As is evident in Listing 10.14, the function makes use of the modulus operator to check the current clock tick against two global variables named duration and rate. A modulus value of 0 indicates that a multiple of the given clock tick has been reached, which triggers an appropriate Note-On or Note-Off message. Also note that *doClock()* turns an LED on each quarter note (clock_ticks % 24) and turns the LED off on each half note. The function also checks for MIDI start, continue, and stop commands.

Listing 10.14 doClock() method

```
void doClock(byte b)
{
    if(b == CLOCK)
    {
        clock_ticks++;
        //Handle note-off
        if(clock_ticks % duration == 0)
        {
            arpEngine.sendLastNoteOff();
        }
        //Handle note-on
        if(clock_ticks % rate == 0 && arpEngine.getNumNotes() > 0)
```

```
            {
                switch(currentPattern)
                {
                    case up: arpEngine.doUpwardArp(reps); break;
                    case down: arpEngine.doDownwardArp(reps); break;
                    case random_order: arpEngine.doRandomArp(reps); break;
                    case wrap: arpEngine.doWrap(reps, 2); break;
                }
            }
            //Turn LED on beats:
            if(clock_ticks % 24 == 0)
            {
                clock_ticks = 0;
                if(alignIndex)
                {
                    current_index = 0;
                    arpEngine.restartArp();
                    alignIndex = false;
                }
                    //Turn LED on
                    digitalWrite(LED_PIN, HIGH);
            }
            //Turn LED off on 8ths
            if(clock_ticks == 12)
            {
                digitalWrite(LED_PIN, LOW);
            }
        }
```

The main sketch provides a global Boolean variable named *internalClock* that tracks internal and external clock modes. The internal clock is handled by a timer initialized in the *setup()* function and updated in a function named *trackTempoPot()*. Since voltage levels tend to fluctuate slightly when read from a potentiometer, an "if" statement provides a way to filter small tempo changes that would be produced by such fluctuations (see Listing 10.15):

Listing 10.15 Internal timer

```
//Set up timer:
// Tempo = 60bpm (1000000)/24
Timer1.initialize(1000000/24);
Timer1.attachInterrupt(timerCallback);
void trackTempoPot()
{
    static int last_value = 0;
    int val = analogRead(TEMPO_PIN);
```

CHAPTER 10 INTERACTIVE MIDI ARPEGGIATOR 155

```
    if(val > last_value + 4 || val < last_value - 4)
    {
        last_value = val;
        //Calculate a new tempo and update the timer
        tempo = map(val, 0, 1023, 30, 400);
        unsigned long microSecDelay =
        (MICROSECONDS_PER_BEAT / tempo) /24;
        Timer1.setPeriod(microSecDelay);
    }
}
```

Tip: Listing 10.15 introduces the unsigned keyword. Where signed integers represent a finite range of positive and negative numbers, unsigned integers represent only positive numbers, so a greater range of positive numbers can be represented with an unsigned integer. The unsigned keyword can be combined with other keywords such as unsigned short or unsigned long. Unsigned integers (or long integers) are a good choice when tracking time since micro- or milliseconds add up quickly and the values are positive.

As with MIDI functions, the Teensy timer mechanism is handled with a callback function that is called each time the timer fires. As is evident in Listing 10.16, the internal timer callback simply calls *doClock()* and sends a byte representing a clock message:

Listing 10.16 Timer callback function

```
void timerCallback()
{
    if(isActive && internalClock == true)
    {
        doClock(CLOCK);
    }
}
```

External MIDI clock messages are handled in a similar way in response to incoming MIDI real-time system messages (see Listing 10.17):

Listing 10.17 Handling MIDI Clock messages

```
void handleRealTimeSystem(byte b)
{
    if(isActive && internalClock == true)
    {
        doClock(b);
    }
}
```

SOUND & MUSIC PROJECTS FOR EURORACK AND BEYOND

Handling Song Position Messages

The remaining MIDI handler functions are responsible for adjusting the current position (stored in *clock_ticks*). This is useful when using the arpeggiator in conjunction with a hardware or software sequencer. As shown in the listing, the functions are responsible for initializing the clock position at the start of a sequence, sending Note-Off messages when the sequence stops, and adjusting the number of clock ticks to an incoming song-position message (which are adjusted to align to a quarter-note boundary).[6]

Listing 10.18 Song Position Handlers

```
void handleStart(void)
{
        clock_ticks = 0;
        //Comment out this line for "floating" starts
        arpEngine.restartArp();
}

void handleStop(void)
{
    arpEngine.allNotesOff();
}

void handleSongPosition(uint16_t pos)
{
    clock_ticks = pos * 6; //Six MIDI clocks per beat
}
```

CONNECTING ARPENGINE TO A USER INTERFACE

It is easy to connect *ArpEngine* to a user interface using switches, rotary switches, or rotary encoders. For example, this iteration of IMA utilizes momentary switches for input but the functions for tracking pattern selection, duration, rate, and other parameters could be adapted to work with other forms of input. Given that the code for tracking momentary switches is similar to the code presented in earlier chapters, we will focus on a single function named *trackDurationButtons()*. The code for rate, repeat, and pattern selection is similar and available for download from the OUP website.

Tracking Momentary Switches

As discussed in previous chapters, the Teensy Bounce class provides a convenient way to debounce and track the status of a momentary switch. Instances of the Bounce class are declared as global variables and the constructor takes two parameters representing the switch and the number of milliseconds to be used for debouncing the switch.

```
//Pins 10 and 11 with 10ms debounce
Bounce decDurationBtn = Bounce(10, 10);
Bounce incDurationBtn = Bounce(11, 10);
```

It is important to remember to configure the pins for input and turn on the internal pull-up resistor in the *setup()* function in order for the switch to function with the Bounce class:

```
pinMode(10, INPUT_PULLUP);
pinMode(11, INPUT_PULLUP);
```

Listing 10.19 shows how a pair of momentary switches are configured to set the duration of arpeggiated notes from 1 to the current playback rate. In this example, a global variable named duration stores the current duration.

Listing 10.19 Tracking duration with a pair of momentary switches

```
void trackDurationButtons()
{
    //Track the duration decrease switch
    decDurationBtn.update();
    if(decDurationBtn.fallingEdge())
    {
        duration--;
        if(duration <1)
        {
            duration = 1;
        }
    }

    //Track the duration increase switch
    incDurationBtn.update();
    if(incDurationBtn.fallingEdge())
    {
        duration++;
        if(duration > rate)
        {
            duration = rate;
        }
    }
}
```

Using the Arpeggiator

As with other projects in the book that utilize *usbMIDI*, it is easy to configure the arpeggiator to work with a DAW or free online sequencer. Select the Teensy as a MIDI device for input and output in the preferences of your application and be sure that the DAW is configured to send MIDI clock messages. Select one track to output MIDI to the Teensy and configure a second track as a virtual synthesizer to receive messages from the Teensy (see Figure 10.4). While it is convenient to use a DAW to test and explore the arpeggiation project, the arpeggiator is a good choice as a stand-alone MIDI UART device.

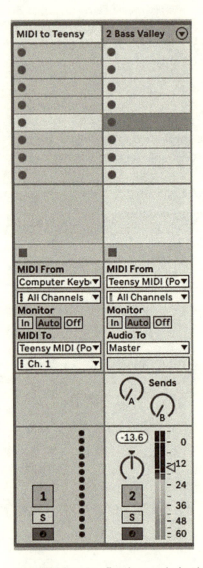

FIGURE 10.4 Configuring tracks in Ableton Live to interact with the Teensy arpeggiator

Summary

Although modern DAWs typically provide arpeggiators, there is something liberating about using a stand-alone arpeggiator. Not only is the IMA fun to use, but it also works well in the context of Eurorack setups and can be easily adapted to output UART MIDI or control voltages. Another benefit of the modular approach is that multiple arpeggiators could be incorporated in a Eurorack rig and arpeggiation streams could be coordinated by a single clock (either by building multiple arpeggiators or adapting the code to handle multiple instances of *ArpEngine*). Finally, the IMA provides a convenient way to develop customized arpeggiation patterns beyond the limited number of patterns available in a typical DAW. As with other projects in the book, readers are encouraged to visit the OUP website for demonstration videos and source code and to adapt the code for their own use.

CREATIVE CHALLENGE

Arpeggiators are fun to use, and they can be applied to many styles of music-making. Consider some of the following activities to get your creative juices flowing:

- Arpeggiate a chord from a scale or mode and use the scale as a resource to improvise a melody.
- Arpeggiate a chord but use the output to trigger percussive sounds.
- Stack two contrasting triads to create interesting polychords.
- Use the arpeggiator to perform a sequence of chords from a jazz or classical composition for a unique boundary-crossing experiment.
- Arpeggiate a simple triad and change one note at a time to create a linear progression of chords.
- Configure an arpeggiator or repetitive pattern in a DAW and select external synchronization on the IMA to create interactive patterns. Setting a different subdivision on the IMA can create interesting polyrhythmic effects.
- Add code to the IMA to output intervals or chords for each note of the arpeggiation.
- Add code to the IMA to create random velocities.
- Configure the IMA to respond to an alternative clock source such as a specific MIDI note, any Note-On event, and so on.
- Or, for the ultimate creative challenge, use motion tracking of a fish to control the arpeggiator.[7]

CHAPTER 11

GENETIC STEP SEQUENCER

> ... and if I had my life to live over again, I would have made a rule to read
> some poetry and listen to some music at least once every week.[1]
>
> CHARLES DARWIN

Evolutionary algorithms (EAs) provide a fascinating avenue of exploration for electronic musicians. Dating back to the 1970s with the work of John H. Holland and David E. Goldberg, the so-called "American School" of *genetic algorithms* provides a rich framework for utilizing biological procedures for problem solving and creative applications. Genetic algorithms, a subclass of evolutionary algorithms, are modeled on natural systems and utilize stochastic search techniques.[2] However, unlike the chance or aleatoric explorations associated with composers including John Cage, Karlheinz Stockhausen, and others, the stochastic elements of a genetic algorithm provide variety in the context of evolutionary or biological processes. In applying genetic algorithms to music composition, the output can sound organic, not random.

Evolutionary algorithms are a natural extension of Charles Darwin's theory of natural selection, where variations or mutations of inheritable traits provide the adaptability that allows some fit individuals to survive and pass useful traits to their progeny. Interestingly, "survival of the fittest" doesn't necessarily mean survival of the strongest or most aggressive: Scientists Brian Hare and Vanessa Woods posit that friendly partnerships have been an important component of evolution for some species including dogs—the people-loving descendants of wolves—and bonobos who, unlike warring chimpanzees, are governed by females and "engage in sex to maintain a peaceful collective temperament."[3]

This chapter details the use of genetic algorithms to drive a MIDI *step sequencer* with ever-changing genetic modifications. Primitive sequencers, dating from the early days of analog synthesis, generally consisted of eight or sixteen *steps* that provided a repeating pattern of voltages characteristic of the music of Kraftwerk and others (and more recently popularized in the soundtrack to *Stranger Things*, a hit Netflix series).[4] Although some early step sequencers had provisions for modifying playback (such as playing an entire sequence backwards), microcontroller technology provides an opportunity for innumerable variations including artificial intelligence and the EAs described in this chapter.

Components required to build the genetic step sequencer:

- Teensy 3.2 or 4.0 microcontroller.
- Breadboard for prototyping.
- Hookup wire.
- Four through-hole tactile switches.
- One rotary encoder.

Sound & Music Projects for Eurorack and Beyond. Brent Edstrom, Oxford University Press. © Oxford University Press 2024.
DOI: 10.1093/9780197514504.003.0011

Developing a Biological Model

Figure 11.1 illustrates a general iterative process for an EA consisting of:

1. An initial population.
2. Selection of parents.
3. Recombination and/or mutation of the chromosomes of fit parents.
4. Evaluation of offspring in the context of a new population.[5]

This pseudo-Darwinian model forms the basis for the genetic step sequencer and will guide the creation of a virtual habitat for the algorithms to adapt and flourish.

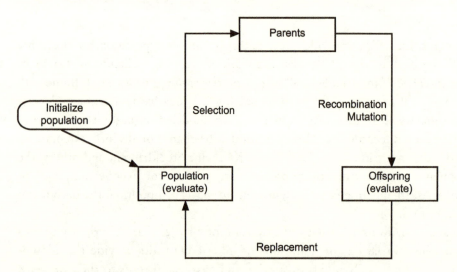

FIGURE 11.1 General evolutionary algorithm (based on an illustration in Evolutionary Computer Music)

GENETIC REPRESENTATION

In biology, DNA consists of *chromosomes* that are made of *genes*—the sequences of proteins that determine traits.[6] In a similar way, a collection of chromosomes provides the underlying musical characteristics of the genetic sequencer. In this application, multiple chromosomes are combined into a *genotype* representing the initial population which is, in turn, decoded into a *phenotype*—the set of observable characteristics.

There are myriad ways to approach a genetic representation including using numbers and characters or, in the case of music, notes and durations. Complex encodings containing a mixture of characters, numbers, and rules are also possible and are the approach used in the genetic sequencer project. In this case, an unsigned 16-bit integer represents a chromosome containing the musical traits shown in Figure 11.2. Characteristics include the index of a lookup table of notes, dynamic level, on or off status, and function; and the characteristics are encoded in the individual bits of the chromosome. Although the chromosome requires bit-level manipulation, a set of templatized bit-manipulation functions are provided in *bit_tools.h*, one of the project header files available for download from the Oxford University Press website. Strategies for bit manipulation are described in a sidebar at the end of the chapter.

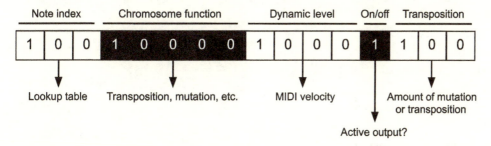

FIGURE 11.2 A 16-bit musical chromosome

Using the Chromosome

The first three bits of the chromosome encode an index to a lookup table that is stored as part of the *genome* containing the complete set of genes. The lookup table, which consists of eight bytes representing a palette of MIDI notes, provides the musical set that forms a foundation for evolutionary processes. Since three bits are used to encode the index, the index will always fall in the range of 0–7—the maximum value that is possible with three bits.

The next five bits store the value of a chromosome function. As you will see in the code that follows, functions include various transpositions and mutations—including a permanent cancer mutation that alters the underlying lookup table.

The final four bits represent the on or off status of the chromosome and a transposition value—a number that is used in conjunction with some of the transposition functions.

CODING THE CHROMOSOME

The data structure for the chromosome is shown in Listing 11.1—a complete listing of the *Chromosome.h* header file. Note how the *struct* contains a single unsigned 16-bit integer representing the chromosome and how an enumeration lists ten possible functions consisting of eight transpositions and two mutations. Of course, additional functions—including more adventuresome transformations—are possible depending on aesthetic taste. However, the functions used in this chromosome tend to produce music that sounds organic. Strident mutations are infrequent and often sound surprisingly intentional given the stochastic techniques incorporated in the algorithms. Incidentally, function values outside of the range of the enumeration do not provide any real-time modification, so the chance of transposition or mutation is approximately 31% given the range of values from 0–31 that are possible with the five bits allocated for chromosome function.

Listing 11.1 Chromosome.h

```
#ifndef __CHROMOSOME
#define __CHROMOSOME

#include <Arduino.h>

struct Chromosome
{
    uint16_t chromosome;

    //Function enumeration
    enum{octave_up, octave_down, fifth_up, fourth_down,
        upper_neighbor, lower_neighbor, transpose_up,
        transpose_down, mutate, permanent_mutation};

    //Default constructor
    Chromosome();

    //Setters
    void setNoteIndex(const uint16_t index);
    void setFunction(uint16_t f);
    void setDynamic(uint16_t dynamic);
    void setNoteOnStatus(bool on);

    //Getters
    bool noteOn();
    int getTransposition();
    uint16_t getNoteIndex();
    uint16_t getFunction();
    uint16_t getDynamic();
    int getFitness();
};

#endif
```

CONSTRUCTOR

The *Chromosome* struct contains a default constructor that calls *random()* to assign a random value to the chromosome when it is constructed (see Listing 11.2). Looking ahead, it is important to note that the genotype does restrict the randomness when objects are initialized in the genotype's constructor.

Listing 11.2 Chromosome constructor

```
Chromosome::Chromosome()
{
    //Randomize on construction
    chromosome = random(65535);
}
```

SETTERS

Most of the grunt work of the *struct* involves setting individual bits or converting a series of bits into an integer representing an index, dynamic level, or function. All of the member functions involving bit setting rely on functions found in *bit_tools.h* (described in the sidebar at the end of the chapter) and have a similar format, so we will focus on the *setNoteIndex()* method shown in Listing 11.3 to see how the process works. In this example, a *for loop* iterates through the first three bits of the chromosome and changes the values of individual bits, as needed, based on the value of the first three bits of the *index* parameter.

Listing 11.3 setNoteIndex()

```
void Chromosome::setNoteIndex(const uint16_t index)
{
    for(int i = 0; i <= 2; i++)
    {
        if(isBitSet(index, i))
        {
            setBit(chromosome, i);
        }else{
            clearBit(chromosome, i);
        }
    }
}
```

The other "setter" functions for setting chromosome function, dynamics, and MIDI Note-On status function similarly.

Getters

The "getter" member functions are similarly simple and rely on the *getValue()* function found in *bit_tools.h*. As shown in Listing 11.4, *getNoteIndex()* calls *getValue()* to convert the first three bits (0–2) into an integer.

Listing 11.4 getNoteIndex()

```
uint16_t Chromosome::getNoteIndex()
{
    return getValue(chromosome, 0, 2);
}
```

One function deserves more discussion: *getDynamic()* calls *getValue()* to read bits 8–11, converting the bits into one of sixteen possible dynamic levels (see Listing 11.5). For aesthetic reasons, the dynamics are handled as an offset, so the function always returns a dynamic that is at least *mezzo-piano* (approximately 64 in terms of a MIDI velocity level). Musicians rarely play with consistently sudden and extreme dynamic changes, so constraining dynamics in this way provides character without sacrificing a pleasing over-arching dynamic level.

Listing 11.5 getDynamics()

```
uint16_t Chromosome::getDynamic()
{
    uint16_t dynamic = getValue(chromosome, 8, 11);
    //Use an offset so MIDI velocity is at least 64
    return 64 + (dynamic * 4);
}
```

Fitness Function

The real fun of the *Chromosome* struct is found in its *fitness function* shown in Listing 11.6. The fitness function is called by the genome to determine which chromosomes will create offspring, so the method with which chromosomes are rated has a significant impact on the output of the genetic algorithm.

Listing 11.6 Fitness function

```
int Chromosome::getFitness()
{
    //Add other fitness attributes here
    return getDynamic();
}
```

The chromosome's fitness function uses dynamic level as a measure of fitness, an approach that might be described as "the loudest individuals get to replicate." But many other approaches are possible including random fitness levels (which result in chaotic output), or the use of register, function, note index, or a combination of these or other attributes. For example, the fitness function could use the bits representing chromosome function to prioritize mutations resulting in more frequent and strident changes over time, or the mathematical value of the entire chromosome could be incorporated into the evaluation. It is fascinating to explore varying approaches and listen to the output that is produced through evolutionary processes.

POPULATION STRUCTURE: BIOLOGICAL GENOTYPE

Most of the action in the genetic sequencer happens in the *Genotype* data structure shown in Listing 11.7. As is evident in the listing, the structure contains an array containing eight chromosomes and a second array containing the eight notes that form the palette of notes available to the chromosomes. The default values form a G7sus chord, but the notes can be changed via MIDI input as described later in the chapter.

CHAPTER 11 GENETIC STEP SEQUENCER   167

Listing 11.7 Genotype declaration from Genotype.h

```
#ifndef __GENOTYPE
#define __GENOTYPE

#include "bit_tools.h"
#include "Chromosome.h"

struct Genotype
{
    enum{numChromosomes = 8};

    Chromosome chromosomes[numChromosomes];
    int activeStep;

    //Default to a G7sus
    uint8_t noteArray[numChromosomes] = {55, 60, 62, 65, 67, 65,
        69, 67};

    //Default constructor
    Genotype();

    MIDINote nextNote(bool ignore_note_off);
    void evaluateChromosomes(int &best_index, int &second_best_index,
        int &least_index);
    void applyFunction(int function, MIDINote &n);
};


#endif
```

The *Genotype.h* file also implements a simple *MIDINote* struct, shown in Listing 11.8, that provides a convenient way to pass MIDI information to and from the genotype. The struct contains bytes representing MIDI channel, note, and velocity as well as a default constructor that initializes the MIDI message to default starting values:

Listing 11.8 MIDINote structure

```
struct MIDINote
{
    byte channel;
    byte note;
    byte velocity;

    MIDINote(): channel(1), note(60), velocity(100){};
};
```

Overview of Evolutionary Process

The evolutionary process encoded in the *Genotype* data structure can be described with the following pseudo-code, adapted from a process described in *Algorithmic Composition: Paradigms of Automated Music Generation*, by Gerhard Nierhaus:[7]

1. Create a partially randomized starting population of chromosomes. (Note: Although dynamic level, function, and Note-On status are randomized, each of the chromosomes is assigned an index to a note in a lookup table of MIDI note values.)
2. Calculate the fitness of each chromosome.
3. Select the fittest individuals.
4. Use crossover and/or mutation to generate a new individual based on the chromosomes of the fittest individuals.
5. Optionally force periodic mutation on some chromosomes.
6. Create the next generation and return to step 2.

Of the steps listed above, the process of *crossover* is particularly intriguing. In a truly biological process, two chromosomes can break and connect in different ways, resulting in "an exchange of genes, called genetic recombination."[8] The locus for the crossover, shown in Figure 11.3, can vary resulting in equal or unequal crossover—a process that is mimicked in the genetic sequencer with randomized crossover points.

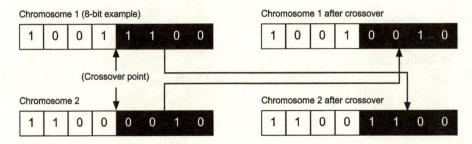

FIGURE 11.3 Genetic crossover

Construction

As shown in Listing 11.9, the *Genome* constructor loops through the set of chromosomes and assigns each chromosome an index to one of the notes in the lookup table. The process could be randomized, but I prefer to use the initial set of notes for aesthetic reasons. (Remember that the other bits have been previously randomized in the chromosome's constructor.)

Listing 11.9 Genome constructor

```
Genotype::Genotype(): activeStep(0)
{
    for(int i = 0; i < numChromosomes; i++)
    {
        //Assign each chromosome an index to the lookup table
        chromosomes[i].setNoteIndex(i);
    }
}
```

Evaluation

Hierarchical evaluation of chromosomes is handled by the *evaluateChromosomes()* function, a member of the *Genotype* data structure. Three parameters representing the index of the best, second-best, and least-best chromosomes are passed to the function *by reference*, so changes to those variables "stick" when the function returns—an approach described in more detail in Chapter 3. As is evident in Listing 11.10, the function uses a series of "if" statements to track and sort the fitness status of the chromosomes.

Listing 11.10 evaluateChromosomes() member function

```
void Genotype::evaluateChromosomes(int &best_index,
        int &second_best_index, int &least_index)
{
    int best = 0;
    int second_best = 0;
    int least = 0;
    best_index = 0;
    second_best_index = 0;
    least_index = 100;

    //Find top two chromosomes and least-fit chromosome
    for(int i = 0; i < numChromosomes; i++)
    {
        int fitness = chromosomes[i].getFitness();
        if(fitness > best)
        {
            best = fitness;
            best_index = i;
        }else if(fitness > second_best)
        {
            second_best = fitness;
            second_best_index = i;
        }
        if(fitness < least)
        {
            least = fitness;
            least_index = i;
        }
    }
}
```

Function Application

As described in the Chromosome section of this chapter, each chromosome uses five bits to encode a function representing a transposition or genetic mutation, and the *Genome* structure applies these functions to a MIDI note in its *applyFunction()* method. The method takes an integer parameter representing the given function and a *MIDINote* struct as a reference. As with the function for evaluating chromosomes, changes to the *MIDINote* struct are maintained when the function returns. Most of the alterations are applied in a similar way, so only the first two transformations are shown in Listing 11.12.

Listing 11.11 applyFunction() excerpt

```
void Genotype::applyFunction(int function, MIDINote &n)
{
    if(function == Chromosome::octave_up)
    {
        n.note += 12;

    }else if(function == Chromosome::octave_down)
    {
        n.note -= 12;
    }
    .
    .
    .
```

The code for handling mutations is shown in Listing 11.12, part of the *applyFunction()* method. In the case of a single mutation, the function randomly toggles one of the sixteen bits of the chromosome and refreshes the MIDI note (in case the mutation altered the index of the lookup table). The second mutation adds the interval of a *perfect fourth* (five semitones) to the underlying lookup table—permanently altering the table.

Listing 11.12 code for handling genetic mutations (part of the applyFunction() method)

```
else if(function == Chromosome::mutate)
{
    toggleBit(chromosomes[activeStep].chromosome,
            random(0, 16));
    n.note = noteArray[activeStep];
}else if(function == Chromosome::permanent_mutation)
{
    noteArray[activeStep] = noteArray[activeStep] + 5;
    n.note = noteArray[activeStep];
}
```

Of course, innumerable approaches could be used to mutate the genetic content of the chromosomes, but these mutations provide an output that could be described as interesting but subtle. More extreme mutations might include randomizing the transposition of permanent mutations (or using the transposition value encoded in the chromosome), randomizing chromosome function, or some other approach. As with the fitness function described in the Chromosome section of this chapter, it is fascinating to experiment with a variety of approaches to genetic mutation. As you will see in the next section, the genome also includes a provision to force genetic transformations on some chromosomes.

nextNote()

The final method of the *Genotype* data structure is *nextNote()*, a method that returns a *MIDINote* struct on each tick of an internal or external clock source. Although the function is long, it follows the steps shown in Figure 11.4 consisting of preparation of the *MIDINote* struct based on the values of the active chromosome, incrementing the index of the active sequence step, evaluation and application of crossover and mutation, and periodic mutation of chromosomes.

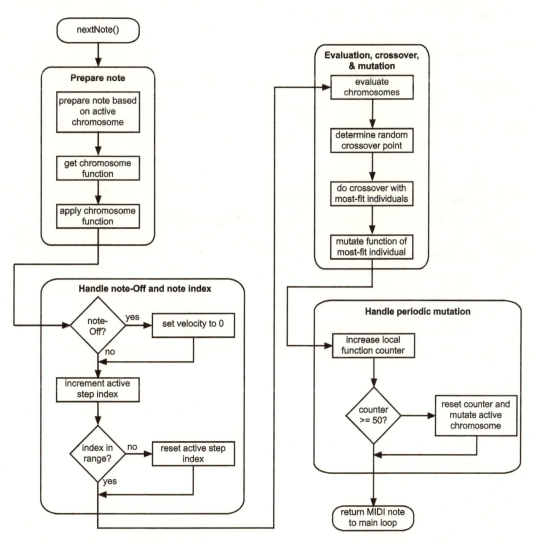

FIGURE 11.4 nextNote() algorithm

Most of the steps of the *nextNote()* algorithm utilize the chromosome's member functions including *getNoteIndex()*, *getDynamic()* and *getFunction()* in conjunction with the genome methods for evaluating chromosomes and applying functions, so we will focus on the second half of the function shown in Listing 11.13. Here, indices are provided for the most-fit individuals and a randomized crossover point is determined. The crossover point retains at least one bit of the original chromosome but, as with other algorithms in the genome, it is interesting to experiment with different values. For example, the crossover could be limited to a range of bits representing the lookup table or chromosome function.

172   SOUND & MUSIC PROJECTS FOR EURORACK AND BEYOND

Crossover, the exchange of genetic material, is handled by the *crossover()* function—another of the functions provided in *bit_tools.h*. The function takes a reference to two integers and a crossover point and exchanges the relevant bits between the two integers.

The *nextNote()* method also performs a subtle mutation on the most-fit chromosome by randomizing the chromosome's function. A more aggressive mutation is performed in the last section of the function: When an internal counter reaches fifty iterations, the function of the active chromosome is randomized, a random bit is toggled, and all the bits are inverted resulting in a modified chromosome. This is yet another place where experimentation will yield many interesting aesthetic possibilities.

Listing 11.13 getNextNote() excerpt

```
MIDINote Genotype::nextNote(bool ignore_note_off)
{
    .
    .
    .

    //Evaluate chromosomes and get indices to
    //most- and least-fit individuals
    evaluateChromosomes(best_index, second_best_index, least_index);

    //Determine crossover point
    int crossover_point = random(1, 16);

    //Do the crossover
    crossover(chromosomes[best_index].chromosome,
        chromosomes[second_best_index].chromosome, crossover_point);

    //Mutate the function of the best chromosome
    chromosomes[best_index].setFunction(random(0, 32));

    //Force a extreme randomized mutation every 50 iterations
    counter++;
    if(counter >= 50)
    {
        counter = 0;
        chromosomes[activeStep].setFunction(random(0, 32));
        toggleBit(chromosomes[best_index].chromosome,
            random(0, 16));
        invert(chromosomes[activeStep].chromosome);
    }

    //Return the MIDI note
    return n;
}
```

Output

Although it was interesting to listen to the varied output of the genetic sequencer, I was curious to see the distribution of notes produced by the algorithm and entered the scale shown in Figure 11.5—colloquially known as a "bebop" scale, a Mixolydian scale with a passing tone between the subtonic and tonic.

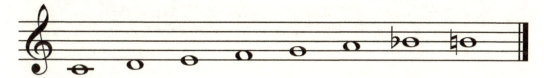

FIGURE 11.5 C-"bebop" scale

Figure 11.6 is a histogram that shows the distribution of notes over 700 iterations of the algorithm. It is interesting that, while twenty notes were produced by the genome, only one new *pitch class* was introduced—presumably through the mechanism for permanent genetic mutation encoded in the genome.

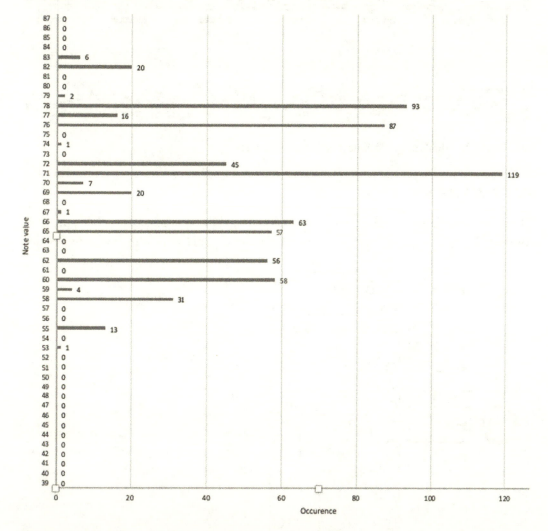

FIGURE 11.6 Histogram of 700 iterations of the genetic algorith

Figure 11.7 illustrates some of the rhythmic and melodic permutations that occurred over twelve measures when the lookup table was initialized with the notes of a C-Dorian scale. Interestingly, a permanent mutation evidently occurred in the first bar since E-natural isn't one of the notes contained in a C-Dorian scale. Alternatively, the note might have been produced by the transposition of another tone in the scale.

FIGURE 11.7 Rhythmic permutations (first three measures)

HARDWARE

The genetic sequencer can be built on a breadboard using the components shown in Figure 11.8. Although I used a Teensy LC to test the code, the project should work with any Teensy model.

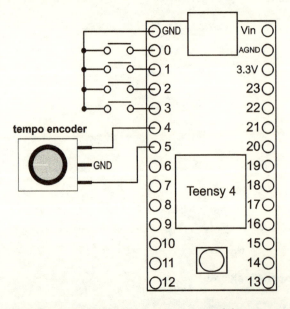

FIGURE 11.8 Hooking up pushbuttons and the rotary encoder

To experiment with the project, configure the Teensy as a MIDI device from the Tools . . . USB Type menu in the Arduino IDE and select it as a MIDI source in a DAW or other sequencer. While the sequencer utilizes USB MIDI, very few changes would be required to reconfigure the project for UART MIDI as described in Chapter 8. A configuration for Ableton Live is shown in Figure 11.9.

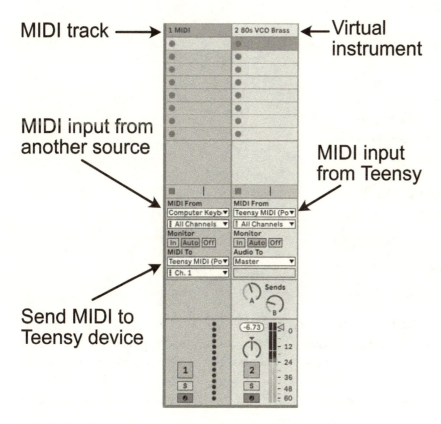

FIGURE 11.9 Using the genetic step sequencer with Ableton Live

MAIN SKETCH

The main sketch is built around four pushbuttons and a rotary encoder. Given that those electronic components have been covered in previous chapters, we will focus on aspects of the code that are unique to the genetic sequencer.

The four pushbuttons toggle the states shown in Table 11.1.

TABLE 11.1 Function of pushbuttons.

Pushbutton	Description
Playback	Toggles between playback and standby modes.
Rhythm	When active, the main sketch plays all notes returned by the genome—even if the chromosome Note-On bit is off.
Clock source	Switches between internal clock (in beats-per-minute) and an external MIDI clock source (in pulses per quarter note—PPQN).
Record mode	Incoming MIDI Note-On messages are stored in the genome's note array when record mode is active.

As expected, the main sketch declares four Boolean variables to track the status of the menu pushbuttons described above. Additional variables are provided to handle tempo and MIDI clock rate, and to track incoming MIDI clock ticks. In addition to the expected *Bounce* and *Encoder* objects that are used to track pushbutton and encoder status, three class objects—*Genome, Metro,* and *MIDINote*—are also instantiated (see Listing 11.14).

Listing 11.14 Global variables

```
bool playing = false;
bool ignore_rhythm = true;
bool recording = false;
bool internal_clock = true;
int bpm = 240;
int rate = 6;
int clock_ticks = 0;
byte last_note = 0;

Genotype genotype;
MIDINote note;
Metro metro = Metro(60000/bpm);
```

The *Genotype* and *MIDINote* data structures have already been described in this chapter, but the *Metro* object deserves mention: the *Metro* library, a component of the default Teensyduino installation, was created by Thomas Ouellet Fredericks and provides a convenient class for scheduling "events to occur at regular intervals."[9] In addition to the constructor shown in Listing 11.14, the class provides the three methods shown in Table 11.2.

TABLE 11.2 Metro Library methods.

Method	Description
Check()	Check if the interval has elapsed. Returns true if it has, false if it has not (yet).
Interval()	Change to a new interval setting.
Reset()	Reset the interval.

A practical example of the *Metro* library can be seen in the main loop of the genetic sequencer shown in Listing 11.15. In this example, a function called *tick()* is called whenever the *metro* object returns true and the sequencer clock is set to internal. Note how the *reset()* method of the *Metro* object is called to force the object to restart the timer.

Chapter 11 Genetic Step Sequencer 177

Listing 11.15 Main loop of the genetic sequencer

```
void loop()
{
    while (usbMIDI.read()) {
    }

    if(metro.check() == 1 && internal_clock == true)
    {
        tick();
        metro.reset();
    }

    trackPlayBtn();
    trackIgnoreRhythmBtn();
    trackRecordBtn();
    handleInternalBtn();
    handleTempoEncoder();
}
```

MIDI Clock

MIDI Clock messages were covered in detail in Chapter 10, so a summary of the use of MIDI Clock messages in the genetic sequencer project will be sufficient. The *setup()* function, in addition to configuring digital pins, passes five MIDI callback function pointers to the *usbMIDI* object (see Listing 11.16). Also note that the *setup()* function is a convenient place to seed the random number generator by reading the value of one of the "floating" digital pins:

Listing 11.16 setup() function

```
void setup()
{
    //Set up pins for pushbuttons
    pinMode(0, INPUT_PULLUP);
    pinMode(1, INPUT_PULLUP);
    pinMode(2, INPUT_PULLUP);
    pinMode(3, INPUT_PULLUP);

    //Configure MIDI callback functions
    usbMIDI.setHandleNoteOn(onNoteOn);
    usbMIDI.setHandleRealTimeSystem(handleRealTimeSystem);
    usbMIDI.setHandleStart(handleStart);
    usbMIDI.setHandleStop(handleStop);
    usbMIDI.setHandleSongPosition(handleSongPosition);

    //Seed the random number generator
    randomSeed(analogRead(10));
}
```

The MIDI Clock callback functions are shown in Listing 11.17 and provide similar functionality to the arpeggiator project from the previous chapter. The function handles incoming MIDI clock messages, resets the beat when the clock is started, sends a Note-Off message in response to a stop message, and recalculates the active position in response to a *song position* MIDI message.

Listing 11.17 MIDI Clock callback functions

```
void handleRealTimeSystem(byte b)
{
    //Ignore if sequencer is not active or
    //running on internal clock
    if(!playing || internal_clock == true)
    {
        return;
    }
    doClock(b);
}


void handleStart(void)
{
        clock_ticks = 0;
}


void handleStop(void)
{
    usbMIDI.sendNoteOff(last_note, note.velocity, note.channel);
}


void handleSongPosition(uint16_t pos)
{
    //Convert position to ticks (6 MIDI clocks per beat)
    clock_ticks = pos * 6;
}
```

As shown in Listing 11.18, the *doClock()* function handles various states of the MIDI clock and calls *allNotesOff()* when the clock is stopped—a strategy that helps to minimize "stuck" notes that can occur when a given Note-On message is not followed by a corresponding Note-Off message.

CHAPTER 11 GENETIC STEP SEQUENCER   179

Listing 11.18 doClock() function

```
void doClock(byte b)
{
    if(b == CLOCK)
    {
        if(clock_ticks % rate == 0)
        {
            tick();
        }
        clock_ticks++;
    }

    if(b == START)
    {
        clock_ticks = 0;
    }

    if(b == CONTINUE)
    {
        //Use this for LED on or other functionality
    }

    if(b == STOP)
    {
        usbMIDI.sendNoteOff(last_note,
                note.velocity, note.channel);
    }
}

//Call this function to prevent stuck notes
void allNotesOff()
{
    for(int n = 0; n < 127; n++)
    {
        usbMIDI.sendNoteOff(n, 0, 1);
    }
}
```

tick() function

The *tick()* function is the heart of the genetic sequencer and is called by either the internal clock or external MIDI clock (depending on the status of the *interal_clock* Boolean variable). The function receives a MIDINote object from the genome, sends a MIDI Note-Off message corresponding to the last MIDI Note-On message, and emits the new note provided by the genome (see Listing 11.19):

Listing 11.19 tick() function

```
void tick()
{
    if(playing)
    {
        note = genotype.nextNote(ignore_rhythm);
        if(note.velocity!= 0)
        {
            usbMIDI.sendNoteOff(last_note, note.velocity, note.channel);
            usbMIDI.sendNoteOn(note.note, note.velocity, note.channel);
            last_note = note.note;
        }
    }
}
```

Summary

Aside from the code that is required to handle the pushbuttons and rotary encoder, a surprisingly modest amount of code is needed to produce a fascinating, genetically based MIDI step sequencer. The use of classes to encapsulate the chromosome and genotype means the code can be more easily modified and incorporated in other applications ranging from sound-design projects to genetically based composition tools. Miranda and Biles' *Evolutionary Computer Music* is an excellent source for more conceptual information on the musical application of evolutionary algorithms. I also found the "Genetic Algorithms" chapter of *Algorithmic Composition*, by Gerhard Nierhaus, to be a helpful introduction to the subject. The book also provides information on chaos and self-similarity, artificial neural networks, artificial intelligence, and related paradigms of automated music generation.

CREATIVE CHALLENGE

The creative potential of genetic algorithms is virtually limitless. Consider some of the following creative applications of the technology:

- Revise source code to personalize the fitness function.
- Use the output of the sequencer to trigger drum tracks.
- Alter the genetic functions to include alternative transpositions or other modifiers.
- Apply more strident genetic mutations by increasing the likelihood of a mutation in the genetic functions or incorporating more randomness.
- Use the MIDI output of the sequencer to generate melodic and harmonic content for a contemporary art composition.
- Use the MIDI output of the sequencer in conjunction with a traditional DAW production.
- Utilize two or more sequencers (either synchronized or free-running) to explore polyrhythmic effects.

CHAPTER 11 GENETIC STEP SEQUENCER   181

- Use the concepts from the chapter to inform your own unique approach to the genetic generation of melody, harmony, rhythm, or some other musical attribute.

Sidebar: Bit Twiddling Your Inner Geek with bit_tools.h

An understanding of bit manipulation (beyond the use of the functions in *bit_tools*.h) is not required to understand and utilize the concepts presented in this chapter. However, bit-level manipulation is not uncommon in microcontroller programming and some readers may benefit from reading this sidebar to get a feel for bit manipulation and the use of C++ templates.

The Arduino environment provides a useful set of functions for working with the individual bits of integers. However, there is an overhead in calling library functions—albeit small—so a custom set of bit manipulation tools that could be compiled directly with Teensyduino sketches seemed appropriate. In my tests, *setBit()* from *bit_tools*.h was 15–18% faster than the overhead of calling *bitWrite()* in the Arduino library. I also wanted a library that would work with integers ranging from 8 to 32 bits and that would provide convenience functions to handle genetic crossover, determine values from an arbitrary range of bits, and print non-truncated binary numbers for debugging purposes.

BITWISE OPERATORS

The functions in *bit_tools.h* rely on three common *bitwise operators* that perform Boolean algebra on individual bits and are shown in Table 11.3. Each of the operators takes two arguments and produces a result.[10]

TABLE 11.3 Results of Bitwise Operators.

a	b	a & b (AND)	a ∧ b (Exclusive OR)	a|b (OR)
0	0	0	0	0
0	1	0	1	1
1	0	0	1	1
1	1	1	0	1

Setting a Bit

A specific bit can be set by combining the bitwise *OR* operator with the left-shift (<<) operator where x represents the bit to be set (from 0–15) in a 16-bit integer:

```
number |= (1 <<x);
```

It is easy to wrap the operation in a function that takes two parameters: an integer as a reference and another number representing the bit to be set (see Listing 11.20). As previously described, parameters that are passed by reference can be modified by a function:

Listing 11.20 Simple setBit() function

```
void setBit(uint16_t &val, const int bit)
{
    val |= (1 <<bit);
}
```

But what happens if you want to work with an 8-bit byte or a 32-bit integer? One approach is to use the C++ mechanism for *overloading* functions. With this approach, multiple versions of the function can be created to take a variety of integer types. However, that approach is redundant and cumbersome for this application. Enter the concept of a *template*.

C++ TEMPLATES

C++ provides a beautiful solution known as a template. As the name implies, the template mechanism can be used to develop a function while deferring a commitment to a specific data type until compile time. To quote author Bruce Eckel:

> Instead of reusing object code, as with inheritance and composition, a template reuses source code.[11]

Applying the concept of a template to the *setBit()* function in Listing 11.20 involves using the *template* keyword in conjunction with *typename* to specify the type of object that is returned by the function (or the types of parameters passed to the function). Listing 11.21 demonstrates how the *setBit()* function could be templatized to handle 8-, 16-, or even 32-bit integers:

Listing 11.21 Templatized setBit() function

```
template <typename T>
void setBit(T &val, const int bit)
{
    val |= (1 << bit);
}
```

Clearing a Bit

An individual bit can be cleared by using the NOT (~) operator in conjunction with bitwise AND as shown in Listing 11.22. Once again, the use of the *template* keyword means that this single function can be used on multiple integer types:

Listing 11.22 clearBit() function

```
template <typename T>
void clearBit(T &val, const int bit)
{
    val &= ~(1 << bit);
}
```

CHAPTER 11 GENETIC STEP SEQUENCER 183

Toggling a Bit

Individual bits can be toggled between 0 and 1 using the Exclusive OR bitwise operator in conjunction with a left-shift (<<) as shown in Listing 11.23:

Listing 11.23 toggleBit() function

```
template <typename T>
void toggleBit(T &val, const int bit)
{
    val ^= (1 << bit);
}
```

Checking the Status of a Bit

The genetic sequencer project makes frequent use of *isBitSet()*, one of the functions in the *bit_tools.h* library, to see if a given bit is set. Checking the value of a single bit can be achieved using bitwise AND in conjunction with a left-shift. (Note that this approach is similar to the *clearBit()* function but no assignment is made.)

Listing 11.24 isBitSet() function

```
template <typename T>
bool isBitSet(const T val, const int bit)
{
    if(val & (1 << bit))
        return true;
    return false;
}
```

Getting the Value of a Range of Bits

A convenience function, *getValue()*, makes it easy to determine the value of an arbitrary range of bits. The function takes a templatized number as a parameter as well as integers representing the start and end values for the given range of bits. As shown in Listing 11.25, the function declares a template variable (*T val = 0*) and iterates through the bits of the parameter named *number* setting or clearing bits, as needed, so the leftmost bits in *val* match the range of bits in the *number* variable. This provides a convenient way to, say, check the value of the first three bits of a number to determine an index that is encoded in those bits. Alternatively, the function could be used to check the range of bits representing dynamics in the *Chromosome* class described earlier in the chapter. It is also interesting to note that the syntax for returning a templatized variable—typename *T* in this example—is similar to the use of a template function parameter.

184   SOUND & MUSIC PROJECTS FOR EURORACK AND BEYOND

Listing 11.25 getValue()

```
template <typename T>
T getValue(const T number, const int start_bit,
       const int end_bit)
{
    T val = 0;
    int val_bit = 0;
    for(int i = start_bit; i <= end_bit; i++)
    {
        if(isBitSet(number, i))
        {
            setBit(val, val_bit);
        }
        val_bit++;
    }
    return val;
}
```

Performing Genetic Crossover on Two Integers

Although there are a few other functions contained in the library (which can be downloaded from the OUP website), we conclude the chapter with a look at the *crossover()* function that is used to exchange individual bits representing genetic material between two integers. Unlike other function templates described in this section, the function needs to know the size of the integer to perform the crossover. One approach, shown in Listing 11.26, is to use the *sizeof()* function to determine the number of bytes contained in the parameters and multiply that number by 8 to determine the number of bits. The function also creates two temporary variables of type *T* and assigns the value of the two parameters to each variable. A "for" loop iterates through each bit, starting at the crossover point, and sets or clears individual bits in the temporary variables to exchange the genetic material (see Listing 11.26).

Listing 11.26 crossover() function

```
template <typename T>
void crossover(T &val1, T &val2, const int crossover)
{
    int bits = sizeof(T) * 8;
    T temp1 = val1;
    T temp2 = val2;

    for(int i = crossover; i < bits; i++)
    {
        if(bitSet(val1, i))
        {
            setBit(temp2, i);
        }else{
            clearBit(temp2, i);
```

```
            }
            if(bitSet(val2, i))
            {
                setBit(temp1, i);
            }else{
                clearBit(temp1, i);
            }
        }
    val1 = temp1;
    val2 = temp2;
}
```

Looking Ahead

The final section of the book, "Eurorack Concepts and Projects," covers Eurorack-specific concepts ranging from designing modules and front panels to circuits for analog mixing, and the creation of custom embedded digital signal processors on the Teensy platform. The final chapters detail the code and circuitry for three complete Eurorack projects including a digital signal processor, MIDI to control voltage converter, and FM synthesizer.

PART III
EURORACK CONCEPTS

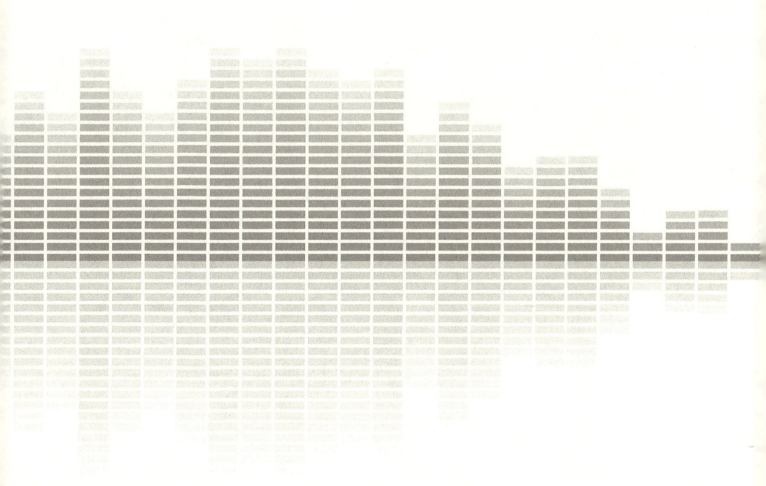

CHAPTER 12
MAKING CONNECTIONS

Microcontroller I/O

> Building synthesizers is clearly a circular affair. You must jump into the circle somewhere and keep spinning around and around until everything falls into place.[1]
>
> Thomas Henry, Author of *Build a Better Music Synthesizer*

Overview

One advantage of modular synthesizers is the myriad ways modules can be connected and configured (see Figure 12.1). But modular flexibility presents design challenges. While banks of patch points provide many avenues of exploration, connective flexibility assures that circuits will be connected in ways the designer did not intend. The goal of this chapter is to provide strategies for taming the input and output signals that are typically encountered in Eurorack systems—audio, gate, trigger, and control voltage—and introduce strategies to minimize the risk of damage that can occur when circuits are connected in unconventional ways.

FIGURE 12.1 Commercial Eurorack modules and custom modules designed by the author

Sound & Music Projects for Eurorack and Beyond. Brent Edstrom, Oxford University Press. © Oxford University Press 2024.
DOI: 10.1093/9780197514504.003.0012

Warning: Although some Teensy microcontrollers are 5V tolerant, the pins on 32-bit Teensy 3.x and 4.x microcontrollers will be damaged if exposed to voltages above 3.3V or below 0V. Always use a multimeter to verify the output of experimental circuits before attempting to connect them to a microcontroller.

STUDYING SCHEMATICS

Eurorack is a unique space inhabited by musicians, engineers, hobbyists, music technologists, and others, and a strong DIY undercurrent is evident in the many videos and descriptions of custom projects on the web. The liberation of musicians into the realm of electronic instrument design provides opportunities for expanding our creative palette and is, in my opinion, one of the most fascinating and compelling aspects of the maker movement. Although commercial manufacturers are understandably hesitant to provide open-source schematics of their designs, several Eurorack manufacturers are deliberate in contributing to the open-source space. I am deeply grateful to Émilie Gillet (Mutable Instruments) and Matthew Skala (North Coast Synthesis) for their commitment to providing documentation for their products. Their designs have been a gift to me and other musicians who have learned from their work. I have also benefited from the writings of Hal Chamberlin, Thomas Henry, Delton T. Horn, Ray Wilson, and others who have shared their knowledge of analog and digital synthesis in articles and books. Circuit study is akin to score study for musicians, and I commend the practice as an aid in understanding how building-block circuits can be modified and combined to solve specific problems.

Audio Output

Unlike pro audio signals that peak around 1.74V,[2] Eurorack audio signals are often significantly "hotter" and may peak as high as +5V ($10V_{pp}$).[3] One reason for the increase in audio level is that audio signals are sometimes used as modulation sources and larger voltages allow more options for modular control. How can an audio signal be amplified or attenuated so it can be safely read by a microcontroller? Enter the op amp.

OP AMPS

Operational amplifiers or "op amps" are one of the most useful categories of integrated circuits available for electronic music projects. A typical op amp provides inverting and non-inverting inputs and an output, and they can be used as the basis for circuits ranging from active filters to amplifiers, buffers, and comparators. One of the most common configurations, shown in Figure 12.2, is an inverting amplifier. The gain, which describes the output voltage (V_O), is determined by the ratio of resistors R_2 and R_1:

$$gain = -\frac{R2}{R1}$$

Applying the resistor values from Figure 12.2 to the equation indicates that the circuit provides a gain of –2.

A Few Words About Negative Feedback

It is helpful to remember that, when configured as an inverting amplifier, op amps want to keep their inverting and noninverting inputs at the same voltage. To do so, the op amp pushes or pulls a varying amount of current at its output to balance its inputs. One way to visualize the process is to apply Ohm's law (current = voltage/resistance):

$$I = \frac{V}{R}$$

To paraphrase a useful description by author, Ray Wilson, consider a 1V signal applied to the inverting input of the op amp through the 10k input resistor: 1V/10,000 ohms = 0.0001 amps (or 0.1 milliamps). The op amp will need to produce −2V at its output to pull 0.1 mA through the 20k feedback resistor (R2) *away* from the input for a net current of 0, which matches the non-inverting input. Similarly, with an input voltage of −2V, 0.2 mA is flowing away from the inverting input, so the op amp will output +4V to provide 0.2 mA (through R2) *towards* the input for a net current of 0 at the inverting input. This balancing act is a fundamental characteristic of op amps and, as will be evident in the following pages, enables these versatile integrated circuits to perform many useful tasks. As detailed in the following paragraphs, additional components—including a 1k output resistor—are usually added to the circuit when it is used to amplify the output of a synthesizer.

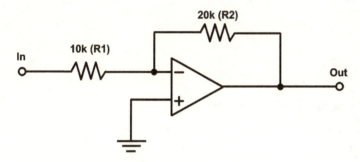

FIGURE 12.2 Basic inverting Amplifier

SIDEBAR: POWERING OP AMPS

By convention, power connections are not shown on schematics involving op amps—a convention that can be frustrating to those of us who do not come from an electrical engineering background. It is generally understood that op amps are powered by a dual (or bipolar) power supply such as the +12V and −12V rails provided by a Eurorack power supply. This configuration allows a signal to oscillate around ground (see Figure 12.3):

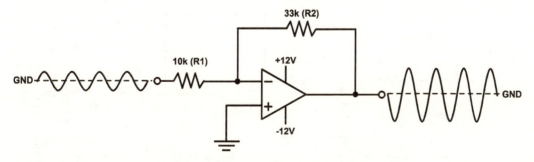

FIGURE 12.3 Dual supply op amp oscillating around ground (output is inverted)

In contrast, op amps are sometimes configured to run from a single (unipolar) supply such as 5V or 3.3V (see Figure 12.4). Depending on the function of the op amp, a pair of resistors may provide a *reference voltage* that enables a signal to oscillate around the mid-point between ground and the supply voltage (e.g., 2.5V in reference to ground) for a single-supply op amp powered from 5V. This is a good time to stress that op amps with *rail-to-rail* output are used for this and other single-supply circuits in the chapter. Rail-to-rail op amps can drive their output all the way to the supply rails (0–5V in this example) instead of clipping the output at a narrower range.

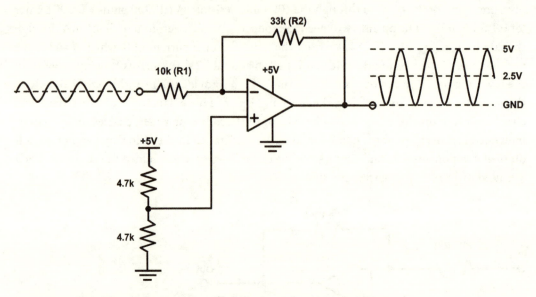

FIGURE 12.4 Single-supply op amp oscillating around virtual ground

AUDIO OUTPUT CIRCUIT

Figure 12.5 illustrates a more nuanced inverting op amp circuit that might be used to amplify the output of a DAC or a related task. The example, which is based on a circuit from a commercial product, provides a point of reference for understanding a common op amp configuration. As with other examples in the book, the intent is to detail a building-block circuit that can be used as a starting point and adapted for the unique needs of a given project. The dotted lines in the illustration indicate circuit segments that are described in the following paragraphs.

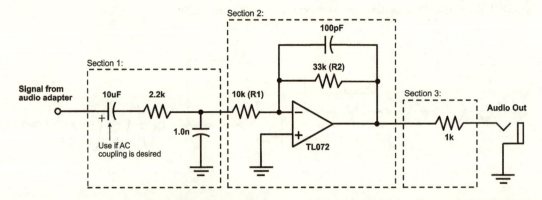

FIGURE 12.5 Modified inverting amplifier circuit

AUDIO OUTPUT CIRCUIT ANALYSIS

Section 1: AC coupling

The 10 µF capacitor in section 1 is an *AC coupling capacitor.* Coupling capacitors are sometimes used to remove DC offset (i.e., direct current on which the signal "sits") from audio signals, but many Eurorack modules utilize DC coupling. Depending on the configuration of a circuit, the DC component can cause an amplifier to saturate and distort, but DC coupling can be desirable if the device is to do double duty as a modulation source—something that is becoming increasingly common even in the world of professional audio.[4] The nuances of coupling capacitors are worthy of an entire chapter, but it will be helpful to consider a few observations.

- Electronics engineer Douglas Self provides clear advice regarding electrolytic blocking capacitors: "For small-signal use, as long as the signal voltage across the capacitor is kept low, non-linearity is not normally detectable. The capacitance value is non-critical, as it has to be, given the wide tolerances of electrolytics."[5]
- Bigger capacitor values can reduce distortion in some contexts.[6]
- Electrolytic capacitors are polarized, and the plus side should point to the "more positive" circuitry.[7]
- Reverse voltage of approximately 1.5V is probably acceptable.[8]

Putting these ideas into practice, the orientation of the blocking capacitor in Figure 12.5 is correct for an application such as amplifying the output of a DAC with a positive reference—a signal that swings above ground. The real rub, as far as I am concerned, are scenarios where it is less clear which side of an AC connection is "more positive." My best advice for those of us without an advanced degree in electronics is to use an empirical approach. Electronics simulators are helpful for getting a feel for voltage and current levels in circuits, and a multimeter and breadboard can also provide valuable insights. Other options include using non-polarized electrolytic capacitors or placing two electrolytics back-to-back in opposing orientation (positive-negative, negative-positive).

Low-pass Filter

I have always enjoyed the fact that such a wide variety of useful circuits can be created with simple electronic components, and there probably isn't a circuit that is as useful and easy to create as a passive low-pass filter. Low-pass filters are often used to remove high-frequency artifacts from DACs, and various cutoff frequencies can be attained by varying the amount of resistance and/or capacitance. An extreme example is shown in Figure 12.6 for illustrative purposes. Note how the resistor and capacitor alter the harmonic spectrum of the square wave.

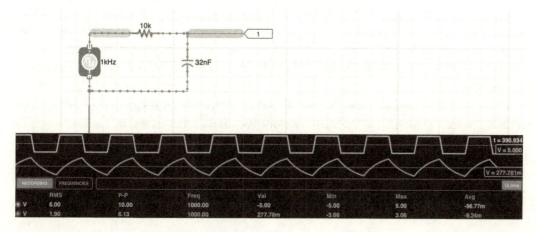

FIGURE 12.6 Low-pass filter simulation

Moving back to section 1 of Figure 12.5, the 2,200 ohm resistor and 1.0 nF capacitor form a low-pass filter with a cutoff frequency of 72.4 kHz—the point at which the filter reaches –3 dB of attenuation. The cutoff frequency (f_C) of a low-pass filter is calculated with the following formula where R is the amount of resistance and C is capacitance:

$$fc = \frac{1}{2\pi RC}$$

To apply the formula, convert the resistance to ohms and the capacitance to farads. For example:

    2.2k = 2,200 ohms
    1.0nF = 1×10^{-9} farads

    f_C = $1/(2 \times 3.14 \times 2200 \times 1\times10^{-9})$
    f_C = 72.4kHz

In actuality, the cutoff frequency will be somewhat higher due to loading in the following section, but approximate values will suffice in this context.

Although audio filtering is usually applied in the audible range, DACs can generate out-of-band noise above the Nyquist frequency (half the sample rate) which can create problems with downstream circuitry. My layman's way of visualizing the problem is that inaudible harmonic content can be aliased into the audible spectrum and cause distortion. The 72.4 kHz cutoff frequency was used on the output of a DAC in a commercial product, and I have noted similar cutoff frequencies prescribed in books and datasheets that address DAC output.

Section 2: Amplification

The op amp in section 2 is a TL072 powered by a bipolar ±12V supply and configured as an inverting amplifier. The gain formula, $gain = -\frac{R2}{R1}$ indicates a gain of –3.3. However, be aware that the components from section 1 decrease the gain of the circuit. This is another case where electronics simulation or multimeter tests can provide a quick answer to a complex circuit analysis task.

HIGH FREQUENCY STABILITY

The small capacitor in the feedback loop of section 2 is a *compensation capacitor* that "ensures HF stability if there are excess phase-shifts due to stray capacitance."[9] Unwanted oscillations sometimes occur—often above 100 kHz—and can create noise at the output of the op amp.[10] The feedback resistor and capacitor essentially form another low-pass filter with the cutoff frequency determined by f_C = $1/2\pi RC$. In this case, the cutoff is around 48kHz.[11]

This is a good place to stress that, while building block circuits can be applied to many tasks, strive to be mindful of the way components interact. For example, small changes to the value of the seemingly innocuous feedback capacitor can have a big impact on the frequency response of the circuit. Coming from the perspective of an electronics autodidact, I find it helpful to experiment with new concepts on a breadboard to better understand and internalize how canonic circuits function. With that said, it is not always possible to accurately test for high frequency stability on a breadboard since stray capacitance can change when a project is built in another way such as on a PCB. For this reason, I tend to err on the side of using feedback capacitors in PCB designs if I am concerned about stability of a given op amp. That approach provides the opportunity to use, change, or omit the capacitor as needed.

Section 3: Output

Although not standardized, it is not uncommon to see a 1 kΩ resistor (or similarly low output impedance) at the output of Eurorack modules. The approach enables the output of the device to be combined with compatible modules through a passive multiple (or "mult"). But the primary reason for including a resistor on the output is that it provides some protection against a short circuit between the output and ground.[12]

Figure 12.7 shows a sine wave in its original form (top) and its amplified form (bottom) after passing through the inverting op amp configuration described in the proceeding section.

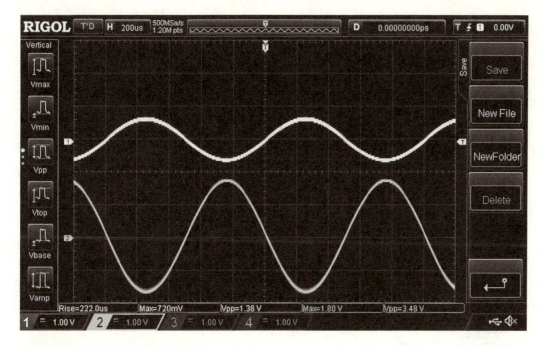

FIGURE 12.7 Amplified audio output

Audio Input

The Teensy Audio Adapter is based around an SGTL5000 Low-Power stereo codec. Many functions for controlling the device are available and detailed in the Audio System Design Tool, including a *lineInLevel()* API function to set analog voltage input sensitivity levels ranging from 0.24V to 3.12V.

Warning: Audio signals to the Audio Adapter should stay between 0.3V below ground and 0.3V above the supply voltage. Voltages over 3.3V and negative voltages (e.g., a bipolar signal that swings positively and negatively around 0V) can damage the device.

Given that negative voltages and voltages above 3.3V are problematic, a single-supply op amp running at 3.3V can provide some protection from over- and undervoltage. As Douglas

Self states in his seminal book, *Small Signal Audio Design*, "bullet-proof protection against input over-voltages is given by running the driving opamp from the same supply rails as the analogue section of the ADC, the opamp saturation voltages ensuring that the input can never reach the supply rails, never mind exceed them."[13] But it is important to note that, depending on context, circuit configuration, and choice of op amp, the op amp inputs might need to be protected by diodes or another voltage mitigation strategy.

A Texas Instruments document provides a helpful starting point for creating a single-supply inverting op amp that can attenuate incoming signals.[14] As shown in Figure 12.8, two 100k resistors form a voltage divider that creates a reference voltage to bias the non-inverting input of the op amp. The voltage divider enables the incoming signal to swing around ≈1.65V, the midpoint between ground and 3.3V.

A capacitor strips the DC component from the incoming signal, which is attenuated by the ratio of resistors R_2 and R_1.

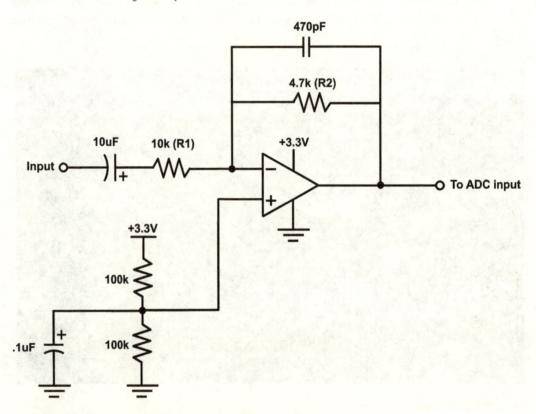

FIGURE 12.8 Single-supply (3.3V) inverting op amp for audio input

As with the circuit for audio output, it is easy to adjust the gain if a different amount of attenuation is desirable. The attenuation in this example allows hotter signals to be processed by the circuit, but very little attenuation would be needed for a typical line-level audio signal. As you will see in the final section of the book, the circuit can also be combined with an attenuating potentiometer. Figure 12.9 illustrates the clipping that occurs when a 10V peak-to-peak signal was processed by the circuit shown in Figure 12.8. While clipping is generally a bad thing in audio, it is desirable in this instance since the goal is to protect the pins on the microcontroller.

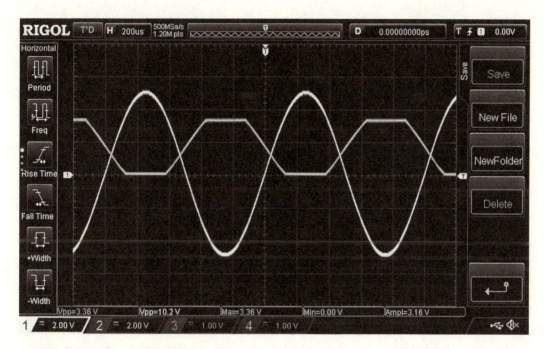

FIGURE 12.9 Clipped audio input signal

Gate and Trigger Input

Gate and trigger signals are a ubiquitous part of Eurorack music making and are used for many tasks ranging from triggering VCAs to distributing clock pulses. Unfortunately, gate and trigger signals are typically at voltages that can easily damage the pins of a Teensy microcontroller.

Using Transistors

An NPN transistor can condition incoming gate signals and provide some protection against overvoltage. Although a detailed discussion of transistors is beyond the scope of this book, a brief overview of the function of an NPN transistor will provide context for the gate shown in this section.

NPN TRANSISTOR

The NPN (N-type) transistor is a common transistor form under the broader heading of bipolar junction transistors (BJT). Although the term transistor might have old school associations with portable radios of yore, they are useful for many electronic tasks ranging from logic gates to switching and amplification. As shown in the conceptualized illustration of Figure 12.10, an NPN transistor consists of a base, collector, and emitter. Transistors can be configured to handle several tasks, but a key concept for this discussion is that transistors can function like a switch where a small signal at the base turns on the electrical path from the collector to the emitter.

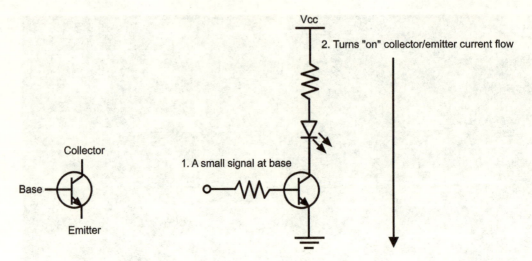

FIGURE 12.10 NPN transistor

Figure 12.11 illustrates how the collector of an NPN transistor can be configured to provide 3.3V to a digital input pin on a microcontroller. The incoming gate connects to the base of the transistor, and a large-value resistor minimizes current. As shown, a diode helps to protect against negative voltage. It is important to note that the microcontroller will read low when a positive signal is applied to the base and high when no signal is present at the base. Although this might seem counterintuitive, it makes sense when you consider that current will flow from the 3.3V supply to the microcontroller pin when the transistor is "off." A sufficient signal at the base causes current to flow between the collector and the emitter and draws current away from microcontroller pin. One disadvantage of this circuit that I have noticed is that the supply voltage appears to float when higher voltages are applied to the input.

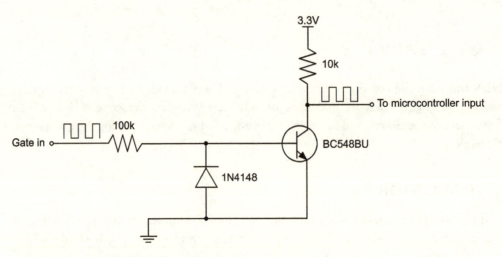

FIGURE 12.11 NPN transistor circuit

USING OP AMPS TO PROCESS GATE SIGNALS

A more robust strategy is shown in Figure 12.12. This example, which is based on a schematic for the Mutable Instruments Plaits module, provides an interesting approach that utilizes an op amp to process incoming gate signals. In this simplified example, a gate or trigger signal is processed by an MCP6002 op amp running on a single supply of 0–3.3V. The MCP6002 is a good choice for this application since it is a rail-to-rail op amp that works well on a single-supply voltage. The analog inputs of the op amp are also more robust than some other op amps.

Émilie Gillet, the designer of the Mutable Instrument product line, uses an interesting approach to process incoming gate signals. The circuit utilizes a negative reference that enables the rail-to-rail op amp to handle signals in the range of about −1V to 8V and, since the rails are powered by a 3.3V single-supply, the circuit will output microcontroller-safe voltages in the range of 0–3.3V. The negative reference voltage is provided by a shunt which is described in more detail in Chapter 13. This circuit scales the incoming signal, and the original voltages can be calculated by the microcontroller as shown at the end of the chapter and detailed in Chapter 17. It is worth noting that the 1nF feedback capacitor and 33k feedback resistor provide a cutoff frequency of 4.8kHz, a value that is too low for audio but can prevent aliasing on slow-moving control voltages. But the value can, of course, be changed for different applications. For example, changing the feedback capacitor to 100 pF provides a 48.25 kHz cutoff frequency in conjunction with the 33k feedback resistor. Note that a higher value resistor may be needed for Rs if the negative reference voltage is shared across multiple inputs.

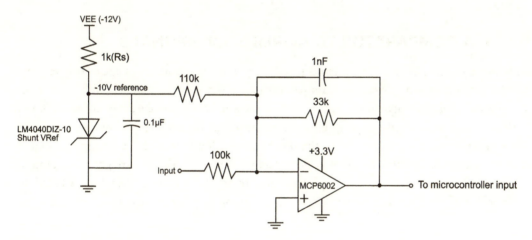

FIGURE 12.12 Gate input based on Mutable Instruments schematic

A document by Texas Instruments, titled *Single-supply Op Amp Design*, provides insights into the function of a similar circuit based around a TLV2471 op amp (see Figure 12.13).[15] Here we see the pair of resistors, R_{G1} and R_F that would typically provide the gain or attenuation for an inverting op amp. V_{REF} provides a reference bias through R_{G2}.

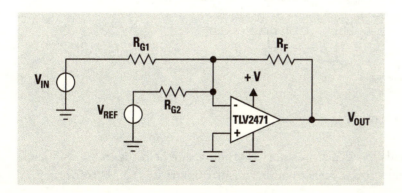

FIGURE 12.13 Scaling circuit (image from Texas Instruments Incorporated document)

$$Vout = -Vin\left(\frac{RF}{RG1}\right) - Vref\left(\frac{RF}{RG2}\right)$$

Applying the terms of the preceding circuit yields the following output for a 5V gate or trigger signal:

$$Vout = -5V\left(\frac{33k}{100k}\right) - -10V\left(\frac{33k}{110k}\right)$$

$$Vout = 1.35$$

As with the transistor gate described in the preceding section, this circuit inverts the gate signal. However, unlike the NPN transistor circuit that is configured as an on-off switch, this circuit provides a range of values that can be useful for implementing velocity sensitivity or other functions. Using an op amp in this way also provides an opportunity to implement a user-selectable trigger level.

Gate Out

USING A COMPARATOR TO AMPLIFY 3.3V SIGNALS

Although a digital pin on a 3.3V microcontroller can provide adequate voltage to trigger some 5V devices, a single-supply op amp comparator provides a way to ensure the voltage is at an appropriate level. A comparator works by comparing a reference voltage at the inverting input with a voltage at the non-inverting input. The output of the comparator swings low when the non-inverting input is lower than the reference, and high when the same input is higher than the reference. In this way, an arbitrary reference (such as 1.6V) can trigger an op amp to output a +5V signal in response to a specific signal threshold. Figure 12.14, which is based on a Microchip Technology Inc. document, illustrates an op amp configured as a comparator.[16]

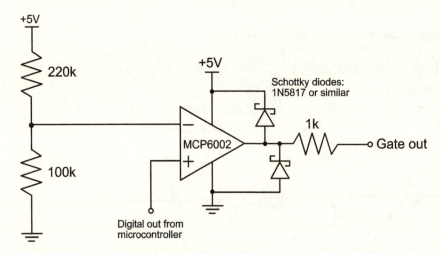

FIGURE 12.14 Comparator 3.3V to 5V gate output

Use the following formula to calculate resistor values for a threshold trigger voltage that is about half the voltage of a digital output pin on the microcontroller (e.g., ≈1.6V for a 3.3V microcontroller):

$$R1 = R2\left(\frac{5V}{1.6V} - 1\right)$$

Select a nominal value for R2 such as 100k and solve for R1. Note that larger value resistors are used in this example to avoid a large current draw from the voltage divider.

$$R1 = 100,000\left(\frac{5V}{1.6V} - 1\right)$$

$$R1 = \approx 220k$$

A Word about Diodes

A comparator such as the one shown in Figure 12.14 does not require diodes to function. However, an MCP6002 op amp can be damaged by overvoltage or negative voltage applied to its output. Given the wide range of voltages found in a Eurorack setup, it is prudent to protect the output pin with diodes. In the case of the comparator, a voltage that exceeds 5V applied to the *output* will cause the upper diode to conduct and shunt current to the 5V supply. Similarly, negative voltages will cause the second diode to conduct.

USING A NON-INVERTING OP AMP FOR GATE OUTPUT

One disadvantage of the previous circuit is that a large voltage connected to the output can cause supply voltage to float if a protection diode shunts current into a lightly loaded supply. Another approach, illustrated in Figure 12.15, is to use an op amp powered by the ±12V power supply in a non-inverting configuration. This approach has the benefit of being more robust to an inadvertent connection of an output to the output of the circuit, and it also provides an opportunity to adjust the ratio of the input and feedback resistors to customize the output voltage. This example will amplify a 3.3V microcontroller signal at its input to about 5.1V and provide a gain of approximately 1.5: (10k/18k) + 1. The feedback capacitor and resistor provide a cutoff frequency of approximately 72kHz.

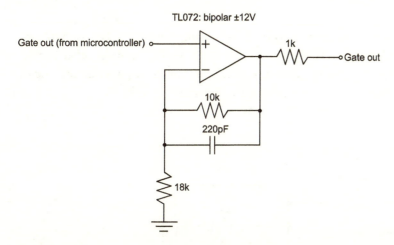

FIGURE 12.15 Non-inverting op amp for gate output

Control Voltage Output for Fluctuating Signals

Where gate and trigger signals are generally used for on/off events, control voltage can also provide varying voltage for control of parameters including pitch, amplitude, filter cutoff, and resonance. Chapter 16 details the process of using a dedicated 12-bit DAC to output control voltages suitable for pitch control and related tasks, and this section provides a circuit framework for sending and receiving voltages generated by a DAC.

Although it is possible to directly connect the output of the DAC to another device, it is not advisable since loading by downstream devices will be particularly evident in unbuffered DAC signals. A better approach is to use one or more op amps to protect and buffer the DAC. Op amps can also be configured to amplify the output providing a greater range of voltages.

One approach is to output 0–2V from a DAC and amplify the signal with a pair of op amps. In Figure 12.16, the output of a DAC is amplified by –5X in the first stage and inverted by the second op amp, which has a gain of –1. The feedback resistor and capacitor of the second op amp provide a cutoff frequency of approximately 72.4 kHz. One unusual aspect of the circuit is the 1k output resistor that is placed *inside* the feedback loop, an approach that can help to mitigate CV errors that are particularly undesirable when controlling the pitch of an oscillator. This circuit is a good choice when combined with an internally referenced DAC, and it has worked well in my tests and projects.

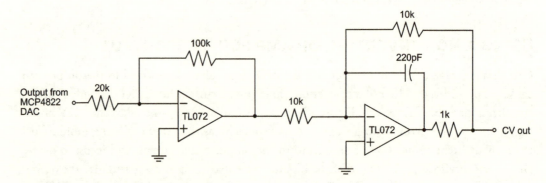

FIGURE 12.16 Non-inverting CV amplifier

Control Voltage Input

A final circuit challenge is to consider how to read fluctuating control voltages (suitable for pitch control and other tasks) with a 3.3V microcontroller. As with most of the other circuits in this chapter, a trusty op amp comes to the rescue in the form of the attenuating circuit shown in Figure 12.17, a variation of the gate-input circuit from Figure 12.12.

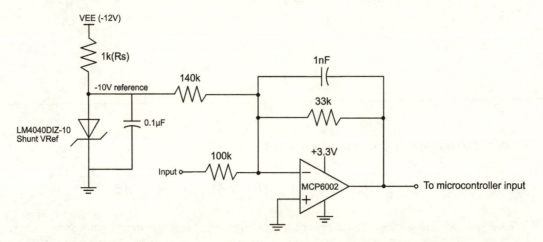

FIGURE 12.17 CV input circuit

As with Figure 12.12, a negative reference biases the incoming signal, and this iteration of the circuit can process signals in the range of approximately –3V to 7V.

SCALING CONTROL VOLTAGE

The circuit works by scaling control voltages down to 0.33V per octave from the common 1V per octave (V/oct) value. This enables a 3.3V microcontroller to safely read the voltage, and it is a simple matter for the microcontroller to interpret or reconstruct the scaled value mathematically. Table 12.1 shows the scaled voltages for a range of inputs from –3V to 7V based on the equation:

$$Vout = -Vin\left(\frac{RF}{RG1}\right) - Vref\left(\frac{RF}{RG2}\right)$$

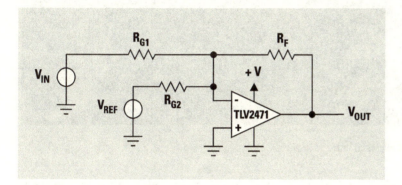

The control voltage inputs can be reconstructed by dividing the scaled input by 0.33. The only snag is that the op amp inverts the signal—a detail that can be handled by the microcontroller by subtracting the reconstructed voltage from the maximum expected input voltage.

TABLE 12.1 Scaled voltages

Voltage in	Scaled voltage	Reconstructed voltage = Scaled voltage / 0.33	Re-inverted voltage = 7V – reconstructed voltage
7	0.047	0.14	6.86
6	0.377	1.14	5.86
5	0.707	2.14	4.86
4	1.037	3.14	3.86
3	1.367	4.14	2.86
2	1.697	5.14	1.86
1	2.027	6.14	0.86
0	2.357	7.14	–0.14
–1	2.687	8.14	–1.14
–2	3.017	9.14	–2.14
–3	3.347	10.14	–3.14

Figure 12.18 illustrates a "hot" control voltage signal that has been scaled and clipped by the preceding circuit.

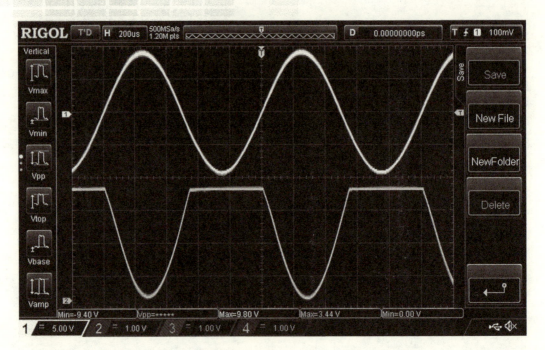

FIGURE 12.18 Scaled (and clipped) voltage input

We revisit the CV input circuit in Chapter 18, where we combine code and circuitry to create a simple MIDI to CV converter.

Summary

Revisiting Thomas Henry's quote from the start of the chapter, this tour of input and output circuits might feel like a circular affair. But rest assured that comprehension will be enhanced through experimentation. Construct the circuits (sans microcontroller) on a solderless breadboard and test a variety of inputs and outputs with a multimeter or oscilloscope. Although the chapter has emphasized more theory than others, the concepts will provide a useful foundation for the Eurorack projects that are detailed in the final chapters of the book. It is also helpful to know that these circuits will open the door to innumerable creations ranging from custom synthesizer modules and effects processors to MIDI/CV converters.

CHAPTER 13

POWERING EURORACK MODULES

Getting Started

This chapter represents a transition from breadboard experimentation to the exciting realm of custom Eurorack instruments. Just like a building needs a strong foundation, Eurorack projects are built around a reliable power source. The discussion includes strategies for powering your modules from commercial Eurorack power supplies, using a voltage regulator to provide +5V, using a shunt to provide a stable reference voltage, and using diodes to prevent damage from reverse polarity.

COMMERCIAL POWER SUPPLIES

Some manufacturers offer Eurorack cases with built-in power supplies, but prices can be prohibitively expensive. An approach that has worked well for me is to build my own Eurorack case and purchase rails and a separate power supply such as the Tip Top uZeus shown in Figure 13.1. While a small external supply will not be able to power multiple racks of gear, they are a good choice for a first power supply—and you will likely use the power supply for prototyping if you eventually purchase a commercial rack with built-in power or build your own supply.

Sound & Music Projects for Eurorack and Beyond. Brent Edstrom, Oxford University Press. © Oxford University Press 2024.
DOI: 10.1093/9780197514504.003.0013

FIGURE 13.1 Economical Eurorack power supply

Power Pinout

Figure 13.2 shows the common power pinouts provided by a power bus or flying power distribution bus. Note that the −12V pins align with the red stripe on a typical sixteen- or ten-pin Eurorack ribbon power cable, although it is always best to double-check voltages with a multimeter before connecting power to a module.

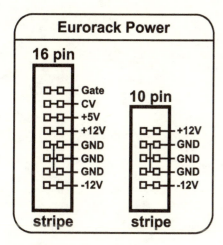

FIGURE 13.2 Power pinout

In many instances, modules are connected to the power bus via a sixteen- to ten-pin ribbon cable such as the one shown in Figure 13.3. As you will see in the pages that follow, the ten-pin connection is a good choice for many DIY Eurorack projects.

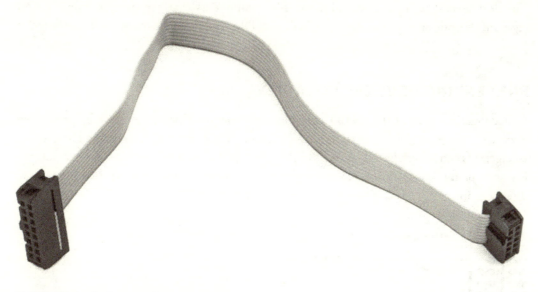

FIGURE 13.3 16-pin to 10-pin power cable

Shrouded Headers

While it is easy to use a commercial power supply to power one or more Eurorack modules, it is also easy to destroy the module (and possibly downstream modules) by accidentally reversing the polarity of the power supply. Although some Eurorack musicians prefer to use unshrouded header pins on their modules, I prefer shrouded headers like the one shown in Figure 13.4. Reverse polarity is still possible from a mis-wired cable or design error, but I do like the mechanical deterrent that is provided by the shroud.

FIGURE 13.4 Shrouded header

Powering A Module

The next several paragraphs detail electronic components that can protect, smooth, and regulate the power that has been applied to a DIY Eurorack board from a commercial power supply.

PREVENTING REVERSE POLARITY

A diode rectifier such as the 1N4002 can provide some protection to a device by preventing electric charge from flowing in the wrong direction. While rectifiers drop a small amount of voltage, this should not be a problem and the potential for protection against reverse polarity is worth the modest cost of the components. Note how the rectifiers are oriented in opposite directions for positive and negative voltage (see Figure 13.5).

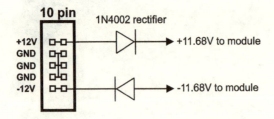

FIGURE 13.5 Using rectifiers to protect against reverse polarity

One benefit of using a ten-pin Eurorack power supply is that the rectifying diodes should protect the module if the orientation of a cable is reversed (see Figure 13.6). Such protection is more difficult to create when using sixteen-pin connections since the +5V pins will swap with a pair of GND pins when the connector is reversed.

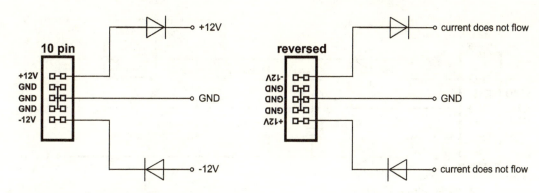

FIGURE 13.6 Reversed power connection

SMOOTHING THE POWER SUPPLY

Two pairs of capacitors (see Figure 13.7) help to filter ripple and immunize the circuit from transients and other noise problems.[1] The polarized electrolytic capacitors should be rated for 35V or more[2] and the ceramic capacitors rated for 50V.[3]

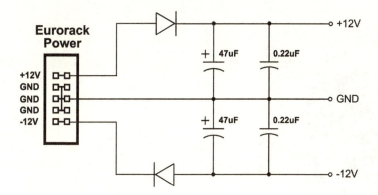

FIGURE 13.7 Smoothing capacitors

5V REGULATION

One disadvantage of a ten-pin Eurorack power connection is the lack of 5V power—a necessary feature for any microcontroller project. However, adding 5V power to a Eurorack module couldn't be easier and the module will be more flexible since it won't require an external 5V power source—something that is not available on all Eurorack power supplies.

A 7805-voltage regulator is all that is required to create a stable 5V supply for a microcontroller. As is evident in Figure 13.8, connect +12V to the input of the regulator and ground to ground and the regulator will provide +5V at the output. Two capacitors are added but the datasheet states that "although no output capacitor is needed for stability, it does help transient response. (If needed, use 0.1-μF, ceramic disc)."[4]

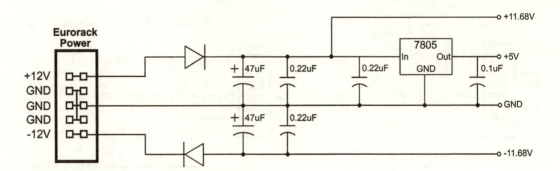

FIGURE 13.8 7805 voltage regulator

Building a Desktop Voltage Regulator

The voltage regulator circuit provides an opportunity to build the helpful mini project shown in Figure 13.8. Here, a shielded Eurorack power header and voltage regulation circuit are affixed to a small solder board to form a desktop 5V regulator. The project provides +/−12V reverse polarity protection and +5V when connected to a ten-pin Eurorack power supply, and I have found the circuit to be handy when breadboarding circuits.

FIGURE 13.9 Desktop 5V voltage regulator

PROVIDING A −10 VOLT REFERENCE

One final component deserves mention in this section. As you will learn in the following chapter, a −10V reference voltage is useful when using an op amp to scale control voltages to levels that can be safely read by a 3.3V microcontroller. The reference voltage is provided by a *shunt* diode connected to −12V on a Eurorack power supply. Figure 13.10 illustrates the shunt circuitry in the context of a completed power section that can be used for many Eurorack projects:

CHAPTER 13 POWERING EURORACK MODULES

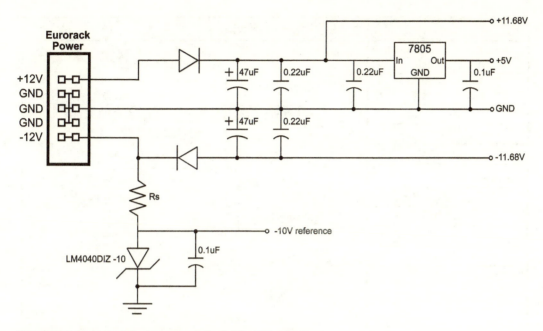

FIGURE 13.10 Completed power section with -10V reference

The datasheet for the LM4040DIZ provides information regarding the calculation of the R_S value, but Texas Instruments provides a handy spreadsheet calculator that is useful in exploring a range of values.[5] The idea is to select a resistance that is small enough to supply the minimum current through the shunt (I_Q) when the supply voltage is at its minimum and load current is at maximum. But R_S should also be big enough to limit current through the shunt to less than 15 mA when the supply voltage is at its maximum.[6]

As an example, consider a shunt that provides a reference voltage to six 140k resistors that are each a part of an op amp circuit. (Such a circuit is described in the next chapter.) In this case, the resistors are in parallel for a total resistance of 23.3k. Using Ohm's law $I = V / R$ a reference voltage of 10V and resistance of about 23.3k yields a load current of approximately 0.43 mA.

$$I = \frac{10V}{23,333\,ohms}$$

As is evident in Figure 13.11, a 1k resistor provides acceptable current levels with an input voltage in the range of 10.6V to 12V while 500 ohms of resistance would enable the circuit to work on just 10.3V of input voltage.

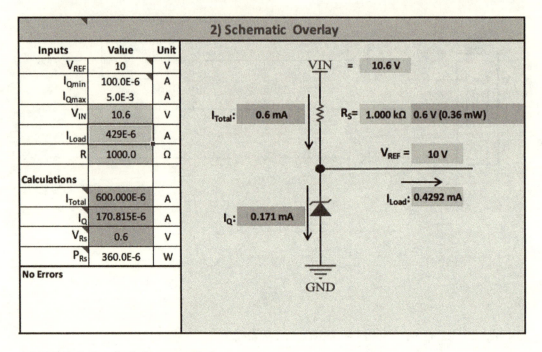

FIGURE 13.11 R_s calculation: example 1

Figure 13.12 provides another way to view the range of values. In this case, a resistance between approximately 400 and 500 ohms will produce acceptable current levels for a supply voltage in the range of 10.3V–12V and load current of 0.1 mA to 0.5 mA:

1) Rs Quick Start				
	Value		Unit	
Reference Voltage (V_{REF})	10		V	
	Min	Max	Unit	
Voltage Supply Bounds	10.30	12.00	V	
Load Current Bounds	100.0E-6	500.0E-6	A	
I_Q Bounds	100.0E-6	5.0E-3	A	
	Value	Nearest 1%	Nearest 5%	
R_{S_MIN}	392.2 Ω	402.0 Ω (10.0 mW)	430.0 Ω (9.3 mW)	
R_{S_MAX}	500. Ω	499.0 Ω (8.0 mW)	470.0 Ω (8.5 mW)	

No Errors

FIGURE 13.12 R_s calculation: example 2

Moving to PCB or Solder Board

There are a few considerations when creating a Eurorack power section on a PCB or solder board. Bear in mind that capacitors need to be close to the power source to do their job, so I usually mimic component schematics when determining the physical location of such parts (see Figure 13.3). In this example, notice how the capacitors are located next to their respective diodes and the capacitors follow the layout of the original schematic. Also, note the thickness of the power traces on the left in contrast to the audio traces on the right. Finally, be sure to check that components have an appropriate rating for their function in the circuit.

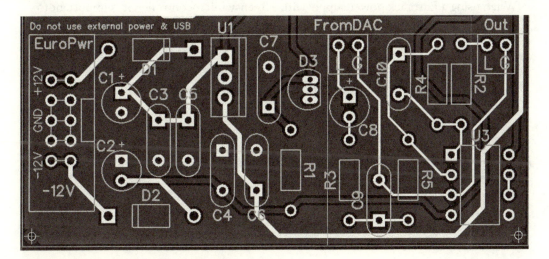

FIGURE 13.13 Power and audio sections of a PCB

Warning 1: Reverse Power

Always use a multimeter to check the voltages of any new Eurorack power bus (see Figure 13.4) since reversing the connection may damage a module and/or Teensy microcontroller. Similarly, it is never a good idea to trust the orientation of the stripe of a Eurorack power ribbon cable. Always ensure that the correct voltage is applied to the correct pin.

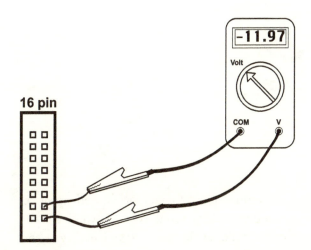

FIGURE 13.14 Using a multimeter to check the voltage of a Eurorack power bus

Warning 2: Using a Teensy with External Power and USB

When using a Eurorack power supply with a Teensy microcontroller, it is important to separate the power provided from the USB cable from power that is provided via the Vcc (+5V) pin to avoid potential damage to your computer. Also, as documented on the PJRC website, reverse polarity power or greater than 6 volts can damage Teensy.[7] PJRC provides three options but, for our purposes, the first option will be appropriate for most projects:

Cutting "5V" Pads Apart

To separate USB power from +5V power, use a knife to carefully cut the trace that connects the 5V pads (see). Severing the 5V trace disconnects USB power from the circuit board, and PJRC provides additional information about how to disconnect power from several types of Teensy boards.

FIGURE 13.15 Cutting 5V pads apart

Summary

Although this chapter is brief, the concepts will form a useful foundation for many projects and enable designs to be moved from a breadboard to a stage or studio. As you will see in the next chapter, these concepts drive a range of useful building block circuits to handle gate and trigger signals, control voltages, and audio input and output.

A NOTE ABOUT DIY POWER SUPPLIES

This book is all about hands-on experimentation, so I was intentional in *not* addressing DIY power supplies since there is a real danger of electrocution whenever mains power is involved. A middle ground is to use a 12V AC to AC wall wart and incorporate rectification and +/−12V voltage regulation. One such project is detailed in an article by Ray Wilson on the *Music from Outer Space* website.[8] My own take on Wilson's design is shown in Figure 13.16. Another option is to use a DC wall wart in conjunction with a switching regulator. Of course, there are also many fine books and articles that detail power supply design should you want to explore that aspect of electronics.

FIGURE 13.16 Custom Eurorack power supply by the author

CHAPTER 14

BUILDING EURORACK MODULES

Part I: Stripboard

Overview

Eurorack is a modular format built on the DIN 41494 standard used in industrial applications. The format was introduced for musical applications in 1996 by Dieter Doepfer of Doepfer Musikelektronik and popularized with the A-100 series modules.[1] Today, Eurorack is running strong with dozens of manufacturers offering Eurorack products. Given the wide variety of modules and the potential for original creations built around microcontrollers and other technologies, Eurorack provides a modular framework with a vast potential for creative expression, expansion, and adaptation.

Stripboard vs Printed Circuit Boards

There are two primary approaches to consider when moving a project from a solderless breadboard to a permanently soldered circuit: components can be soldered to solderable protoboard/stripboard, or the design can be transferred to a professionally manufactured printed circuit board (PCB). Benefits of the first approach include simplicity, flexibility and, in some cases, a slight cost saving. While PCBs represent a more complex design process involving sophisticated software, PCBs provide an opportunity to control every aspect of component layout and are surprisingly inexpensive to produce. PCBs are also a good choice for complex layouts where many components need to fit in a small space. One other advantage of PCBs is that components such as encoders and potentiometers are affixed by soldering mounting tabs in addition to pins—an approach that provides the best long-term strength and stability. We will focus on stripboard in this chapter.

The chapter also introduces the Eurorack format including dimensions, mounting, and other design considerations. Chapter 15 continues the conversation and details the design and creation of custom printed circuit boards. As with other sections of the book, the chapter details a practical project—a handy monophonic mixer—that is inexpensive to build and will provide a useful addition to any Eurorack setup. Although the design concepts are applied to an analog project, core concepts apply to the embedded microcontroller projects described in other chapters, and the design concepts inform the demonstration projects in the final chapters of the book.

A bill of materials (BOM) for the audio mixer is available for download from the OUP website.

Sound & Music Projects for Eurorack and Beyond. Brent Edstrom, Oxford University Press. © Oxford University Press 2024.
DOI: 10.1093/9780197514504.003.0014

Dimensions

Doepfer Musikelektronik provides a useful overview of the construction details for their A-100 modular system.[2] A-100 front panels are three units (3U) high where each unit is 44.45 mm. Thus, the front panel height for a 3U module is 133.4 mm. However, the final panel height is somewhat smaller (≈128.5 mm) to account for the rim of the mounting rails.

Module width is calculated in horizontal pitch (HP) where 1 HP = 5.08 mm. However, as with the calculation of module height, the front panel width "is a few tenth[s] of a mm less than the calculated value" for assembly tolerance.[3]

Table 14.1, adapted from the Doepfer website, shows calculated and actual module widths for a variety of module sizes:

TABLE 14.1 Eurorack module widths

Module width [HP]	Calculated module width [mm] = multiples of 5.08 mm	Actual module width [mm]
1	5.08	**5.00**
1.5	7.62	**7.50**
2	10.16	**9.80**
4	20.32	**20.00**
6	30.48	**30.00**
8	40.64	**40.30**
10	50.80	**50.50**
12	60.96	**60.60**
14	71.12	**70.80**
16	81.28	**80.90**
18	91.44	**91.30**
20	101.60	**101.30**
21	106.68	**106.30**
22	111.76	**111.40**
28	142.24	**141.90**
42	214.36	**214.00**

MOUNTING HOLES

As shown in Figure 14.1, the horizontal position of the 3.2 mm mounting holes is found by centering the leftmost hole 7.5 mm from the left edge and placing additional mounting holes N × 5.08 mm from the starting hole. The lower holes are centered 3 mm from the bottom of the module and the top holes are located 125.5 mm from the bottom or 3 mm from the top—assuming a module height of 128.5 mm. With that said, pre-drilled blank

Eurorack panels can be purchased for a minimal cost and are a convenient option for many projects.

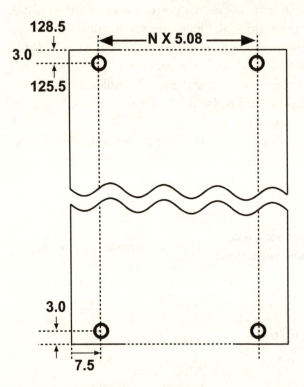

FIGURE 14.1 Position of mounting holes

Tip: Always print drill holes and other cutouts before cutting an aluminum front panel. This will help to prevent mistakes that are all too easy to make when working with a variety of components. A laminator, if available, is particularly useful since holes can be drilled in the material and the semi-rigid printout can be overlayed on the components that form the user interface to check for size and position.

MOUNTING AND SCREWS

As the Doepfer documentation indicates, a pair of mounting holes (top and bottom) is sufficient for modules up to 10 HP and four (or more) mounting holes are used for larger modules. M3 × 6 oval-head Phillips screws are recommended.

POWERING A MODULE

The Doepfer approach to power bus pinout, shown in Figure 14.2, has emerged as a de facto standard. Ribbon cables with female sockets connect the two rows of eight-pin headers to the module, and either sixteen- or ten-pins are provided on the module. Ten-pin headers are used for most of the projects in the book, but a 5V supply can be easily provided with a voltage regulator as described in Chapter 13.[4]

CHAPTER 14 BUILDING EURORACK MODULES   219

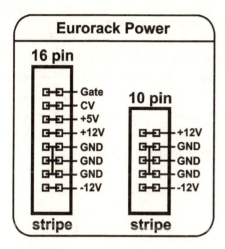

FIGURE 14.2 Eurorack power pinout

Figure 14.3 shows a ribbon connection to a custom Eurorack module. Note how the stripe corresponds to the −12V connection.

FIGURE 14.3 Ribbon cable connecting to a custom Eurorack module

Building a Eurorack Mixer: Stripboard Version

The monophonic mixer utilizes the circuit shown in Figure 14.4. The circuit, based on an example in Ray Wilson's *Make: Analog Synthesizers*, uses a pair of op amps (contained in a single IC) to mix and buffer multiple audio channels. Op amps such as the TL072 are a good choice for this project.[5]

Reading the schematic from left to right, audio signals arrive at input jacks and flow through 10k potentiometers that attenuate the signal. A 0.1 µF capacitor blocks the DC component—that is, an offset that would cause the signal to swing *above* ground instead of swinging *around* ground. Given that the input resistor and feedback resistor of the first op amp are both 100k, the op amp provides a gain of -1. As described in Chapter 13, gain can be adjusted by altering the ratio of the input and feedback resistors. The signal flows through a second inverting buffer and another AC coupling capacitor. Wilson recommends using a 10 µF aluminum bipolar/non-polarized capacitor, but some designs may utilize higher-value electrolytics.[6] As with the input capacitor, the output capacitor blocks the DC offset that has been contributed by the op amps.

Tip: *The same circuit can also be used to mix control voltages (which rely on the DC component) by omitting the capacitors shown in Figure 14.4.*

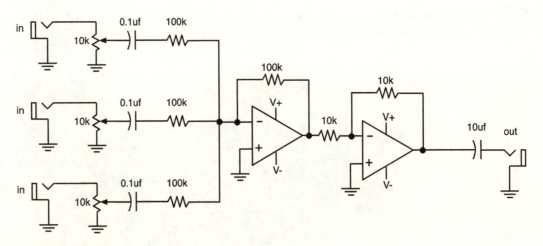

FIGURE 14.4 Simple mixer circuit

USING STRIPBOARD

For readers who are new to the term, stripboard is a type of prototyping board used for soldering components where a series of holes are connected by strips forming an electronic node or bus.[7] For example, GND could be connected to one strip and 3.3V to another strip providing multiple connection points for components. The conductive side of the strips can be partially drilled out, as needed, to break an electrical connection along the node—**a necessary step when using integrated circuits and microcontrollers to avoid shorting the pins** (see Figure 14.5). I generally prefer stripboard over protoboard board for most projects. My preference might come from a background in recording where buses are used to route channels, sends, and returns. But that is just a personal preference. Protoboard is just as effective although it usually results in spaghetti wiring for this author.

CHAPTER 14 BUILDING EURORACK MODULES

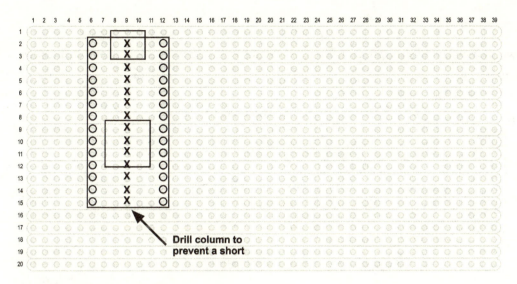

FIGURE 14.5 Drilling out stripboard nodes

HOOKUP WIRE

22-gauge solid hookup wire is a good choice for connecting signals between components, and I like to purchase multi-colored kits to make it easier to differentiate power, ground, audio, and other signals—especially when I need to revisit a circuit at a later date to fix or update a project.

TRANSFERRING A BREADBOARD DESIGN TO A STRIPBOARD

Stripboard is a close cousin to a solderless breadboard and provides a familiar layout for soldering resistors, capacitors, and other components (see Figure 14.6). The following paragraphs provide a brief description of each section of the circuit.

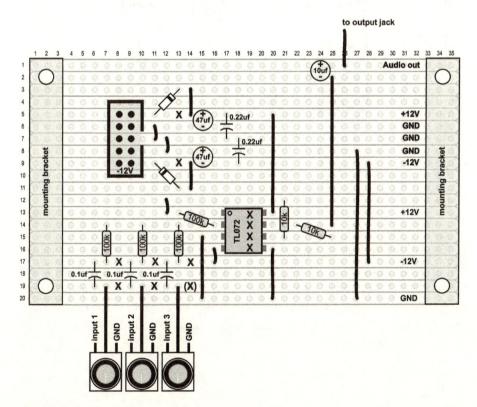

FIGURE 14.6 Mixer circuit (stripboard version)

Power Section

Power is provided by a Eurorack header and circuitry described in the previous chapter (see Figure 14.7).

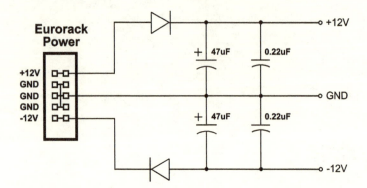

FIGURE 14.7 Power section

Note how the stripboard version of the circuit follows a similar layout (see Figure 14.8). While it is not necessary to follow the schematic in this way, the orderly layout is easily recognizable, and the capacitors are in reasonable proximity to the power source. Also, note the holes marked with an X. These should be partially drilled out on the conductive side of the board to prevent power from reaching the circuit without first passing through the protective diodes.

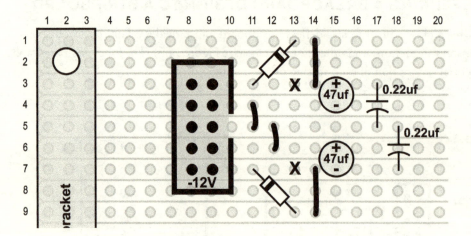

FIGURE 14.8 Power section (stripboard)

Audio Input

As with the power section, the layout of audio input components follows the schematic. Here, three input jacks feed the input pins of three potentiometers (see Figure 14.9) and the signal continues through the coupling capacitor and resistor to combine on row 14 (which feeds the first op amp). As with the previous section, partially drilled holes prevent the signals from interacting until they have passed through the coupling capacitors and 100k resistors.

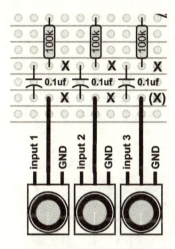

FIGURE 14.9 Audio input section

Op Amp Section

The op amp section is easier to visualize by comparing its pinout (see Figure 14.10) with the circuit. Just like the original circuit, the feedback resistors straddle each output and their respective inverting inputs.

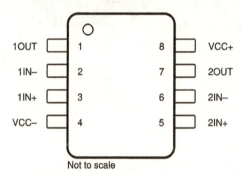

FIGURE 14.10 TL072 pinout (Texas Instruments)

Less clear is the small jumper wire that passes the output of the first op amp to a 10k resistor feeding the inverting input of the second op amp (see Figure 14.11). The signal travels on row 12, through the 10k resistor, and arrives at the inverting input. The illustration also shows the output of op amp 2 (pin 7) that feeds a capacitor (shown in Figure 14.6) providing audio to the output jack.

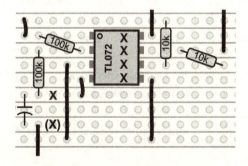

FIGURE 14.11 Op amp section

Tip: I always use sockets for integrated circuits and microcontrollers since it is so easy to damage a component while soldering pins. Sockets also make it easy to replace a damaged part or borrow a component for use in another project.

The completed circuit is shown in Figure 14.12. Although the circuit could be completed with traditional perforated board, stripboard often requires fewer wires and I have found it easier to use.

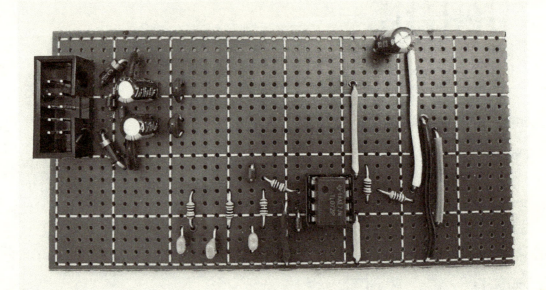

FIGURE 14.12 Completed circuit

FRONT PANEL

The front panel houses potentiometers, jacks, and other through-hole components that form an interface to the circuit. Seeing a design come to life in the form of a new instrument or audio tool can be exciting and is a part of Eurorack design that inspires me to keep exploring this aspect of music making. Not only do front panels provide visual clues to the form and function of a module, but custom panels provide another outlet for creative expression.

Front Panel Design

I like to work on front panel design in conjunction with circuit layout since the panel and circuitry obviously need to be compatible. For example, the first iteration of the mixer circuit included four input channels, but I quickly realized I could not fit the components on the Eurorack panel I intended to use for the project.

One effective approach is to use graphic design software to determine the location of all front-panel components. Layers, if they are available in your design software, are convenient for separating printable elements from board outlines, design notes, and other non-printing elements. It is also helpful to add a graphic layer with dimensional outlines of each component to ensure that there is enough space for each item.

I designed the following mixer shown in Figure 14.13 around a 6HP Eurorack panel.

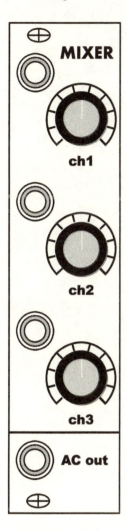

FIGURE 14.13 Mixer design

Front Panel Milling

Once your panel design is ready there are several options for milling and printing panel graphics. The top-of-the-line approach is to upload the design to a company that specializes in manufacturing front panels. Although the results can look fantastic, the costs are prohibitive. Some DIYers use acrylic, wood, or other materials or design custom PCBs to function as a front panel—a less expensive option than dedicated panel manufacturing facilities (see Figure 14.14). PCB front panels are particularly convenient for projects that involve cutouts—which are difficult to create with hand tools. See Chapter 15 for an overview of creating PCB front panels.

FIGURE 14.14 PCB front panel

Blank Front Panels

One cost-effective method is to purchase blank Eurorack panels. With this approach, holes are drilled with a hand drill or drill press and graphics are transferred to the module from clear laser or inkjet sticker paper. Figure 14.15 shows the mixer design with just the outline and hole layers showing.

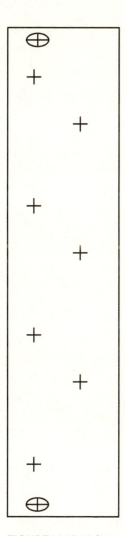

FIGURE 14.15 Hole position layer (not to scale)

Use painter's tape to attach a printout of the hole positions to the panel and use a punch to mark the position of each hole on the panel. The holes can then be drilled with a hand drill or drill press (see Figure 14.16). Be sure to use clamps to hold the panel and wear protective eyewear! A small file or hole reamer can clean up any burrs—a necessary step when painting or applying a clear sticker to the panel.

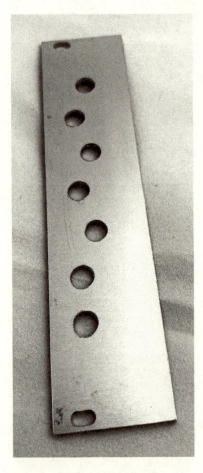

FIGURE 14.16 A milled panel

Front Panel Printing

Individuals with an artistic bent may enjoy painting a front panel design directly on the milled Eurorack panel. However, I prefer using graphic design software to print designs to clear sticker paper available from several manufacturers.

Figure 14.17 shows the completed panel. Although the results don't rival a professionally manufactured panel, homemade panels can still look attractive.

CHAPTER 14 BUILDING EURORACK MODULES   229

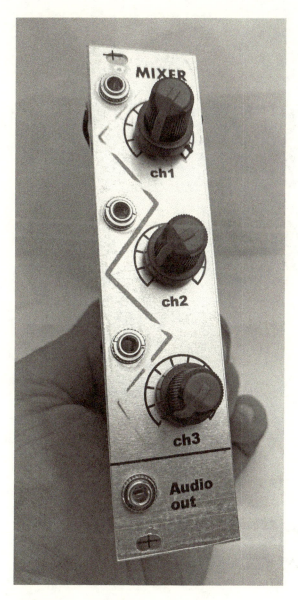

FIGURE 14.17 Completed panel with graphics

PUTTING IT ALL TOGETHER

The final step is to mount the circuit to the panel and connect the components to the circuit. A common approach for DIY designers is to create an L-shaped mounting bracket like the one shown in Figure 14.18. The bracket can be held in place with potentiometers, switches, or other through-hole components and the circuit affixed with nuts and bolts. Brackets can be fashioned from metal (but be sure to isolate the circuit to prevent a short), or they can be printed from a 3D printer if one is available.

FIGURE 14.18 L-shaped mounting bracket

Wires (see Figure 14.19) are typically used to connect pots and other components to a circuit.

FIGURE 14.19 Using wires to connect components to stripboard

Although wires can look messy, they provide a few advantages for DIY Eurorack projects:

- Protoboard-friendly components such as audio jacks can be difficult to source.
- It is generally not necessary to match the off-the-board height of components.
- It is easier to replace components (e.g., swap out a linear potentiometer for a logarithmic potentiometer), and fix mistakes.

Summary

Figure 14.20 shows the completed stripboard mixer ready for action in a Eurorack setup. Although there are limitations to the approach—particularly for complex projects—building custom Eurorack modules using through-hole components and stripboard certainly fits with the DIY ethos of the platform. And, unlike PCB-based projects, you can build a module in a single day from existing parts—something that is impossible for PCB projects unless you happen to have access to a PCB manufacturing facility.

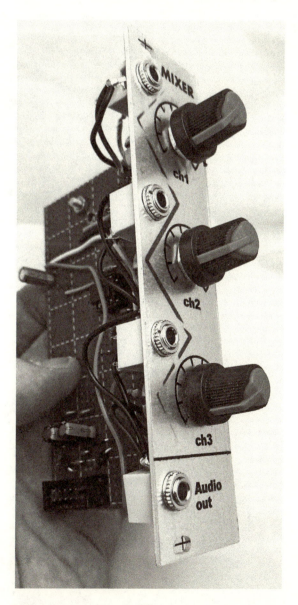

FIGURE 14.20 Completed stripboard Eurorack mixer

CREATIVE CHALLENGE

The simple audio mixer has been a handy extension to my Eurorack setup and is economical to build. Although this version of the project is intended to mix audio signals, the circuit can also handle DC mixing tasks by removing the DC-blocking capacitors. Other revisions might include providing an access jack after the first op amp (described as an "attenuverter" in Eurorack parlance), altering resistor ratios to provide gain, or revising the circuit to accommodate switches to toggle between AC and DC mixing.

CHAPTER 15

BUILDING EURORACK MODULES WITH PCBS

Chapter 14 introduced the topic of custom Eurorack modules with a focus on the use of stripboard and through-hole components. This chapter looks at the same project—an analog mixer—through the lens of a custom printed circuit board (PCB). Printed circuit boards have several advantages over solderable prototyping boards (and some disadvantages) as shown in Table 15.1.

TABLE 15.1 *PCBs vs prototyping boards*

PCB Pro	PCB Con
Access to a broader range of parts including tactile switches and rotary encoders.	Requires the use of specialized software.
Ability to utilize smaller components and fit more parts in less space.	Larger PCBs can be expensive.
Streamlined soldering process (components are clearly labeled on the PCB face).	Manufacturing takes time.
Potential cost savings.	Hard or impossible to fix circuit errors.
Potential for more professional outcomes.	Hole placement for front panel is unforgiving.

A bill of materials (BOM), Gerber files (for printing PCBs), and other resources are available for download from the OUP website. Project PCBs can be printed for a few dollars from budget manufacturers and components purchased from electronics parts vendors if desired.

Getting Started

Unlike protoboard projects that utilize wires to connect front-panel components to circuitry, PCB projects typically utilize pots, switches, jacks, and other components that are soldered directly onto a PCB. While this can result in tighter spacing of components, it does bring up two important questions: How will the PCB be attached to the front panel and how can components of varying heights be made to fit between a PCB and front panel?

Sound & Music Projects for Eurorack and Beyond. Brent Edstrom, Oxford University Press. © Oxford University Press 2024.
DOI: 10.1093/9780197514504.003.0015

ATTACHMENT ISSUES

PCBs can be attached perpendicular or parallel to a front panel. With the perpendicular approach, right-angle potentiometers and jacks are positioned to extend beyond the edge of the PCB and the front panel can, in some cases, be attached with nuts on threaded components. The right-angle connection can be bolstered with additional threaded right-angle terminals or other mounting hardware as necessary.

Vertical-mount components such as pots and jacks are used when the PCB is mounted parallel to the front panel. As with right-angle mounting, threaded components may help to hold the front panel in place. However, four (or more) threaded standoffs are recommended for most projects and can be incorporated into a PCB design using the process for creating mounting holes detailed later in the chapter.

HEIGHT ISSUES

One of the challenges of designing a parallel-mount PCB is selecting parts that have complementary heights. I typically start with component datasheets and use graphic design software to create approximations of the parts and place them on a virtual PCB. This makes it easy to see if the standoff height needs to be adjusted or other components sourced for the project. For example, in Figure 15.1 it is clear that component 7 is too tall to fit standoff height (S). Incidentally, I often use 10 mm threaded standoffs for Eurorack projects since they are a good match for my most-used components.

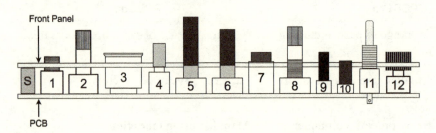

FIGURE 15.1 Comparing component heights on a virtual PCB

Designing PCBs: A Crash Course in DipTrace

This section provides a gentle introduction to DipTrace, a popular PCB-design application, and details the use of the software to create a PCB version of the Eurorack mixer shown in Figure 15.2.[1] While the chapter is built around DipTrace, it is important to stress that there are many fine applications including Eagle, Kicad, and others. The point is not to emphasize or encourage the use of specific software but rather to provide an overview of a process that will be common to most PCB design applications. The choice of PCB design software will include considerations including cost, capability, operating system, and ease of use; and the concepts presented in this chapter will be useful in introducing key concepts to readers who are new to the process.

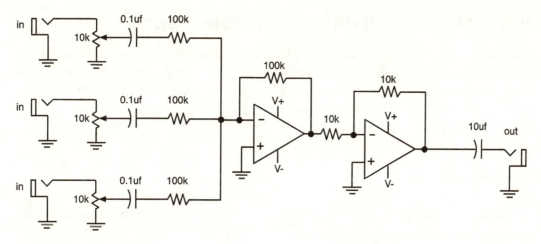

FIGURE 15.2 Mixer circuit

Although DipTrace or other PCB applications can be complex, it is not unduly difficult to learn the basics and you will be rewarded with a useful skill and the ability to create more professional Eurorack projects. This introduction will be necessarily brief, but the "over the shoulder" look at a simple project will provide familiarity with the core functions of the program and tasks that are similar among all PCB design applications. A comprehensive tutorial is provided at the DipTrace website as are many video tutorials created by individuals who use the program on a regular basis. In the spirit of encouragement, I don't mind saying I am fairly new to DipTrace and it isn't unduly difficult to learn the basics once you develop a feel for the underlying paradigms of PCB design—concepts that will apply to other PCB design applications.

WHY DIPTRACE?

While there are many excellent PDB design applications, DipTrace represents a good blend of power, ease of use, and flexible licensing options. You may even find that DipTrace Lite—the free version that provides support for 500 holes and two layers—will be sufficient for many projects. And additional functionality is available for the cost of a modest upgrade. However, the primary reason I use the program is that the application fits *my* workflow better than some other options. Like choosing a DAW or score writer, the selection of PCB design software can be subjective—so use the concepts in the chapter to find the software option that works best for you!

CREATING A SCHEMATIC

DipTrace can be thought of as a suite of tools that provide the ability to:

- Create schematics.
- Design PCBs based on a schematic.
- Create custom components for use in the schematic designer.
- Create custom patterns for use in the PCB designer.

POPULATING A SCHEMATIC WITH COMPONENTS

The first step usually involves running DipTrace and selecting the Schematic Capture tool to create a schematic. Drag the components shown in Table 15.2 into the main window of the schematic design tool. Each component can be found by selecting the library category (shown near the top left of the window) and selecting the given component in the bottom selection list (see Figure 15.3).

TABLE 15.2 *Mixer components*

Component Library	Component	Number of Components
Discreet	RES400	4
Discreet	CAP200	2
Discreet	POLCAP	1
Con Phone Jacks	MJ-3536NG	2
ST Micro 1	TL072IN or similar	1 (one part contains two op amps)

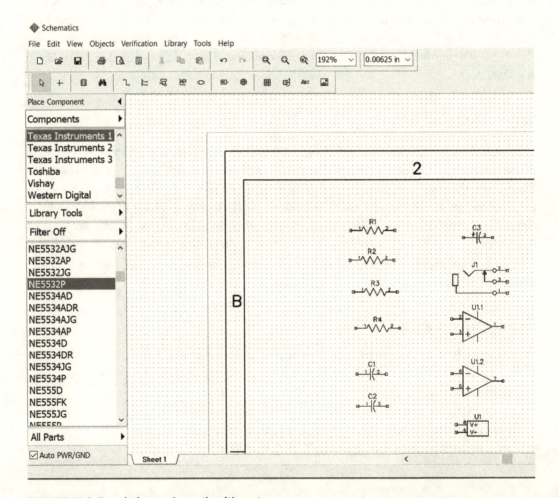

FIGURE 15.3 Populating a schematic with parts

DESIGNING CUSTOM SCHEMATIC PARTS

In a perfect world, all the necessary parts would be available to place in the schematic, but it is sometimes necessary to design custom components for use in the schematic and PCB design tools. In the case of the mixer schematic, I was unable to find the side-adjust Bourns potentiometer (PTV09A-2020F) I had selected for the project, so I used the steps outlined in the following section to create a schematic symbol and PCB footprint for the part. I used the same process to create a custom power header so voltage and ground connections could be clearly shown on the schematic.

To create a custom part, run the DipTrace Launcher and select the Component Editor tool. Use the Library . . . New menu option to create a new library (e.g., Eurorack) or use the Library . . . Open option if you have previously created a library you wish to use. Use the Component . . . Add New menu to start the process of creating a new component. Bear in mind that the goal of the Component Editor tool is to create a visual representation of the component for the schematic view, so a stock graphic can often be used for the purpose—particularly with discreet components such as resistors and capacitors. A variety of templates are available from the Template dropdown menu in the Component Properties window shown in Figure 15.4:

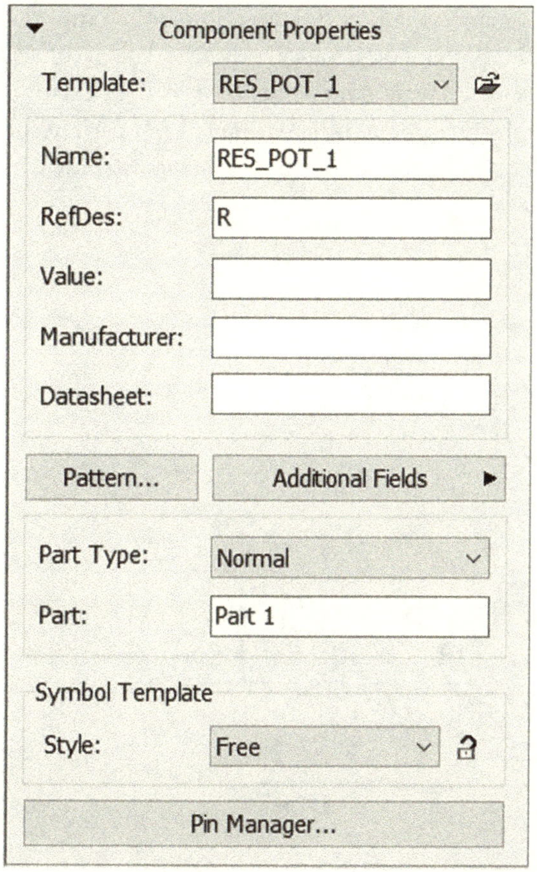

FIGURE 15.4 Selecting a visual template in the Component Editor

Double-click on each pin, relabel as desired, and provide a name (such as PTV09A-2020F-A103). My simple adaptation of the potentiometer template is shown in Figure 15.5.

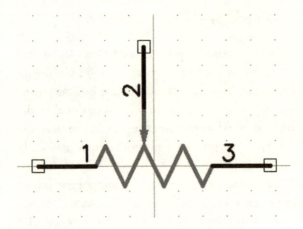

FIGURE 15.5 Completed schematic component

DESIGNING A CUSTOM PCB PART

The final step in creating a custom component is to design a PCB pattern in the Pattern Editor (also available from the DipTrace Launcher). Ideally, patterns are linked to schematic components so the completed schematic can generate the PCB file used to manufacture the PCB. Part patterns for PCBs may have a combination of holes, solder pads, text, and graphics.

Run the pattern editor from the launch screen, create a new library or load an existing library, and select Pattern . . . Add New to begin the process of designing a PCB pattern for the part. Component datasheets will provide information about hole spacing as shown in Figure 15.6.

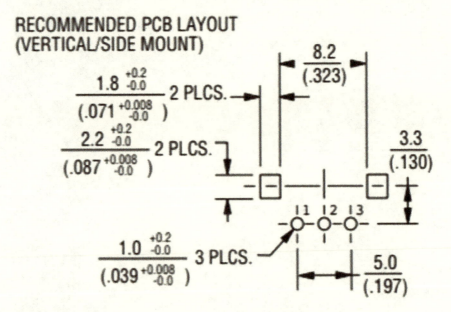

FIGURE 15.6 Hole spacing information from component datasheet

Select the "place pad" icon and click to add one or more pads to the pattern. I usually drop the necessary number of pads in a rough approximation of their location and double-click each pad with the selection tool to enter the pad position and properties—which are available by selecting Pattern's Pad Properties as shown in Figure 15.7.

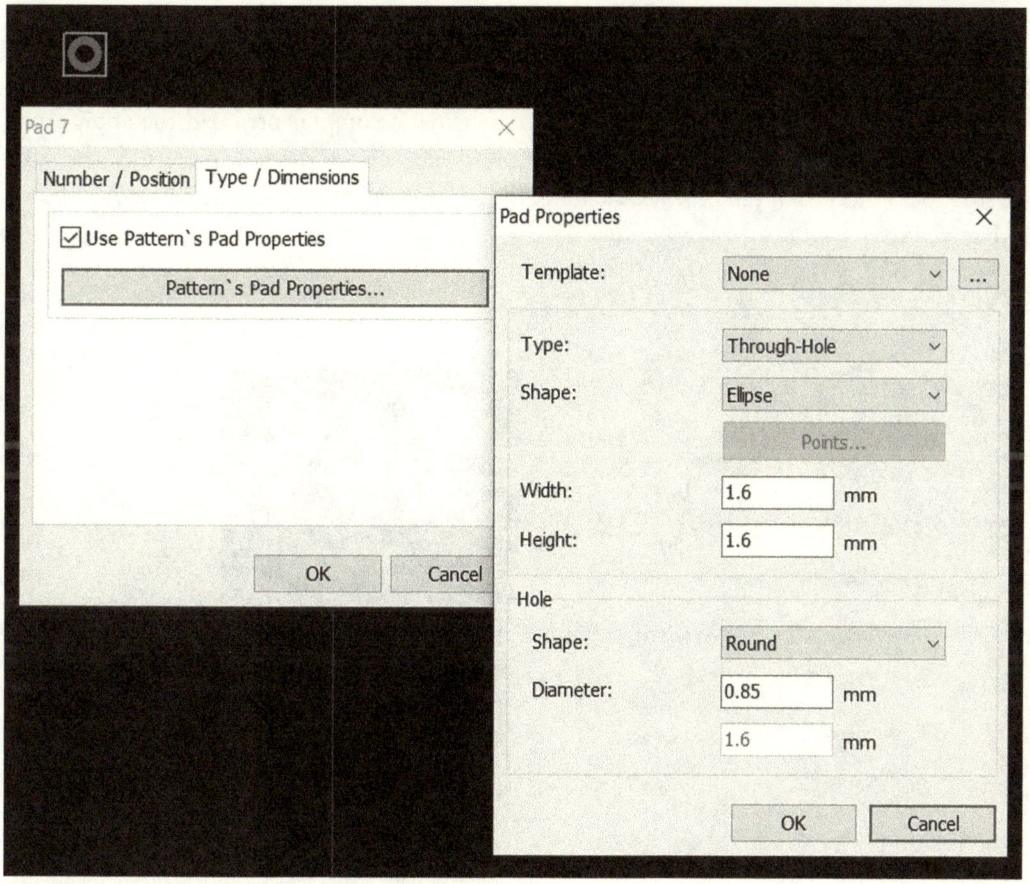

CHAPTER 15 BUILDING EURORACK MODULES WITH PCBS 239

FIGURE 15.7 Editing pad properties and location

The process may feel cumbersome at first, but you will soon get a feel for the workflow and develop shortcuts (such as lassoing multiple pads and right-clicking to align the pads). Be sure to closely follow the location and pad sizes that are provided by the datasheet and consider using the graphic tools to provide information that may be useful when viewing a pattern on an unpopulated PCB. A completed pattern, named Side-mount pot, is shown in Figure 15.8.

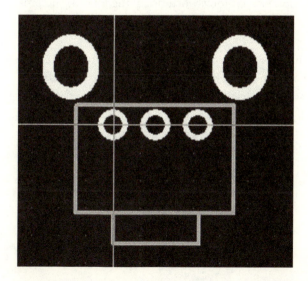

FIGURE 15.8 Finished pattern for a side-mount potentiometer

CONNECTING A PATTERN TO A SCHEMATIC COMPONENT

Save your work and re-start the Component Editor to complete the process of linking the newly created pattern to the previously created schematic component. Load the appropriate library, select the part, and click on the Pattern button to attach the new pattern to the part. Be sure to connect each pin on the schematic to the appropriate pad on the pattern as shown in Figure 15.9:

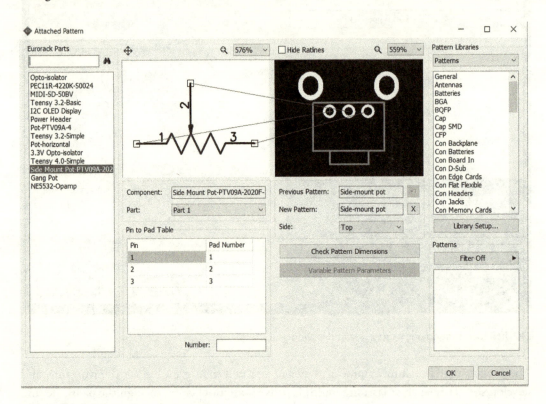

FIGURE 15.9 Connecting pins to pads

Save your work and return to the Schematic Capture tool to complete the schematic.

Although it might feel awkward to jump between tools when designing a PCB, the process is easy to visualize:

1. Start a schematic and populate it with necessary components.
2. Use the Component Editor to create custom schematic symbols for any missing parts. In most cases, an existing template, available from the Template dropdown of the Component Properties dialog, can be used with little or no editing.
3. Use the Pattern Editor in conjunction with an appropriate datasheet to create a PCB pattern for the component.
4. Return to the Component Editor and use the Pattern button to connect the pattern to the selected schematic component.
5. Return to the Schematic Capture Tool to complete the schematic.

COMPLETING THE CIRCUIT SCHEMATIC

Now that the necessary parts are available, it is a relatively simple process to drag components to a suitable location and use the Place Wire tool to connect components in the Schematic Capture tool. Note that the R key provides a convenient way to rotate components, and many additional operations (such as flipping a component) are available by right-clicking. Figure 15.10 shows a completed audio channel with the newly created side-mount potentiometer part.

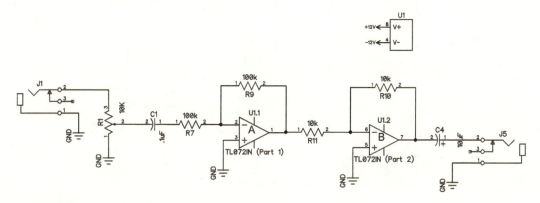

FIGURE 15.10 A completed channel

USING NETS

One final tip is to consider the use of Nets to simplify the visual appearance and logic of the schematic. As shown in Figure 15.11, pins such as those that power the op amp (see the U1 graphic) or headers (see the +12V, GND, and –12V pins) can be added to a "net" by right-clicking on a pin and selecting the "Add to Net" option. Select a net from the dropdown menu or click the + button to create a new net. For example, there is no reason to route separate wires for each ground and power connection when they only serve to clutter the schematic. This section of the schematic also illustrates a custom Eurorack power header that was created using the part-creation steps detailed in the previous section.

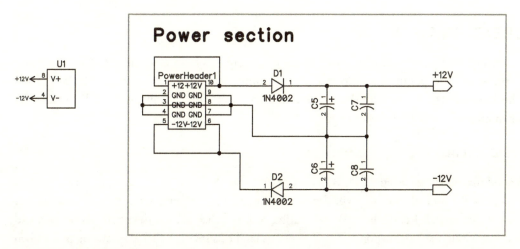

FIGURE 15.11 Using nets for power and ground

The final iteration of a mixer schematic is shown in Figure 15.12. Additional channels were created by copying and pasting the first channel and connecting the output of the channel using the Place Wire tool.

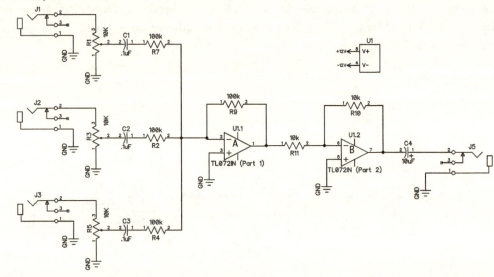

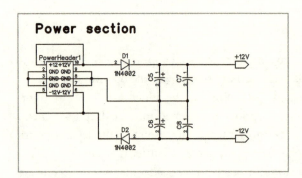

FIGURE 15.12 Completed schematic

CREATING A PCB

Assuming that patterns are attached to all the components in a schematic, the Schematic Capture tool can populate a PCB layout with components. Select Verify . . . Electrical Rule Check to check for issues with the circuit and then select File . . . Convert to PCB to hand the schematic off to the PCB Layout tool.

Board Outline

A good first step when using the PCB Layout tool is to use the Place Board Outline tool to create an outline for the circuit board. You will also want to use the View menu to set units to your preference (e.g., millimeters). Select the Place Board Outline tool and click around the perimeter of the board to create a rough approximation of the dimensions (and be sure to re-click the starting point when you have completed the outline). Right-click and select Board Points to enter the exact coordinates of the board—a process that is easier than attempting to create an outline using mouse clicks. Be aware that small changes in size can have a dramatic impact on the cost. For example, I used values of 100 mm by 50 mm for the AC Mixer which prices out at $4.95 (total) for *ten* PCBs from a popular vendor, but a 105 mm by 50 mm board costs about four times as much from the same vendor.

Figure 15.13 shows the completed board outline with components provided by the Schematic Capture tool.

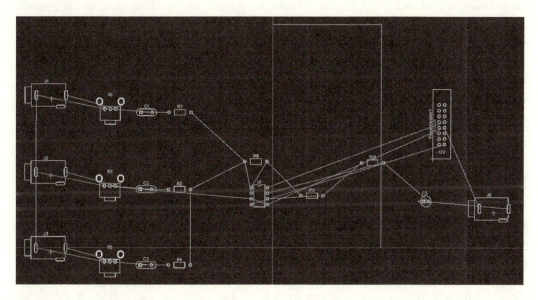

FIGURE 15.13 Board outline with "raw" PCB layout from Schematic Capture tool

Placing Components

Readers who enjoy puzzles will love the next step in the process—placing components and routing the traces between components. Consider the placement and orientation of parts and use the R key to rotate, as needed, to minimize long traces or awkward connections. This part of the process involves both art and skill, and professionals who do the work on a regular basis would make short work of a simple PCB like the mixer. For the rest of us, a good first step is to organize parts into functional units: for example, power section, amplifier section, and so on. Keep in mind that multiple parts can be selected by shift-clicking, and right-clicking can be used to access alignment options. Figure 15.14 shows the component placement I used for the first iteration of the mixer project.

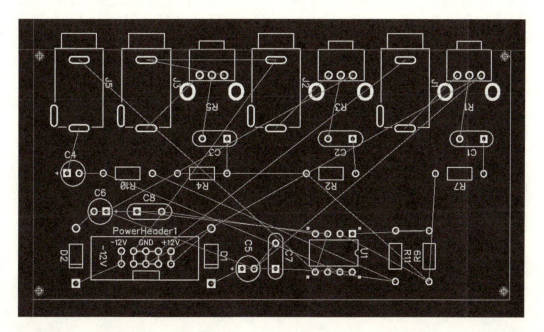

FIGURE 15.14 Basic layout of components

TRACE WIDTHS

Trace widths are measured in a unit called a *mil* or *thou* (1/1000th of an inch) and typically range from 6 to 30 mils.[2] While trace widths are crucial for high-frequency or high-power circuits, they are less crucial for relatively low-power Eurorack projects with a few caveats: power traces should be closer to 30 mils or even higher if space permits, and signal traces should be comfortably larger than the manufacturer's listed minimum trace width. I typically use 12 mils (.305mm) or larger for signals and at least 24 mils (.61mm) for Eurorack power rails, but you will want to increase power trace widths for higher amperage applications.[3] Fortunately, many online trace-width calculators are available to help determine ideal trace widths.[4]

Creating a Ground Plane

It is generally advisable to create a ground plane on the bottom layer to mitigate electrical noise and other problems.[5] Given that many components are connected to the ground, adding a ground plane will simplify trace routing on the top layer. Select the bottom layer and use the Place Copper Pour tool to create the plane. The process is like creating a board outline—click along the perimeter of the board to create the outline for the ground plane and make a final click at the starting point to complete the outline. A dialog box (which is also available by right-clicking the newly created Copper Pour) is used to configure parameters for the plane. Also, be sure to click the Connectivity Tab and connect the pour to the GND net. The last step will effectively absorb any GND connections on the bottom layer (but any non-GND ratlines or traces will be visible on the layer). Looking ahead, *vias* can be used to connect surface-mount components to the ground plane.

> **Tip:** *It can be tricky to click precisely when creating a bounding box for the ground plane. I generally create a rough approximation with the mouse and enter dimensions in the Copper Pour dialog box. A copper pour that is 0.5mm smaller than the PCB works well for most projects.*

Running Traces

You will notice the many *ratlines* that show electrical connections between components. However, the ratlines are just a visualization of those connections—not the actual traces that will be present on the finished PCB. That work is done with the Route Manual tool. Although my layout skills are a far cry from those of a professional electrical engineer, I have found the process can be relaxing and somewhat akin to solving a puzzle.

Use the appropriate dropdown menu to select the top layer and select the Route Manual option to begin the process of drawing traces. Hover the mouse to determine component connections and use the routing tool to connect the appropriate pads. It may take several tries to find a workable routing for all traces, so save incremental versions of the file and don't be shy about making frequent use of the undo option. And enjoy the smug satisfaction that your first routing will likely be better than what the auto-router will produce.

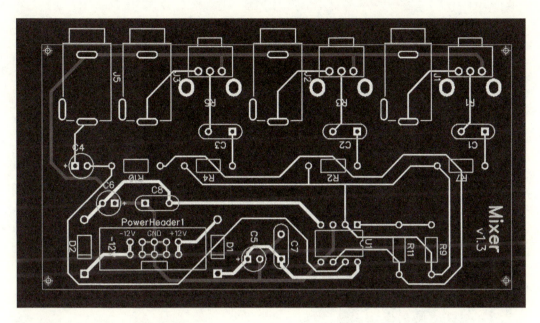

FIGURE 15.15 Traces on the top layer

Tip: Increase the default width of traces that carry power. Although a discussion of trace-width calculation is beyond the scope of this book, I used a default of ≈0.305 mm signal trace and 0.7 mm (or wider) power trace for many of the projects in the book.

Text and Mounting Holes

Select the Top Silk layer from the dropdown menu and use the text tool to add information to be printed on the top layer of the PCB. Mounting holes can also be added, if desired, by clicking the Add Mounting Holes icon. As with component holes, mounting hole properties are adjusted by right-clicking on the hole.

3D Preview

The Tools . . . 3D Preview menu provides a 3D representation of the PCB. Although I don't usually take the time to create 3D models of parts to be rendered by the viewer, the 3D tool can be a great asset in finding problems such as missing text or alignment issues (see Figure 15.16).

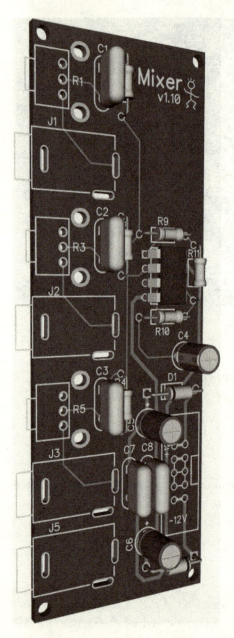

FIGURE 15.16 Virtual 3D view of PCB

PREPARING FILES FOR FABRICATION

The final step of the process is to create Gerber files that are used to manufacture the PCB. The process can be as simple is as simple as selecting File . . . Export . . . Gerber but—and this is important—follow the instructions of your vendor to make any necessary setting adjustments before exporting the Gerber files. You will also need to export a drill pattern using the appropriate export option such as Export . . . NC Drill. Again, follow the instructions provided by the PCB manufacturer.

A final step is to create a .zip file containing the exported drill file and Gerber layers. This is easily achieved on a PC by placing the files in a folder, selecting the files, right-clicking and selecting Send To . . . Compressed (zipped) folder. It is also possible to export Zipped Gerber and drill files directly from the Gerber Export dialog.

AVOIDING ERRORS

Although it can be surprisingly inexpensive to order PCBs, it is frustrating, time-consuming, and wasteful to order PCBs that contain errors. The following tips may be useful in preventing some errors and added expenses:

- Diptrace provides diagnostic tools to check for unconnected nets and trace-spacing issues. There is also an option to check the PCB against the original schematic. Get in the habit of running the diagnostic tools as a second pair of eyes before exporting Gerber files.
- Use a Gerber reader such as gerbv.exe to check each layer of the PCB before ordering.
- Print the PCB design on paper and place parts on the printout. Some layout problems such as tight spacing or colliding knobs may be caught by this step. You can also press parts such as potentiometers and switches through the paper into the conductive foam to check for dimensional accuracy.
- Double-check the top and bottom layers for overlapping parts: It is all too easy to place components such that they are unduly hard or impossible to solder.
- Double-check the taper of any pots: Remember that the taper curves shown on datasheets show resistance, *not* signal level. And yes, I did order a batch of PCBs where pots were wired in the wrong direction. Not a problem in a microcontroller project where such an error can be "fixed in the mix," but a disappointing problem for a project like the PCB mixer.
- Be mindful of Eurorack metrics and PCB cost. A 100 mm height generally provides a nice compromise between PCB cost and maximal between-the-rails coverage for a Eurorack project.
- Consider the front panel before ordering PCBs: Attachment method, aesthetics, availability of components, and space between parts are primary considerations.

While protoboards such as stripboard can be a good option for DIY Eurorack projects, I have found that learning to design custom PCBs is liberating and has opened a new world of options. Not only do the PCBs provide a cleaner and more professional foundation for my builds, but I can also incorporate a wider variety of parts including surface-mount components.

CREATING PCB FRONT PANELS

An attractive front panel can be created using the "DIY" steps detailed in Chapter 14, but this is a good time to look at repurposing Diptrace's PCB designer for front-panel design. Although PCB front panels are not on a par with professionally manufactured panels, they can still look very good and are relatively inexpensive to manufacture. Another benefit is that PCB front panels can be manufactured with hole tolerances that are impossible to achieve with a hand drill or drill press. And most PCB manufacturers offer a variety of background colors beyond the classic "PCB green." Although PCB design tools leave a lot to be desired in terms of graphic design, it is possible to achieve good results.

PLACE HOLES

For a front panel that is *perpendicular* to potentiometers, jacks, and other components, use the datasheet for each component to determine the height of the component hole in relation to the PCB. Place holes so they are at the same point on the Y-axis of the component board and use the vertical component hole height to determine the component's hole position on the X-axis of the front panel (see Figure 15.17).

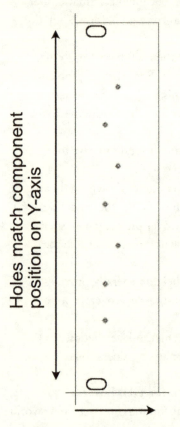

FIGURE 15.17 Placing holes for a perpendicular front panel

Resize the newly created holes so they are big enough to easily accommodate the given component (see Figure 15.18).

CHAPTER 15 BUILDING EURORACK MODULES WITH PCBS 249

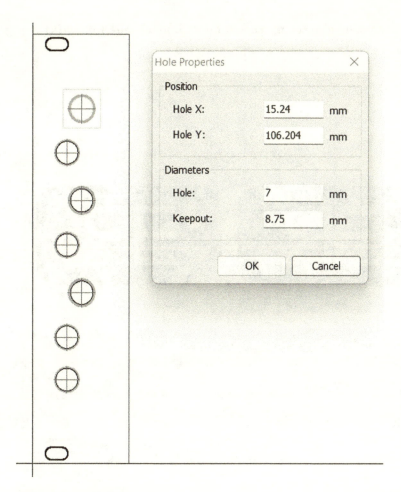

FIGURE 15.18 Resizing holes

Tip: I always print a paper copy of the front panel and check the alignment with components before ordering a manufactured front panel. When designing a front panel for a component PCB that has not yet been manufactured, print a copy of the component PCB, and place it on semi-firm static dissipative foam. Potentiometers and other components can be pressed into the foam to check the alignment of holes against the front panel.

For a front panel that is *parallel* to components, save a *copy* of the completed interface PCB and rename the file as myfile-FRONT-PANEL or similar. Select the mounting tool icon and carefully place mounting holes so they align with the centers of any potentiometer shafts, jacks, LEDs, rotary encoders, switches, and the like. Carefully remove the circuitry and traces from the original board and you should have a front panel with holes that are perfectly aligned with the underlying component PCB.

ADD GRAPHICS

Graphics can be added to the top (and bottom) silkscreen layers. I generally use the built-in text editor for text and numbers and use graphic design software to create logos, specialty fonts, potentiometer markings, or other graphic elements. Graphics can be imported (and resized) using the graphic tool in Diptrace (see Figure 15.19).

Front panel tip: Create a ground plane on the back of the PCB front panel if you prefer a darker and richer color.

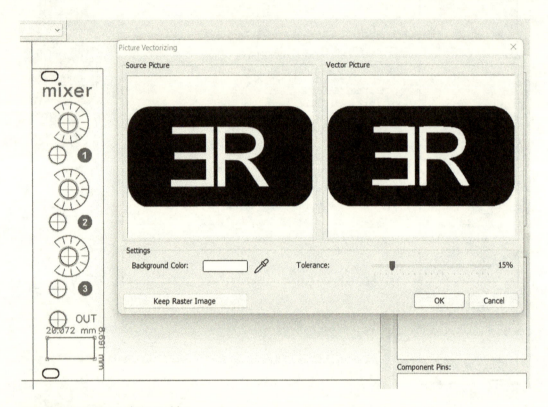

FIGURE 15.19 Importing graphics

Final Front Panel Check

- Print a copy of the original PCB and the newly created front panel.
- Double-check that holes on the original interface align with the newly created front panel.
- Preview the front panel in the Diptrace 3D viewer to check for proper alignment of graphics and components.
- Export Gerber files and submit the files to a PCB manufacturer.

Tip: *Since the front panel is a PCB sans circuitry, it might be tempting to order a single-side PCB. Don't do it unless you prefer "retro brown" for your PCB front panel. I have also ordered a few PCBs that appear to have been automatically changed to single-side by the manufacturer's pre-production process. This does make sense when you consider that front panels don't contain circuitry. I have noticed that I have never had the issue when I use pads (that are conductive on both sides of the board) to create the mounting holes shown in Figure 15.19.*

COMPLETING THE MIXER PROJECT

Once the PCB arrives from a manufacturer, check the fit of all parts and solder components to the PCB. When possible, attach the front panel *before* soldering potentiometers, LEDs, and related components to ensure proper alignment of the parts (see Figure 15.20).

FIGURE 15.20 Using a front panel to align components prior to soldering

It may be helpful to use a multimeter to check for shorts before powering the unit—particularly when minimal space exists between solder points. A final step is to verify the circuit's function by powering it from a +/− 12V Eurorack power source.

Summary

The finished project is shown in Figure 15.21. Although the simple analog mixer won't win any awards for innovation, the project does illustrate many core concepts that can be applied to a wide variety of microcontroller projects. And the project provides a handy mixer that will be a useful addition to almost any Eurorack kit.

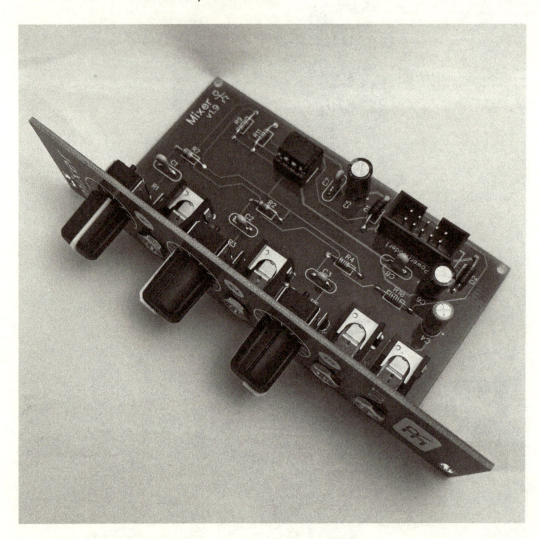

FIGURE 15.21 Completed PCB mixer

CHAPTER 16

VOLTAGE CONTROL, GATES, AND TRIGGERS

Getting Started with Voltage Control

It is interesting that voltage control, a concept pioneered by Robert Moog and Don Buchla in the 1960s, has reemerged as a popular feature of synthesizers in the new millennium.[1] While MIDI has many advantages over voltage control including support for polyphonic performance and a wide array of parameters for real-time control and synchronization, using voltage to control synthesizers can open the door to new expressive opportunities—particularly in the realm of modular synthesis where analog signals are connected and processed in unique ways. To quote Hal Chamberlin, author of *Musical Applications of Microprocessors*:

> The real power of the voltage-control concept lies in the realization that the only difference between a signal voltage and a control voltage is the typical rates of change.[2]

So, what *is* voltage control? Simply put, voltage can be applied to synthesizer components such as a voltage-controlled oscillator (VCO), voltage-controlled filter (VCF), and voltage-controlled amplifier (VCA). Figure 16.1 illustrates a common scenario where the frequency of a voltage-controlled oscillator (VCO) is controlled by a voltage generated at the output of a low-frequency oscillator (LFO).

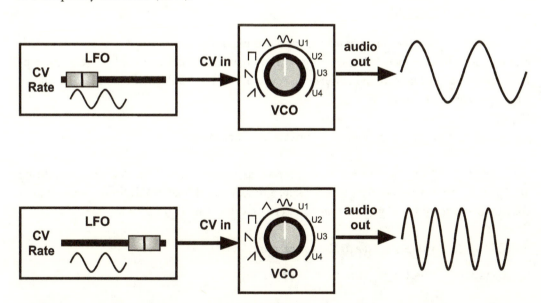

FIGURE 16.1 Applying control voltage to an oscillator

Voltage is also used for triggers, gates, and clock pulses but, unlike MIDI where messages are tied to specific functions, voltage control—even with its many limitations—can provide unique opportunities for creative application including using a voltage source to modulate another voltage source. As you will learn in the pages that follow, manufacturers have approached voltage control in different ways, so it will be important to check product specifications to determine if the device can be safely connected to a given voltage level.

Control Voltage Schemes

Control voltage isn't just used for modulation, gates, and triggers, it also provides a mechanism for pitch control where specific frequencies are output by applying voltage to the input of a VCO. Historically, two approaches were devised to correlate voltage levels and pitch: *volts per octave*, and *Hertz per volt* as shown in Figure 16.2. Although we will consider both forms, the volts per octave approach is used in the world of Eurorack.

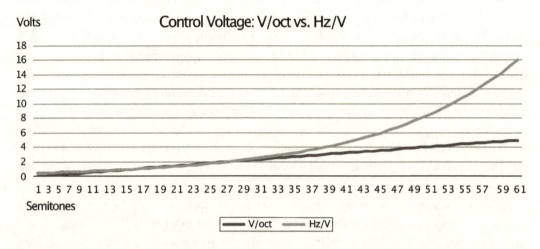

FIGURE 16.2 Volts per Octave vs. Hertz per Volt

VOLTS PER OCTAVE

As the name implies, the volts per octave approach divides a voltage range into octaves—with one volt per octave (V/oct) being the most common and the easiest to work with. A conceptually simple approach is to divide the octave (usually 1V) by twelve to determine the voltage that represents each semitone:

```
1V / 12 semitones = 0.083333 volts per semitone
```

Although we will look at a more nuanced approach to voltage control later in the chapter, listing 16.1 provides an overview of the process. Here, a function multiplies a MIDI note (representing the number of semitones) by a constant representing voltage in 1/12th of an octave.

Listing 16.1 Volt per octave MIDI conversion

```
const float voltage_step = 0.083333;

float voltsPerOctave(int midi_note)
{
    return (float) midi_note * voltage_step;
}
```

Table 16.1 illustrates the relationship between MIDI note, voltage, and frequency for several notes.

TABLE 16.1 Volts per octave examples

MIDI Note	Voltage	Frequency
21 (A0)	1.75	27.5 Hz
33 (A1)	2.75	55 Hz
45 (A2)	3.75	110 Hz
47 (B2)	3.92	123.47 Hz
48 (C3)	4	130.81 Hz

HERTZ PER VOLT

A contrasting scheme, implemented in some synthesizers manufactured by Korg and others, utilizes a specific number of Hertz per volt (Hz/V). A slope of 55 Hz/V is common with the Hertz per volt approach (see Table 16.2).[3]

TABLE 16.2 Hertz per volt

Volt	Frequency	Note
0	55 Hz	A1
1	110 Hz	A2
2	165 Hz	E3
3	220 Hz	A3
4	275 Hz	C#4

Fortunately, it is easy to convert from volts per octave to Hertz per volt using the following equation:

$$V_{hz} = 2^{Voct-1}$$

The code for the conversion is shown in Listing 16.2.

Listing 16.2 Converting volts per octave to Hertz per volt

```
float VPOtoHPV(float voltage)
{
    return pow(2, voltage -1.0);
}
```

Applying these calculations to several MIDI notes yields the results shown in Table 16.3:

TABLE 16.3 Hertz per volt examples

MIDI Note	Voltage	Frequency
21 (A0)	0.5	27.5
33 (A1)	1.0	55
45 (A2)	2.0	110
47 (B2)	2.24	123.47
48 (C3)	2.38	130.81

Outputting Control Voltage

Now that we have considered the underlying theory of using voltage to control pitch, it is a relatively simple task to move to a practical application—a 3.3V microcontroller that outputs control voltage over an approximately eight-octave range.

USING A DAC

A digital analog converter (DAC) forms the backbone for this voltage control experiment. Many digital analog converters are available, but I utilized a 12-bit MCP4821 DAC for several reasons including ease of use, relatively low cost, and inclusion of an internal voltage reference. A 12-bit DAC can provide precise output and has adequate resolution to support course and fine-tuning and pitch bend. Note that later examples utilize an MCP4822 containing two output channels instead of the single output provided by the MCP4821.

Serial Peripheral Interface

Microcontrollers communicate with the MCP4821 DAC via a Serial Peripheral Interface (SPI) bus. In some respects, SPI functions in a similar way to MIDI in that multiple devices can receive messages from a single MIDI port while ignoring messages that are intended for another device. As is evident in Figure 16.3, at least three signals are required to connect an SPI master device to an SPI slave:

- SCLK (System Clock).
- MOSI (Master Out Slave In).
- SS (Slave Select).

An optional fourth signal, the Master In Slave Out (MISO) connection, is not used by the MCP4821.

CHAPTER 16 VOLTAGE CONTROL, GATES, AND TRIGGERS   257

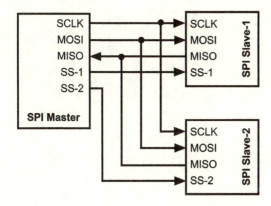

FIGURE 16.3 Master to SPI Slave connections

One potential source of confusion is that several naming schemes are used to describe SPI pins, so note that pins 2–4 in Figure 16.4 (CS, SCK, and SDI) use alternative names for the SS, SCLK, and MOSI connections found on some other devices.

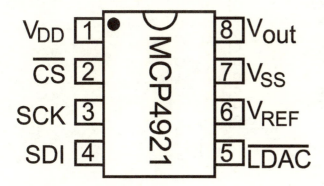

FIGURE 16.4 MCP4821 DAC

DAC WIRING

Figure 16.5 illustrates the SPI connections for a single DAC. The SCLK and MOSI/SDI pins (as well as +3.3V and GND) are connected to *all* SPI devices, but each device will have its own unique CS connection to the microcontroller.

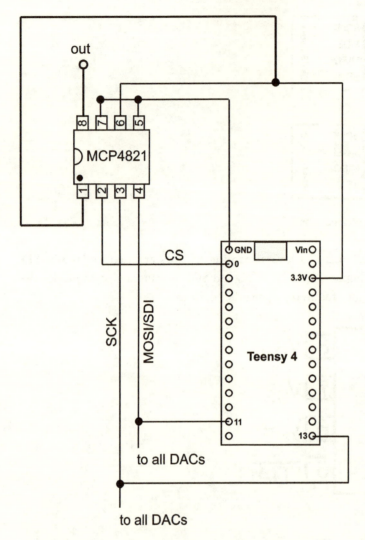

FIGURE 16.5 Connecting an MCP4821 to Teensy 4 (or similar)

TABLE 16.4 DAC pin assignments

MCP4821 PIN	Teensy 4.0 Pin
1-Vdd	+3.3V
2-CS	D0 (assignable)
3-SCK	13
4-SDI	11
5-LDAC	GND
6-SHDN	+3.3V
7-Vss	GND
8-Vout	Connect to op amp output circuit

AMPLIFICATION CIRCUITRY

One approach to outputting control voltage is to produce a narrow range of voltages from a DAC and amplify the output with a pair of op amps. For this experiment, an MCP4821 DAC is configured to output voltages in the range of 0–2.048V. The output of the DAC passes through the circuit shown in Figure 16.6, which amplifies the output by 5x. With precision resistors, this approach has provided excellent accuracy in my tests and can be adjusted up or down about 3 volts with a biasing potentiometer. A 20k input resistor works with the 100k feedback resistor to provide –5x amplification via the first inverting op amp. The second op amp inverts the signal back to its original orientation and does not provide additional gain.

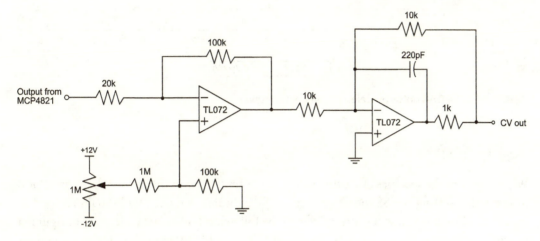

FIGURE 16.6 Amplification circui

A voltage control amplifier circuit is shown in Figure 16.7 and was previously detailed in Chapter 12. Figure 16.8 illustrates the accuracy of control voltages measured, in reference to ground, after passing through the circuit. Note that resistors with 1% precision were used for this test.

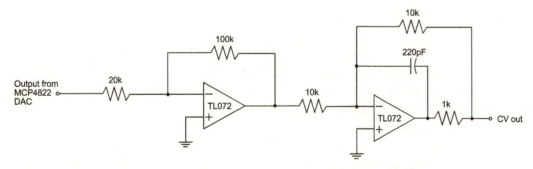

FIGURE 16.7 Simplified CV amplification circuit

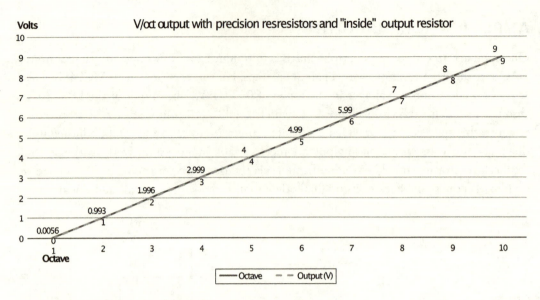

FIGURE 16.8 2V DAC outputs scaled 5X over nine octaves

Prepping for SPI

We will look at the specifics of writing values to the DAC later in the chapter, but it is helpful to know that setting the SS (or CS) pin to LOW indicates that the DAC should respond to incoming SPI data. You will want to refer to the following boilerplate code that configures a microcontroller pin for output, sets the pin to HIGH (which signals the DAC to ignore incoming values), and begins SPI communication with a call to *SPI.begin()* (see Listing 16.3):

Listing 16.3 Boilerplate code for SPI setup

```
#include <SPI.h>

const int cs_pin = 0;

void setup()
{
    //Set pins for output and default to HIGH
    //(pins go low only for writing data)
    pinMode(cs_pin, OUTPUT);
    digitalWrite(cs_pin, HIGH);

    //Start SPI communication
    delay(10);
    SPI.begin();

}
```

UPDATING THE DAC

The output of the MCP4821 is configured through commands sent via the Serial Peripheral Interface. As described in the datasheet, communication is initiated by setting the CS pin

CHAPTER 16 VOLTAGE CONTROL, GATES, AND TRIGGERS

low and clocking configuration and data bits into the SDI pin. The write-command register, shown in Figure 16.9 and described in Table 16.4, is comprised of four configuration bits (bits 15–12) and twelve data bits representing the 12-bit word (bits 11–0). Phrased another way, the DAC takes a 16-bit integer containing both a 4-bit configuration header and a 12-bit value.

W-x	W-x	W-x	W-0	W-x	W-x	W-x	W-x	W-x	W-x	W-x	W-x	W-x	W-x	W-x	W-x
0	—	$\overline{GA}$	SHDN	D11	D10	D9	D8	D7	D6	D5	D4	D3	D2	D1	D0
bit 15															bit 0

FIGURE 16.9 Write Command Register for MCP4821

TABLE 16.5 Write Command Register descriptions (adapted from datasheet)

Bit	Settings
15	0 = Write to DAC register1 = Ignore this command
14	Don't Care
13	**GA:** Output Gain Selection bit1 = 1x (VOUT = VREF * D/4096) 0 = 2x (VOUT = 2 * VREF * D/4096), where internal VREF = 2.048V.
12	**SHDN:** Output Shutdown Control bit 1 = Active mode operation. VOUT is available.0 = Shutdown the device. Analog output is not available. VOUT pin is connected to 500k (typical).
11-0	**D11:D0:** DAC Input Data bits.

Listing 16.4 shows a function, *updateDAC()*, that handles communication with the DAC. The function takes an integer representing the chip select pin and an unsigned integer containing the requested 12-bit voltage level. Sending the CS pin as a parameter enables the function to work with more than one DAC connected to the Serial Peripheral Interface. An approach for outputting to a two-channel DAC is shown later in the chapter.

Listing 16.4 updateDAC() function uses Vref (2.048V) as max DAC output

```
void updateDAC(int cs, uint16_t value)
{

    uint16_t out = (0 << 15) | (0 << 14) | (1 << 13) | (1 << 12) | (value);

    //Set chip select LOW and transfer a 16-bit
    //value as two bytes:
    digitalWrite(cs, LOW);
    SPI.transfer(out>>8);
    SPI.transfer(out & 0xFF);
    //End transmission by setting chip select HIGH
    digitalWrite(cs, HIGH);
}
```

The first line of the *updateDAC()* method packs the incoming voltage value into the lower twelve bits of a 16-bit integer and uses bit twiddling to set each of the highest four bits to 0 or 1.

```
uint16_t out = (0 << 15) | (1 << 14) | (1 << 13) | (1 << 12) | (voltage);
```

In this case, the left-shift operator writes a digital '1' or '0' to bits 12–15 and those bits are "ORed" together with the bitwise OR operator. One way to visualize the process is to think of the bitwise OR operator as "glue" that groups individual bits together. Each bit is set using the shift operator where *value* is the value—either "1" or "0"—and *bit* is the location of the bit from 0–15:

```
(value << bit)
```

The remaining lines of code look like other SPI transactions in that the following steps are required to send data to the DAC:

1. The Slave Select (or Chip Select) pin is set to LOW to indicate the DAC is about to receive incoming data.
2. Data is transmitted to the DAC.
3. The SS pin is reset to HIGH so that the SPI device will ignore any additional messages until the SS pin is set LOW.

One potentially confusing aspect of the transaction shown in Listing 16.4 is that the 16-bit value must be transmitted in two 8-bit bytes. The right-shift operator (*out>>8*) provides a way to retrieve the high byte, and binary masking (*out & 0xFF*) provides convenient access to the low byte.

Don't worry if bit manipulation, shifting, and masking look unfamiliar. The low-level details are less important than understanding that specific bits need to be set to configure the DAC and 16-bit values must be broken into two 8-bit bytes when transmitting to the DAC.

EXAMPLE: SIMPLE MIDI TO CV CONVERSION

The 12-bit DAC and amplification circuitry makes quick work of the task of converting MIDI Note-On messages to control voltages, and the code for sending control voltages is just as easy. The trick is to be mindful of the units for each stage of the conversion process. The DAC takes 12-bit values in the range of 0–4095 and, as configured, outputs a maximum of 2.048 volts. The two-volt range is amplified five times by the pair of op amps and provides control voltages in the range of 0 to approximately eight volts. For example, the *amplified* DAC outputs 5V for a 12-bit input of 2000, so a 12-bit value of 400 (2000/5) produces 1 volt at the output (see Table 16.6). Hence, a semitone is equivalent to the floating-point number 33.33 (400/12) in this 12-bit DAC system.

TABLE 16.6 Control Voltage unit examples

DAC Input (12-bit)	DAC Output	Amplified Output
2000	1V	5V
1000	0.5V	2.5V
400	0.2V	1V
33.33	0.016V	0.0833V

The code for outputting volts per octave is shown in Listing 16.5. Although the floating point values are rounded when they are sent to the *updateDAC()* function, accuracy was acceptable when I tested the output with a multimeter.

Listing 16.5 Volts per octave output using 5x amplification (setup code not shown)

```
float volt = 2000.0 /5;
float semitone = volt / 12.0;

void noteOnHandler(byte channel, byte note, byte velocity)
{
    float n = note;
    //Convert note to voltage representing a semitone
    float voltage = n * semitone;
    //Send the voltage to the DAC
    updateDAC(cs_pin_1, voltage);
}


void updateDAC(int cs, uint16_t value)
{
    uint16_t out = (0 << 15) | (0 << 14) | (1 << 13) |
        (1 << 12) | (value);

    //Set chip select LOW and transfer 16-bit value
    //as two bytes
    digitalWrite(cs, LOW);
    SPI.transfer(out>>8);
    SPI.transfer(out & 0xFF);

    //End transmission by setting chip select HIGH
    digitalWrite(cs, HIGH);
}
```

MIDI Velocity to CV Conversion

The code in Listing 16.5 can be adapted to handle the conversion of MIDI velocities. One approach is to scale incoming velocities (which are in the range of 0–127) to a 12-bit value. For example, the following pseudo-code translates MIDI velocity to a 0–5V range using the circuitry described in this section:

```
float velocity_percent = velocity / 127;
float velocity_cv = velocity_percent * 2000; // 2000 = 5V output
```

Reading Control Voltages

Chapter 12 details a circuit for processing incoming control voltages (see Figure 16.10). The circuit uses an inverting op amp running on 3.3V to bias and scale control voltage input to levels that may safely be read by the analog inputs of a microcontroller. More circuit details are provided in Chapter 12.

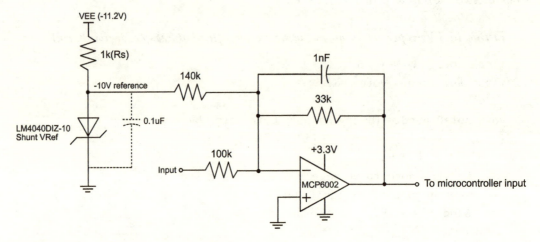

FIGURE 16.10 Control voltage input circuit

The first step in the conversion process is to configure the analog pins to read at 12-bits (0–4095) instead of the default 8-bit input (0–1023) as shown in Listing 16.5.

Listing 16.6 Configuring analog pins to read at 12 bits

```
void setup()
{
    //Set input resolution to 12 bits
    analogReadResolution(12);
}
```

Next, we use the concept of equivalent ratios to convert the incoming 12-bit values provided by the ADC into floating point numbers representing the 0–3.3V range provided by the scaling circuit:

$$\frac{x}{3.3V} = \frac{val}{4096}$$

EXAMPLE

$$\frac{x}{3.3V} = \frac{416}{4096}$$

$$x = \left(\frac{416}{4096}\right)3.3V$$

$$x = 0.335V$$

Listing 16.7 shows a simple function that converts 12-bit ADC values into 3.3V floating-point numbers:

Listing 16.7 Converting 12-bits to 3.3V

```
float convert12BitTo3V(float value)
{
    return (value/4096) * 3.3;
}
```

A final step is to plug the scaled 3.3V value into the formula shown below to tease out the full-range input voltage that was received by the circuit (see Figure 16.11). The circuit and formula are described in a helpful Texas Instruments document titled "Single-supply Op Amp Design."[4]

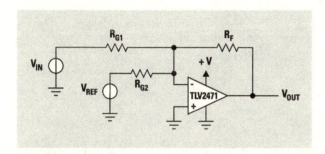

FIGURE 16.11 CV input circuit

$$Vout = -Vin\left(\frac{RF}{RG1}\right) - Vref\left(\frac{RF}{RG2}\right)$$

TABLE 16.7 Circuit values

Component or level	Value
RG1	100K
RG2	140K
Rf	33K
Vref	–10V
Vin	unknown

EXAMPLE

To determine the unknown input voltage, apply the values representing the reference voltage and resistance and solve. For example, the following full-range input voltage was determined from a scaled output value of 2.043V using the component values shown in Table 16.7:

$$2.043Vout = -Vin\left(\frac{33k}{100k}\right) - -10Vref\left(\frac{33k}{140k}\right)$$

$$2.043Vout = -Vin(0.33) + 2.357Vref$$

$$2.043Vout + Vin(0.33) = +2.357Vref$$

$$Vin(0.33) = 2.357Vref - 2.043Vout$$

$$Vin = \frac{0.314}{0.33}$$

$$Vin = 0.9215$$

Listing 16.8 demonstrates an approach to calculating full-range input voltage levels using the previous formula.

Listing 16.8 Function for converting scaled voltages back to full-range levels

```
float convert3Vto10V(float v_out_3v)
{
    /* Using 33k feedback resistor, 100k input resistor,
     * and 140k bias resistor with -10V reference
     */
    return ((2.357 - v_out_3v) / 0.33);
}
```

Depending on the precision of the resistors used in the scaling circuit, it may be necessary to multiply the results with a tuning constant. For example, when I used a combination of resistors with 5% and 1% accuracy, calculated inputs were slightly off from the known input level. In this case, multiplying each calculated value by a tuning constant improved the scaling accuracy of the circuit. Of course, utilizing resistors with 1% precision will improve performance. Table 16.8 shows the results of the conversion of eight octaves of volt-per-octave input:

TABLE 16.8 Control voltage input test (tuning constant applied)

Octave	Keyboard Volts	Difference	Scaling Circuit Volts	Difference	12-bit ADC Input	Difference
0	0.0027		0.00		2982	
1	0.995	−0.9923	0.99	−0.99	2570	412
2	1.994	−0.999	2.00	−1.01	2152	418
3	2.992	−0.998	3.01	−1.01	1734	418
4	3.991	−0.999	4.01	−1.00	1319	415
5	4.98	−0.989	5.01	−1.00	902	417
6	5.98	−1	6.01	−1.00	487	415
7	6.98	−1	7.01	−1.00	70	417
	Average step size	−0.996757143		−1.00		416
	Accuracy	−0.996757143		−0.998573466		

Tip: As you will see in Chapter 19, the combination of an external ADC, separate 3.3V power supply, and precision resistors provides the best accuracy—which is desirable for V/oct inputs.

Gates and Triggers

In contrast to V/oct control voltage, gates and triggers are "on or off" voltages that are typically used to transmit timing clocks or trigger an envelope generator. Eurorack synthesizers utilize an approach called V-Trigger (Voltage Trigger), which uses zero volts to indicate off and a positive voltage such as +5V to signify that the gate or trigger is active. Bear in mind that other strategies have been used by manufacturers including higher voltage levels and even negative voltage, so it is important to check manufacturer specifications before attempting to connect components.[5]

HOW ARE GATES AND TRIGGERS USED?

Where a trigger is a momentary signal lasting perhaps one millisecond, gates are often on for the duration of an event such as a keypress. However, this isn't entirely standardized, and some overlap exists between the terms trigger and gate depending on the manufacturer. Figure 16.12 provides a visualization of the relationship between a typical v-trigger and gate signal:

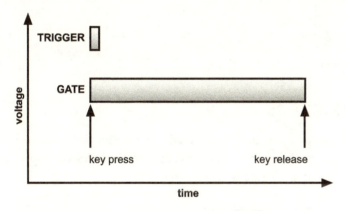

FIGURE 16.12 Typical trigger pulse and gate signal

While a trigger might be used to initiate a component such as an attack-decay envelope generator, a gate can keep the envelope in sustain mode until a key or other controller is released (see Figure 16.13).

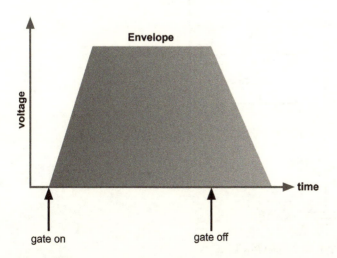

FIGURE 16.13 Using a gate to indicate the release phase of an envelope

A benefit of separating gate and trigger signals can be seen in Figure 16.14, an illustration based on an article by Gordon Reid in *Sound on Sound*.[6] Here, it is easy to see how re-triggering can be useful in initiating a new transient for each note. Assuming a performance of several legato notes, the envelope would be "stuck" at the sustain level without the attacks provided by additional triggers. Of course, this is all dependent on the capability and configuration of a given instrument. Although Eurorack synthesizers generally do not separate gates and triggers, these logical signals can work together as partners in other contexts.

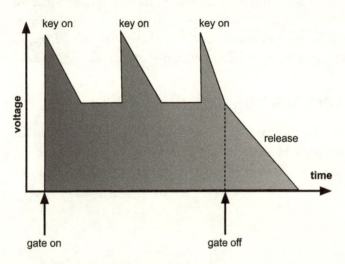

FIGURE 16.14 Re-triggering and envelope

SENDING GATES AND TRIGGERS

Chapter 12 details the use of a non-inverting op amp configuration for outputting gates and triggers (shown again in Figure 16.15). In this configuration, the op amp produces an approximately 5.1V output for a typical 3.3V signal from a microcontroller.

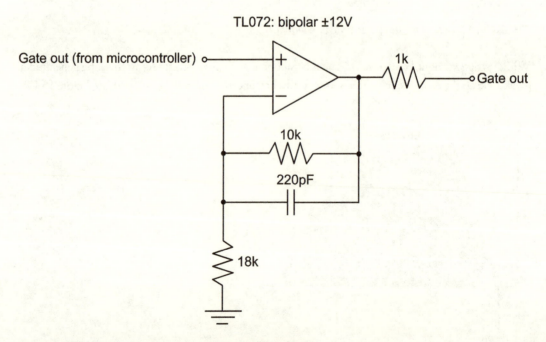

FIGURE 16.15 A non-inverting gate output amplifier circuit

As shown in Listing 16.9, a simple call to *digitalWrite()* is all that is required to send gate messages. These functions would also likely include additional code to toggle LEDs or related tasks.

Listing 16.9 Source code to output a gate or trigger

```
void gateOn(int gate_pin)
{
    digitalWrite(gate_pin, HIGH);
}

void gateOff(int gate_pin)
{
    digitalWrite(gate_pin, LOW);
}
```

Receiving Gates and Triggers

As detailed in Chapter 12, an op amp can also be configured to receive triggers and gates (see Figure 16.16).

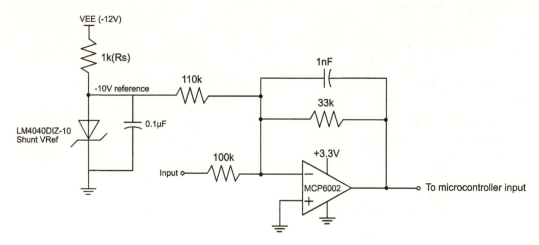

FIGURE 16.16 Gate input circuit

The output of the gate is inverted, so "off" means "on" and vice versa when using a transistor in this way (see Listing 16.10).

Listing 16.10 Reading (inverted) gate signals

```
void trackGate(int gate_pin)
{
    if(digitalRead(gate_pin) == LOW)
    {
        //Gate is on: do something interesting here
    }else if (digitalRead(gate_pin) == HIGH)
    {
        //Gate is off: stop doing something interesting here
    }
}
```

Practical Application: A Simple MIDI to Control-Voltage Converter

One useful application of the concepts detailed in this chapter is a MIDI to Control-Voltage converter. Surprisingly, it takes less than 100 lines of code to create a simple converter. This project forms the basis for the Eurorack MIDI to CV converter, one of the projects in the final section of the book.

PREAMBLE

A brief "preamble" includes header files for SPI and MIDI communication, establishes constants representing digital pins, and defines several variables to handle DAC conversion and trigger type (see Listing 16.10). A final step is the creation of a UART MIDI object created with the MIDI_CREATE_INSTANCE directive as covered in Chapter 8.[7]

Listing 16.11 MIDI to Control Voltage "preamble"

```
#include <SPI.h>
#include <MIDI.h>

//Chip select and gate pins
const int cs_pin = 1;
const int gate_out_pin = 2;

//Volt and semitone using 12-bit DAC and 5x amplification
float volt = 2000.0 /5;
float semitone = volt / 12.0;

//Tuning offset
float tuning_offset = 0.0;

//Store last_note to prevent extraneous offs
//for legato playing
int last_note = 0;

MIDI_CREATE_INSTANCE(HardwareSerial, Serial1, MIDI);
```

SETUP() AND LOOP() FUNCTIONS

The *setup()* and *loop()* functions, shown in Listing 16.11, configure the microcontroller for SPI and MIDI communication using the boilerplate code from this and other chapters. Note that *MIDI.read()*, called each iteration of the main loop, will automatically call the appropriate MIDI handler for any Note-On or Note-Off message.

CHAPTER 16 VOLTAGE CONTROL, GATES, AND TRIGGERS   271

Listing 16.12 MIDI to Control Voltage sketch

```
void setup()
{
    //Set up SPI for the DAC
    pinMode(cs_pin, OUTPUT);
    digitalWrite(cs_pin, HIGH);

    //Start SPI communication
    delay(100);
    SPI.begin();

    //Start UART MIDI input and set MIDI handlers
    MIDI.begin(MIDI_CHANNEL_OMNI);
    MIDI.setHandleNoteOn(noteOnHandler);
    MIDI.setHandleNoteOff(noteOffHandler);
}

void loop()
{
    MIDI.read();
}
```

MIDI HANDLERS

The MIDI handling functions, described in Chapter 8, are called in response to Note-On and Note-Off events. The Note-On handler shown in Listing 16.12 multiplies the MIDI note number by the calculated semitone value and adds a tuning offset—a useful feature when using multiple synthesizers and voltage control sources. The function updates the DAC by passing the pin number associated with the DAC and calculated 12-bit voltage level. The function also stores the given note as *last_note* to prevent extraneous Note-Off messages that can occur with legato playing. Finally, the function also calls *gateOn()*, from Listing 16.9, which outputs a V-Trigger gate.

Listing 16.13 MIDI note-On handler

```
void noteOnHandler(byte channel, byte note, byte velocity)
{
    float n = note;
    float voltage = (n * semitone) + tuning_offset;
    if(velocity!= 0)
    {
        updateDAC(cs_pin, voltage);
        gateOn(gate_out_pin);
        last_note = note;
    }else{
        //Note-On with velocity of zero = Note-Off
        noteOffHandler(channel, note, velocity);
    }
}
```

The Note-Off function simply checks the given MIDI note against *last_note* and sends a Gate-Off message as appropriate.

Listing 16.14 MIDI note-Off handler

```
void noteOffHandler(byte channel, byte note, byte velocity)
{
    if(note == last_note)
    {
        gateOff(gate_out_pin);
    }
}
```

UPDATEDAC(): TWO-CHANNEL OUTPUT

The *updateDAC()* function is responsible for sending 12-bit values to the DAC via the SPI connection and utilizes code that is similar to Listing 16.4 earlier in the chapter. Listing 16.14 is an adaptation that enables an MCP4822 DAC to provide two channels of output.[8] Although the code is nearly identical to the single-channel example, the fifteenth bit is set or cleared to output from DACB or DACA (see Listing 16.14). The revised code is shown in bold.

Listing 16.15 updateDAC function with two-channel output with an MCP4822 DAC

```
void updateDAC(int cs, int channel, uint16_t value)
{
    uint16_t out = (channel << 15) | (0 << 14) |
        (1 << 13) | (1 << 12) | (value);

    //Set chip select LOW and transfer 16-bit value as two bytes
    digitalWrite(cs, LOW);
    SPI.transfer(out>>8);
    SPI.transfer(out & 0xFF);
    //End transmission by setting chip select HIGH
    digitalWrite(cs, HIGH);
}
```

SUMMARY

While the MIDI to Control Voltage converter described in this section is primitive, it can be built on a solderless breadboard or protoboard and can provide a useful (and inexpensive) addition to a Eurorack setup. Many enhancements are possible including support for polyphonic output or USB MIDI input. Other options could include a potentiometer or encoder to select a tuning offset or support for selectable Hz/V control. It would also make sense to add an LED to indicate incoming MIDI messages and provide a rotary switch or other method for selecting the active MIDI channel. Finally, a monophonic converter would benefit from a second channel of control voltage dedicated to MIDI velocity, which could be applied to many synthesizer parameters to enhance expression. Several of these enhancements are included in the Eurorack MIDI/CV converter project in the final section of the book.

CHAPTER 16 VOLTAGE CONTROL, GATES, AND TRIGGERS

Calibration

One key feature that is missing from the project is a method for calibration. Products such as the Gracious Host from North Coast Synthesis provide a way to fine-tune the output of the device, a desirable feature for a MIDI to CV converter. The Gracious Host performs output calibration by sending control voltages to an external VCO and analyzing the frequency that is returned by the VCO. For a DIY project, brute force calibration could be achieved by testing the output of the DAC with a multimeter and using those measurements to create a lookup table. With that said, the output of the circuits and code detailed in this chapter has been adequate in my tests.

CREATIVE CHALLENGE

Gates, triggers, and control voltage circuits open the door to unique Eurorack controllers, sequencers, and the like. A few of the many possible directions for creative exploration include:

- Apply the concepts from Chapter 1 to create a light-to-CV converter.
- Connect an Arduino nunchuck breakout adapter to a Teensy and output control voltages based on the nunchuck's position.
- Code a stand-alone random CV generator.
- Code a stand-alone polyrhythmic gate generator.
- Create a project that tracks incoming clock signals and subdivides or alters the clock.
- Create a CV effect module that clips, delays, multiplies, or otherwise mangles a control voltage signal.

PART IV
EURORACK PROJECTS

CHAPTER 17

BUILDING A EURORACK EFFECTS UNIT

Practice is the best of all instructions.[1]

BOB KATZ, Author of *Mastering Audio*

Bob Katz provides sage advice. We have covered a lot of ground to prepare to take the training wheels off, and now it is time to apply the concepts to several full-fledged Eurorack projects. For the most part, these final projects are comprised of building-block concepts presented in previous chapters, so consider how you might improve and adapt the projects to your own needs. The beauty of DIY electronics is that the builder is free to envision unique applications of the underlying technologies. Fluency with those technologies will yield a vast creative potential where circuits and code extend the creative palette. As with learning an instrument, practice *is* the best instruction. Take your time, be prepared to learn from mistakes, and enjoy a process that can be deeply satisfying.

Overview of the Eurorack Effects Unit

The Eurorack Effects Unit is a relatively simple project that combines the power and audio circuits from Chapters 13 and 14 with concepts from the Digital Signal Processing chapter (Chapter 7). The unit takes a mono audio signal and provides four effects that are selected via a pushbutton switch. Most of the code is provided by the PJRC Audio System Design Tool, so it is simple to customize the project with other pre-built effects (or roll your own as described in Chapter 7). As shown in Figure 17.1, the unit provides jacks for audio input and output. The device also provides five potentiometers to control input level, output level, wet-to-dry ratio, rate, and depth. (The function of the rate and depth pots depends on the active effect.)

Sound & Music Projects for Eurorack and Beyond. Brent Edstrom, Oxford University Press. © Oxford University Press 2024.
DOI: 10.1093/9780197514504.003.0017

FIGURE 17.1 Completed effects unit

A bill of materials (BOM), Gerber files (for printing PCBs), and other project resources are available for download from the OUP website.

Circuit Design

The effects unit utilizes several subcircuits consisting of a power section, audio input and output section, and control section. As described in the following paragraphs, the project can be built around inexpensive custom PCBs or solder board.

POWER SECTION

The power section was detailed in Chapter 13 and a similar circuit is shown in Figure 17.2. Four capacitors (C1–C4) help to smooth the power supply and a voltage regulator (U1) provides 5 volts to power a Teensy 4. For best results, remember to keep capacitors C5 and C6 close to the input and output of the regulator. Also, remember to connect the individual pins of each section of the power header: +12V to +12V, GND to GND, and –12V to –12V to avoid relying on a single strand of the ribbon cable for power.

Warning: be sure to read PJRC's instructions for Using External Power with USB at https://www.pjrc.com/teensy/external_power.html. Instructions are provided for separating external power from USB power—a necessary step if you want to upload code to the device while it is running from a Eurorack power source.

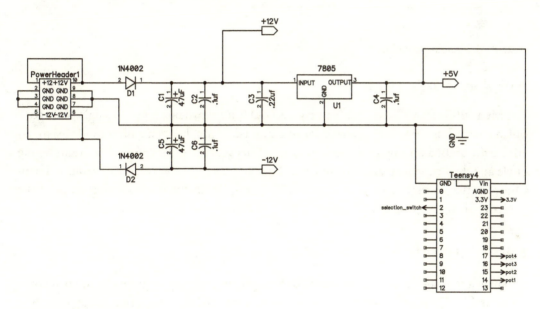

FIGURE 17.2 Power section

AUDIO INPUT

Audio input is handled by the op amp circuit shown in Figure 17.3 and described in Chapter 12. Although low-voltage audio input *can* be handled directly by the audio adapter, the op amp (as configured) provides some protection for the adapter—which can be damaged by voltage levels above its supply voltage or below ground. An MCP6002 op amp is powered by 3.3V and biases the incoming signal around a reference voltage formed from resistors R8 and R9 (see Chapter 13 for more information). A 4.7k feedback resistor works in conjunction with a 10k input resistor to provide a gain of –0.47, and a 10k potentiometer mitigates signal clipping by providing pre-circuit signal attenuation.

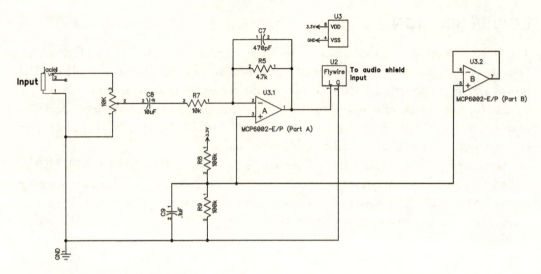

FIGURE 17.3 Audio input circuit

A Word about Unused Op Amps

The MCP6002 op amp (and TL072 in Figure 17.4) feature two op amps in a single package—which is what I prefer to keep on hand for single and dual use. It is generally a good idea to terminate the unused op amp to prevent noise and other problems. An approach for terminating single and dual-supply op amps is shown in Figures 17.3 and 17.4, respectively and relies on a unity buffer configuration for each unused op amp (with the non-inverting input of the single-supply op amp being tied to supply voltage/2).[2]

AUDIO OUTPUT

Although a separate op amp is not required to output an audio signal from the audio adapter, a bipolar TL072 op amp provides an opportunity for signal gain and offers some protection for the output pin.[3] More (or less) gain can be provided, as desired, by altering the ratio of resistors R8 and R5 shown in Figure 17.4. Unlike the input circuit, output levels are handled virtually by adjusting mixer audio objects in response to changes in the position of a potentiometer connected to one of the analog input pins. As with most of the output circuits in the book, a 1k resistor provides protection if the output is inadvertently shorted.

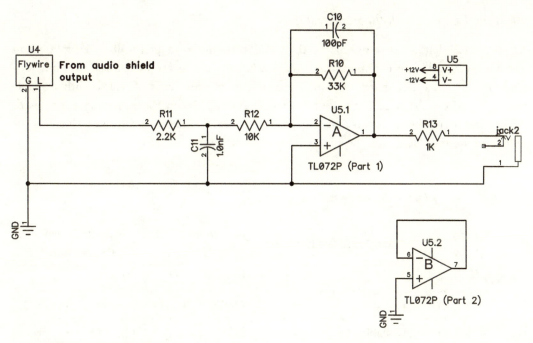

FIGURE 17.4 Audio output circuit

Using Wires

Wired connection points provide a convenient way to route audio signals to and from the audio adapter (located on top of a Teensy microcontroller) to the PCB. Although wires might be considered unprofessional, they can be useful, and I have noticed them in some commercial Eurorack products.

CONTROLS

The interface controls are purposely minimal and consist of a single momentary switch and four potentiometers. The potentiometers provide voltages in the range of GND to +3.3V and are read by analog pins A0–A3.

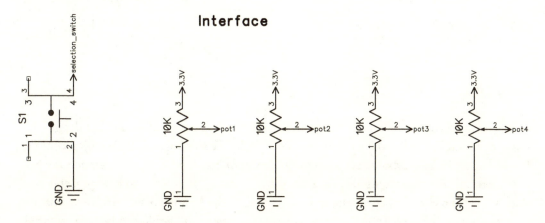

FIGURE 17.5 Momentary switch and potentiometers

SOUND & MUSIC PROJECTS FOR EURORACK AND BEYOND

Avoiding Conflicts with the Audio Adapter

One "gotcha" that is easy to overlook is the fact that the audio adapter utilizes several pins on the Teensy board, so it is important to avoid using those pins for switches, potentiometers, and the like. Table 17.1 shows revision-D pin assignments for Teensy 4 boards with available and optional pins.[4] For example, GPIO pin 6 is available if SPI flash memory is not used. Although the number of inputs and outputs might seem limited with the audio shield, additional inputs and outputs can be added using multiplexers.

TABLE 17.1 *Teensy 4 and Audio Board Rev. D connections*

Teensy 4 Pins		Audio Board Connections	Teensy 4 Pins		Audio Board Connections
GND			Vin	5V	N/A
0	RX1	Available	GND	GND	Used for audio GND
1	TX1	Available	3.3V	3.3V	+3.3V (250 mA max)
2		Available	23	A9	I2S MCLK1
3		Available	22	A8	Available
4		Available	21	A7	I2S BCLK1
5		Available	20	A6	I2S LRCLK1
6		SPI-CS for flash memory	19	A5	I2C (SCL)
7	RX2	I2S OUT1A	18	A4	I2C (SDA)
8	TX2	I2S IN1	17	A3	Available
9		Available	16	A2	Available
10	CS	SPI-CS for SD card	15	A1	Volume pot
11	MOSI	SPI-MOSI	14	A0	Available
12	MISO	SPI-MISO	13	(led)	SPI-SCLK

Designing a PCB

Once circuit schematics have been designed in DipTrace, Eagle, KiCad, or another design tool, the circuits can be used as the basis for a custom PCB. We won't rehash PCB design concepts from Chapter 15, but several concepts are worth mentioning. A primary consideration is where to place the Teensy microcontroller. Readers who are familiar with Arduino have probably used shields—custom circuits that are plugged into the top of the Arduino device. However, that approach is not feasible with Teensy devices without inordinately tall headers. A better approach is to mount the Teensy on the back of the PCB (along with the Eurorack power header) and save the front of the PCB for jacks, potentiometers, and other components (see Figure 17.6). A downside of the approach is that it can be challenging to incorporate jacks, pots, microcontroller, and through-hole components on a single PCB. An alternative approach is to use a second PCB in parallel or at right angles—an approach that is detailed in the chapters that follow.

CHAPTER 17 BUILDING A EURORACK EFFECTS UNIT 283

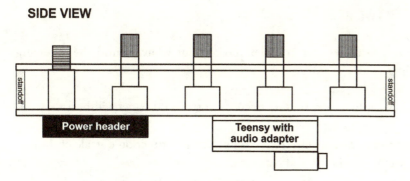

FIGURE 17.6 Mounting a Teensy on the back PCB

Figure 17.7 shows the completed PCB and front panel.

FIGURE 17.7 PCB and front panel

PCB Layout Strategies

It can be a challenge to run traces in a complex project, but I have found the following strategies to be helpful:

- Create the desired PCB outline first. Be sure to consider standard panel widths for Eurorack projects.
- Hide ratlines and drag and organize electronic components by function outside of the outline (e.g., power section, audio in, audio out, etc.).
- Orient each component to best advantage; for example, follow the circuit design and strive to place components strategically to minimize long traces or complex routings.
- Position user-interface components on the PCB and drag functional sections inside the layout.
- Strive to perfect the position of components on the board before running traces.
- Add a ground plane on the bottom layer before running power and signal traces.

The completed PCB design, suitable for use with a 10 HP front panel, is shown in Figure 17.8. Note the use of 3M mounting holes in each corner. The mounting holes provide a way to connect the PCB to a front panel via threaded standoffs and 3M nuts.

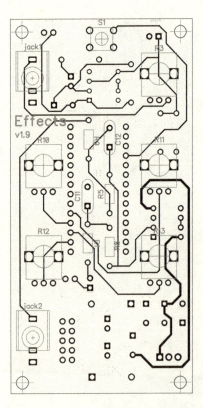

FIGURE 17.8 Completed effects unit PCB outline

Creating a PCB Front Panel

As described in Chapters 15 and 16, blank front panels can be purchased for a few dollars from vendors such as Sweetwater Sound and Amplified Parts. An alternative strategy is to use PCB design software to create the circuit boards *and* front panel. From my perspective, custom

PCB front panels are the best option from the standpoint of cost, aesthetics, and convenience (no drilling, decals, or painting!). The following steps have worked well for me:

1. Save a copy of the completed circuit board and remove all traces. (Look for an "edit selection" option in your software to make quick work of this step.)
2. Carefully add a mounting hole at the center of each front-panel component such as pots and switches and size the hole to leave a suitable margin for the part. I typically measure components with a drill-sizing template and add two sizes to the hole size of the component. Note that this step will only work if hole centers are clearly marked on the PCB components themselves.
3. Delete all components, leaving only the component holes and mounting holes.
4. Add text and graphics to the silkscreen.
5. Print a scale version of the front panel and circuit board and ensure all holes are at the correct location and of the correct size. This is also a good time to ensure that there is adequate room for each component by printing a paper copy of the PCB and setting components in their respective places.

The approach should yield a board with component holes and mounting holes that are in perfect alignment with the underlying PCB (see Figure 17.9).

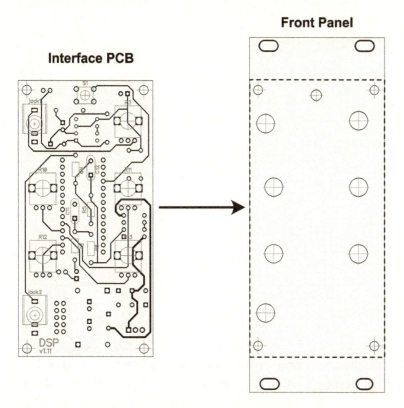

FIGURE 17.9 Deriving a front panel from a project PCB

Adding Graphics

Although it is tempting to import a graphic file for use as an overlay on the PCB, I have had better success importing and copying individual graphics due to scaling issues associated with the rasterization process. For example, use graphic design software to create markings for a single potentiometer and import the graphic to the silk layer of your PCB design. Resize the graphic to a suitable size and copy and paste the graphic to the other potentiometer holes. A similar process can be used for title text and logos, but I tend to use the stock PCB text tool for most text.

The completed front panel is shown in Figure 17.10.

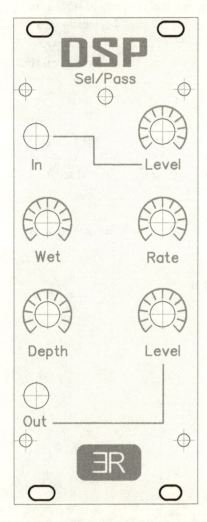

FIGURE 17.10 Completed front panel

Using Solder Board

Although I enjoy the process of creating PCBs, solder board circuits can also be a good option. Figures 17.11 and 17.12 illustrate one approach to circuit layout on a popular solder board form factor. The boards can be mounted using mounting brackets as described in Chapters 14 and 15:

CHAPTER 17 BUILDING A EURORACK EFFECTS UNIT 287

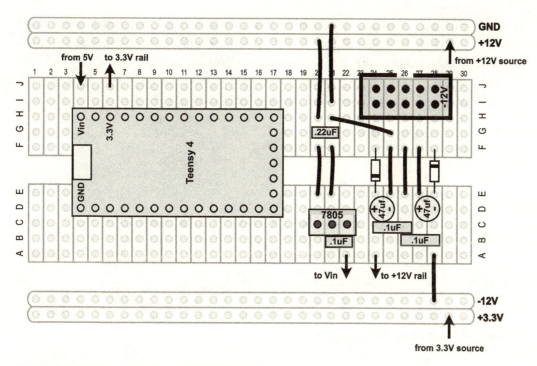

FIGURE 17.11 Solder board version (main board)

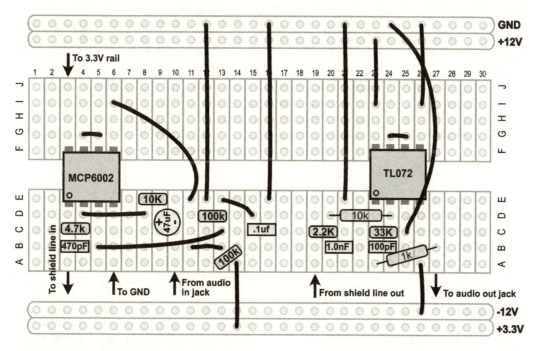

FIGURE 17.12 Solder board version (sub board)

Audio System Design Tool

We have already covered the ins and outs of using the audio design tool for DSP projects in Chapter 7, but it will be helpful to view the audio components used in this project to get a feel for the function of the effects unit (see Figure 17.13).[5] Monophonic audio enters the unit via the line input which passes the stream to a flanger, reverb, bit crusher, and delay effect. The effects are routed to the effects mixer (which functions as a switcher in code), and another copy of the "dry" signal is sent directly to the *effectsMixer* object, which provides a convenient method for blending the wet and dry signals. The blended signal arrives at the *main_mix* object which is controlled by the position of the output level potentiometer. Note that the Eurorack effects project is available from the OUP website.

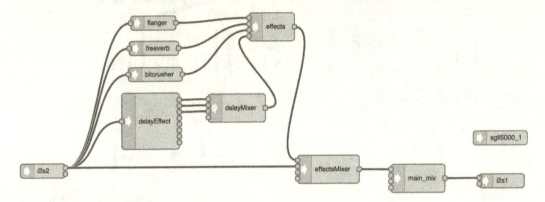

FIGURE 17.13 Audio Design Tool components

Main Loop

Given that the project relies on the Audio System Design Tool, the code for the Effects Processor is quite simple and consists of tracking the selection switch and potentiometers. This functionality is easy to see in the main loop (see Listing 17.1), which calls several handler functions:

Listing 17.1 Main loop

```
void loop()
{
    handleSwitch();
    handleVolumePot();
    handleWetnessPot(pot_sensitivity);
    handleFreqPot(pot_sensitivity);
    handleDepthPot(pot_sensitivity);
}
```

VOLUME

A potentiometer provides values for volume control. As shown in Listing 17.2, the value returned by *analogRead()* is compared to the previous value. If the new value differs from the previous value (plus or minus a sensitivity constant), the input is converted into a fractional value between 0 and 1.0 and applied to the gain of the main mixer object. The sensitivity parameter provides a way to avoid small spurious changes returned by the pot. More sophisticated approaches might involve a stabilization capacitor and/or a simple filtering or averaging.

Listing 17.2 Volume control

```
void handleVolumePot(int sensitivity)
{
    static int last_val = 0;
    //Read the value of the volume pot:
    int val = analogRead(volume_pot);
    //Update gain if the position of the pot has changed.
    if(val < last_val - sensitivity ||
        val > last_val + sensitivity)
    {
        last_val = val;
        level = (float) val / 1023.0;
        main_mix.gain(0, level);
    }
}
```

WETNESS

The wetness control functions similarly but, as wetness increases, it is subtracted from the dry signal—which serves to blend the signals within the 0–1.0 range expected by the audio system (see Listing 17.3).

Listing 17.3 Blending wet and dry signals

```
void handleWetnessPot(int sensitivity)
{
    //Set the ratio of wet and dry signals:
    //wet = percentage of 0-1, dry = 1-wet
    static int last_val = 0;
    int val = analogRead(wetness_pot);

    if(val < last_val - sensitivity || val > last_val + sensitivity)
    {
        last_val = val;
        float wetness = float(val) / 1023.0;
        effectsMixer.gain(1, wetness);
        effectsMixer.gain(0, 1.0 - wetness);
    }
}
```

FREQUENCY AND DEPTH

Frequency and depth controls are handled in a similar way, but the results are scaled as appropriate for each effect. For example, the *handleFreqPot()* function is shown in Listing 17.4. As with the previous functions, the potentiometer value is scaled to a range of values from 0–1.0 and that percentage is applied, as appropriate, for each effect. For simplicity, each effect is updated whenever the potentiometer changes position—regardless of its active status.

SOUND & MUSIC PROJECTS FOR EURORACK AND BEYOND

Listing 17.4 Updating frequency

```
void handleFreqPot(int sensitivity)
{
    //This pot sets flanger frequency, reverb room size,
    //and delay amount.

    static int last_val = 0;
    int val = analogRead(freq_pot);
    float percent = (float) val / 1023.0;

    if(val < last_val - sensitivity || val > last_val + sensitivity)
    {
        last_val = val;
        //=====Update flanger frequency=====
        if(current_effect == flanger_effect ||
          current_effect == tremolo_effect)
        {
            s_freq = 10.0 * percent;
            if(s_freq < 0.05)
            {
                s_freq = 0.05;
            }

            AudioNoInterrupts();
            flanger.voices(s_offset,s_depth,s_freq);
            tremolo.setFrequency(s_freq);
            AudioInterrupts();
            last_val = val;
        }

        //=====Update reverb room size=====
        if (current_effect == reverb_effect)
        {
            AudioNoInterrupts();
            freeverb.roomsize(room_size);
            AudioInterrupts();
        }

        //=====Update delay amount=====
        if(current_effect == delay_effect)
        {
            AudioNoInterrupts();
            first_delay = 200.0 * percent;
            delayEffect.delay(0, first_delay);
            delayEffect.delay(1, first_delay * 2.0);
            AudioInterrupts(); }
    }
}
```

SELECTING AN EFFECT

A single momentary switch cycles through the four effects and relies on a global enumeration for effect selection. Pressing the switch moves the global variable *current_effect* to the next effect and wraps around to the first effect as necessary (see Listing 17.5):

Listing 17.5 Selecting effects

```
//Enumeration to handle effect selection (global variables)
enum{reverb_effect, flanger_effect,
bitcrusher_effect, delay_effect};
int current_effect = reverb_effect;.
.
.
.

void handleSwitch()
{
    selectionSwitch.update();
    if(selectionSwitch.fallingEdge())
    {
        current_effect++;
        if(current_effect > delay_effect)
        {
            current_effect = reverb_effect;
        }
        selectEffect(current_effect);
    }
}
```

SELECTEFFECT()

The *selectEffect()* function is responsible for activating the selected effect. This is done with a loop that turns each channel off or on depending on the active effect:

Listing 17.6 selectEffect() function

```
void selectEffect(int effect)
{
    //Turn on the appropriate effect channel
    for(int i = 0; i < 4; i++)
    {
        if(effect == i)
        {
            //Turn active effect on
            effects.gain(i, level);
        }else{
            //Turn other effects off
            effects.gain(i, 0);
        }
    }
}
```

Summary

Although the Eurorack Audio Effects project is relatively small, it does illustrate a capable Eurorack module that is fun to use and relatively inexpensive to build. It also demonstrates just one of many approaches that could be taken with the project, so consider how you might adapt the project to your own needs. The project can be constructed on a solderless breadboard, or as was mentioned at the top of the chapter, Gerber files, BOM, and other resources are available from the OUP website should you want to order PCBs from a manufacturer.

CREATIVE CHALLENGE

I purposely kept this project simple to emphasize the application of core concepts, but many enhancements are possible, including several that I have incorporated into later iterations of the project. Many technical and creative options are possible, including:

- Adding multiple LEDs to indicate the active effect.
- Adding a retro toggle switch for passthrough mode.
- Enhancing code and circuitry for stereo input and output.
- Adding support for multi-effects.
- Coding new custom DSP components or incorporating other components from the Audio System Design Tool.
- Providing voltage control inputs to control volume, wetness, and other parameters.

CHAPTER 18

MIDI TO CONTROL-VOLTAGE CONVERTER

First make it work, then make it neat.[1]

ROBERT GROSSBLATT

Overview

The MIDI to Control-Voltage Converter project provides a useful addition to any Eurorack setup. While control voltages predominate in Eurorack systems, MIDI to control-voltage conversion opens the door to using computers, MIDI keyboards, and other devices as sources of voltage control.

The converter is comprised of a modest collection of circuits and code detailed in previous chapters and includes V/oct and gate/trigger output, onboard 5V power supply, and MIDI input. Since core concepts have been detailed in previous chapters, this chapter summarizes the building block elements and focuses on attributes that are unique to the project.

PROJECT DESCRIPTION

The module, shown in Figure 18.1, features a single five-pin MIDI input port and two pairs of 3.5mm outputs for transmission of control voltage and gate/trigger signals. Two operating modes and CV output types are selected via a pair of toggle switches. For this iteration of the project, operating mode 1 features a monophonic operation where incoming MIDI Note-On messages generate control voltages representing pitch and velocity, and incoming MIDI clock messages are translated into trigger signals sent from the second gate. Mode 2 features duophonic output where V/oct and gate signals are generated in response to MIDI messages on channels 1 and 2.

As with other projects in the book, source code, Gerber files, demonstration videos, and other resources are available from the OUP website.

Sound & Music Projects for Eurorack and Beyond. Brent Edstrom, Oxford University Press. © Oxford University Press 2024.
DOI: 10.1093/9780197514504.003.0018

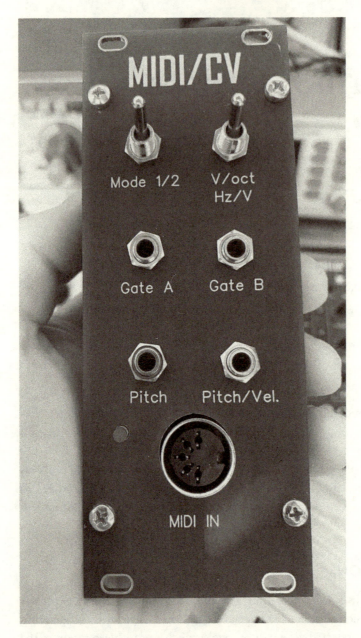

FIGURE 18.1 MIDI to control voltage converter

To this point, the projects and experiments presented in the book have been reasonable to build using stripboard or solder board. However, as projects increase in complexity, they can become more challenging to build on solder board—particularly within the size constraints of a typical Eurorack module. Given the modest cost of manufacturing printed circuit boards (PCBs), they make an attractive option and will be used in the final chapters of the book. With that said, core concepts can still be applied to a solderless breadboard for experimentation and development.

Developing a Eurorack Prototyping System

In this section, we look at an extensible approach to hardware design where a PCB "backpack" connects to a second PCB "interface." With this approach, the backpack houses a microcontroller and circuitry for 5V power and signal processing, and the interface PCB provides switches, jacks, LEDs, potentiometers, and other components that form the user interface. Signals, power, and ground are shared between PCBs via a set of pins and female headers, so the interface PCB can incorporate additional circuitry as needed. This approach, which is conceptually similar to Arduino *shields* and BeagleBone *capes*, makes it easy to use common circuitry as a foundation for multiple Eurorack projects by simply swapping out the interface and uploading new code. The approach is also economical. For example, 5–10 PCBs can be manufactured for about $5 at current budget PCB manufacturing rates.[2]

In the sections that follow we will explore the design, form, and function of the backpack and interface boards in the context of the MIDI to Control Voltage Converter project. Chapter 19 details a similar approach to an extensible Eurorack FM synthesizer.

A TYPICAL EXAMPLE

Figure 18.2 illustrates how the MIDI to Control Voltage backpack can function as a foundation for a typical MIDI-based Eurorack project. In this example, the backpack provides power to the Teensy and handles MIDI input and control voltage and gate output. While the interface PCB contains jacks and switches, the *same* backpack could just as easily be connected to an interface for a step sequencer, arpeggiator, or other instrument that features MIDI input, V/oct, and gate/trigger output.

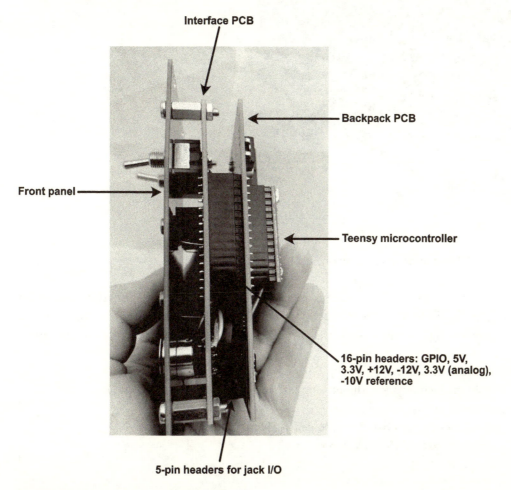

FIGURE 18.2 Backpack and interface PCBs

SURFACE MOUNT COMPONENTS? SAY IT ISN'T SO!

Through-hole components are convenient to use for prototyping and are a great choice for many projects, but there are a few distinct disadvantages: Through-hole components are generally larger than surface-mount devices (SMDs), they complicate or preclude population of components on both sides of a PCB, through-hole components are becoming harder to source, and some through-hole components are more expensive than equivalent SMDs. For these reasons, SMDs make sense for the Eurorack backpacks detailed in the final chapters of this book. Rest assured that SMDs can be just as easy to solder as through-hole components and, in some instances, they can be faster.[3] For example, 1206-size SMD resistors and capacitors don't require bending and snipping leads like most through-hole components (see Figure 18.3).

FIGURE 18.3 Hand-soldering a surface-mount resistor (1206 package)

While detailed instruction on surface-mount soldering is beyond the scope of this book, video tutorials are available at the OUP website as well as many fine tutorials on the web. With that said, the following tips have worked well for me when soldering SMD resistors and capacitors:

- Clean the surface of the PCB with 99% isopropyl alcohol.
- To avoid mistakes, work with only one capacitor or resistor value at a time.
- Apply no-clean flux to one or more pads.
- Apply a small amount of 0.3 mm solder to the tip of a soldering iron.
- Use tweezers to hold the part in position.

CHAPTER 18 MIDI TO CONTROL-VOLTAGE CONVERTER 297

- Use the solder tip to gently tack one side of the component into position.
- Hold 0.3 mm solder at right angles to the opposing side and solder.
- Repeat the previous step to solder the "tacked" side.

Use an appropriately sized soldering tip for SMD work. I use a beveled 1.5 mm tip and 0.3 mm solder wire when soldering SMDs with my Hakko iron. A lighted magnifying glass is also helpful unless you have amazing eyesight. Aside from developing a feel for tacking components in place, you might be surprised to find how easy it is to solder SMD parts.

Developing a Backpack Board

The backpack board shown in Figure 18.4 houses a Teensy microcontroller and provides access to the Teensy pins via two sixteen-pin headers. As shown in the illustration, the bottom-most outer pads also provide access to +12V, –12V, and a –10V reference as described in previous chapters. A 3.3V voltage regulator is also provided for analog devices since it can be useful to provide a separate power source for (noisy) digital and (sensitive) analog components. The outer rows of pads also provide access to +5V, +3.3V (Teensy power), and ground in addition to the GPIO pins. An inner set of pads provides a way to house a Teensy 4.0 microcontroller on fourteen-pin headers. Finally, the five pads at the bottom of the board provide a conduit for sending signals between the backpack and interface boards.

FIGURE 18.4 Backpack board (with Teensy)

Warning: Be sure to disconnect +5V USB power from external power as shown in Figure 18.5. The process will vary slightly depending on the board, and details are described on the PJRC website. Disconnecting USB power enables the module to be programmed from a computer while connected to Eurorack power.

FIGURE 18.5 Disconnecting 5V USB power from external power

POWER SECTION

As with other projects, the power section features protection diodes, smoothing capacitors, and 5V voltage regulation for the microcontroller. The power section also includes an optional −10V reference provided by an LM4040CIM3-10.0 shunt. Although the reference voltage isn't used in this project, the reference is useful for projects that read incoming voltages to provide tuning offset, pitch bend, or other functions (see Figure 18.6).

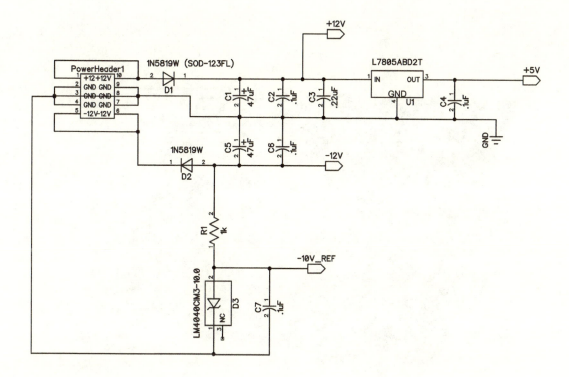

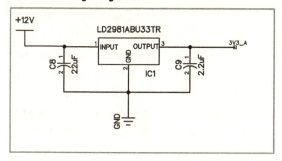

FIGURE 18.6 Power section with optional -10V reference

PCB DESIGN

A primary design goal was to minimize PCB costs and maximize versatility, so I chose an outer dimension of 100x49 mm. The 49 mm width is narrow enough to fit a 10 HP Eurorack module, and 100 mm is a common maximum dimension for budged PCB pricing. Once the outline was established, M3 mounting holes were added to the corners of the board. While mounting holes are not required when the PCB is used as a backpack, they do enable the boards to be more easily incorporated into interfaces utilizing through-hole components. For example, Figure 18.7 shows the use of wire connections and right-angle mounting with an early MIDI to CV prototype.

FIGURE 18.7 Fly wires connecting signals on a right-angled backpack

Headers and Pins

The backpack provides a pair of fourteen-pin headers to house the Teensy Microcontroller. A custom Teensy component was created in Diptrace and provided the footprint for the microcontroller.[4] A second custom part provides the footprint for a pair of sixteen-pin holes and a five-pin header (see Figure 18.8). The sets of header pads were combined into a single part in the Diptrace component editor to ensure perfect alignment between the backpack and interface.

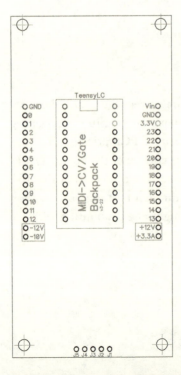

FIGURE 18.8 Teensy footprint and signal/power headers on base board

Pins can be soldered to the back of the backpack and connected to headers soldered to the back of an interface PCB as shown in Figure 18.9.

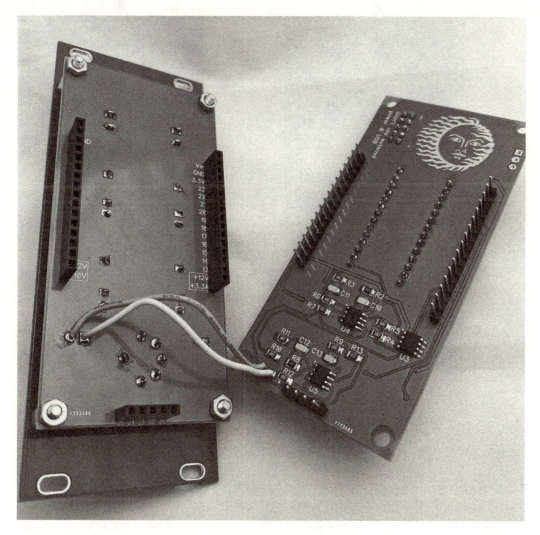

FIGURE 18.9 Pins and headers connecting backpack and interface

Caution: In Diptrace, the composite header component is placed on the top layer of the backpack PCB, but pins are soldered to the back of the backpack. However, the same composite header component is placed on the back of the interface PCB and headers are soldered to the back of the interface. As shown in Figure 18.9, this configuration maintains the proper orientation of pins for interconnection.

COMPONENT PLACEMENT

As described in previous chapters, components are placed in a logical arrangement following the original circuit design. Note how wider traces are used for power connections and ground pins are tied together into a copper pour on the back of the board (see Figure 18.10). Vias—small holes that provide a connection between the top and bottom layers—are useful for connecting surface mount components to the ground layer.

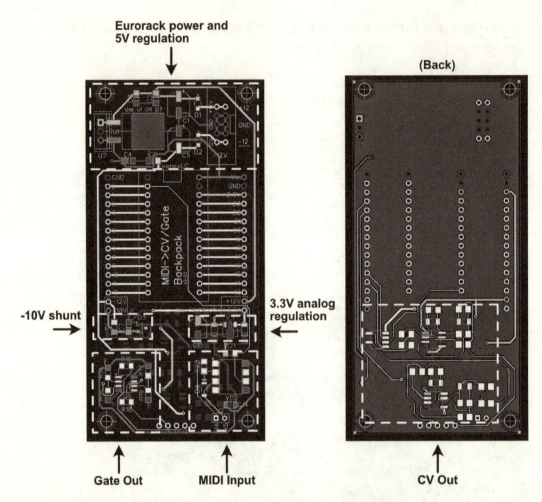

FIGURE 18.10 Component placement and traces (functional sections circled)

Experienced coders often use object-oriented programming to create reusable objects, and the backpack is, in many respects, a circuit-based form of that paradigm. The backpack provides a functional block that provides power, MIDI input, gate, and control voltage output. It can connect directly to a variety of interface boards, it can function with through-hole interface components via wires, and the backpack can also work as a stand-alone board for prototyping in conjunction with a solderless breadboard.

MIDI Processing

Figure 18.11 illustrates how incoming MIDI signals are processed and converted by circuitry attached to the microcontroller:

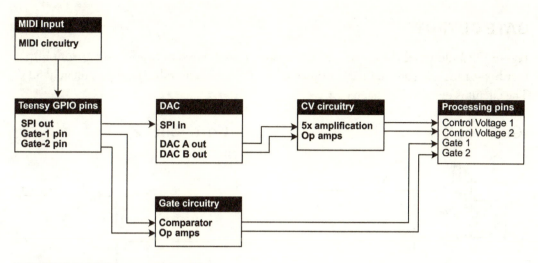

FIGURE 18.11 MIDI converter signal flow

TWO-CHANNEL DAC

Two channels of control voltage output are provided by a dual-channel MCP4822 DAC and a pair of dual op-amp integrated circuits (see Figure 18.12).[5] As described in Chapter 16, each pair of op amps provides a non-inverting gain of 5x—so the 2V output of the DAC can provide nearly ten octaves of voltage control. The MCP4822 features an internal voltage reference and has provided good results in my tests when used with precision resistors.

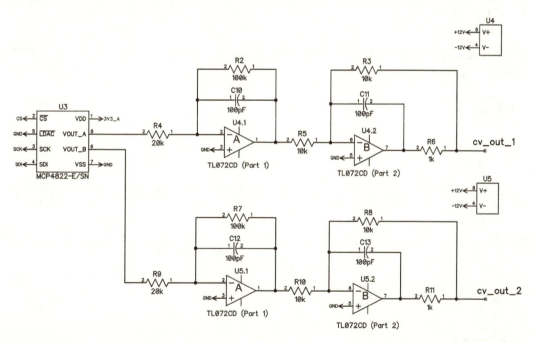

FIGURE 18.12 Control voltage output circuit

GATE OUTPUTS

Figure 18.13 illustrates the use of a pair of op amps, configured as control voltage amplifiers, that boost the 3.3V gate and trigger signals from the microcontroller to approximately 5.1V. The circuit is detailed in Chapter 12.

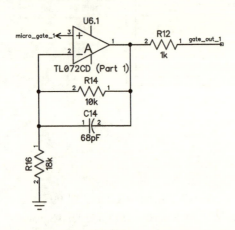
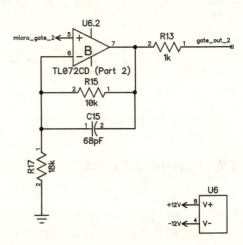

FIGURE 18.13 Gate output circuit

MIDI Input

MIDI input is provided by the circuit shown in Figure 18.14—an approach recommended by PJRC and described in Chapter 8.

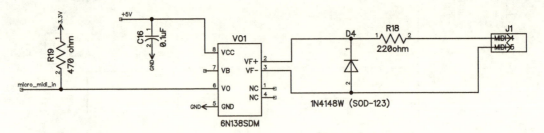

FIGURE 18.14 MIDI input circuit

INPUT AND OUTPUT

It is important to stress that incoming MIDI and outgoing CV and gate signals *must* be routed through the backpack via the five-pin header and MIDI wires. In this way, the backpack functions as a signal processor to the microcontroller.

Designing a User Interface Board

Although fly wires can be used to connect the backpack to through-hole components on a front panel, I prefer to use a separate PCB to house jacks, potentiometers, and the like. This approach provides access to a greater variety of interface components, facilitates tighter component spacing, and provides space for additional circuitry if needed.

INTERFACE COMPONENTS

The user interface for the MIDI to Control Voltage Converter consists of two toggle switches, two pairs of jacks for gate and control-voltage output, and a single five-pin DIN MIDI input jack. No additional circuitry is required beyond a current limiting resistor for the LED, so the components on the interface PCB connect directly to pins on the microcontroller through the backpack headers (see Figure 18.15).

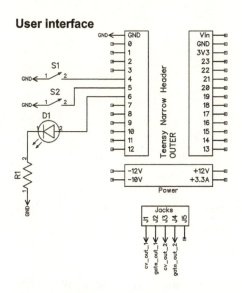

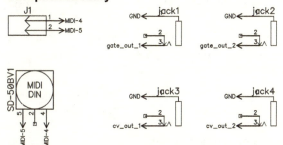

FIGURE 18.15 Interface circuit

MOUNTING HOLES

Four M3 mounting holes provide a convenient way to attach the interface PCB to a front panel. Assuming the front panel shares the same hole size and spacing, standoffs can be used to connect the interface (with attached backpack) to the front panel. Although the approach is not as elegant as the hidden mounting studs used on some commercial products, the method is inexpensive and provides a strong connection between the interface and the front panel (see Figure 18.16).

FIGURE 18.16 Using standoffs to connect a front panel to the user interface PC

FRONT PANEL

Attractive front panels can be designed using the methods outlined in previous chapters. For this project, I created a PCB front panel as detailed in Chapter 15. A benefit of the approach is that I received several copies of the PCBs and made multiple MIDI to CV converters for the price of a Teensy and a few components.

Although it took some time to design the MIDI/CV backpack, the reward is the ease with which other projects can be created by connecting the backpack to new interface boards.

Code Logic

The MIDI to CV converter has a few basic tasks to handle in code:

- Track the modes of operation and voltage control type via toggle switches.
- Respond to MIDI Note-On and Note-Off messages.
- Respond to MIDI clock messages.
- Turn on an LED to provide visual feedback in response to MIDI messages.

Given that relevant code has been provided in previous chapters, we will move to diagrams to provide a conceptual view of the operation of the unit. Ideally, this approach will facilitate the adaptation of core concepts for new applications. As with other projects in the book, the source code is available for download from the OUP website.

OPERATION AND CONTROL VOLTAGE MODES

Operation modes are handled with an if/else statement as shown in Figure 18.17, and the modes are stored in the global variable *active_mode*.

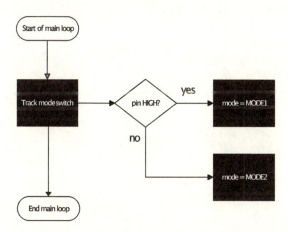

FIGURE 18.17 Operation mode and gate type selection

HANDLING NOTE-ON MESSAGES

The Note-On message handler lights the activity LED and passes the message to the appropriate Mode 1 or 2 handler. As shown in Figure 18.18, MIDI Note-Off messages are sometimes sent as Note-On messages with a velocity of zero, so that option is also handled by the algorithm:

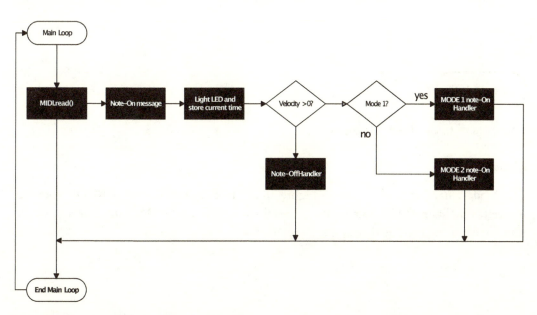

FIGURE 18.18 Note-On handler and LED status

Mode-1

The logic for handling MIDI messages when operating in Mode 1 is illustrated in Figure 18.19. Here, Note-On messages and velocities are output as control voltages and the gate-1 output is set to high to signal the Note-On event. As described in Chapter 16, the DAC receives values that are scaled to 1/5 the desired output level since the 2V output of the DAC is amplified 5x by a pair of inverting op amps.

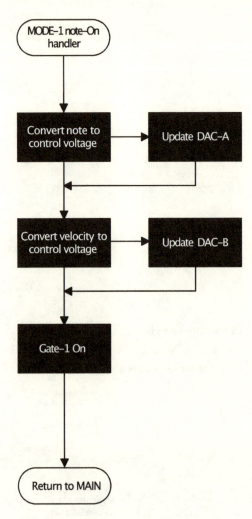

FIGURE 18.19 Mode-1 Note-On handler

Mode-2

The Mode-2 handler is illustrated in Figure 18.20. In this case, incoming MIDI Note-On messages on channels 1 or 2 are sent as control voltages from the DAC and gate signals are simultaneously emitted by their respective gate pins.

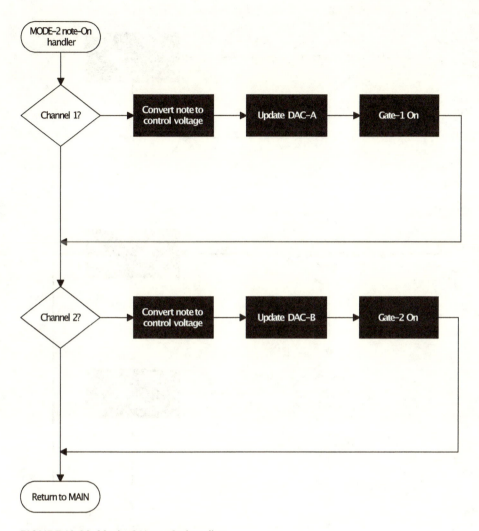

FIGURE 18.20 Mode-2 Note-On handler

Handling Note-Off Messages

Tracking gate status for Note-Off MIDI messages is complicated by the fact that Mode-1 functions as an omni mode and will respond to *any* MIDI Note-On messages. By contrast, Mode-2 messages must occur on channels 1 *or* 2 in this iteration of the firmware. This distinction is handled by three variables that track the most recently received omni note and any Note-On messages received from channels 1 and 2 (see Figure 18.21).

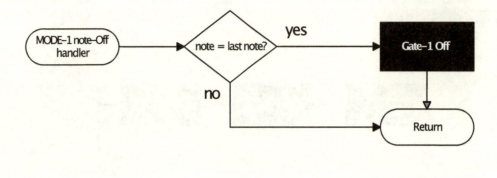

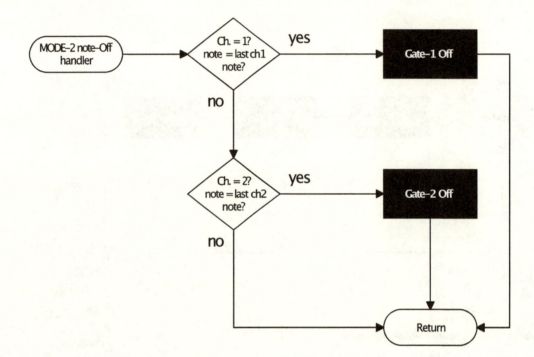

FIGURE 18.21 Handling Note-Off messages

HANDLING MIDI CLOCK

While operating in Mode-1, incoming clock messages are sent as trigger signals from the gate-2 jack. This enables the unit to drive Eurorack sequencers, arpeggiators, drum machines, and other units that respond to clock signals. As shown in Figure 18.22, the main loop tracks the duration of any active trigger signals and limits the duration to the time value stored in the global variable *clock_duration*. Although not shown, a similar algorithm handles LED durations.

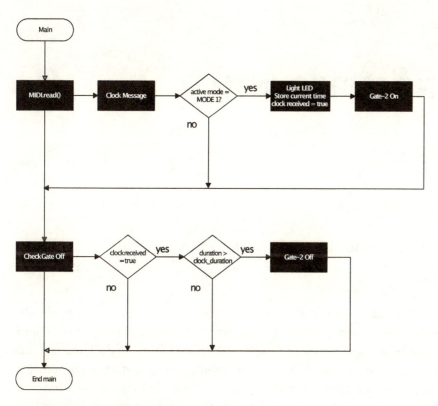

FIGURE 18.22 Clock on and off logic

Summary

Although one reason for building a custom MIDI to CV converter is to personalize its form and function, the project is also economical to build. The modular approach to the MIDI to CV backpack enables its use in a variety of projects such as custom sequencers, arpeggiators, or real-time controllers. The unit provides similar functionality to some commercial products, and the provision of an onboard voltage reference opens the door to projects that integrate control-voltage inputs for tuning offsets or another purpose.

CREATIVE CHALLENGE

The MIDI to Control-Voltage Converter has proved to be a helpful addition to my Eurorack kit, but there are many enhancements and creative applications to consider:

- Revise code and circuitry to create additional channels of CV and gate output.
- Adapt the project to use a Teensy 4.1 with USB host capability.
- Apply the concepts from the polyphony chapter (Chapter 9) to create distributed control voltages over multiple CV outputs.
- Enhance the project to output control voltages based on continuous controller messages.
- Add MIDI thru or MIDI out capability to distribute MIDI clock or other types of messages.
- Provide one or more jacks to support external controllers such as a light, distance, or pressure sensing; nunchuck control; or volume pedal.
- Incorporate CV input circuitry and provide a utility algorithm to tune CV outputs from the unit.

CHAPTER 19

BUILDING EUROSYNTH

If it takes time to build, it takes time to understand.[1]

ROBERT GROSSBLATT

We conclude with *Eurosynth*, a fun and powerful frequency-modulation synthesizer built on concepts presented throughout the book (see Figure 19.1). Although source files, bill of materials (BOM), and related resources are available for download from the OUP website, this is an especially good project on which to abandon the training wheels and adapt the concepts to your own creative vision. For example, the interface would be well-suited to other forms of music synthesis described in the first section of the book. Other enhancements might include circuits for MIDI input, menu items for patch storage, or other features.

FIGURE 19.1 Eurosynth

Project Description

The FM synthesizer project, one of my favorites in this book, has provided hours of enjoyment and demonstrates one of many ways that electronic musicians can tap into the power of inexpensive modern microcontrollers. The synthesizer is surprisingly capable given the modest amount of code and electronic components that are required to build the project:

- Four rotary encoders with built-in pushbuttons.
- Two channels of Gate and CV input.
- OLED display.
- Four FM operators.
- Ten algorithms (the connections between operators).
- Course and fine-tuning/modulation control for each operator.
- Adjustable output level for each operator.
- Adjustable feedback level for each operator.

A Backpack for CV Input

Eurosynth relies on a custom backpack PCB to process incoming V/oct and gate signals. The backpack also houses a DAC with amplification circuitry for audio output. As with the project detailed in Chapter 18, the backpack in this chapter can function as a foundation for a variety of music synthesizers, and all that is required is to use wires or headers to connect the backpack to a user interface.

POWER SECTION

The power section, shown in Figure 19.2, uses the same circuitry from Chapter 18 which includes a 5V regulator, a –10V shunt reference, and a dedicated 3.3V analog regulator.

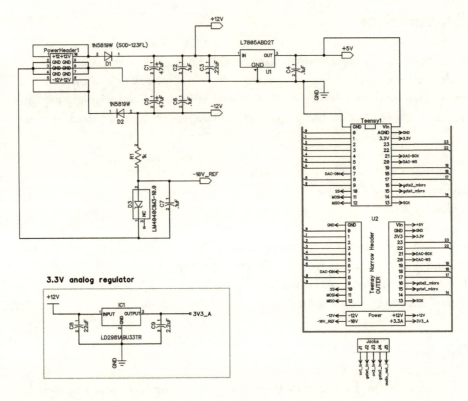

FIGURE 19.2 Power section

GATE INPUT CIRCUIT

Incoming trigger/gate signals are processed by the circuit shown in Figure 19.3. As described in Chapter 12, the circuit utilizes a resistor network, negative voltage reference, and rail-to-rail MCP6002 op amp powered by 3.3V to scale the signal to a level that can be safely read by the GPIO pins on the microcontroller. Although the output is inverted, it is trivial to handle the logic in code as shown later in the chapter.

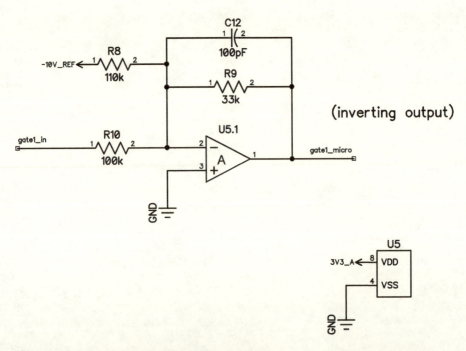

FIGURE 19.3 Trigger/gate input (one channel shown)

V/OCT INPUT CIRCUIT

Control voltages are handled by the scaling circuit shown in Figure 19.4 and described in previous chapters. The circuit is similar to the circuit used to scale incoming gates and the −10V reference and resistor network enables the circuit to scale negative and positive voltages into a 0–3.3V range.[2] (See Chapter 12 for more information.) The V/oct processing circuitry uses an external MCP3202 12-bit SPI analog-to-digital converter. While the analog inputs on the Teensy can be configured for 12-bit input, I achieved the best results using an external ADC powered by a separate regulated 3.3V supply.

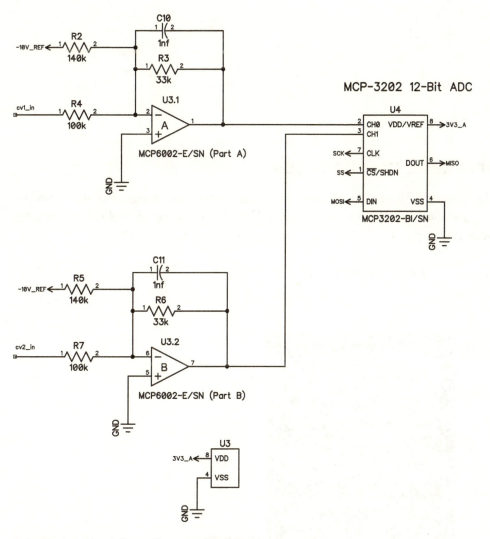

FIGURE 19.4 Circuit for scaling control voltages

AUDIO OUTPUT: INTRODUCING THE PT8211 DAC

The backpack features an integrated PT8211 DAC for audio output.[3] The SPI DAC, which is available from PJRC or eBay, works seamlessly with the Teensy Audio Library and is a good choice for projects that don't require the full capabilities of a Teensy Audio Shield. As you will see in a moment, all that is required to use the PT8211 is to select a PC8211 as a destination object in the Audio System Design Tool. Figure 19.5 also illustrates an amplification circuit that can be tailored by adjusting the ratio of R14 and R15. An electrolytic capacitor strips the DC component and a passive low-pass filter removes high-frequencies to suppress residual noise.

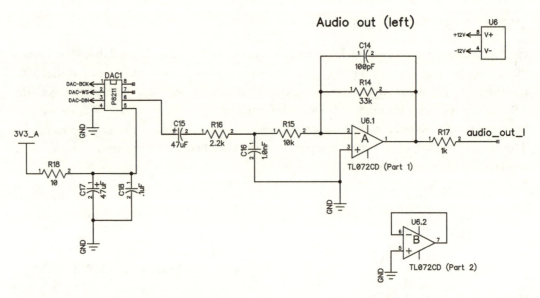

FIGURE 19.5 PT8211 DAC with amplification

SMD PLACEMENT AND TRACES

As stated in previous chapters, it is helpful to arrange components in logical groups according to circuit function. The approach provides several benefits including streamlined trace routing and minimal footprint. Figure 19.6 illustrates each logical section of the PCB.

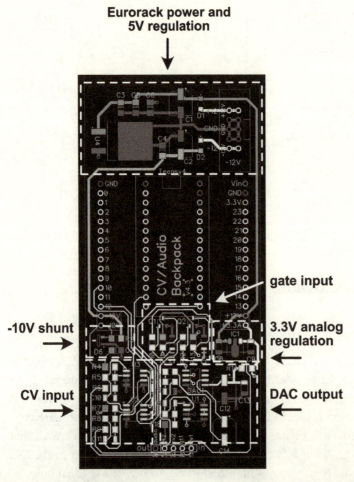

FIGURE 19.6 PCB function

Warning: As described previously in the book, be sure to disconnect external power when programming the microcontroller or follow the instructions provided by PJRC to disconnect USB power from the external 5V source.[4] It is also important to note that incoming gate and control voltage signals must be processed by the input circuitry since the microcontroller can be damaged by over- or under-voltages.

Eurosynth Interface

A primary benefit of using a custom backpack is the ease with which a new interface can be developed. In this case, all that is required to create a PCB interface is to place a few components and route traces to the appropriate pins on the backpack. The interface and CV-input backpack share the same composite headers, which ensures alignment of headers and pins and provides access to the Teensy pins and signal-processing circuitry (see Figure 19.7). The schematic for the user interface consists of an OLED display, four combination switch/rotary encoders, and jacks for audio output and V/oct and gate input.

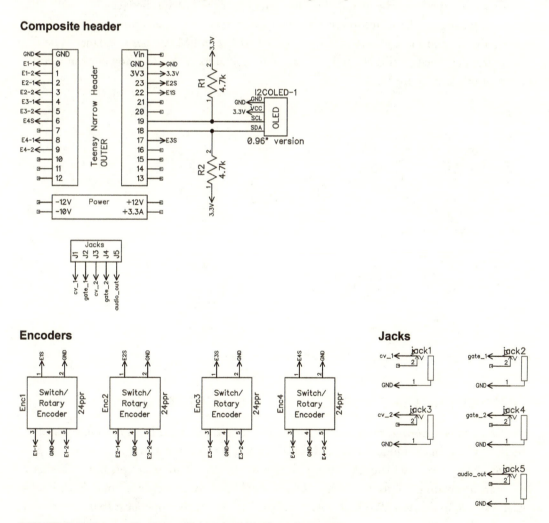

FIGURE 19.7 Eurosynth composite header with pin assignments

Coding Eurosynth

The code for the Eurosynth project is more complex than other projects in the book, but the code is built on building-block concepts that have been presented in previous chapters. And it is helpful to remember that the concepts are scalable. Readers who are relatively new to programming can download source code and incorporate small revisions to suit their personal taste, and readers with more experience might consider how the concepts in this final chapter could be applied to custom creations.

OPERATORS AND ALGORITHMS

The term *operator* is often used to describe the modulators and carriers that are used in a frequency modulation synthesizer. Where terms like *carrier* and *modulator* imply a specific function, the term *operator* implies a more generic audio object that can function as a carrier *or* modulator—or both. Operators can also include individual envelopes although, for the sake of clarity, envelopes won't be included in this iteration of the FM synthesizer.

Configuring oscillators to function as modulators or carriers opens the possibility of connecting the operators in a variety of ways called *algorithms* in FM synthesis parlance. The FM synthesizer described in this chapter provides four operators with the following connections or algorithms (see Figure 19.8).

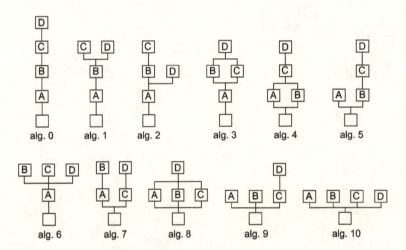

FIGURE 19.8 Operator algorithms in the FM Synthesis project

CONFIGURING THE AUDIO SYSTEM DESIGN TOOL

The first step is to configure the audio objects in the Audio System Design Tool. For clarity, the FM Synthesizer is monophonic and features a single voice, but additional voices are possible by adding more oscillator and mixer objects and incorporating concepts from Chapter 7.

Start by creating the four *AudioSynthWaveformModulated* objects and four *AudioMixer4* objects shown in Figure 19.9. These objects are the basis of the four operators that form a voice and make it possible to configure the synthesizer for the algorithms listed above. The output of each oscillator is connected to a corresponding input on each mixer. Also, note how the output of each mixer (labeled OPMIX1A-D) provides feedback to the input of each oscillator (labeled OP1A-D) and the output of each oscillator is *also* routed directly to a VOICE1MIXER object. Finally, the output of the voice mixer is connected to an envelope object, providing a convenient way to alter attacks and releases of the voice.

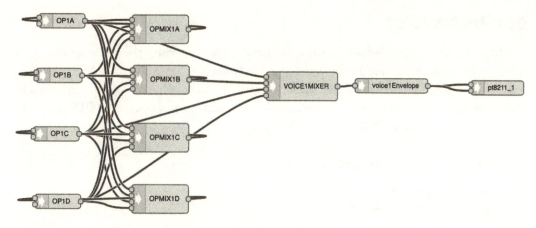

FIGURE 19.9 FM components created in the Audio Design Tool

CODING AN OPERATOR

Two custom data structures (*FMOperator* and *FMVoice*) work together to provide the functionality of an FM operator in this project. *FMOperator* is a structure defined in *FMOperator.h*, one of the project files available for download from the OUP website. The purpose of the struct, shown in its entirety in Listing 19.1, is to track variables associated with an operator including coarse and fine tuning (or modulation level), output level, feedback level, and output channel. The struct also provides a default constructor to initialize those variables to reasonable defaults. Essentially, the coarse-tuning variable provides an integer modulation factor, and the fine-tuning variable provides fractional tuning or modulation. For example, values of 1 and 0.5 for coarse- and fine-tuning modulates the operator that follows by 1.5 times the fundamental frequency.

Listing 19.1 FMOperator.h

```
struct FMOperator
{
    public:
    int coarseTuning; //Octave
    float fineTuning; //0.0-1.0
    float outputLevel;
    float feedback;
    int outputChannel;

    //Default constructor
    FMOperator()
    {
        coarseTuning = 1;
        fineTuning = 0.0;
        outputLevel = 0.25;
        feedback = 0.0;
        outputChannel = 0;
    }
};
```

CODING FMVOICE

A related class, *FMVoice*—found in the *FMVoice.h* file—provides the software glue that manages the oscillator and mixer objects created in the Audio System Design Tool. The class uses enumerations to represent each of the four operators. Although MIDI input is not used in this iteration of the project, the class also contains data members to track the MIDI Note-On and Note-Off (see Listing 19.2).

Listing 19.2 FMOperator: enumerations and data members

```
#include <Audio.h>
#include "FMOperator.h"

class FMVoice
{
    enum{OpA = 0, OpB, OpC, OpD};
    enum{numOperators = 4};

    public:
    bool note_on;
    int lastNoteOn;
    .

    .

    .
```

Using Pointers to Objects

The class also defines pointers and pointer arrays representing objects created in the Audio System Design Tool (see Listing 19.3).

Listing 19.3 Defining arrays of object pointers

```
//Arrays of pointers for oscillators and mixers
AudioSynthWaveformModulated *pOperator[numOperators];
AudioMixer4 *pOpMixer[numOperators];
AudioMixer4 *pVoiceMixer;
AudioEffectEnvelope *pEnvelope;
```

As detailed in Chapter 3, pointers provide a convenient way for a class such as the *FMVoice* class to access and manipulate objects that are created outside of the class. Bearing in mind that the Audio System Design Tool produces cut-and-paste code that defines and instantiates objects, pointers provide a way to access and manipulate those objects without needing to hard-code the object names. Thus, multiple instances of the *FMVoice* class can be created to interface with additional objects *without any changes to the underlying code*.

Attaching Objects

The audio objects generated by the Audio System Design Tool are passed to *FMVoice* using several "attach" functions such as the *attachSines()* function shown in listing 19.4. In this example, four pointers to oscillator objects are passed to the function and assigned to the pointers stored in the pointer array named *pOperator*.

CHAPTER 19 BUILDING EUROSYNTH 321

Listing 19.4 attaching audio objects

```
void attachSines(AudioSynthWaveformModulated *pA,
      AudioSynthWaveformModulated *pB,
      AudioSynthWaveformModulated *pC,
      AudioSynthWaveformModulated *pD)
{
    pOperator[0] = pA;
    pOperator[1] = pB;
    pOperator[2] = pC;
    pOperator[3] = pD;
}
```

Pointers to other objects from the main sketch (such as the four operator mixers, voice mixer, and envelope generator) are attached to the *FMVoice* class using similar functions found in the source code available from the OUP website.

ARRAY OF FMOPERATOR OBJECTS

The *FMVoice* class also contains an array of *FMOperator* objects that were described earlier in the chapter, and these objects track the status of each operator including output and feedback level, course and fine tuning, and output channel (see Listing 19.5). Incidentally, the *public* keyword indicates that these data members will be visible beyond the class without the need for accessor methods.

Listing 19.5 Instantiating an array of FMOperator objects contained by FMVoice

```
public:
    //Array of operators
    FMOperator operators[numOperators];
    int fundamentalFrequency;
```

UPDATING OBJECTS

The *FMOperator* objects provide the glue that coordinates operator values entered in the main sketch with the actual audio objects (which have no knowledge of application-specific parameters such as tuning offsets or mixer channels). Thus, *FMVoice* provides several update methods that can be called to change the state of each oscillator. For example, the method *updateOperatorOutputLevel()* iterates through each oscillator and adjusts the amplitude by the value stored in the corresponding *FMOperator* object (see Listing 19.6):

Listing 19.6 Updating operator amplitude

```
void updateOperatorOutputLevel()
{
    for(int i = 0; i < numOperators; i++)
    {
        //Update sine objects with values from FMOperator
        pOperator[i]->amplitude(operators[i].outputLevel);
    }
}
```

The other update methods, *updateTuning()* and *updateFeedbackLevel()*, use a similar process.

CONFIGURING ALGORITHMS

The *updateAlgorithm()* method is responsible for configuring the operator outputs in the ten algorithms described earlier in the chapter. The method does this by manipulating the output level of each operator mixer to form new connections between the operators.

The first step is to reset the voice to a normalized state using the helper function *turnOffInputs()*. This method, shown in Listing 19.7, simply turns off the gain of each operator and mixer channel:

Listing 19.7 turnOffInputs() method

```
void turnOffInputs()
{
    //Turn off each operator
    for(int i = 0; i < numOperators; i++)
    {
        for(int chan = 0; chan < 4; chan++)
        {
            pOpMixer[i]->gain(chan, 0.0);
        }
    }
    //Turn off the mixer channels
    pVoiceMixer->gain(OpA, 0.0);
    pVoiceMixer->gain(OpB, 0.0);
    pVoiceMixer->gain(OpC, 0.0);
    pVoiceMixer->gain(OpD, 0.0);
}
```

Once the mixer levels are reset, the *updateAlgorithm()* method configures the connections to match one of the ten algorithms. For example, algorithm-0 (see Figure 19.10) is created using the code snippet shown in Listing 19.8.

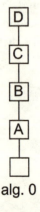

alg. 0

FIGURE 19.10 Algorithm-0

Listing 19.8 Configuring mixers for algorithm-0

```
if(alg == 0)
{
    pOpMixer[OpA]->gain(OpB, level);
    pOpMixer[OpB]->gain(OpC, level);
    pOpMixer[OpC]->gain(OpD, level);
    pVoiceMixer->gain(OpA, 1.0);
}
```

Working from the top to the bottom, note how the operator A mixer is configured to receive input from its operator B channel, operator B receives input from its operator C channel, and so on. In the final line, the *voice mixer* is configured to receive input from operator A (which is the last operator in the series). In this way, the operator mixers and voice mixers work together to route signals to match a given algorithm.

Let's look at another example. In Listing 19.9, note how operator B receives input from operators C and D and operator A receives input from operator B. This configuration follows the algorithm shown in Figure 19.11. The other algorithms follow a similar process.

Listing 19.9 Configuring mixers for algorithm-1

```
if(alg == 1)
{
    pOpMixer[OpA]->gain(OpB, level);
    pOpMixer[OpB]->gain(OpC, level);
    pOpMixer[OpB]->gain(OpD, level);

    pVoiceMixer->gain(OpA, 1.0);
}
```

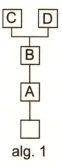

FIGURE 19.11 Algorithm-1

MAIN SKETCH

Although there are more than 500 lines of code in the main sketch, much of the code will be familiar after reading previous chapters. The primary tasks include setting up the audio system, displaying text on the OLED display, handling input from the switches and encoders, and responding to V/oct and gate input. Thus, this section of the chapter provides

324   SOUND & MUSIC PROJECTS FOR EURORACK AND BEYOND

a 20,000-foot overview of the main logic with a discussion of core features that are unique to the project.

Setup

The main sketch instantiates an *FMVoice* object and uses its "attach" methods to connect pointers of the audio objects created by the Audio System Design Tool (see Listing 19.10). The *setup()* function also configures the OLED display, Teensy audio system, menu buttons, and (optional) MIDI callback functions, but that code is not shown since it is so similar to the boilerplate code in previous chapters.

Listing 19.10 Instantiation of an FMVoice object and the setup() function

```
FMVoice voice1;

void setup()
{
    //Attach objects to FMVoice object
    voice1.attachSines(&OP1A, &OP1B, &OP1C, &OP1D);
    voice1.attachMixers(&OPMIX1A, &OPMIX1B, &OPMIX1C, &OPMIX1D);
    voice1.attachVoiceMixer(&VOICE1MIXER);
    voice1.attachEnvelope(&voice1Envelope);

    //Configure the FMVoice
    voice1.setADSR(20, 10, 0.8, 100);
    voice1.updateAlgorithm(currentAlgorithm);
    voice1.updateOperatorOutputLevel();
    voice1.updateFeedbackLevel();
    voice1.updateTuning();
    .
    .
    .
```

Logic of the Main Loop

Figure 19.12 illustrates the logic of the main loop.

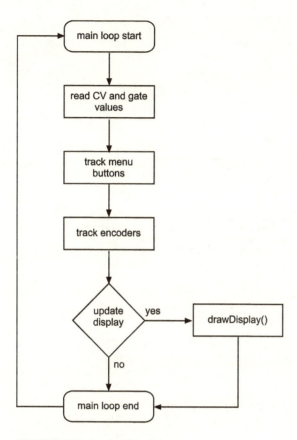

FIGURE 19.12 Logic of main loop

You might be surprised to see that there are just four primary tasks in the main loop. This brings up an important point: Strive for clarity and simplicity in your code. To quote Bruce Eckel, author of *Thinking in C++*:

> *Always keep it simple. Little clean objects with obvious utility are better than big, complicated interfaces.*[5]

Although the FM Synthesizer project is complex, note how the core functionality can be distilled into a few primary tasks.

Tracking Menu Pushbuttons

The button-tracking functions provide a means for selecting the modes of operation of the FM Synthesizer. Again, the underlying code (see Listing 19.11) is unremarkable and similar to that seen in previous chapters, but note that most of the buttons use the logic shown in Figure 19.13 to toggle between modes such as the coarse- and fine-tuning modes shown in this example.

One detail to be aware of is that operational modes can be freely selected at any time but toggling between sub-modes (such as coarse- and fine-tuning) only occurs after the tuning function is selected. This approach enables the menu pushbutton to function in a more intuitive way:

326   SOUND & MUSIC PROJECTS FOR EURORACK AND BEYOND

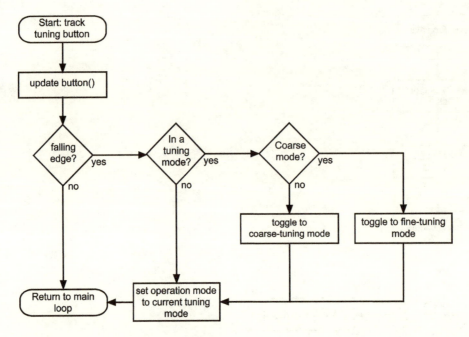

FIGURE 19.13 Tuning button toggle logic

Listing 19.11 Code for using a pushbutton to toggle an operation mode

```
void trackTuningBtn()
{
    static int tuning_mode = coarse_tuning_mode;
    btn1.update();
    if(btn1.fallingEdge())
    {
        //Only toggle if we are already in a tuning mode
        if(currentMode == coarse_tuning_mode ||
           currentMode == fine_tuning_mode)
        {
            //Toggle between modes
            if(tuning_mode == coarse_tuning_mode)
            {
                tuning_mode = fine_tuning_mode;
            }else if(tuning_mode == fine_tuning_mode)
            {
                tuning_mode = coarse_tuning_mode;
            }
        }
        currentMode = tuning_mode;
        updateDisplay = true;
    }
}
```

Tracking Encoders

Encoder-tracking presents an interesting programming challenge. Where the menu pushbuttons toggle between one or two menu selections, the encoders *simultaneously* update parameters including tuning, output level, and algorithm selection (depending on the active operation mode).

I previously stated that pointers and references are used infrequently in this book, but we will use them here (surprise!) to solve this programming conundrum. The beauty of references is that the *same* code can be used for *all* the encoders. Instead of writing a block of logic and repeating it for each encoder, we simply write the code once and pass each encoder to the function as a reference. Although we have previously looked at encoder-handling functions, let's take a brief look at how encoders are handled in the FM synthesizer sketch.

The *handleEncoder()* function takes a reference to an *Encoder* object, a pointer to an *FMOperator* object, and a reference to an integer representing the last encoder position:

```
void handleEncoder(Encoder &rEncoder, FMOperator *pOperator,
    long &last_position);
```

The pointers enable a level of abstraction so the function can update values for any encoder and operator pairs that it receives (See Figure 19.14). Although the behavior of the function is complex (four encoders updating five or more parameters depending on the active mode), the underlying logic is simple and can be described with just a few steps:

1. Read the encoder position.
2. Calculate the difference if the encoder is at a new position.
3. Apply the difference to the appropriate parameter.

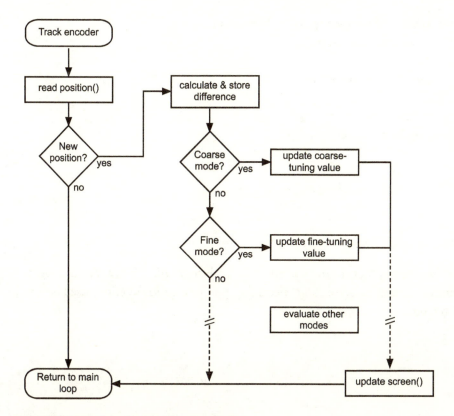

FIGURE 19.14 Encoder tracking algorithm

Translating this algorithm to code is straightforward and involves reading the encoder to determine the difference in its position (see Listing 19.12). A series of "if" statements enable the function to select the correct parameter for updating and, again, note how the function doesn't need to know the name of the specific instance of the *FMOperator* object since it is passed as a pointer.

Listing 19.12 handleEncoder() function (excerpt)

```
void handleEncoder(Encoder &rEncoder, FMOperator *pOperator, long
    &last_position, int index)
{
    long pos = rEncoder.read();

    if(pos == last_position)
    {
        //No need to continue
        return;
    }

    //Calculate the difference:
    long difference = pos - last_position;
    last_position = pos;

    //Update the coarse tuning parameter pointed
    //to by pOperator
    if(currentMode == coarse_tuning_mode)
    {
        pOperator->coarseTuning += difference;
        if(pOperator->coarseTuning < 0)
        {
            pOperator->coarseTuning = 0;
        }
        updateDisplay = true;
        voice1.updateTuning();
    }
    .
    .
    .
```

Drawing Algorithms and Other Screens

The OLED screen-drawing algorithm is similarly straightforward. The functional logic, shown in Figure 19.15, clears the screen and selects the appropriate sub-function based on the current operation mode.

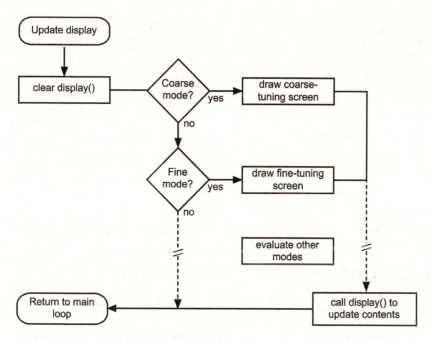

FIGURE 19.15 drawDisplay() algorithm

Responding to Gate and Trigger Signals

EuroSynth uses a gate signal to trigger the attack and release phase of the envelope. Listing 19.13 demonstrates how an analog pin can respond to signals from the gate processing circuitry. Although the analog pins can function as digital pins, the analog inputs provide an opportunity to define a threshold level incoming gate signals. As is evident in the listing, the function calls the appropriate *noteOn()* and *noteOff()* methods. The global variable *note_on* tracks the status of the pin to prevent multiple calls to the envelope when the gate is on or off. The only quirky aspect of the code is the fact that the gate processing circuit returns an inverted voltage: values below the threshold indicate the start of the envelope and values above the threshold indicate that *noteOff()* should be called.

Listing 19.13 Gate-1 tracking code (OLED update code not shown)

```
void trackGate1()
{
   //=====Track gate 1
   int gate_1 = analogRead(gatePin1);
   if(gate_1 <= gate_threshold)
   {
      if(note_on == false)
      {
         note_on = true;
         voice1Envelope.noteOn();
      }
   } else if (gate_1 > gate_threshold)
```

```
        {
            if(note_on == true)
            {
                note_on = false;
                //Note: optionally set releaseNoteOn()
                //to reduce clicks or pops.
                voice1Envelope.noteOff();
            }
        }
    }
```

The second gate could be used for a variety of purposes such as implementing a second voice.

TRANSLATING CONTROL VOLTAGE TO FREQUENCY

The backpack also processes incoming voltages for V/oct pitch control. As described in previous chapters, the circuitry scales the voltage so it can be safely read by the microcontroller. The *trackCV1()* function uses a handy library, created by Souvik Saha, to read 12-bit values from the MCP3202 ADC.[6] The library is available for download from the Teensyduino Tools . . . Manage Libraries menu. To use the library, add an include directive at the start of the sketch, create an instance of the MCP3202 object, and call the object's *begin()* method in the *setup()* function as shown in the boilerplate code in Listing 19.14:

Listing 19.14 Using the MCP3202 library

```
#include <MCP3202.h>

const int chip_select = 10;
MCP3202 adc = MCP3202(chip_select);

void setup()
{
    adc.begin();
}
```

The *trackCV1()* function, shown in Listing 19.15, reads a 12-bit value from the ADC, converts the value back to its full range, and converts the control voltage to frequency using the following formula where F = frequency, V is voltage, and $F0$ is the bas'e frequency:

$$F = 2^V F0$$

Also shown in the listing are two convenience functions for converting the 12-bit values returned by the ADC into 3.3V values and "un-scaling" the values provided by the circuitry.

Listing 19.15 trackCV1() function (OLED update code not shown)

```
void trackCV1()
{
    static unsigned long last_input;

    //Read CV1
    unsigned long val = adc.readChannel(0);
    int window = 3;
    if(val < last_input - window || val > last_input + window)
    {
        last_input = val;
        float volts3V = convert12BitTo3V((float)val);
        float volts10V = convert3Vto10V(volts3V);
        float freq = basis_frequency * pow(2.0, volts10V);
        voice1.setFundamentalFrequency(freq);

        if(currentMode == utility_mode)
        {
            updateDisplay = true;
            cv1_volts = volts10V;
        }
    }
}


float convert12BitTo3V(float value)
{
    return (value / 4096.0) * 3.3;
}


float convert3Vto10V(float v_out_3v)
{
    /* Using 33k feedback resistor, 100k input resistor,
    * and 140k bias resistor with -10V reference
    */
    return ((2.357 - v_out_3v) / 0.33) * circuit_tuning_constant;
}
```

CV Tracking Accuracy

In my tests, the voltage control scaling circuitry and code worked well in translating V/oct signals from commercial products. Figure 19.16 shows the results of processing one octave of semitone inputs from a Keystep 37 keyboard.

Eurosynth Control Voltage Accuracy Test
1-octave output from a commercial keyboard processed by 3.3V Eurosynth scaling circuitry

Note	C	C#	D	D#	E	F	F#	G	G#	A	A#	B	C
Eurosynth calculated volts	0.960	1.050	1.130	1.210	1.300	1.380	1.460	1.550	1.630	1.710	1.800	1.880	1.970
Keystep37 volts	0.994	1.077	1.160	1.243	1.326	1.409	1.493	1.576	1.659	1.742	1.825	1.908	1.991

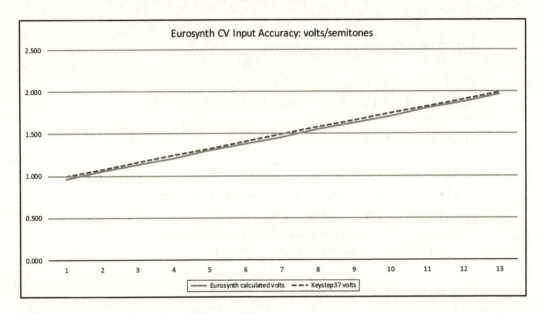

FIGURE 19.16 Eurosynth CV input accuracy test

PUTTING IT ALL TOGETHER

Listing 19.16 shows the pedestrian tasks that are handled by the main loop including reading gate and V/oct, tracking the pushbuttons, tracking the encoders, and updating the display. Under the hood, all signal generation and processing are transparently handled by the powerful Teensy Audio Library.

Listing 19.16 Main loop

```
void loop()
{
    //Handle incoming CV
    trackGate1();
    trackGate2();
    trackCV1();
    trackCV2();

    //Handle the menu buttons
    trackTuningBtn();
    trackAlgorithmBtn();
    trackLevelBtn();
    trackUtilityBtn();
```

```
    //Handle the four encoders
    handleEncoder(encoder1, &voice1.operators[0], 0);
    handleEncoder(encoder2, &voice1.operators[1], 1);
    handleEncoder(encoder3, &voice1.operators[2], 2);
    handleEncoder(encoder4, &voice1.operators[3], 3);

    if(updateDisplay == true)
    {
       drawDisplay();
       updateDisplay = false;
    }
}
```

To complete the project, download the most recent code from the OUP website and upload the project to a Teensy 4 microcontroller with PT8211 shield and input circuitry, or use the backpack detailed in this chapter.

A BOM and Gerber files are available for download and can be used to manufacture inexpensive PCBs. Alternatively, the circuitry can be built on a solderless breadboard or finalized on solder board or stripboard, with hookup wire providing a connection between a breadboard and the user interface. Figure 19.17 shows the completed project in action in a Eurorack setup.

FIGURE 19.17 EuroSynth in action

Other Enhancements

The second voltage control input and gate are currently unassigned and could be used for many functions including adding a second voice, external pitch or amplitude modulation, or dynamic control. Another option might include assignable voltage control parameters, which could be incorporated into the device's menu system. Be sure to visit the OUP website for video demonstrations of this and other projects in the book and consider your own creative adaptations of EuroSynth.

CREATIVE CHALLENGE

I have spent many enjoyable hours designing sounds with EuroSynth, and my primary suggestion is to have fun and experiment with the synthesizer. With that said, the following strategies may be useful as you get a feel for the instrument:

- Select the first algorithm and use the level page to turn the volume of operators 2–4 to zero. Press the level button a second time to view the feedback page and adjust the feedback level of operator 1. A surprisingly wide array of sounds can be produced with a single operator in a feedback loop.
- Select the first algorithm and turn down the volume of operators 3 and 4. Use the coarse-tuning page to experiment with the changes to operators 1 and 2. You will notice that increasing the frequency of operator 1 produces wild bell-like timbres as sidebands are produced from modulating operator 2, while changes to operator 2 are heard as partials or harmonic color.
- Continue with the first algorithm but turn up the level of the third operator. Adjust the tuning and level of each operator to see the impact it has on the other operators and timbre. Experiment with levels, feedback, and fine-tuning as you craft unique sounds.
- Bring up the level of the fourth operator and continue to experiment. What happens when you turn feedback on (or off) on each operator? What happens when tunings are inharmonic, or levels are subtly different? Although small changes can create wildly differing timbres, it is gratifying to get a feel for the sound-design potential of a single FM algorithm.
- Buckle your seat belt and select another algorithm. Listen to how the timbre changes and visualize how each operator is functioning in the algorithm. Does the operator function as a harmonic or a modulator? How does feedback affect the sound? What about fine-tuning? Continue to experiment with parameters and lose track of time. You are in the FM zone.

Conclusion

We have covered much ground in this text, ranging from music synthesis to circuitry and programming. Along the way, we looked at ways to apply those concepts to custom Eurorack modules and considered design strategies that apply to a wide range of DIY projects. Any complex endeavor will take time to absorb and apply, and that is perhaps even more germane to the realm of microcontrollers. Speaking from an avocational perspective, the concepts *will* become comfortable with regular practice and experimentation. Play with the concepts you are comfortable with and expand those boundaries as you incorporate new ideas, and you will enjoy an expanded creative palette that enables you to envision and build new instruments that are suited to *your* style of music-making.

APPENDIX A

DATA TYPES

TABLE A.1 *Common data types*

Data Type	Example	Description
boolean (8 bit)	bool on = true;	Simple logical true/false.
byte (8 bit)	byte data_byte = 60;	Unsigned number from 0–255.
char (8 bit)	char ch = 'a';char ascii = 97;	Signed number from -128 to 127. The compiler will attempt to interpret this data type as a character in some circumstances, which may yield unexpected results.
unsigned char (8 bit)	unsigned char note = 60;	Same as "byte"; if this is what you're after, you should use "byte" instead, for reasons of clarity.
word (16 bit)	word a = 65535;	Unsigned number from 0–65535.
unsigned int (16 bit)	unsigned int b = 65535;	The same as "word". Use "word" instead for clarity and brevity.
int (16 bit)	int c = 32767;int d = -32768;	Signed number from -32768 to 32767. This is most commonly what you see used for general purpose variables in Arduino example code provided with the IDE.
unsigned long (32 bit)	unsigned long e = 4294967295;	Unsigned number from 0–4,294,967,295. The most common usage of this is to store the result of the *millis()* function, which returns the number of milliseconds the current code has been running.
long (32 bit)	long f = 2147486647;	Signed number from -2,147,483,648 to 2,147,483,647.
float (32 bit)	float pi = 3.14159;	Signed number from -3.4028235E38 to 3.4028235E38.

Source: "Data Types in Arduino," Sparkfun, https://learn.sparkfun.com/tutorials/data-types-in-arduino, accessed June 13, 2023.

APPENDIX B

PRIMARY AUDIO OBJECTS

Waveform

The waveform object encapsulates the functionality of a multi-waveform oscillator in an easy-to-use object. Waveforms include sine, sawtooth, reverse sawtooth, square, triangle, variable triangle, arbitrary, pulse, and sample/hold waves.

Clicking on a waveform object (or other object) in the Audio Design Tool provides useful information about the object and its methods. The examples in this section are based on information provided from the PJRC website and are listed here for convenience.[1]

Method	Description
begin(waveform)	Configure the waveform type to create.
begin(level, frequency, waveform)	Output a waveform and set the amplitude and frequency.
frequency(freq)	Change the frequency.
amplitude(level)	Change the amplitude. Set to 0 to turn the signal off.
offset(level)	Add a DC offset, from -1.0 to +1.0. Useful for generating waveforms to use as control or modulation signals.
phase(angle)	Cause the generated waveform to jump to a specific point within its cycle. Angle is from 0 to 360 degrees. When multiple objects are configured, *AudioNoInterrupts()* should be used to guarantee all new settings take effect together.
pulseWidth(amount)	Change the width (duty cycle) of the pulse.
arbitraryWaveform(array, maxFreq)	Configure the waveform to be used with WAVEFORM_ARBITRARY. Array must be an array of 256 samples. Currently, the data is used without any filtering, which can cause aliasing with frequencies above 172 Hz. For higher frequency output, you must bandwidth limit your waveform data.

Mixer

The mixer object combines up to four signals (indicated by "channel" numbers that range from 0 to 3) and provides a single *gain()* method as described in the Audio Design Tool documentation:

Method	Description
gain(channel, level)	Adjust the amplification or attenuation: "channel" must be 0 to 3 and "level" may be any floating-point number from 0 to 32767.0. 1.0 passes the signal through directly. Level of 0 shuts the channel off completely. Between 0 to 1.0 attenuates the signal, and above 1.0 amplifies it. Negative numbers may also be used, to invert the signal. All four channels have separate gain settings.

i2s

i2s (often referred to as "I-two-ess") takes a left and right channel as inputs and streams the audio to the i2s component of the Teensy board. Note that you can connect a single output to both inputs to hear a mono sound in both sides of a pair of headphones. The i2s object does not provide any methods.

sgtl5000

The sgtl5000 object is responsible for handling input and output streams and is used to stream audio to the headphone jack. The primary methods are listed below:

Method	Description
enable()	Start the SGTL5000. This function should be called first.
volume (level)	Set the headphone volume level. Range is 0 to 1.0, but 0.8 corresponds to the maximum undistorted output for a full scale signal. Usually 0.5 is a comfortable listening level. The line level outputs are *not* changed by this function.
inputSelect(input)	Select which input to use: AUDIO_INPUT_LINEIN or AUDIO_INPUT_MIC.
micGain(dB)	When using the microphone input, set the amplifier gain. The input number is in decibels, from 0 to 63.

APPENDIX C

USING POLYPHONE TO CREATE CUSTOM WAVETABLES

The AudioSynthWavetable object is designed to work with samples derived from SoundFont2 samples.[1] Soundfonts, which were originally designed to store sound sets for computer sound cards, can be downloaded from a variety of resources on the web—but be aware that many of the sample packages are too large to be used with the memory constraints of a microcontroller. For this example, we will create a custom SoundFont2 based on a wave file. An overview of the process of using SoundFont2 with a Teensy wavetable project includes:

- downloading or creating a SoundFont2 (sf2) file;
- decoding the SoundFont2 using Teensy SoundFont2 Decoder, a Python application;
- importing the header (.h) and source (.cpp) files created by the decoder into a Teensyduino project; and
- connecting one or more wavetable oscillators to the digital audio data referenced in the decoded header file.

Tips for Creating a Looping Wave File

A first step is to record or edit a digital file and save the file as a mono wave file. Be aware that the sample will need to be short to fit the limited memory space of the microcontroller. One tip, if you intend to create a looping sample, is to use a DAW or other audio editing software to cut the recording into two segments. Move the first segment *after* the second segment and use a cross-fade to splice the boundaries between the two segments. The start and end of the recording will loop seamlessly since the ends were on either side of the cut, and the crossfade should result in a smooth transition between the original start and end of the sample. The process is illustrated in Figure C.1.

1. Split loop into two parts

2. Swap positions and crossfade the segments

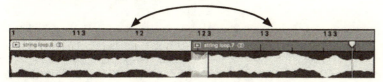

FIGURE C.1 Cutting and splicing audio to create a seamless loop

Once you have prepared a wave file, use an app to pack the wave into a Soundfont. The open-source Polyphone worked well for me, but other options are available. To use Polyphone for the process, select the New Soundfont option and click the "Add Sample icon" as shown in Figure C.2.

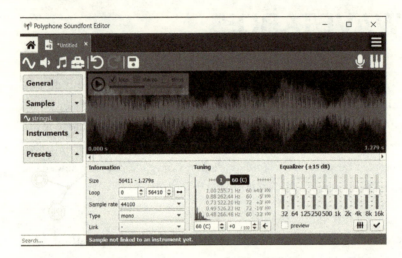

FIGURE C.2 Adding a sample to a Polyphone Soundfont

With the sample selected, click "create instrument icon" and be sure to select the "Link selected samples" option as shown in Figure C.3.

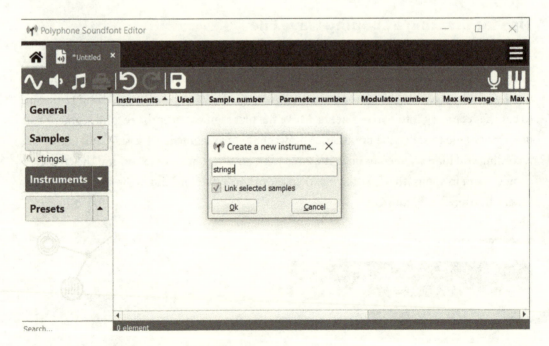

FIGURE C.3 Creating an instrument in Polyphone

Finally, select the musical note icon to create a preset. Enter a name for the preset and save the newly created Soundfont to disk (see figure C.4). Several other editing options are available in Polyphone, but the steps described in this section are sufficient to create a simple Soundfont suitable for use in a Teensy wavetable project.

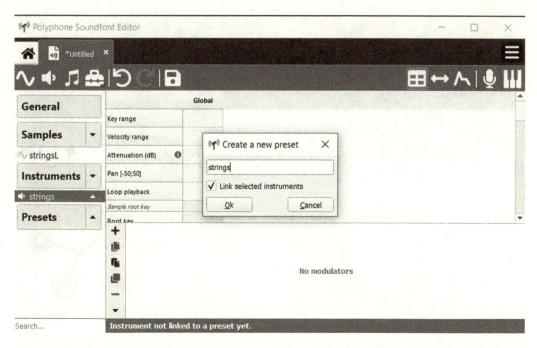

FIGURE C.4 Creating a preset in Polyphone

Using Soundfont Decoder

One final step is required to prepare a Soundfont for use in a memory-based wavetable project. A Python application, Teensy Soundfont Decoder, is provided by PJRC and available on Github.[2] The decoder application provides a way to load a Soundfont file and decode the information into Teensy-friendly header (.h) and source (.cpp) files that can be incorporated into a Teensy sketch. Incidentally, the original Soundfont project was created by a group of students as part of a Portland State University capstone project.

Download the most-recent Python files for the Soundfont Decoder application on Github and, if necessary, install Python from python.org. It is also necessary to install a special Python library named sf2utils before using the Soundfond Decoder application. You may be able to use the "pip" package installer to install the library from the terminal or command line by typing one of the following options:

- pip install sf2utils; or
- pip3 install sf2utils.

Depending on the configuration of your system, you can run the Soundfont Decoder application by loading the bare-bones Python editor IDLE, an application that is typically included with a Python installation. Open IDLE, navigate to the folder containing the Soundfont Decoder Python files downloaded in the previous step, and open and then run the file named *controller.py*. Once the decoder application is running, click the New Soundfont button and use the Browse button to select your newly created Soundfont. Select the instrument from the leftmost panel and then select the relevant sample table on the rightmost column (see Figure C.5).

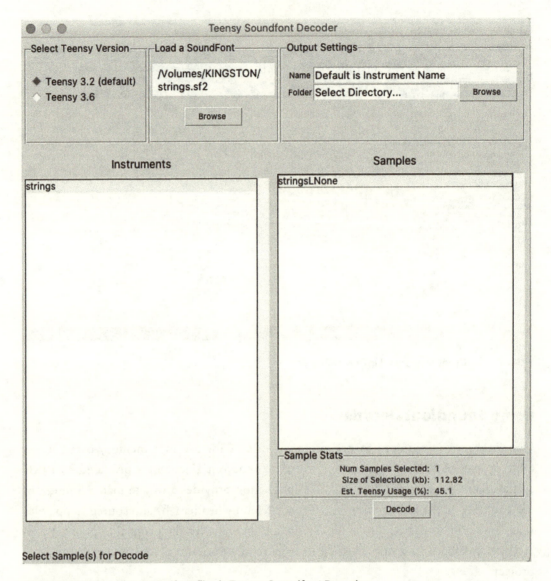

FIGURE C.5 Decoding Soundfont files in Teensy Soundfont Decoder

The Sample Stats section provides useful information including an estimate of the memory usage for the selected Teensy version. For example, the Soundfont in this example is approximately 1.5 seconds in length and uses 45% of available memory on a Teensy 3.2 (or 10.8% on a Teensy 3.6)—clearly memory space is at a premium when using memory-based wavetables on a microcontroller!

Use the Browse button in Output Settings to select a destination folder and then click the Decode button to create .h and .cpp files that can be used in a Teensyduino project.

Creating a Custom Project with Audio System Design Tool

As described in Chapter 2, run the Audio System Design Tool, and create the objects shown in Figure C.6—the same objects included with the WavetableSynth demonstration sketch from that chapter:

- one AudioSynthWavetable oscillator;
- one AudioEffectEnvelope object;

- one AudioMixer4;
- one AudioOutputI2S to transmit to the Teensy Audio Shield; and
- one AudioControlSGTL5000 object to coordinate I2S audio streams.

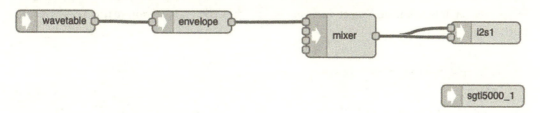

FIGURE C.6 Audio System Design Tool

Importing Components from the Audio System Design Tool

Use the Export button in the Audio System Design Tool and copy the resulting text into memory as shown in Figure C.7. The code and *#include* statements can then be pasted near the top of a newly created Teensyduino project.

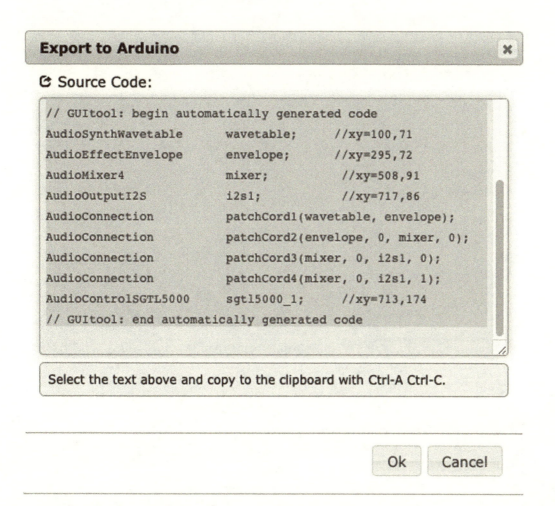

FIGURE C.7 Copying objects from the Audio System Design Tool

Importing Custom Samples

For custom wavetable projects, use the Sketch . . . Add file . . . menu option to add the .h and .cpp files that were created by the Teensy Soundfont Decoder application described in the previous section. It is also necessary to use the *#include* directive to incorporate the newly created header file in the main sketch:

```
#include "strings_samples.h"
```

At this point, the custom wavetable samples are ready for use as described in Chapter 2.

NOTES

Chapter 1

1. Ray Kurzweil, *The Singularity is Near: When Humans Transcend Biology* (London: Viking, 2005), 1.
2. "Soldering Tutorial for Beginners: Five Easy Steps," YouTube, accessed April 1, 2023, https://www.youtube.com/watch?v=Qps9woUGkvI.
3. Simon Monk, *Programming Arduino Next Steps* (New York: McGraw Hill, 2014), 16.
4. "Audio System Design Tool for Teensy Audio Library," PJRC, last modified March 19, 2023, https://www.pjrc.com/teensy/gui/.
5. Kyle Loudon, *C++ Pocket Reference* (Sebastopol, CA: O'Reilly, 2003), 38.
6. "Audio Connections & Memory," PJRC, last modified March 19, 2023, https://www.pjrc.com/teensy/td_libs_AudioConnection.html.
7. Elliot Williams, *Make: AVR Programming* (Sebastopol, CA: Maker Media, 2014), 131.

Chapter 2

1. Victor Lazzarini, *Computer Music Instruments II* (Cham: Springer, 2019), 192–193.
2. Perry R. Cook, *Real Sound Synthesis for Interactive Applications* (Natick, MA: A.K. Peters, 2002), 114–116.
3. Brent Edstrom, *Arduino for Musicians* (New York: Oxford University Press, 2016), 213–233.
4. "Using USB MIDI," PJRC, last modified March 19, 2023, https://www.pjrc.com/teensy/td_midi.html.
5. Ibid.
6. "map()," Arduino, accessed April 10, 2023, https://www.arduino.cc/reference/en/language/functions/math/map/.

Chapter 3

1. Elliot Williams, *Make: AVR Programming* (Sebastopol, CA: Maker Media, 2014), 107.
2. "Bounce Library," PJRC, last modified March 19, 2023, https://www.pjrc.com/teensy/td_libs_Bounce.html.
3. "Adafruit SSD1306," Adafruit, last modified January 8, 2013, https://adafruit.github.io/Adafruit_SSD1306/html/index.html.
4. "Wire Library," PJRC, accessed August 2018, https://www.pjrc.com/teensy/td_libs_Wire.html.
5. "Adafruit SSD1306 OLED Library," PJRC, accessed June 9, 2023, https://www.pjrc.com/teensy/td_libs_SSD1306.html.
6. Kyle Loudon, *C++ Pocket Reference* (Sebastopol: O'Reilly, 2003), 24.
7. Ibid., 27.

Chapter 4

1. John M. Chowning, "The Synthesis of Complex Audio Spectra by Means of Frequency Modulation," *Journal of the Audio Engineering Society* 1, no.2 (1977), 46–54.
2. Perry R. Cook, *Real Sound Synthesis for Interactive Applications* (Natick, MA: A.K. Peters, 2002), 116–119.

3. Ibid., 117.
4. "Audio System Design Tool for Teensy Audio Library," PJRC, accessed August 24, 2022, https://www.pjrc.com/teensy/gui/.
5. "Using USB MIDI," PJRC, accessed August 4, 2022, https://www.pjrc.com/teensy/td_midi.html.
6. Gary P. Scavone, *Midi/Frequency Conversion*, McGill University, accessed June 12, 2023, https://www.music.mcgill.ca/~gary/307/week1/node28.html.
7. Ibid.

Chapter 5

1. Perry R. Cook, *Real Sound Synthesis for Interactive Applications* (Natick, MA: A. K. Peters, 2002), 45.
2. Daniel R. Mitchell, *BasicSynth: Creating a Music Synthesizer in Software* (Morrisville, NC: Lulu Press, 2008), 197–201.
3. Eduardo Miranda, *Computer Sound Design: Synthesis Techniques and Programming*, 2nd ed. (Woburn: Focal Press, 2002), 51.
4. Samuel Pellman, *An Introduction to the Creation of Electroacoustic Music* (Belmont, CA: Wadsworth Publishing Company, 1994), 232–233.
5. Ibid., 211–212.
6. "Audio System Design Tool for Teensy Audio Library," PJRC, accessed August 5, 2022, https://www.pjrc.com/teensy/gui/.
7. "Audio Adaptor Boards for Teensy 3.x and 4.x," PJRC, last modified June 5, 2023, https://www.pjrc.com/store/teensy3_audio.html
8. Kyle Loudon, *C++ Pocket Reference* (Sebastopol, CA: O'Reilly, 2003), 38.
9. Ibid., 24.

Chapter 6

1. Eduardo Miranda, *Computer Sound Design: Synthesis Techniques and Programming* (Woburn, MA: Focal Press, 2002), 101.
2. Perry R. Cook, *Real Sound Synthesis for Interactive Applications* (Natick, MA: A. K. Peters, 2002), 155.
3. "AudioEffectGranular", PJRC, accessed August 4, 2022, https://www.pjrc.com/teensy/gui/index.html?info=AudioEffectGranular.
4. "Granular," PJRC, last modified March 29, 2023, https://github.com/PaulStoffregen/Audio/blob/master/examples/Effects/Granular/Granular.ino.
5. "AudioInputUSB", PJRC, last modified March 19, 2023, https://www.pjrc.com/teensy/gui/?info=AudioInputUSB.

Chapter 7

1. "AudioOutputUSB," PJRC, last modified March 19, 2023, https://www.pjrc.com/teensy/gui/index.html?info=AudioOutputUSB.
2. "AudioInputUSB," PJRC, last modified March 19, 2023, https://www.pjrc.com/teensy/gui/?info=AudioInputUSB.
3. "AudioInputI2S," PJRC, last modified March 19, 2023, https://www.pjrc.com/teensy/gui/?info=AudioInputI2S.
4. "Low Power Stereo Codec with Headphone Amp," NXP Semiconductors, last modified January 2022, https://www.nxp.com/docs/en/data-sheet/SGTL5000.pdf.
5. "AudioEffectFreeverb," PJRC, last modified March 19, 2023, https://www.pjrc.com/teensy/gui/index.html?info=AudioEffectFreeverb.
6. "AudioEffectFlange," PJRC, last modified March 19, 2023, https://www.pjrc.com/teensy/gui/?info=AudioEffectFlange.
7. "Audio Library Processor Usage & Interrupts," PJRC, accessed June 7, 2023, https://www.pjrc.com/teensy/td_libs_AudioProcessorUsage.html.

NOTES   347

8. "Creating New Audio Objects," PJRC, accessed June 7, 2023, https://www.pjrc.com/teensy/td_libs_AudioNewObjects.html.

9. Ibid.

10. "Teensy Audio Library," PJRC, last modified March 19, 2023, https://github.com/PaulStoffregen/Audio.

11. Brent Edstrom, *Arduino for Musicians* (New York: Oxford University Press, 2016), 223–228.

12. Curtis Roads, *Composing Electronic Music: A New Aesthetic* (New York: Oxford University Press), 14.

Chapter 8

1. Paul Griffiths, *A Guide to Electronic Music* (New York: Thames and Hudson, 1980), 27.

2. David Miles Huber, *The MIDI Manual* (Carmel, CA: Sams, 1991), 1.

3. "MIDI Library," PJRC, accessed August 8, 2022, https://www.pjrc.com/teensy/td_libs_MIDI.html.

4. Brent Edstrom, *Arduino for Musicians* (New York: Oxford University Press, 2016), 121.

5. *The Complete MIDI 1.0 Detailed Specification*, 2nd ed. (Los Angeles: The MIDI Manufacturers Association, 2006), 33.

6. Scherz, Paul, and Simon Monk. *Practical Electronics for Inventors*, 3rd ed. (New York: McGraw Hill, 2013), 763–764.

7. "Specification for TRS Adapters," MIDI Association, last modified May 17, 2018, https://midi.org/specification-for-use-of-trs-connectors-with-midi-devices.

Chapter 9

1. Bjarne Stroustrup, *A Tour of C++* (Boston, MA: Addison-Wesley, 2023), 22–24.

2. "Audio System Design Tool for Teensy Audio Library," PJRC, last modified March 19, 2023, https://www.pjrc.com/teensy/gui/.

3. Stroustrup, *A Tour of C++*, 24.

4. "AudioEffectEnvelope," PJRC, last modified March 19, 2023, https://www.pjrc.com/teensy/gui/?info=AudioEffectEnvelope.

5. "Using USB MIDI," PJRC, last modified March 19, 2023, https://www.pjrc.com/teensy/td_midi.html.

Chapter 10

1. Jeff Nilsson, "Albert Einstein: 'Imagination is More Important Than Knowledge'," *The Saturday Evening Post*, March 20, 2010, https://www.saturdayeveningpost.com/2010/03/imagination-important-knowledge/.

2. Bjarne Stroustrup, *A Tour of C++* (Boston, MA: Addison-Wesley, 2023), 25.

3. Karuna Sehgal, "An Introduction to Bubble Sort," last modified February 11, 2018, https://medium.com/karuna-sehgal/an-introduction-to-bubble-sort-d85273acfcd8.

4. "MIDI Library," PJRC, last modified March 19, 2023, https://www.pjrc.com/teensy/td_libs_MIDI.html.

5. Paul Messick, *Maximum MIDI: Music Applications in C++* (Greenwich, NY: Manning, 1998), 132–133.

6. Ibid., 20–21.

7. Shaltiel Eloul, Gil Zissu, Yehiel H. Amo, and Nori Jacoby, "Motion Tracking of a Fish as a Novel Way to Control Electronic Music Performance," *Leonardo* 49 no. 3 (June 2016): 190.

Chapter 11

1. Charles Darwin, *The Autobiography of Charles Darwin* (Amherst, MA: Prometheus Books, 2000), 54.

2. Gerhard Nierhaus, *Algorithmic Composition: Paradigms of Automated Music Generation* (Mörlenbach: Springer, 2009), 157.

348 NOTES

3. Marlene Cimons, "'Friendliest,' not Fittest, Is Key to Evolutionary Survival, Scientists Argue in Book," *Washington Post,* July 20, 2020, https://www.washingtonpost.com/science/friendliest-not-fittest-is-key-to-evolutionary-survival-scientists-argue-in-book/2020/07/17/6f70697e-c5fe-11ea-a99f-3bbdffb1af38_story.html.

4. Delton T. Horn, *Music Synthesizers: A Manual of Design & Construction* (Blue Ridge Summit, PA: Tab Books, 1984), 209.

5. Eduardo Miranda and John Biles, *Evolutionary Computer Music* (London: Springer, 2007), 3–4.

6. Ibid.

7. Gerhard Nierhaus, *Algorithmic Composition: Paradigms of Automated Music Generation* (Mörlenbach: Springer, 2009), 157–159.

8. Ingrid Lobo and Kenna Shaw, "Thomas Hunt Morgan, Genetic Recombination, and Gene Mapping," *Nature,* 2008, https://www.nature.com/scitable/topicpage/thomas-hunt-morgan-genetic-recombination-and-gene-496/.

9. "Metro Library," PJRC, accessed July 30, 2020, https://www.pjrc.com/teensy/td_libs_Metro.html.

10. Brent Edstrom, *Arduino for Musicians* (New York: Oxford University Press, 2016), 394.

11. Bruce Eckel, *Thinking in C++, Vol. 1: Introduction to Standard C++,* 2d ed. (Upper Saddle River, NJ: Prentice Hall, 2000), 696.

Chapter 12

1. Thomas Henry, *Build a Better Music Synthesizer* (Blue Ridge Summit, PA: Tab Books, 1987), vii.

2. "Product Guide: Audio Design," West Penn Wire, last modified December 19, 2021, https://www.westpennwire.com/pdf/16774-Audio-ProductGuide.pdf.

3. "Eurorack and Line Level Signals," Perfect Circuit, accessed June 3, 2021, https://www.perfectcircuit.com/signal/eurorack-line-level.

4. "M2|M4|M6 User Guide," MOTU, manual version 2.0, https://cdn-data.motu.com/manuals/usb-c-audio/M_Series_User_Guide.pdf, 19.

5. Douglas Self, *Small Signal Audio Design*, 2nd ed. (New York: Focal Press, 2015), 65.

6. Ibid., 71–74.

7. Matthew Skala, "Electrolytics for AC Coupling," last modified March 29, 2020, https://northcoastsynthesis.com/news/electrolytics-for-ac-coupling/.

8. Ibid.

9. Self, *Small Signal Audio Design*, 363.

10. Ray Wilson, *Make: Analog Synthesizers* (Sebastapol: Maker Media, 2013), 88.

11. "Active Low Pass Filter," *Electronics Tutorials*, accessed June 20, 2023, https://www.electronics-tutorials.ws/filter/filter_5.html.

12. Henry, *Build A Better Music Synthesizer*, 27–28.

13. Self, *Small Signal Audio Design*, 727.

14. "Single-supply Op Amp Design Techniques," Texas Instruments, last modified March 2001, https://www.ti.com/lit/an/sloa030a/sloa030a.pdf.

15. "Single-supply Op Amp Design," Texas Instruments, last modified 2005, https://www.ti.com/lit/an/slyt189/slyt189.pdf.

16. "3V Tips 'n Tricks," Microchip Technology, last modified 2008, https://ww1.microchip.com/downloads/en/DeviceDoc/chapter%208.pdf.

Chapter 13

1. Thomas Henry, *Build a Better Music Synthesizer* (Blue Ridge Summit: Tab Books, 1987), 132–135.

2. Ibid.

3. Paul Scherz and Simon Monk, *Practical Electronics for Inventors*, 3rd ed. (New York: McGraw Hill, 2013), 706–707.

4. "LM340, LM340A and LM7805 Family Wide V_{IN} 1.5-A Fixed Voltage Regulators," Texas Instruments, last modified 2023, https://www.ti.com/lit/ds/symlink/lm340.pdf.

NOTES 349

5. "Shunt Voltage Reference External Resistor Quick-start Calculator," Texas Instruments, accessed June 12, 2023, https://www.ti.com/tool/SHUNT_VOLTAGE_REFERENCE_RESISTOR_CALCULATOR.

6. "LM4040-N/-Q1 Precision Micropower Shunt Voltage Reference," Texas Instruments, last modified June 2016, https://www.ti.com/lit/ds/symlink/lm4040-n-q1.pdf?ts=1686550757659.

7. "Using External Power and USB," PJRC, accessed June 12, 2023, https://www.pjrc.com/teensy/external_power.html.

8. Ray Wilson, "Wall Wart Power Supply (+/-9V to +/-15V)," Music from Outer Space, last modified, June 2010, http://musicfromouterspace.com/analogsynth_new/WALLWARTSUPPLY/WALLWARTSUPPLY.php.

Chapter 14

1. Mark Vail, *The Synthesizer* (New York: Oxford University Press, 2014), 251–252.

2. "A-100 Construction Details," Doepfer, accessed April 15, 2022, http://www.doepfer.de/a100_man/a100m_e.htm.

3. Ibid.

4. "Technical Details A-100," Doepfer, last modified July 1, 2019, https://doepfer.de/a100_man/a100t_e.htm.

5. Ray Wilson, *Make: Analog Synthesizers* (Sebastopol, CA: Maker Media, 2013), 131–132.

6. Douglas Self, *Small Signal Audio Design*, 2nd ed. (New York: Focal Press, 2015), 71–74.

7. "Stripboard," *Electronics Club*, last modified April 13, 2023, https://electronicsclub.info/stripboard.htm.

Chapter 15

1. "Welcome to DipTrace," DipTrace, last modified July 20, 2022, https://diptrace.com/books/tutorial.pdf.

2. "Picking the Right Trace Width," MacroFab, last modified October 25, 2017, https://macrofab.com/blog/picking-right-trace-width/.

3. Douglas Self, *Small Signal Audio Design*, 2nd ed. (New York: Focal Press, 2015), 39–40.

4. "PCB Trace Width Calculator," 4PCB, last modified May 4, 2023, https://www.4pcb.com/trace-width-calculator.html.

5. Roger Hu, *PCB Design and Layout Fundamentals for EMC* (Las Vegas: Independently published, 2019), 80–81.

Chapter 16

1. Jeff Pressing, *Synthesizer Performance and Real-Time Techniques* (Madison, WI: A-R Editions) pp. 8–9.

2. Hal Chamberlin, *Musical Applications of Microprocessors*, 2nd ed. (Hasbrouck Heights, IN: Hayden), 40.

3. Jean-Michel Réveillac, *Electronic Music Machines: The New Music Instruments* (Hoboken, NJ: John Wiley & Sons, 2019), 315.

4. "Single-supply Op Amp Design," Texas Instruments, last modified 2005, https://www.ti.com/lit/an/slyt189/slyt189.pdf.

5. Ray Wilson, *Make: Analog Synthesizers* (Sebastopol, CA: Maker Media, 2013), 40.

6. Gordon Reid, "Envelopes, Gates & Triggers," *Sound on Sound*, November 1999, https://www.soundonsound.com/techniques/envelopes-gates-triggers.

7. "MIDI Library," PJRC, last modified March 19, 2023, https://www.pjrc.com/teensy/td_libs_MIDI.html.

8. "MCP4802/4812/4822," Microchip Technology, last modified January 27, 2015, https://ww1.microchip.com/downloads/en/DeviceDoc/20002249B.pdf.

Chapter 17

1. Robert A. Katz, *Mastering Audio*, 2nd ed. (Burlington, MA: Taylor and Francis, 2007), 22.
2. Edward Mullins, Ian Williams, Giuseppe Lo Voi, and Raphael Puzio, "How to Properly Configure Unused Operational Amplifiers," Texas Instruments, last modified September 2018, https://www.ti.com/lit/an/sboa204a/sboa204a.pdf.
3. "TL07xx Low-Noise FET-Input Operational Amplifiers," Texas Instruments, last modified July 7, 2021, https://www.ti.com/lit/ds/symlink/tl072.pdf.
4. "Audio Adaptor Boards for Teensy 3.x and 4.x," PJRC, last modified June 5, 2023, https://www.pjrc.com/store/teensy3_audio.html.
5. "Audio System Design Tool for Teensy Audio Library," PJRC, last modified March 19, 2023, https://www.pjrc.com/teensy/gui/.

Chapter 18

1. Robert Grossblatt, *Creative Circuit Design* (Blue Ridge Summit, PA: TAB books, 1992), 41.
2. "Price Comparison," PCB Shopper, accessed June 12, 2023, https://pcbshopper.com.
3. Simon Monk, *Make Your Own PCBs with Eagle* (New York: McGraw Hill, 2014), 164.
4. "DipTrace Tutorial," DipTrace, last modified July 7, 2020, https://diptrace.com/books/tutorial.pdf.
5. "MCP4802/4812/4822," Microchip Technology, last modified January 27, 2015, https://ww1.microchip.com/downloads/en/DeviceDoc/20002249B.pdf.

Chapter 19

1. Robert Grossblatt, *Creative Circuit Design* (Blue Ridge Summit, PA: TAB books, 1992), 11.
2. Mutable Instruments, "Plaits v50," accessed June 9, 2023, https://pichenettes.github.io/mutable-instruments-documentation/modules/plaits/downloads/plaits_v50.pdf.
3. "PT8211 16-Bit Digital to Analog Converter," Princeton Technology Corp, last modified February 2012, https://www.pjrc.com/store/pt8211.pdf.
4. "Using External Power and USB," PJRC, accessed June 12, 2023, https://www.pjrc.com/teensy/external_power.html.
5. Bruce Eckel, *Thinking in C++*, 2nd ed. (Upper Saddle River, NJ: Prentice Hall, 2000), i:56.
6. Souvik Saha, "MCP3202 Library," GitHub, last modified April 21, 2021. https://github.com/souviksaha97/MCP3202.

Appendix B

1. "Audio System Design Tool," PJRC, last modified March 19, 2023, https://www.pjrc.com/teensy/gui/.

Appendix C

1. "Create a Soundfont from scratch," Polyphone, last modified March 5, 2022, https://www.polyphone-soundfonts.com/documentation/en/tutorials/create-a-soundfont-from-scratch.
2. "Teensy Wavetable Synthesis," GitHub, last modified winter 2017, https://teensyaudio.github.io/Wavetable-Synthesis/html/index.html.

BIBLIOGRAPHY

4PCB. "PCB Trace Width Calculator." Last modified May 4, 2023. https://www.4pcb.com/trace-width-calculator.html.

Adafruit. "Adafruit SSD1306." Last modified January 8, 2013. https://adafruit.github.io/Adafruit_SSD1306/html/index.html.

Adafruit. "Monochrome OLED Breakouts." Last modified July 29, 2012. https://learn.adafruit.com/monochrome-oled-breakouts/overview.

Berlin, Howard M. *Design of OP-AMP Circuits with Experiments*. Indianapolis: Howard W. Sams & Company, 1977.

Boulanger, Richard, and Victor Lazzarini. *The Audio Programming Book*. Cambridge, MA: The MIT Press, 2011.

Chamberlin, Hal. *Musical Applications of Microprocessors*, 2nd ed. Hasbrouck Heights, IN: Hayden, 1985.

Chowning, John M. "The Synthesis of Complex Audio Spectra by Means of Frequency Modulation." *Journal of the Audio Engineering Society* 1, no.2 (1977): 46–54.

Cook, Perry R. *Real Sound Synthesis for Interactive Applications*. Natick, MA: A.K. Peters, 2002.

Coulter, Doug. *Digital Audio Processing*. Lawrence, KS: R&D Books, 2000.

Cowles, Laurence G. *Transistor Circuits and Applications*. Englewood Cliffs, NJ: Prentice Hall, 1974.

Cullen, Charlie. *Learn Audio Electronics with Arduino*. New York: Routledge, 2020.

DipTrace. "DipTrace Tutorial." Last modified July 7, 2020. https://diptrace.com/books/tutorial.pdf.

DipTrace. "Welcome to DipTrace." Last modified July 20, 2022. https://diptrace.com/books/tutorial.pdf.

Doepfer. "A-100 Construction Details." Accessed June 7, 2023. http://www.doepfer.de/a100_man/a100m_e.htm.

Doepfer. "A-100 DIY page." Last modified September 2004. http://www.doepfer.de/DIY/a100_diy.htm.

Eckel, Bruce. *Thinking in C++*, 2nd ed. Upper Saddle River, NJ: Prentice Hall, 2000.

Edstrom, Brent. *Arduino for Musicians*. New York: Oxford University Press, 2016.

Eggleston, Dennis L. *Basic Electronics for Scientists and Engineers*. Cambridge: Cambridge University Press, 2011.

Electronics Tutorials. "Active Low Pass Filter." Accessed June 20, 2023, https://www.electronics-tutorials.ws/filter/filter_5.html.

Griffiths, Paul. *A Guide to Electronic Music*. New York: Thames and Hudson, 1980, 27.

Henry, Thomas. "Build a MIDI to Logic Controller the Easy Way." *Nuts and Volts*, October 2012: 32–37.

Henry, Thomas. *Build a Better Music Synthesizer*. Blue Ridge Summit, PA: Tab Books, 1987.

Horn, Delton T. *Music Synthesizers a Manual of Design & Construction*, 2nd ed. Blue Ridge Summit, PA: Tab Books, 1984.

Horowitz, Paul, and Winfield Hill. *The Art of Electronics*, 3rd ed. New York: Cambridge University Press, 2015.

Hu, Roger. *PCB Design and Layout Fundamentals for EMC*. Las Vegas: Independently published, 2019.

Huber, David Miles. *The MIDI Manual*. Carmel, CA: Sams, 1991.

Hughes, J.M. *Practical Electronics: Components and Techniques*. Sebastopol, CA: O'Reilly, 2015.

Katz, Robert A. *Mastering Audio*, 2nd ed. Burlington, MA: Taylor and Francis, 2007.

LaMothe, André, John Ratcliff, Mark Seminatore, and Denise Tyler. *Tricks of the Game Programming Gurus*. Indianapolis, IN: Sams, 1994.

Lancaster, Don. *Active-Filter Cookbook*. Carmel, CA: Howard W. Sams & Company, 1975.

Lazzarini, Victor. *Computer Music Instruments II*. Cham: Springer, 2019.

Lindley, Craig A. *Digital Audio with Java*. Upper Saddle River: Prentice Hall, 2000.

Loudon, Kyle. *C++ Pocket Reference*. Sebastopol, CA: O'Reilly Media, 2003.

MacroFab. "Picking the Right Trace Width." Last modified October 25, 2017. https://macrofab.com/blog/picking-right-trace-width/.

Margolis, Michael. *Arduino Cookbook*. Sebastopol, CA: O'Reilly Media, 2011.

McComb, Gordon. *Robot Builder's Bonanza*, 4th ed. New York: McGraw-Hill, 2011.

Messick, Paul. *Maximum MIDI: Music Applications in C++*. Greenwich, NY: Manning, 1998.

Meyers, Scott. *Effective Modern C++*. Sebastopol, CA: O'Reilly Media, 2015.

Microchip Technology. "MCP3202: 2.7V Dual Channel 12-Bit A/D Converter with SPI Serial Interface." Last modified August 2, 2011. https://ww1.microchip.com/downloads/aemDocuments/documents/APID/ProductDocuments/DataSheets/21294E.pdf.

Microchip Technology. "MCP4801/4811/4821 8/10/12-Bit Voltage Output Digital-to-Analog Converter with Internal VREF and SPI Interface." Last modified January 5, 2010. https://ww1.microchip.com/downloads/en/DeviceDoc/22244B.pdf.

Microchip Technology. "MCP4802/4812/4822." Last modified January 27, 2015. https://ww1.microchip.com/downloads/en/DeviceDoc/20002249B.pdf.

Microchip Technology. "3V Tips 'n Tricks." Last modified 2008. https://ww1.microchip.com/downloads/en/DeviceDoc/chapter%208.pdf.

MIDI Association. "Specification for TRS Adapters." Last modified May 17, 2018. https://www.midi.org/midi-articles/trs-specification-adopted-and-released.

MIDI Manufacturers Association. *The Complete MIDI 1.0 Detailed Specification*, 2nd ed. Los Angeles: The MIDI Manufacturers Association, 2006.

Miranda, Eduardo. *Computer Sound Design: Synthesis Techniques and Programming*, 2nd ed. Woburn, MA: Focal Press, 2002.

Miranda, Eduardo, and John Biles. *Evolutionary Computer Music*. London: Springer, 1997.

Mitchell, Daniel. *BasicSynth: Creating a Music Synthesizer in Software*. Morrisville, NC: Lulu, 2009.

Monk, Simon. *Make Your Own PCBs with Eagle*. New York: McGraw Hill, 2014.

Monk, Simon. *Programming Arduino Next Steps*. New York: McGraw Hill, 2014.

Moog, Robert A. "Voltage-Controlled Electronic Music Modules." *Audio Engineering Society*, October 1964. https://www.moogfoundation.org/wp-content/uploads/AES-1964-No0320-Modules.pdf.

MOTU. "M2|M4|M6 User Guide." Manual version 2.0, https://cdn-data.motu.com/manuals/usb-c-audio/M_Series_User_Guide.pdf, 19.

Mullins, Edward, Ian Williams, Giuseppe Lo Voi, and Raphael Puzio. "How to Properly Configure Unused Operational Amplifiers." Texas Instruments. Last modified September 2018. https://www.ti.com/lit/an/sboa204a/sboa204a.pdf.

Mutable Instruments. "Elements v02." Accessed June 9, 2023. https://pichenettes.github.io/mutable-instruments-documentation/modules/elements/downloads/elements_v02.pdf.

Mutable Instruments. "Plaits v50." Accessed June 9, 2023. https://pichenettes.github.io/mutable-instruments-documentation/modules/plaits/downloads/plaits_v50.pdf.

Mutable Instruments, "tides2 v40." Accessed June 9, 2023. https://pichenettes.github.io/mutable-instruments-documentation/modules/tides_2018/downloads/tides_v40.pdf.

Mutable Instruments. "Warps v30." Accessed June 9, 2023. https://bgr360.github.io/assets/pdf/mutable_instruments/warps_v30.pdf.

Mutable Instruments. "Yarns v03." Accessed June 9, 2023. https://pichenettes.github.io/mutable-instruments-documentation/modules/yarns/downloads/yarns_v03.pdf.

Nagle, Paul. "Modular Profile: Dieter Doepfer." *Sound on Sound*, April 2017. https://www.soundonsound.com/people/modular-profile-dieter-doepfer.

Nierhaus, Gerhard, *Algorithmic Composition: Paradigms of Automated Music Generation*, Mörlenbach: Springer, 2009.

Nilsson, Jeff. "Albert Einstein: 'Imagination is More Important Than Knowledge.'" *The Saturday Evening Post*, March 20, 2010. https://www.saturdayeveningpost.com/2010/03/imagination-important-knowledge/.

Novarm. "DipTrace Tutorial." Last modified July 20, 2022. https://diptrace.com/books/tutorial.pdf.

NXP Semiconductors. "Low Power Stereo Codec with Headphone Amp." Last modified January 2022. https://www.nxp.com/docs/en/data-sheet/SGTL5000.pdf.

Owen, Mark. *Practical Signal Processing*. Cambridge: Cambridge University Press, 2007.

PCB Shopper. "Price Comparison." Accessed June 12, 2023, https://pcbshopper.com.

Pellman, Samuel. *An Introduction to the Creation of Electroacoustic Music*. Belmont, CA: Wadsworth Publishing Company, 1994.

Perfect Circuit. "Eurorack and Line Level Signals." Accessed June 3, 2021. https://www.perfectcircuit.com/signal/eurorack-line-level.

Pithadia, Sanjay, and Shridhar More, "Grounding in Mixed-Signal Systems Demystified, Part 1." Last modified 2013. https://www.ti.com/lit/an/slyt499/slyt499.pdf?ts=1686106673405&ref_url=https%253A%252F%252Fwww.google.com%252F.

PJRC. "Adafruit SSD1306 OLED Library." Accessed June 9, 2023, https://www.pjrc.com/teensy/td_libs_SSD1306.html.

PJRC. "Audio Adaptor Boards for Teensy 3.x and 4.x." Last modified June 5, 2023. https://www.pjrc.com/store/teensy3_audio.html.

PJRC. "Audio Connections and Memory." Accessed July 14, 2020. https://www.pjrc.com/teensy/td_libs_AudioConnection.html.

PJRC. "Audio Library Processor Usage & Interrupts." Accessed June 7, 2023. https://www.pjrc.com/teensy/td_libs_AudioProcessorUsage.html.

PJRC. "Audio System Design Tool for Teensy Audio Library." Last modified March 19, 2023. https://www.pjrc.com/teensy/gui.

PJRC. "AudioEffectEnvelope." Last modified March 19, 2023. https://www.pjrc.com/teensy/gui/index.html?info=AudioEffectEnvelope.

PJRC. "AudioEffectFlange." Last modified March 19, 2023. https://www.pjrc.com/teensy/gui/index.html?info=AudioEffectFlange.

PJRC. "AudioEffectFreeverb." Last modified March 19, 2023. https://www.pjrc.com/teensy/gui/index.html?info=AudioEffectFreeverb.

PJRC. "AudioEffectGranular." Accessed August 4, 2022. https://www.pjrc.com/teensy/gui/index.html?info=AudioEffectGranular.

PJRC. "AudioInputI2S." Last modified March 19, 2023. https://www.pjrc.com/teensy/gui/index.html?info=AudioInputI2S.

PJRC. "AudioInputUSB." Last modified March 19, 2023. https://www.pjrc.com/teensy/gui/index.html?info=AudioInputUSB.

PJRC. "AudioOutputUSB." Last modified March 19, 2023. https://www.pjrc.com/teensy/gui/index.html?info=AudioOutputUSB.

PJRC. "Bounce Library." Accessed June 7, 2023. https://www.pjrc.com/teensy/td_libs_Bounce.html.

PJRC. "Creating New Audio Objects." Accessed June 7, 2023. https://www.pjrc.com/teensy/td_libs_AudioNewObjects.html.

PJRC. "Granular." Last modified March 29, 2023. https://github.com/PaulStoffregen/Audio/blob/master/examples/Effects/Granular/Granular.ino.

PJRC. "Metro Library." Accessed November 25, 2021. https://www.pjrc.com/teensy/td_libs_Audio.html.

PJRC. "MIDI Library." Last modified March 19, 2023. https://www.pjrc.com/teensy/td_libs_MIDI.html.

PJRC. "Naming Conventions for Audio Objects." Accessed August 7, 2020. https://www.pjrc.com/teensy/td_libs_AudioNamingConvention.html.

PJRC. "PT8211 Audio Kit for Teensy 3.x." Accessed June 7, 2023. https://www.pjrc.com/store/pt8211_kit.html.

PJRC. "Teensy Audio Library." Last modified March 19, 2023. https://github.com/PaulStoffregen/Audio.

PJRC. "Teensy Wavetable Synthesis." Accessed June 7, 2023. https://teensyaudio.github.io/Wavetable-Synthesis/html/md_additional_pages_soundfontDecoder.html.

PJRC. "Using External Power and USB." Accessed June 12, 2023. https://www.pjrc.com/teensy/external_power.html.

PJRC. "Using USB MIDI." Last modified March 19, 2023. https://www.pjrc.com/teensy/td_midi.html.

PJRC. "Wire Library." Accessed June 9, 2023. https://www.pjrc.com/teensy/td_libs_Wire.html.

Pressing, Jeff. *Synthesizer Performance and Real-Time Techniques*. Madison, WI: A-R Editions, 1992.

Price, Simon. "Granular Synthesis." *Sound on Sound*, December 2015. https://www.soundonsound.com/techniques/granular-synthesis.

Princeton Technology Corp. "PT8211 16-Bit Digital to Analog Converter." Last modified February 2012. https://www.pjrc.com/store/pt8211.pdf.

Python Packaging Authority (PyPA). "The Python Package Installer." Accessed June 7, 2023. https://pip.pypa.io/en/stable/.

Reid, Gordon. "An Introduction to Additive Synthesis." *Sound on Sound*, June 2000. https://www.soundonsound.com/techniques/introduction-additive-synthesis.

Reid, Gordon. "An Introduction to Frequency Modulation." *Sound on Sound*, April 2000. https://www.soundonsound.com/techniques/introduction-frequency-modulation.

Reid, Gordon. "Envelopes, Gates & Triggers." *Sound on Sound*, November 1999. https://www.soundonsound.com/techniques/envelopes-gates-triggers.

Réveillac, Jean-Michel. *Electronic Music Machines: The New Music Instruments*. Hoboken, NJ: John Wiley & Sons, 2019.

Roads, Curtis. *Composing Electronic Music: A New Aesthetic*. New York: Oxford University Press, 2015.

Robinson, Kevin. *Practical Audio Electronics*. New York: Focal Press, 2020.

Saha, Souvik. "MCP3202 Library." GitHub. Last modified April 21, 2021. https://github.com/souviksaha97/MCP3202.

Scherz, Paul, and Simon Monk. *Practical Electronics for Inventors*, 3rd ed. New York: McGraw-Hill, 2013.

Sehgal, Karuna. "An Introduction to Bubble Sort." Last modified February 11, 2018. https://medium.com/karuna-sehgal/an-introduction-to-bubble-sort-d85273acfcd8.

Self, Douglas. *Small Signal Audio Design*, 2nd ed. New York: Focal Press, 2015.

Shacklette, L.W., and H.A. Ashworth. *Using Digital and Analog Integrated Circuits*. Englewood Cliffs, NJ: Prentice Hall, 1978.

Skala, Matthew. "Design Mistakes in Synth Schematics." Last modified February 28, 2020. https://northcoastsynthesis.com/news/design-mistakes-in-synth-schematics/.

Skala, Matthew. "Electrolytics for AC Coupling." Last modified March 29, 2020. https://northcoastsynthesis.com/news/electrolytics-for-ac-coupling/.

Skala, Matthew. "PCB Design Mistakes." Last modified October 4, 2020. https://northcoastsynthesis.com/news/pcb-design-mistakes/.

Slone, G. Randy. *Tab Electronics Guide to Understanding Electricity and Electronics*, 2nd ed. New York: McGraw-Hill, 2000.

Sparkfun. "Data Types in Arduino." Accessed June 7, 2023. https://learn.sparkfun.com/tutorials/data-types-in-arduino.

Sparkfun. "Pull-up Resistors." Accessed June 7, 2023. https://learn.sparkfun.com/tutorials/pull-up-resistors/all.

Stroustrup, Bjarne. *A Tour of C++*, 3rd ed. Boston, MA: Addison-Wesley, 2023.

SyntherJack. "Eurorack Module DIY Tutorial (2)." Last modified September 18, 2017. https://syntherjack.net/eurorack-module-diy-tutorial-2-graphics/.

Texas Instruments. "LM4040-N/-Q1 Precision Micropower Shunt Voltage Reference." Last modified June 2016. https://www.ti.com/lit/ds/symlink/lm4040-n-q1.pdf?ts=1686550757659.

Texas Instruments. "Shunt Voltage Reference External Resistor Quick-start Calculator." Accessed June 12, 2023. https://www.ti.com/tool/SHUNT_VOLTAGE_REFERENCE_RESISTOR_CALCULATOR.

Texas Instruments. "Single-supply Op Amp Design." Last modified 2005. https://www.ti.com/lit/an/slyt189/slyt189.pdf.

Texas Instruments. "Single-supply Op Amp Design Techniques." Last modified March 2001. https://www.ti.com/lit/an/sloa030a/sloa030a.pdf.

Texas Instruments. "Tips and Tricks for Designing with Voltage References." Last modified 2021. https://www.ti.com/lit/eb/slyc147a/slyc147a.pdf?ts=1686114925640.

Texas Instruments. "TL07xx Low-Noise FET-Input Operational Amplifiers." Last modified July 7, 2021. https://www.ti.com/lit/ds/symlink/tl072.pdf.

Traister, Robert J., and Jonathan L. Mayo. *44 Power Supplies for Your Electronic Projects*. Blue Ridge Summit, PA: Tab Books Inc., 1987.

Vail, Mark. *The Synthesizer*. New York: Oxford University Press, 2014.

Vincent, Robin. "Modular Interfacing." *Sound on Sound*, September 2020. https://www.soundonsound.com/techniques/modular-interfacing.

West Penn Wire. "Product Guide: Audio Design." Last modified December 19, 2021. https://www.westpennwire.com/pdf/16774-Audio-ProductGuide.pdf.

Williams, Elliot. *Make: AVR Programming*. Sebastopol, CA: Maker Media, 2014.

Wilson, Ray. *Make: Analog Synthesizers*. Sebastopol, CA: Maker Media, 2014.

Wilson, Ray. "Wall Wart Power Supply (+/−9V to +/−15V)." *Music from Outer Space*. Last modified June 2010. http://musicfromouterspace.com/analogsynth_new/WALLWARTSUPPLY/WALLWARTSUPPLY.php.

Zumbahlen, Hank. "Staying Well Grounded." *Analog Dialogue* 46. Last modified June 2012. https://www.analog.com/en/analog-dialogue/articles/staying-well-grounded.html.

INDEX

Tables and figures are indicated by an italic *t* and *f* following the page/paragraph number.

--, decrement operator, 148
#include directive, 12, 36, 78
++, increment operator, 148
<<, left shift operator, 183, 262
>>, right shift operator, 105, 262
1N4002 diode, 208
1N5819W diode, 314*f*
7404 hex inverter, 116
7805 regulator, 209
8.24 fixed-point number, 102
8.8 fixed-point number, 100

A-100 modular system, 216
Ableton Live
 with audio projects, 60, 82
 with MIDI projects, 27
AC coupling, 193, 220
Adafruit SSD1306 OLED library, 38, 39, 54
additive synthesis, 62–63
ampersand, use in programming, 42, 44, 68, 69
amplitude
 amplitude modulation, 64
 amplitude of carrier, 56
 amplitude of modulator, 50, 53
 converting MIDI velocity, 57
 updating harmonics, 70
amplitude(), function, 10, 70–71, 72
analog pin, 13, 25–26, 329
analogRead(), function, 13–19, 28–29, 288
AND, logical operator, 182
Arduino IDE
 board manager, 4
 editor, 6
 installation, 4
 programming with, 7
 setting USB type, 14
 uploading code, 8
Arduino shields, 294–95
arpeggiation
 arpeggiator, 142
 configuring with a DAW, 154
 patterns, 144, 147
arrays
 audio block, 40, 68, 96, 144
 of objects, 321
 passing as a parameter, 40, 46

artifacts, audio, 94, 98, 193
asterisk, use in programming, 42
attack(), function, 29–30, 134
attenuation, 194, 196, 199, 202, 279
Audio Adapter Board
 avoiding conflicts, 282
 avoiding overvoltage, 90
 boilerplate initialization, 12
 soldering options, 3
audio objects
 creating custom objects, 96
 initialization, 12
 methods, 10
 modulation, 65
 organizing data structures, 129
 pointers to, 69
 primary audio objects, 337
audio signals
 amplification and attenuation of, 190
 clipping, 196
 effects, 277
 granular processing, 76
 input, 279
 level, 190
 output, 280
 setting amplitude, 104
Audio System Design Tool
 configuring for USB audio, 82
 copying code, 12, 53
 description of, 11
 exporting code, 12
 incorporating custom samples, 26
 making sound, 11
 overview of, 11
 pointers to objects, 69
 renaming objects, 53
AUDIO_INPUT_LINEIN, 90
AUDIO_INPUT_MIC, 90
AudioControlSGTL5000 object, 65, 89, 130
AudioEffectEnvelope, 65, 130
AudioEffectFlange, 92
AudioEffectFreeverb, 95
AudioEffectGranular, 77, 81
AudioEffectGranular, functions, 77*t*
AudioEffectMultiply, 65
AudioInputI2S, 60

358 INDEX

AudioInputUSB, 82, 89
AudioInterrups(), function, 94
AudioMemory(), function, 10
AudioMemoryUsageMax(), function, 10
AudioMixer4, 65, 78, 130, 318
AudioNoInterrupts(), function, 94
AudioOutputI2s, 65, 78, 89, 130
AudioOutputUSB, 14, 60, 82
AudioStream, 93
AudioSynthWaveform, 65, 69, 130, 131
AudioSynthWaveformModulated, 53, 318
AudioSynthWavetable, 30, 65, 78, 339

band-pass filter, 15
beginFreeze(), function, 80
beginPitchShift(), function, 80
bias, op amp, 196, 259, 279
bill of materials, 216, 233, 278, 312, 333
binary masking, 262
bipolar power supply, 191
bit depth, 22
bit manipulation, 162–63
bit twiddling, 181, 262
bits, retrieving values, 183
bitwise operators, 181
BOM. *See* bill of materials
Boolean algebra, 181
boolean type, 335*t*
Bounce class, 34, 67
brackets, use in programming, 7
break statement, 42
breakout modules, 36
bubble sort algorithm, 147
buffer
    adding notes to, 146
    audio, 220
    DAC, 202
    fixed length, 147–48
    memory, 79, 142, 144
    op amp, 190
    sorting, 147
    unity, 280
byte, 335*t*

callback function, 27, 56, 72, 116
carrier wave, 50, 53, 318
case statement, 42
char, 335*t*
chorus effect, 89
circuits
    –10V reference, 210
    audio input, 195, 279
    audio output, 192
    comparator gate, 200
    CV amplifier, 201–2, 259
    CV input, 202, 263–64, 314, 315
    DAC, 258*f*
    gate input, 198–99, 314
    gate output, 201, 304
    mixer, 220
    transistor gate, 198

class
    constructor, 132
    C++ programming, 34, 68, 131
    data members, 144
    default constructor, 132, 164
    inheritance, 146
    member functions, 10, 132–33
    methods, 10
    virtual functions, 146
clearDisplay(), function, 39–40
clipping, 95*f*, 96, 191–92, 196, 279
comparator, 200
compensation capacitor, 194
compiling code, 6, 8, 60, 181
component placement, 243, 301, 316
composite header, 301, 317
constants, 9, 10, 90, 144
container class, 129, 134
control voltage
    calibration, 270
    control voltage schemes, 254
    description, 201–2
    input, 203, 263–64
    MIDI to CV conversion, 262
    output, 202, 259
    scaling, 203
copper pour, PCB design, 244, 301
coupling capacitors, 193, 220, 222
cross fade, 339
CS pin, 260–61
cutoff frequency, 15, 194, 199, 201
cycle, of a waveform, 22, 98, 337

DAC
    conceptualization, 23
    configuration bits, 260–61
    dual channel, 303
    loading, 202
    overview, 15
    updating, 260–61
    usage, 256
    wiring, 257
    write-command register, 260–61
damping(), function, 91, 95
data structures, 68, 129, 131, 163, 319
data types
    common, 335*t*
    containing in a struct, 68
    deferred commitment, 182
    example, 9
    logical grouping, 68
    user-defined class, 34
DAW. *See* digital audio workstation
DC
    DC component, 193, 196, 220, 315
    DC coupling, 193
    DC offset, 193, 337
debouncing, switches, 34, 156
decrement operator, 148
delay, audio effect, 89, 164, 290
delay(), function, 10
development process, 6

digital audio workstation, 14, 27, 60, 72, 82, 89
digital pin, 9, 33–34, 35
digital signal processing
 custom object template, 93
 depth control, 289
 effect selection, 291
 overview, 87, 277, 287–88
digitalWrite(), pin function, 10, 263
DIN 41494, standard modular format, 216
DIN, MIDI, 27, 118, 305
diode rectifier, 208
diodes, 195–96, 198, 201, 298
DipTrace
 Component Editor, 237, 240
 designing parts, 238
 overview, 234
 Pattern Editor, 238, 240
 PCB Layout, 242
 place board outline, 242
 place copper pour, 244
 Schematic Capture, 241, 242
distortion, 93, 97, 193, 194
Doepfer Musikelektronik, 216
dot notation, calling class methods, 100
dot notation, fixed-point math, 100
DSP. *See* digital signal processing
dual power supply, op amps, 191
dynamic contour, 66

EAs. *See* evolutionary algorithms
economy of selection, 103
effects, creating custom, 93, 96
elapsedMillis, timing object, 19
electrolytic capacitors, 193, 209, 220, 315
Encoder class, 36, 54, 67
encoder handling, 37, 44, 81, 323
enumerations, 41, 132, 320
envelope generator, 267, 321
envelopes, 21, 28, 29, 66, 72, 131
Eurorack
 5V regulation, 190, 209
 avoiding reverse power connections, 208
 building modules, 219, 233
 creating front panels, 224, 247
 dimensions, 217
 DIN41294 module standard, 216
 DIY power supplies, 215
 mounting holes, 217–18
 overview, xii, 216
 power pinout, 206
 power supplies, 205, 208
evolutionary algorithms
 biological model, 162
 chromosomes, 162, 168, 170
 crossover, 168, 171–72
 crossover function, 184
 DNA, 162
 fitness function, 166
 genes, 162
 genotype, 162
 hierarchical evaluation, 169
 mutation, 162, 166, 168

overview, 161
 phenotype, 162
 population structure, 166
 recombination, 162
exclusive OR, 183

fallingEdge(), function, 35, 40
feedback capacitor, 194–95, 199
feedback resistor, 199, 220, 259, 279
filters
 calculating cutoff frequency, 194
 configuration of, 16
 filtering DAC noise, 194
high-pass filter, 15
 low-pass, 193, 315
 object, 15
 resources for designing digital filters, 107
 setting cutoff frequency, 18
 setting resonance, 19
 subtractive synthesis, 14
fixed-point numbers, 24, 100, 107
flanger, DSP effect, 89
float. *See* floating point numbers
floating pin, 33–34
floating point numbers, 9, 29, 40, 335*t*
flying power distribution bus, 206
FM. *See* frequency modulation
for loop, examples of, 70, 98, 135, 165
frequency(), method, 10, 70
frequency and periodicity, 22
frequency modulation
 algorithms, 60, 318
 coding a simple example, 53
 configuring the Audio System Design Tool, 53
 custom project, 313
 modulator and carrier, 50
 operators, 318
 overview, 50
 sidebands, 50
front panels
 adding graphics, 249
 blanks, 226
 design of, 224, 247
 dimensions, 217
 milling, 225
 PCB design, 225, 247, 284–85
functions
 description, 7
 overloading, 182
 pointers to, 116, 177
 return values, 9
 visualization of, 8*f*
 void keyword, 9

gates
 input, 197, 198–99, 263, 329
 output, 200, 201, 263
 overview, 197
 usage, 263
Gerber files, 246, 333
gerbv.exe, 247
global variables, 19, 28, 41, 45, 79

GND. *See* ground
GPIO, 282, 297, 314
granular synthesis, 76
ground
    button wiring, 33–34
    connecting to a solderless breadboard, 16–17,
       25–26
    ground plane, 244
    loops, 116
    MIDI wiring, 116
    nets in circuit diagrams, 241
    OLED wiring, 38
    potentiometer wiring, 25–26
    powering op amps, 191
    rotary encoder wiring, 35
    short circuit, 195
    with stripboard, 220

harmonic spectrum, 14, 51, 62, 193
harmonics, 51, 63, 68
header
    backpack board, 297
    female, 294–95
    pins, 3–4
    shrouded headers, 207
header file, 26, 34, 36, 54
Hertz per volt, 254, 255
HF stability, 194
HIGH keyword, 10
high-pass filter, 15
histogram, 173
hookup wire, 16–17, 41, 116, 221
horizontal pitch, 217, 218, 284, 299
HP. *See* horizontal pitch

i2s object, 12
IDE. *See* Integrated Development Environment;
    Arduino IDE
if statement, 10, 169, 307, 323
increment operator, 148
increment, pitch shifting, 76
indexing, examples, 24, 42, 70
inharmonic spectra, 52
INPUT keyword, 9
INPUT_PULLUP, 34–35, 157
instructions, use in coding, 7
int, 335*t*
integer, 9
Integrated Development Environment
    board manager, 4
    editor, 6
    installation, 4
    programming with, 7
    setting USB type, 14
    uploading code, 8
internal clock, 149, 151
interpolation, 98
inverting amplifier, 190, 192, 260, 263–64

LD2981ABU33TR 3.3V regulator, 314*f*
LDR. *See* light-dependent resistor
LED, 8, 9, 142

left-shift operator, 183, 262
legato, 271
LFO. *See* low-frequency oscillator
light-dependent resistor, 11, 15
line input, 90, 287–88
LM4040DIZ shunt diode, 211, 298
loading, DAC output, 202
long integer, 9, 37, 335*t*
lookup table, 23, 162–63, 168
loop(), function, 7, 10
LOW keyword, 10
low-frequency oscillator, 50, 64, 100,
    253
low-pass filter, 15, 193–94, 315

M3, mounting holes and screws, 190, 299,
    305–6
map(), scaling function, 29
MCP3202 ADC, 315, 326
MCP4821 DAC, 256, 260–61
MCP4822 DAC, 256, 269, 303
MCP6002 op amp, 198–99, 201, 279
memory address, 42
memory allocation, 7, 10, 79
Metro object, 176
MIDI
    clock, 147, 171, 176
    clock callback, 178
    clock handling, 151, 166, 310
    control voltage conversion, 262, 277
    converting to frequency, 57
    DIN, 116
    message types, 112
    note handler, 27, 271
    note struct, 167
    omni mode, 309
    overview, 111
    ports, 116
    program change, 113
    raw input, 115
    synchronization, 144, 149
    UART input, 116, 118
    UART output, 116, 127
    USB input, 26, 28, 56, 72, 116
    USB output, 111
    velocity, 165–66
MIDIDevice object, 114
mil, PCB measurement, 244
MISO, 256, 282*t*
modular synthesis, 189, 216, 253
modulated signal, 50
modulator, 50, 53, 318
modulus operator, 148, 151
momentary switch, 156, 281, 291
MOSI, 256, 257, 282*t*
mounting bracket, 229
mounting holes, 217–18
mounting screws, 218
mult. *See* passive multiple
multimeter, 190, 193, 206, 213
multiplexer, 282
Mutable Instruments, 198–99

negative voltage reference, 199, 298, 314
nets, use in circuit design, 241
non-volatile variables, 37, 55, 78
NOT operator, 182
note prioritization, 129, 132, 133
Nyquist frequency, 194

Ohm's law, 190–91, 211
OLED
   configuration, 39
   drawing, 39, 328
   overview, 37–40
   pin assignments, 38*t*
op amp
   description, 190
   gain, 190, 220, 280
   negative feedback, 190–91
   open collector, 124–25
   power, 191
   rail-to-rail, 191–92
   TL072 pinout, 223
operator, frequency modulation
   coding, 319
   configuration, 322
   creating in the Audio Design Tool, 319*f*
   overview, 318
opto-isolator, 116–24
OUTPUT keyword, 9
output resistor, 191, 202
overflow, 105, 106
overtone, 63
overvoltage, 64, 90, 190, 195–96, 317

pad
   applying flux, 296
   cutting, 214
   PCP design, 238–40
   routing traces to, 232
parameters
   passing a reference, 40
   passing an array, 46
   passing values, 9, 27, 40
   passive multiple, 195
passthrough, 89, 94
PCB. *See* printed circuit board
periodic signal, 50
periodicity, 22
photoresistor, 11, 13, 15
pinMode(), function, 9, 10, 34–35, 67
pip, package installer, 341
pitch class, 164
pitch shifting, 76
pitch, voltage control of, 254–63
pointers, 27, 42, 69, 93, 131, 320
Polyphone, 339
polyphony, 129
positive voltage, 25–26, 263, 315
potentiometers, 21, 24–26, 142
potentiometer, sensitivity, 93–94, 288
power
   bus, 206, 213, 218
   commercial power supplies, 205

pinout, 206, 218
   power section, 241, 279, 313
   separating USB from 5V, 214
   testing voltage, 213
PPQN. *See* pulses per quarter note
printed circuit boards
   adding graphics, 285–86
   attaching to a front panel, 234, 282
   avoiding errors, 247
   backpack, 294–95, 313, 317
   developing a user interface, 305
   drill pattern, 246
   layout strategies, 284
   preparing for fabrication, 246
   pro and con, 233*t*
   silkscreen, 249, 285
programming, writing sketches, 8, 9
pseudo code example, 148
PT8211 DAC, 315, 333
public, keyword, 68, 131, 135
pull-up resistor, 33–34, 38, 157
pulses per quarter note, 175
pulseWidth(), function, 10
pushbutton, 33, 41, 174*f*, 321
Python, 341
Python, IDLE editor, 341

random(), function, 164
ratlines, 244, 284
read() functions
   Encoder read() function, 37, 44
   MIDI.read(), 119
   usbMIDI.read(), 28, 55, 115
receiveReadOnly(), function, 96
receiveWritable(), function, 96
reference voltage, 191–200, 210, 261, 279, 298
references, use in programming, 40, 42, 68, 169
release(), function, 29–30
resistance
   filter cutoff, 193–94
   limiting shunt current, 211
   Ohm's law, 190–91
   path of least resistance, 17
   potentiometer taper, 247
   variable, 25
resistors
   breadboard example, 13
   calculating comparator threshold, 200
   feedback, 191, 201
   input, 220
   inside feedback loop, 202
   with MIDI circuits, 116
   minimizing current, 198
   network, 314–15
   output, 195
   with shunt diode, 199
return keyword, 9
reverb, digital effect, 89, 90–91, 287–88
reverse polarity, 207–8
ribbon cable, 207
right-shift operator, 105, 262
ripple, in power supplies, 209

362 INDEX

roomsize(), function, 95
rotary encoders, 35, 36, 174*f*

sample rate, 21–23, 104, 194
sample table, 21, 341
samples, importing, 26, 344
sawtooth wave, 63
scaling values, 29
schematics
  creating, 235
  populating, 236
  representation, 13*f*
  signal flow, 220
  studying, 190
  translating to a breadboard, 116–24
  translating to PCBs, 212–13
  translating to stripboard, 222
  SCLK, 256
Serial Peripheral Interface
  ADC, 315
  Audio DAC, 315
  boiler plate setup, 260
  communication with a DAC, 256, 260
  connections, 257*f*
  flash memory, 282
  setup code, 270
  transaction overview, 262
  transfer() function, 261, 263
  wiring, 257
setCursor(), OLED function, 39–40
setSpeed(), granular synthesis function, 81
setup(), function, 7
sgtl5000 object, 10, 12, 195
short circuits, 17, 116, 195
short integer, 96
shunt diode, 199, 210
sidebands, 50, 53, 334
Signal, online application, 27, 60
single supply power, 191–92, 198–99
sketch, basics of, 6–9
SMD. *See* surface mount device
sockets, 4*f*, 224
solder board, 193, 210, 286
solder wire, 297
soldering tip, 297
solderless breadboards
  examples of, 3, 16*f*, 25, 41, 124, 142, 221
  laying out circuits, 124
  translating circuit diagrams to, 116
  usage, 12–17
  using potentiometers, 25, 89*f*
  using pushbuttons, 33–34, 89*f*
  using rotary encoders, 35
sound design, FM synthesis, 334
sound grain, granular synthesis, 77
SoundFont, 24–25, 26, 339
SoundFont2 Decoder, 339, 341
source files, 26, 96
SPDIF, 77
SPI. *See* Serial Peripheral Interface
square wave, 63
SS, SPI slave select, 256

standoffs, 234, 305–6
static constants, 144
static variables, 37, 44, 55
step sequencer, 161
stereo codec, 10
stochastic techniques, 161, 163
String object, 40
stripboard, 216, 220
structure, user-defined data type
  chromosome example, 163
  default constructor, 167
  description, 68
  MIDI example, 144
  structure vs class, 134
subclass, 148–49
subtractive synthesis, 14
surface mount device
  1206 form factor, 296
  introduction to, 296
  placement of, 316
  soldering, 296
switch statement, 42
switching regulator, 215

tactile switch, 33, 233*t*, 277. *See also* pushbutton
Teensy 3.2, 14
Teensy 4, 3
Teensy Audio Library, 11, 23, 77, 82, 89
Teensy, DAW configuration, 60, 82
templates, C++, 181, 182
tempo, calculation of, 176
thou, PCB measurement, 244
through hole components, 224, 229, 284–85, 296
timer callback function, 155
timer, initialization of, 154
timestamps, 131, 133
TL072, op amp, 194, 219, 280
toggle switch, 305
trace widths, 244
traces, running, 244
transients, in voltage regulation, 209
transistor
  NPN, 197
  overview, 197
  switching, 197
tremolo, DSP effect, 93, 97
trigger
  input, 197, 263, 329
  output, 200, 202, 263
  usage, 263
  See also gates
TRS jack, 118
typename, template return type, 182

UART MIDI, 111, 116, 118
undervoltage, 64, 190, 195–96, 317
unipolar power supply, 191–92
unsigned int type, 155, 335*t*
unsigned keyword, 155
unsigned long type, 155, 335*t*
update(), audio object, 93, 95, 102

update(), Bounce function, 35, 40
USB Audio, 60, 77, 82, 89
USB MIDI, 26, 27, 56, 80, 111, 116
USBHost object, 114
usbMIDI.read(), function, 28, 55, 115, 138

V-Trigger, 263, 271
V/oct. *See* volts per octave
value, returning from a function, 9
variable resistor, 25. *See also* potentiometer
variables, use in programming, 9, 10
velocity sensitivity, 200
via, use in PCB design, 244, 301
virtual ground, 192*f*
virtual void, use in programming, 93
void keyword, 9
voltage, calculating input level, 199
voltage control, 253. *See also* control voltage
voltage regulation, 3.3V, 297, 313
voltage regulation, 5V, 209, 218, 279
voltage to frequency conversion, 326
voltage-controlled amplifier (VCA), 253
voltage-controlled filter (VCF), 253
voltage-controlled oscillator (VCO), 253

volts per octave
   accuracy, 331
   control voltage schemes, 254
   converting to Hertz per volt, 255
   input example, 313
   jacks, 317
   output circuit, 303
   scaling, 203
   semitones, 254
   translating to frequency, 326
volume, adjusting with a potentiometer, 288
volume(), *AudioInputUSB* function, 82
volume(), *sgtl5000* function, 12, 13, 19, 26

wave file, looping, 339
waveform object, 10, 11, 65, 337
waveform, overview of a sample, 21
waveshaping, 24
wavetable oscillator, 23, 78
wavetable synthesis, 21, 76
wetness, digital signal processing, 91, 289
word, keyword, 335*t*

Yamaha DX7, 50